Administrative Law

EXAMPLES & EXPLANATIONS

EXAMPLES & EXPLANATIONS

Administrative Law

Seventh Edition

William F. Funk
Lewis & Clark Distinguished Professor of Law Emeritus
Lewis & Clark Law School

Richard H. Seamon
Margaret Schimke Distinguished Professor of Law
University of Idaho College of Law

ASPEN PUBLISHING

To contact Customer Service, e-mail customer.service@aspenpublishing.com, call 1-800-950-5259, or mail correspondence to:

Aspen Publishing
Attn: Order Department
1 Wall Street
Burlington, MA 01803

Printed in the United States of America.

2 3 4 5 6 7 8 9 0

ISBN 979-8-8920-7359-2

Library of Congress Cataloging-in-Publication Data application is in process.

About Aspen Publishing

Aspen Publishing is a leading provider of educational content and digital learning solutions to law schools in the U.S. and around the world. Aspen provides best-in-class solutions for legal education through authoritative textbooks, written by renowned authors, and breakthrough products such as Connected eBooks, Connected Quizzing, and PracticePerfect.

The Aspen Casebook Series (famously known among law faculty and students as the "red and black" casebooks) encompasses hundreds of highly regarded textbooks in more than eighty disciplines, from large enrollment courses, such as Torts and Contracts to emerging electives such as Sustainability and the Law of Policing. Study aids such as the *Examples & Explanations* and the *Emanuel Law Outlines* series, both highly popular collections, help law students master complex subject matter.

Major products, programs, and initiatives include:

- **Connected eBooks** are enhanced digital textbooks and study aids that come with a suite of online content and learning tools designed to maximize student success. Designed in collaboration with hundreds of faculty and students, the Connected eBook is a significant leap forward in the legal education learning tools available to students.

- **Connected Quizzing** is an easy-to-use formative assessment tool that tests law students' understanding and provides timely feedback to improve learning outcomes. Delivered through CasebookConnect.com, the learning platform already used by students to access their Aspen casebooks, Connected Quizzing is simple to implement and integrates seamlessly with law school course curricula.

- **PracticePerfect** is a visually engaging, interactive study aid to explain commonly encountered legal doctrines through easy-to-understand animated videos, illustrative examples, and numerous practice questions. Developed by a team of experts, PracticePerfect is the ideal study companion for today's law students.

- The **Aspen Learning Library** enables law schools to provide their students with access to the most popular study aids on the market across all of their courses. Available through an annual subscription, the online library consists of study aids in e-book, audio, and video formats with full text search, note-taking, and highlighting capabilities.

- Aspen's **Digital Bookshelf** is an institutional-level online education bookshelf, consolidating everything students and professors need to ensure success. This program ensures that every student has access to affordable course materials from day one.

- **Leading Edge** is a community centered on thinking differently about legal education and putting those thoughts into actionable strategies. At the core of the program is the Leading Edge Conference, an annual gathering of legal education thought leaders looking to pool ideas and identify promising directions of exploration.

For our wives and best friends, for putting up with us while we write,
Renate Funk
Holly V. Dawkins

— W.F.F. & R.H.S.

Summary of Contents

Contents

Preface to Seventh Edition

If you are like us when we were law students, you enrolled in a course on administrative law without knowing exactly what the course would be about or understanding what an administrative agency is. The mysteriousness is understandable. Administrative law is like the air we breathe: invisible yet pervasive. Administrative agencies affect so many areas of our lives that we take them for granted. They are part of the atmosphere of modern life, and, like the physical atmosphere, they are necessary (at least in some form) to sustain modern life, but they get little attention from most people. Nonetheless, law students need to learn about them because most lawyers must deal with them.

The near-invisibility and pervasiveness of administrative agencies make administrative law an exciting and challenging subject to learn. Just as students of science learn that the air is made up of many different elements that serve various life-sustaining functions, students of administrative law learn that "the bureaucracy" is made up of many different administrative agencies that serve various governmental functions. Nonetheless, just as all types of physical matter are subject to laws of science (such as the law of gravity), administrative agencies are governed by principles of administrative law. Unfortunately, just as seemingly simple laws of science have hidden complexities, seemingly straightforward principles of administrative law can be difficult to apply in particular situations.

Indeed, administrative law is an especially challenging subject because you must learn both the similarities, as well as differences, in the way government agencies operate. All agencies, for example, must obey the U.S. Constitution, as well as the statutes that create them. The Constitution stays the same, of course, regardless of the agency, but the statute that creates one agency will differ from the statute that creates another agency. In a course on administrative law, you will learn legal principles that are broadly applicable to many or most government agencies. To do so, however, you will study material, including judicial opinions, statutes, and regulations that deal with particular agencies. It can be difficult—but it is critically important—to distinguish the broadly applicable principles from the principles that just apply to a particular agency. For that reason, in a course on administrative law, even more so than in other law school courses, you must be able to see the forest as well as the trees.

This book will help you do that. In the 22 years since the first edition, thousands of law students have used this book. The need for a seventh edition is a result of student demand. The first two chapters give you a lay of the land by providing an overview of (1) what the subject of administrative law is all about, (2) what administrative agencies are, and (3) how they fit into the government structure. Later chapters go into detail about the two major activities in which administrative agencies engage: rulemaking and adjudication. Following the chapters on rulemaking and adjudication are two chapters that will give you a detailed and carefully organized picture of a subject that is near and dear to the hearts of administrative law professors: judicial review of agency action. Finally, we discuss two additional agency activities that are covered in some courses on administrative law: information gathering and information disclosure. We have organized the book as a whole, as well as each chapter, to supply you with a detailed map of the administrative law terrain that should be useful in virtually every administrative law course that uses one of the national casebooks.

In addition to helping you see the big picture, this book is designed to help you understand the details. In every chapter, we discuss each topic in enough depth to facilitate a sophisticated understanding of the topic. These discussions include descriptions of all of the major, relevant decisions of the U.S. Supreme Court (through June 2024), as well as descriptions of the major doctrinal approaches taken by lower federal courts. Our discussion of each topic is followed by examples that enable you to test your understanding of the topic, and by explanations of the examples that, we hope, will deepen your understanding of the topic. Many of these examples are based on actual cases that have been decided by federal courts. This format will bring the sometimes abstract principles of administrative law down to earth.

You can use this book either to prepare for class or to prepare for exams, or for both purposes. The chapters are self-contained, and each chapter is carefully organized to enable you to quickly and easily to locate the topics that you cover in your course. Thus, you do not need to read the book from cover to cover, nor do you need to read the chapters in the order in which they are presented. In particular, you can read our general discussion of a topic to clear up things that remain unclear from class or your casebook, or to review topics at the end of the semester. You can also, during or at the end of the semester, consult the examples and explanations for the topics covered in your course to make sure that you have a handle on that topic or to get additional, concrete illustrations of topics. We hope you find this book helpful. We welcome your comments and suggestions for improvement.

William F. Funk
Richard H. Seamon

September 2024

Administrative Law

CHAPTER 1

Introduction to Administrative Law

Administrative law, though often dreary, can be of huge importance to the day-to-day lives of Americans.

—Washington Post *editorial, June 23, 2001*

I. ADMINISTRATIVE LAW—THE COURSE

Administrative law is largely about procedure—the procedure that government agencies must follow in order to take action that affects private parties. Administrative law as taught in American law schools is a basic course that, despite the approximately 19 different casebooks in the field, does not differ greatly among schools or teachers. All the courses focus on federal administrative law, although some may touch on state administrative law in the particular state in which the course is given. All focus on the federal Administrative Procedure Act (APA), rather than on the myriad other federal statutes that govern the various agencies' activities. Moreover, despite the focus on the APA, administrative law courses are invariably taught through the case method, relying almost exclusively on judicial opinions to explicate the law. All cover the procedural requirements agencies must follow in taking various actions; all include the relationships among the branches of government, making administrative law sort of an advanced political science or constitutional law course; and all address how courts review agency action.

Government regulation of private conduct and constitutional due process also figures heavily in all administrative law courses.

Professors, depending upon their background and point of view, may stress one of these areas more than others, and the order in which they are addressed may differ, but ultimately the courses have more in common than they differ.

As the introductory quotation from the *Washington Post* suggests, the subject of administrative law has rarely been considered intrinsically interesting. Unlike torts, for instance, its subject matter does not often relate to everyday life. At the same time, Executive Branch agencies make rules on matters as diverse as environmental protection, workplace safety, immigration, wholesale electricity price caps, and agricultural price supports. Federal student aid requirements are another example of agency regulations. In addition, federal agencies make individualized decisions affecting some of the most important aspects of people's lives, from health care coverage decisions to decisions on deportation. State agencies make decisions governing who will be admitted to the bar and who will be disbarred, as just one example. In other words, administrative law actually affects you in real life. Moreover, if you care at all about how your government functions, you should care deeply about administrative law, because it governs most of what government does. It is all about power and how to control it.

Also, administrative law is really not all that difficult; it is not tax law. While there are statutory provisions, most administrative law is determined from judicial opinions. Like most areas of the law that are largely driven by judicial decisions—as opposed to statutory or regulatory text—some administrative law is clear-cut, black-letter material, whereas other parts of it involve clear principles, usually easily stated (often with multipart tests), but the application of which is fraught with fuzziness. Finally, some administrative law is still up for grabs; the courts have not yet worked it out, or legislatures pass new laws that confuse the issues.

This book can help sort out what is clear from what is fuzzy in the law, and through examples and explanations help to reduce the fuzziness in the areas that are not so clear-cut but which rely on a contextual application of a general principle. This book also can identify those areas that are not yet worked out and, in those areas at least, identify the issues that are unclear and the likely range in which an ultimate answer is likely to occur.

II. OVERVIEW OF THE HISTORY OF ADMINISTRATIVE LAW

How the law has developed over time often helps to illuminate how judges are likely to rule today. This may be particularly true of administrative law.

The subject matter of administrative law itself is relatively recent in the law. Professor Felix Frankfurter of Harvard Law School, later Supreme Court Justice, is credited with authoring in 1932 one of the first casebooks on administrative law. Prior to the Great Depression, which began with the stock market crash in 1929, the prevailing wisdom reflected in both courts and legislatures was laissez-faire economic theory. This theory is characterized by the absence of government regulation of business with the exception of public utilities (e.g., gas, water, electricity, and once upon a time telephone companies), that were known as natural monopolies. What "administrative" law existed consisted of the constitutional law doctrine of "separation of powers," which you may already have studied in constitutional law, but which administrative law courses revisit with a particular focus. For example, two-thirds of Frankfurter's casebook covered separation of powers, with the remaining one-third dedicated to particular types of administrative functions—utility regulation, taxation, immigration, and "miscellaneous." Compare that to your casebook.

The Great Depression, however, spawned the New Deal, with its belief in the ability of government regulation of business to cure the excesses of laissez-faire capitalism. To implement this regulation, Congress created agencies that were supposed to be apolitical and have the necessary technical expertise to manage industries in a scientific manner. This led to an explosive growth in business regulation, which, because the agencies in reality were more political and less expert than their ideal conception, in turn led to an explosive growth in litigation in which businesses challenged their regulation. After an initial period in which, on the basis of various constitutional provisions, the Supreme Court resisted wide-scale government regulation of business, the Court acceded to the constitutionality of most of the New Deal agencies and regulations. Instead, the Court now developed a common law to control these agencies. This common law emphasized procedural regularity in agency decision making, often mirroring the procedures of courts, and applied a degree of judicial oversight of the substantive adequacy of the agency's decisions. Business interests, not satisfied with this judicially created regime, lobbied Congress for more protective legislation. In 1946, the Administrative Procedure Act (get used to calling it the APA) was passed as a compromise between business interests and the Executive Branch. At the same time, the American Bar Association and the National Conference of Commissioners on Uniform State Laws approved a Model State APA, which slowly but surely provided the basis for the adoption of administrative procedure acts in almost every state.

The APA in 1946 was hardly a revolutionary law. Rather, it largely codified the developing common law. It has remained largely unamended since that time, but it has been subject to substantial judicial interpretation over the years that has taken the APA well beyond its literal text. In particular, this occurred during the 1970s, the second great wave of government regulation after the New Deal. During the New Deal, most of the government regulation was regulation of particular industries in their economic activities. For example, the Federal Communications Commission (FCC) was created to regulate the broadcast industry, and the Securities and Exchange Commission (SEC) was created to regulate the securities industry. In the 1970s, the thrust was somewhat different; now the emphasis was on protecting the environment or health and safety across industries. For example, the Environmental Protection Agency (EPA) was created to protect the environment; the Occupational Safety and Health Administration (OSHA) was created to protect workers in the workplace; and the Consumer Product Safety Commission (CPSC) was created to protect consumers. Whereas the original APA was enacted almost exclusively to protect the subjects of government regulation—those actually regulated by the government and who lobbied for the APA's passage—the judicial response in the 1970s was primarily (although not exclusively) aimed at protecting the intended beneficiaries of the new regulation: workers, consumers, and those who appreciated the environment.

During the 1970s, there also was explosive growth in what are known as government "entitlements" programs. *Entitlements programs* entitle a person to a government benefit if the person meets certain qualifications. For example, if employed persons become disabled so that they cannot work in any job, they may qualify for Social Security Disability payments. Historically, these types of government benefits were not considered "property" under the Due Process Clause, so that persons receiving them had no procedural protections against government termination of their benefits. The same judicial solicitude for beneficiaries of government regulatory programs also came to be reflected in judicial treatment of beneficiaries of entitlements programs, as the courts expanded the notion of property protected by the Due Process Clause.

More recently, starting in the 1980s and continuing to the present, concerns over the cost and efficacy of various government regulations have led to a number of new laws and Presidential Executive Orders designed to "reform" government regulation, generally to make it more cost-effective, or to eliminate it by deregulating formerly regulated areas. For example, the Interstate Commerce Commission (the first multi-member, independent regulatory agency, created in the nineteenth century to regulate the rates that interstate railroads could charge shippers and expanded later to regulate interstate trucking rates as well) was eliminated in 1996. While as yet the reformers have not actually amended the APA, there have been various attempts to do so, and Congress has passed a number of statutes that create new procedural requirements applicable to various agency actions. For example, the Regulatory Flexibility Act requires agencies to engage in a cost-benefit analysis of any regulation that has a substantial impact on small businesses.

This concern for the cost and efficiency of government regulation has not been limited to the Executive and Legislative Branches. The courts also now seem to be more solicitous of the burdens on industry imposed by government regulations and less solicitous of those who seek to retain their government benefits.

Finally, most recently the Roberts Court has undertaken fundamental reconsiderations of matters long thought settled in administrative law, affecting not only how courts review agency action but also how those agencies may be structured. This has been accompanied by a general distrust of the administrative state by the Court, resulting in its changes to the law raising significant barriers to government regulation and enforcement.

This brief and simplistic history of administrative law may help to explain how the case law has developed over time. In particular, it may help to explain how a court applying a "test" articulated by the courts at an earlier time may reach a result seemingly contrary to what earlier courts might have held.

III. OVERVIEW OF THE ADMINISTRATIVE STRUCTURE

As you learned in school, Congress makes the laws and the President is responsible for executing those laws. Of course, the President himself cannot carry out all those laws; he must utilize the services of the officers and employees of the Executive Branch.

A. Agencies Generally

What is an agency? The APA defines *agency* for purposes of its provisions as "each authority of the Government of the United States, whether or not it is within or subject to review by another agency," and then it exempts various entities, most notably Congress, the courts, and the governments of the District of Columbia and territories. *See* 5 U.S.C. § 551(1). In *Franklin v. Massachusetts*, 505 U.S. 788 (1992), the Supreme Court interpreted the APA also to exclude the President from the definition of an agency. Other than these exceptions, however, the APA's definition is broad, including a vast array of different types of entities. Of course, states and state agencies are not subject to the APA. They are not authorities of the government of the United States.

Historically, the most important agencies were "departments," the heads of which constituted the President's "Cabinet," or closest advisory group. Other than the Attorney General, the heads of Cabinet Departments hold the title "Secretary," and each is appointed by the President after Senate confirmation. Today there are 15 Cabinet-level Departments:

(1) Agriculture
(2) Commerce
(3) Defense, which contains three non-Cabinet-level Departments: Air Force, Army, and Navy

(4) Education
(5) Energy
(6) Health and Human Services
(7) Homeland Security
(8) Housing and Urban Development
(9) Interior
(10) Justice
(11) Labor
(12) State
(13) Transportation
(14) Treasury
(15) Veterans Affairs

The proliferation of Departments and the increasing demands on their heads have undermined the historic importance of the Cabinet as the primary advisory body to the President. In recent years this role has increasingly been assumed instead by White House advisors. These advisors are not subject to the requirement of Senate confirmation that is applicable to heads of agencies, because these advisors have no legal power; they only "advise." However, when an advisor handpicked by the President and situated in the Executive Office of the President "advises" a department or agency head, that advice carries great practical weight.

Departments normally contain a number of agencies. They are too numerous to list, but examples include the Forest Service (USFS) in the Department of Agriculture; the Bureau of the Census in the Commerce Department; the Food and Drug Administration in the Department of Health and Human Services; the Fish and Wildlife Service in the Department of the Interior; the Federal Bureau of Investigation in the Department of Justice; the Federal Aviation Administration (FAA) in the Department of Transportation; and the Internal Revenue Service (IRS) in the Treasury Department. Note the variety of names for these sub-departmental agencies, including "service," "bureau," "administration," and others. The heads of these agencies also have various titles, such as Administrator or Director. Most are appointed by the President with the advice and consent of the Senate. Some other high ranking officers are similarly appointed. Inferior officers can, if authorized by statute, be appointed by the President alone or by the head of a Department. The differences in the names of the agencies and the titles of their heads have no legal significance.

There also are agencies outside of Departments. Some are very important, such as the EPA, the Central Intelligence Agency, and the Social Security Administration. Others are not as well known, such as the Farm Credit Administration, the United States Information Agency, and the United States International Development Cooperation Agency. The heads of these agencies also are appointed by the President with the advice and consent of the Senate.

All of these agencies are considered part of the Executive Branch, meaning they are subject to the direction and control of the President as the head of the Executive Branch.

B. Independent Regulatory Agencies

One category of agencies, while part of the Executive Branch, differ from the previous mentioned agencies because they are intended to be more independent of the President's direction. We call them "independent regulatory agencies."[1] There are about 15 such agencies, including the FCC, the SEC, the Federal Trade Commission (FTC), the National Labor Relations Board (NLRB), the Nuclear Regulatory Commission (NRC), and the Federal Reserve Board. They are called "independent" because they generally share certain characteristics that insulate them from that control by the President to which normal executive agencies are subject. These characteristics typically are: (1) they are headed by multi-member groups, rather than a single agency head; (2) no more than a simple majority of these members may come from one political party; (3) the members of the group have fixed, staggered terms, so that their terms do not expire at the same time; and (4) they can only be removed from their positions for "cause," unlike most executive officials, who serve at the pleasure of the President.

Examples

1. Is the Environmental Protection Agency (EPA) an independent regulatory agency? The EPA was established in the executive branch as an independent agency headed by an Administrator.
2. Is the Consumer Product Safety Commission (CPSC) an independent regulatory agency?

Explanations

1. No, the EPA is not an independent regulatory agency. One way to determine whether an agency is an independent regulatory agency is to find the law that created it and determine whether it has the four characteristics of an independent regulatory agency. The law creating the EPA provides that it is headed by an Administrator. Therefore, it is not headed by a multi-member group and cannot be an independent regulatory agency. Another way

1. Actually, one so-called independent regulatory agency, the Federal Energy Regulatory Commission, is located administratively within the Department of Energy (DOE), but it is not subject to the direction of the Secretary of Energy.

is to look up the definition of *independent regulatory agency* in the Paperwork Reduction Act, 44 U.S.C. § 3502(5). The definition contains a list of all the agencies generally considered to be independent regulatory agencies, and although the legal effect of that definition is limited to the Paperwork Reduction Act, this list is consistent with general understanding. Finally, a pretty accurate shortcut way to determine if an agency is an independent regulatory agency is to check whether the name of the agency contains the title "commission" or "board." If so, the agency is very likely to be an independent regulatory agency, because the title reflects that the agency is led by a multi-member group rather than a single head—Secretary, Administrator, Director, etc.

2. Yes, the CPSC is an independent regulatory agency. It was created by the Consumer Product Safety Act, 15 U.S.C. § 2051 et seq. That act refers to the CPSC as "an independent regulatory commission"; it establishes that the CPSC is governed by five commissioners (including the Chair) appointed by the President with the advice and consent of the Senate; each is appointed for a fixed term of seven years, except that the initial appointments were staggered so that their terms expired over a five-year period, rather than all in the same year; no more than three commissioners can come from the same political party; and the President can remove commissioners "for neglect of duty or malfeasance in office but for no other cause."

Example

What does it mean to say the CPSC is headed by a multi-member group?

Explanation

Five commissioners make up the governing body of the CPSC, compared to the single Administrator of the EPA. Although one is the Chair, the Chair has only one vote, like the other Commissioners. Other independent regulatory agencies may have as few as three members or as many as seven, but most have five members, like the CPSC. In most of these agencies, the members are called "Commissioners" (because they are in a Commission), but in an agency known as a "Board" (such as the NLRB or the Federal Reserve Board), the members are simply "Members of the Board." If the CPSC wishes to decide whether to adopt a new consumer product safety regulation, for example, it would require the votes of a majority of the Commissioners to adopt that regulation. Similarly, whenever the agency sets or changes policy, it decides to do it through the mechanism of a majority vote, like a legislative assembly. In the EPA, on the other hand, there is only a single Administrator; if she wishes to adopt a regulation, she can do so on her own. There are no votes.

Independent regulatory agencies, like Executive Branch agencies, have subordinate officers. In the CPSC, for example, there is an Executive Director and several Associate Executive Directors. These officers generally answer to the entire membership of the Commission or Board as to the performance of their functions, although generally the Chair of the Commission or Board is responsible for internal agency administrative matters.

Example

If the CPSC is an independent regulatory agency and the EPA is not, how is the CPSC more independent than the EPA?

Explanation

The so-called *independence* of independent regulatory agencies refers to their independence from Presidential control. This independence, however, is relative rather than absolute. That is, the independent regulatory agencies are somewhat more independent of Presidential control, and much of that independence is a product of history and culture, not law. First, the fact that the agency is controlled by several persons, rather than one, makes it less amenable to direction; it is simply harder to control several persons than just one. More important, Presidential control and influence over most executive officers, such as the Administrator of the EPA, results from the fact that the President appoints them and may remove them at will. They usually have no fixed term of office. Instead, they serve "at the pleasure of the President." Thus, when President Joe Biden replaced President Donald Trump, he dismissed most of the appointed executive officials who had not already resigned. He then could appoint those persons who shared his vision. Later, if they cease to share that vision, he may simply replace them.

The Commissioners of the CPSC and other independent regulatory agencies, on the other hand, because of their fixed and staggered terms, remain in office when a new President is elected. Generally, the President is restricted by statute from removing them except for "cause," such as malfeasance in office or neglect of duty.[2] Because it takes a number of years for the terms of a

2. Absent such statutory protection, the President may remove at will a person holding an office for a fixed term. The Supreme Court has interpreted the fixed term by itself to be a limit on how long a person may hold the position, not an assurance that the person may keep that position for that term.

majority of the members of a commission to run out, it may take a number of years for the President to be able to appoint a majority of members who support his program. For example, the FCC has five members, each of whom is appointed for a five-year term. Thus, every year one Commissioner's appointment runs out, providing an opportunity for the President to appoint a new Commissioner. At this rate, however, it will take at least three years before a new President can appoint a simple majority of the Commission. Even after appointing them, unlike the Administrator of the EPA, the President cannot simply remove them if he does not like what they are doing.

Finally, the limitation that no more than a simple majority of the Commission be from one party limits whom the President can appoint and ensures that at least some Commissioners will be from a different party than the President. Again using the FCC as an example, imagine that a Democratic President replaces a Republican President who has been in office for eight years. The Republican President will have appointed all the Commissioners in office when the new President is inaugurated. Nevertheless, of the five Commissioners, only three may be Republicans (no more than a simple majority can be from one party), leaving two Democrats on the Commission even under a Republican President. If the Democratic members were the first whose terms ran out, the new Democratic President would have to wait three years before he could make a majority of the Commission Democratic members. If the Republican members were the first whose terms ran out, the Democratic President could in the first year create a Democratic majority, but then would have to appoint Republicans in the next two years, so that no more than three members were Democrats.

These legal restrictions as a practical matter can make independent regulatory agencies somewhat independent of the President, but much of these agencies' independence stems from a perception in the political culture that they are supposed to be more independent than Cabinet Departments. After all, Congress created them with this intent, which is generally respected by the President and protected by Congress in the political arena. For example, when President Reagan issued an Executive Order on regulatory reform in 1981, directing agencies to consider costs and benefits in issuing new regulations, the Attorney General advised him that as a legal matter he could impose it on the independent regulatory agencies as well as on the Executive Branch agencies, but that as a political matter there would be considerable concern about such a Presidential direction to the independent regulatory agencies. As a result, the President did not direct the Order to the independent regulatory agencies. To some extent subsequent executive orders on regulatory reform have been extended to the independent regulatory agencies, but those agencies are still not subject to the same oversight under the orders as are other executive agencies.

The independence of these agencies can be overstated. First, the President does appoint (with the advice and consent of the Senate) the Chairs of the independent regulatory agencies from among their Commissioners. Normally, a newly elected President chooses the new Chair from among those on the Commission. The Chair of the CPSC, like the Chairs of other independent regulatory agencies, is the administrative head of the agency, like the Chair of a committee is the administrative head of a committee. While the Chairs cannot make policy decisions for the agencies, which require majority votes of the Commissioners, their administrative powers give them real, practical power beyond their one vote. For example, the Chairs typically are authorized to hire personnel employed by the agency. Second, although the membership of independent regulatory agencies is required to be bipartisan, Presidents usually can find a member of the opposite party who is friendly to the President's goals. Moreover, at least some of the Commissioners will be from the same party as a new President, and even the Commissioners who are not from the same party may desire to be reappointed to their positions when their terms expire, so they may be receptive to the President's influence.

C. Government Corporations

Sometimes the government charters a nonprofit corporation to provide a service, rather than creating an agency to do it. For example, the National Railroad Passenger Corporation (popularly known as Amtrak) is a federal corporation that operates intercity rail transportation. The Tennessee Valley Authority, which operates a number of hydroelectric dams in the Tennessee Valley area, is likewise a government corporation. Although government corporations have many similarities to government agencies, they are not generally considered "agencies" of the government and therefore are not subject to the procedural requirements of administrative law imposed by statute. As government entities, however, they can still be subject to constitutional limitations. *See Lebron v. National Railroad Passenger Corp.*, 513 U.S. 374 (1995) (statutory declaration that Amtrak is not a government entity is effective for matters within congressional control, but Amtrak remains a government entity with respect to restrictions imposed on government by individual rights provisions of the Constitution).

IV. WHAT AGENCIES DO AND HOW THEY DO IT

A. What They Do

Agencies are the entities that actually execute the laws that Congress passes. For example, the IRS collects taxes; EPA administers, among other laws, the

Clean Air Act and the Clean Water Act; the Social Security Administration is responsible for paying Social Security beneficiaries; and the Occupational Safety and Health Administration (OSHA) administers the Occupational Safety and Health Act that protects workers' safety and health on the job. We can characterize what these agencies do in a number of ways.

One category of activity is regulating private conduct. For example, the EPA regulates industrial and other activities to control pollution; OSHA regulates employers' workplaces to ensure that they are safe for workers; the FTC regulates commercial practices; and the SEC regulates securities brokers, dealers, and issuers.

Another category is disbursing entitlements. For example, in addition to the Social Security Administration, the Centers for Medicare and Medicaid Services in the Department of Health and Human Services are responsible for Medicare and Medicaid, and the Department of Agriculture administers the Supplemental Nutrition Assistance Program (SNAP) through what are commonly called food stamps.

Another category is managing federal property. For example, the National Park Service and the Bureau of Land Management (BLM) in the Department of the Interior manage the national parks and BLM lands, and the USFS in the Department of Agriculture manages the national forests.

There are, nevertheless, many agency activities that do not fall into a neat category—whether it is the Department of State's issuance of passports, the Immigration and Customs Enforcement Agency's admission and deportation of aliens, the National Aeronautics and Space Administration's space shuttle program, or the IRS's collection of taxes. In any case, most of what most agencies do has a substantial and direct effect on private persons, whether it is prohibiting or permitting an activity, granting or denying a benefit, or affecting the environment in ways that can impact those who use it.

What agencies do is defined by statute. It is often said that agencies have no inherent powers. As you will see later, this is not strictly true, but it is true that when agencies act to affect the legal rights of persons, they must be acting pursuant to legal authority granted to them, almost always by statute. This concept is important because, despite the number and importance of judicial decisions in administrative law, an administrative lawyer must always keep an eye on the statutes governing the agency, from the agency's organic act or statutory mandate[3] to the APA.

---

3. An agency's organic act is the law that created the agency. An agency's statutory mandate may be contained in its organic act, or it may be in a separate law. For example, the Consumer Product Safety Act both creates the CPSC and defines its powers and responsibilities. The EPA, however, administers a number of different statutes, including the Clean Air Act, the Clean Water Act, the Safe Drinking Water Act, and others; each of these is a statutory mandate to the agency, both defining its powers under those laws and confining its powers within the constraints of those laws.

The APA is an example of a general statute applicable to all agencies when they engage in certain types of activities. There are many other such laws, and administrative law courses often deal to a lesser degree with some of them. These include the National Environmental Policy Act, which requires agencies to make an Environmental Impact Statement when they take actions significantly affecting the environment; the Regulatory Flexibility Act, which requires agencies to make another kind of impact statement when they take actions affecting small entities; the Federal Advisory Committee Act, which requires agencies to follow certain procedures when they create or use advisory committees; the Paperwork Reduction Act, which requires agencies to meet certain standards and follow certain procedures when they impose reporting or recordkeeping requirements on the public; and the Information Quality Act, which requires agencies to follow certain procedures to ensure the accuracy of their data. An administrative lawyer must be familiar with all the general laws affecting an agency's activities.

At the same time, almost every agency is governed by specific laws applicable to it. Some of these laws are program oriented. For example, EPA administers the Clean Air Act and the Clean Water Act, so their provisions define the nature of what the EPA can do under those laws. Other laws may specifically create and organize a particular agency. For example, the Department of Energy Organization Act creates and organizes the DOE. Not only may these specific laws create the substantive authority and obligations of the agency, they also may specify the particular procedural requirements attendant to carrying out the substantive authority. These specific procedural requirements may eliminate, supplement, or substitute for the procedural requirements found in the general laws. For example, the Clean Air Act specifies the procedures by which the EPA may adopt Clean Air Act standards, and these procedures substitute for those in the APA and replace the EIS requirement in NEPA. The Department of Energy Organization Act specifies that when DOE adopts regulations it must follow certain additional procedures beyond those in the APA. Thus, administrative lawyers dealing with a particular agency or program also must be familiar with the specific laws applicable to that agency or program. However, because each of these laws is specific to a particular agency or program, general courses in administrative law rarely address them, other than to warn students that particular laws may alter the effect of the general laws they are studying.

B. How They Do It

Generally speaking, when agencies act in a way that affects persons outside of government, they act in one of two generic ways: they issue rules, or they issue orders after adjudications. Thus, when agencies regulate private conduct, they might adopt rules that require persons to do something or prohibit them from doing something. For example, the EPA makes rules for specific industries, specifying the amount of various pollutants that companies in that industry are allowed to emit from their smokestacks or from pipes into a river. Another example might be that the FAA makes rules specifying how long pilots can fly without time off for rest. Regulatory agencies also issue orders after adjudications. For example, the FTC might issue a cease-and-desist order to a company using a pyramid marketing scheme after an adjudication that the company's marketing scheme is an "unfair or deceptive act or practice in or affecting commerce." Such acts are declared unlawful by the Federal Trade Commission Act, 15 U.S.C. § 45(a)(1). Another example would be the National Labor Relations Board determining that an employer had engaged in an unfair labor practice and ordering it to stop.

These two generic types of administrative action—promulgating rules and adjudicating cases—are not limited to regulatory agencies. For example, the Social Security Administration promulgates rules defining the terms of eligibility for Social Security disability payments. In addition, it engages in adjudication when a person contests Social Security's determination that the person does not meet the eligibility requirements. The IRS makes rules specifying how to interpret the Internal Revenue Code provisions, and the National Park Service makes rules regarding camping in national parks. Similarly, the Executive Office for Immigration Review engages in adjudication before someone may be deported, and the BLM engages in adjudication when it resolves disputes over the use of public lands by permit holders.

As may be seen, rules adopted by agencies are a lot like statutes passed by Congress: they establish rules for the future on a generic basis, not on an individual basis. In fact, rules even look like statutes, organized by chapter, section, subsection, and so forth, and are often phrased in a legalistic manner. We might say that rules mimic statutes, and agencies engaged in rulemaking mimic Congress making statutes. At the same time, agency adjudication looks a lot like what courts do: agencies decide disputed issues with respect to specific parties, decide contested facts, apply the law to the facts, and conclude with the issuance of an order. Indeed, many administrative adjudicatory proceedings resemble court proceedings, complete with a presiding official called a "judge." So we might say that agency adjudication mimics what courts do in deciding cases.

There is one subset of adjudications that may differ from the contested adversary proceeding format we associate with judicial proceedings; this is called "licensing." An agency engages in licensing whenever it grants permission to someone to do something. For example, the Army Corps of Engineers engages in licensing when it issues a permit to a person to fill a wetland; the Forest Service engages in licensing when it allows a company to operate a ski resort on Forest Service land; the NRC engages in licensing when it grants a license for a civilian nuclear reactor to begin operation; and the FAA engages in licensing when it allows a new type of airliner to be put into service. Licensing often differs from other adjudication in that there are not necessarily adverse parties. A person applies to the agency for a permit or license, and the agency grants the permit or license if it finds in the adjudication that the person meets the criteria for obtaining the permit or license. This is not to say that licensing never involves adverse parties. For example, when the NRC licensed the construction of a new nuclear power station, it was inevitably opposed by local groups opposing the construction.

Agencies would like to issue rules and orders in the most efficient manner. For example, think of law enforcement. Police would probably prefer to be able to take the arrested person directly to prison; from the police perspective, a trial is merely interference in their process, and getting a warrant for a search is just a bother. How much easier their job would be if they did not have to follow the various procedures required by law and the Constitution! Agencies are no different. Persons who may be affected by rules and orders, however, just like persons who might be affected by police operating without procedural restrictions, have an interest in ensuring that agencies do not issue rules or orders unless the agency has gone through a process that to some degree ensures fairness and accuracy. Administrative law is all about that process.

As indicated earlier, the Constitution's Due Process Clause and the APA are the basic, general sources of the required process for federal agencies. In the course of the following chapters, the procedural requirements imposed by the Due Process Clause and the APA will be described. As you will find, deciding what requirements are applicable begins with determining the nature of agency action—is it rulemaking or adjudication?—because the type of procedure required differs depending upon the characterization of the action as rulemaking or adjudication. How to figure out which is which is addressed in Chapter 3, Adjudication, and Chapter 5, Rulemaking.

There is also a category of activity by agencies that does not fit neatly within either the rulemaking or adjudication niches. This category involves investigations or gathering of information. Both may occur as incident or preliminary to rulemaking or adjudication, when the agency seeks information or data to support such actions. For example, an agency may investigate to determine if a person has violated its regulations. If it finds the person has, the agency may begin an adjudication to hold the person in violation and order compliance or assess a penalty or both, depending on the agency's statute. However, agency information gathering is not limited to situations that are preliminary or incident to rulemaking or adjudication. For example, income tax returns are a ubiquitous form of information gathering, and the decennial census is a government information-gathering activity mandated by the Constitution. Such information gathering may impose substantial costs on those who must respond, and it may raise legitimate questions about the government's need for the information compared to those costs. Accordingly, there are procedural requirements agencies must follow in order to gather information.

V. THE ROLE OF THE COURTS

As the overview of the history of administrative law indicated, the courts have always played a strong role in administrative law. In the beginning they created it as a matter of federal common law. However, even after the enactment of the APA, courts have continued to play a significant role. Particularly in the 1970s, the courts took an active part in overseeing agency action with the great expansion of government health, safety, and environmental regulation during that time. You would expect the Supreme Court to be the leader in this activity, and indeed most of the cases in administrative law casebooks come from the Supreme Court. In administrative law, however, the U.S. Court of Appeals for the District of Columbia Circuit (D.C. Circuit) plays almost as important a role because people can always sue the United States in the District of Columbia and because several statutes require judicial review of the agency action in the D.C. Circuit. As a result of its greater-than-normal administrative law caseload, the D.C. Circuit has earned a reputation as being expert in administrative law, and because the Supreme Court necessarily hears only a very small number of cases, the D.C. Circuit's precedents have taken on particular importance.

Courts become involved in administrative law when a person challenges agency action. This can occur in either of two ways: when a person sues the agency, alleging the agency has acted illegally in some way; or when the agency sues a person, purportedly enforcing one of the laws applicable to the agency, and the person defends against the agency by alleging that the agency is acting illegally. As a general matter, in either case, the person normally claims that the agency has acted illegally either because it has violated some procedural requirement or because the substance of its decision is invalid. As you will see, much of administrative law involves the procedures agencies must follow in order to take certain actions. If the agency does not follow the correct procedures, the action can be invalidated.

Example

OSHA adopts a "Cooperative Compliance Program" (CCP), under which employers can avoid a mandatory annual safety inspection from OSHA by agreeing to implement a worker safety program that goes beyond the requirements of the Occupational Safety and Health Act. Employer groups challenge the Program as illegal because OSHA did not go through the required procedures to adopt it: OSHA had not provided notice and an opportunity to comment on the Program before adopting it. The court agrees and enjoins OSHA from initiating the Program.

Explanation

As you will learn in a later chapter, the APA requires agencies in most cases to provide to the public notice of proposed rules and an opportunity for the public to comment on them before they are adopted. In the example, the agency did not provide the notice and opportunity to comment. OSHA failed to comply with its procedural requirements, and as a result the court invalidated the Program. If the agency were to go back and go through the proper procedures, it could then adopt the Program anew.

You might wonder why the agency would fail to follow the proper procedures. In this example, which is an actual case, the agency believed that the Program fit within one of the exceptions to the requirement for notice and comment. *See Chamber of Commerce of U.S. v. U.S. Dept. of Labor*, 174 F.3d 206 (D.C. Cir. 1999). The language of the APA, even after 50 years, is still not clear in all regards, and the court's decision interpreting the language of the exception helps to clarify its meaning. Chapter 5, Rulemaking, deals with this problem in more detail. In addition to challenges based on alleged procedural violations, persons also may bring challenges alleging substantive violations. There are several different types of substantive challenges: one might allege that the agency is acting outside its statutory or constitutional authorization; another might argue that there is an insufficient factual basis for the agency decision; and still another might claim that the agency has failed to explain adequately the justification for its action.

Example

OSHA goes through notice and comment and re-adopts the CCP. This time, employee unions challenge the rule on the ground that it is beyond the agency's authority to waive mandatory inspections, which are designed to ensure compliance with the law, in return for a commitment from employers to go beyond the safety requirements of the law. In the alternative, if the court determines OSHA has the statutory authority to adopt such a program, the unions argue that OSHA has failed to show a reasonable basis for believing that the CCP will increase worker safety.

Explanation

This example is not a real case, although it could be. Here, OSHA has complied with all the required procedures, but unions are arguing that the CCP is unlawful because the Occupational Safety and Health Act, the law that provides the substantive authority for OSHA's actions, does not authorize such a program. They might argue that the Act does not provide any basis for the program and instead requires that minimum safety standards be met. Therefore, OSHA cannot abandon inspections designed to ensure that the Act's standards have been met merely because an employer has agreed to go beyond the Act's standards. How a court might rule on this claim depends on information beyond that provided here. If the court rules in favor of the unions, the court would normally declare the program invalid and enjoin its use.

In the alternative, the unions can argue that even if such a program might be within the statutory authority of the agency (perhaps because it is intended to increase worker safety), the program is still unlawful, because OSHA has failed to provide any evidence that the program will in fact increase worker safety. How a court would rule on this claim depends on the record of OSHA's decision. That is, what information did OSHA have when it made its decision? For instance, did it have any data supporting the idea that commitments to increase safety beyond that required by the Act would in fact increase worker safety? Perhaps the unions had submitted data showing that fear of OSHA inspections was the primary motivation by employers for complying with the Act, so that the elimination of inspections might reasonably be seen as threatening worker safety. If the court agreed with the unions' arguments in this case, it would probably remand the program to the agency to enable OSHA to possibly cure the problems of evidence or justification for the program. Normally, the court would also enjoin the program at least pending the agency's attempt to cure the problems.

A continuing issue in administrative law is the proper relationship between courts and agencies. During the activist period of the 1970s, the D.C. Circuit described courts and agencies as "partners in furtherance of the public interest" engaged in a "collaborative enterprise." *See Natural Resources Defense Council v. SEC*, 606 F.2d 1031 (D.C. Cir. 1979). Since then, however, Supreme Court decisions have suggested that courts have a particular function to play that is separate from the function of agencies. Yet it is clear that the last word has not been spoken on the subject. The nature of the relationship between courts and agencies is reflected in two particular ways: what kind of cases courts will hear, and what level of deference courts give to agency determinations.

You probably have already run across the concept of "standing" in constitutional law; you will encounter it again in administrative law, as well as some other concepts, such as ripeness, finality, exhaustion, and primary jurisdiction, all of which deal with when and whether courts should hear certain cases in light of the proper roles to be played by agencies and courts. However, even when a court hears an administrative law case, there is still the issue of how it should treat a determination made by an agency: should it give the agency some deference, or should it treat the determination *de novo*? You will find that courts often do give deference to agencies' determinations. What is more difficult is determining the circumstances that justify giving deference and how much deference is appropriate.

VI. STATES IN THE FEDERAL ADMINISTRATIVE LAW SYSTEM

The federal administrative law system includes all three branches of government: Congress creating agencies and giving them their mandates; the agencies constituting the Executive in executing the laws; and the courts ensuring fidelity to the law and Constitution. The states as separate sovereigns do not appear to have a role in this system. Indeed, in recent cases, the Supreme Court has made it clear that it is unconstitutional for Congress to command states to act as agencies, even with respect to matters otherwise clearly within the power of Congress under the Commerce Clause of the U.S. Constitution. *See New York v. United States*, 505 U.S. 144 (1992) (Congress cannot require states either to take title to low-level nuclear waste or to provide for its disposal); *Printz v. United States*, 521 U.S. 898 (1997) (Congress cannot require local law enforcement offices to perform background checks on individuals about to purchase guns).

Nevertheless, those same cases affirmed the ability of Congress to provide incentives to states to induce them to act essentially as agencies under federal law. First, Congress can appropriate funds to the states for various purposes and condition the receipt of those funds upon the state's adoption and administration of various laws. *See South Dakota v. Dole*, 483 U.S. 203 (1987) (federal grant of highway funds can be conditioned on states enacting minimum age to purchase alcohol at 21).[4] Second, Congress can offer the states the option of regulating an area under federal guidelines or having a federal agency regulate the area itself. Both of these types of incentives are widely used in modern legislation, often in combination.

Example

Under the Clean Air Act, the EPA adopts National Ambient Air Quality Standards (NAAQS) applicable throughout the United States. These standards establish the minimum necessary quality of the outside ambient air. The Clean Air Act then establishes various requirements by which to meet and maintain those standards. States are encouraged to submit State Implementation Plans (SIPs) to the EPA demonstrating how the state will

4. There are limits to the ability of Congress to induce states to carry out federal programs by appropriating funds for the programs. In *National Federation of Business v. Sebelius*, 567 U.S. 519 (2012), for example, the Court found that Congress unduly coerced the states by requiring them either to accept the expansion of the Medicaid program or to give up the program altogether.

meet those requirements and meet and attain the NAAQS within the state. The EPA reviews these SIPs to determine whether they indeed meet the federal requirements. If an SIP meets the federal requirements, then implementation of the Clean Air Act NAAQS is essentially left to the state, subject to EPA oversight. If a state fails to adopt an SIP or the EPA does not approve its SIP, the state will lose certain federal highway funds, and the EPA is required to adopt and administer a Federal Implementation Plan in the state.

Explanation

This system of utilizing states to administer the Clean Air Act is constitutionally permissible. The states are not required to adopt SIPs, but if they do not, they will lose certain federal funding, and the regulation of local activity to meet Clean Air Act standards will be left to the federal EPA. From the states' perspective, federal highway funds are important additions to local funds for roads. In addition, states widely believe that if a state agency is determining the means by which to achieve the national standards and is enforcing the means chosen, the burdens of achieving those federal standards will be less than if the federal agency were to have primary responsibility. As a result, virtually every state has opted to submit SIPs to the EPA. This level of inducement, which some view as bordering on extortionate, nevertheless allows the state legally to withdraw from the field, which the Supreme Court has said is sufficient to preserve the state's autonomy and sovereignty under the Constitution.

When a state submits an SIP to the EPA, the state must have adopted the plan as a matter of state law so that the state agency will have sufficient authority to carry out the program it is proposing. If the EPA approves the SIP, the SIP also becomes part of federal law so that it can be enforced in federal court as well.

This practice of establishing federal standards that states may choose to implement under a federal agency's oversight is widespread in the environmental area, including not only the Clean Air Act, but also the Clean Water Act, the Resource Conservation and Recovery Act (involving hazardous waste storage and disposal), and the Safe Drinking Water Act, to name but a few. The Occupational Safety and Health Act, designed to protect worker safety, also utilizes a similar system. In the 1990s, there was a significant move toward "devolution," which is the term for transferring previously federal responsibilities to states in new areas. As a result, much administrative law in practice can involve shared responsibilities between federal and state agencies and authorities that fall under both state and federal law.

VII. STATE ADMINISTRATIVE LAW

Because states are not agencies of the United States, federal administrative law does not apply to states or state agencies. This is true even when states are carrying out federal functions as described above. Rather, state agencies are governed by state administrative law. And, as is true of other areas of the law, each state's administrative law is particular to that state. Like federal administrative law, state administrative law generally evolved through court decisions as a matter of common law, but there have been attempts to codify and unify state administrative law principles. Notably, there have been various Model State APAs, most recently one adopted in 2010. Ten states and the District of Columbia have adopted all or parts of this Model Act. Other states have adopted all or parts of earlier Model Acts. Nevertheless, several major states, including California, New York, Texas, and Florida, have APAs that differ notably from the Model State APAs and from other states' APAs.

This variety among state administrative laws is the primary reason why law school casebooks and courses in administrative law almost never cover state administrative law in a meaningful way. It would simply be impossible to cover them in any depth, and for those law schools whose graduates do not necessarily remain in their law school's state (and those schools that emulate them), one simply would not know which states' administrative law to cover. Nevertheless, outside of Washington, D.C., most lawyers who practice administrative law primarily practice state administrative law.

The compromise adopted by most administrative law casebooks, courses, and this book is to focus on federal administrative law and only to highlight the significant differences between federal law and state law generally and to identify where some states are engaged in unique administrative law undertakings. The justification for this compromise is that, first, many lawyers will in fact be exposed to, if not practice in, the area of federal administrative law, and second, federal administrative law is a good model for administrative law generally. The issues and themes that have arisen in and continue to plague federal administrative law are the same themes with which state courts, legislatures, and executives have struggled.

At this point, therefore, it is helpful to highlight some of the general similarities and differences between state and federal administrative law. One similarity is that both involve action by agencies, and states, like the federal government, have a wide variety of agencies (including "independent" agencies) to engage in functions from regulation of economic activity, licensing, and health and safety regulation to administering entitlements programs.

Another major similarity between federal and state administrative law is that both relate to the procedures applicable to rulemaking and adjudication, and the procedures do not differ a great deal between the federal APA and state APAs. Also, both federal and state administrative law involve the same general questions of judicial review of agency action: whether and when courts should review agency action and to what extent courts should defer to agency determinations.

One difference is that in many states some important agencies are headed by elected officials rather than individuals appointed by the chief executive. When a Lieutenant Governor, Attorney General, Secretary of State, and other officials are elected to office, and especially if they come from a different party than the Governor, the political dynamics of the Executive Branch are significantly different than in the federal system where only one elected official, the President, is in charge of the entire executive branch. In states, the elected officials who head agencies may in fact be political rivals of the Governor. Another peculiar feature of state law is the role of municipalities—counties, cities, and other political subdivisions. These entities generally are not considered agencies of the state and are not governed by the state APA. There is no real equivalent to these subordinate entities in the federal system. Those of you in state universities should know that state universities are agencies of the state generally subject to their state's APA.

VIII. THE ORGANIZATION OF THIS BOOK

The following chapters of this book deal with the various subjects found in administrative law courses. Chapter 2, How Agencies Fit into Our System of Separated Powers, deals with the constitutional underpinnings of the administrative state as well as executive and legislative attempts to control, coordinate, or review agency action. Chapter 3, Adjudication, and Chapter 4, Due Process, address the statutory and constitutional procedural requirements incident to adjudication. Chapter 5, Rulemaking, describes the procedural requirements for rulemaking. Chapter 6, The Availability of Judicial Review, and Chapter 7, The Scope of Judicial Review, then deal with judicial review of agency action. Chapter 8, Government Acquisition of Private Information, and Chapter 9, Public Access to Government Information, consider how government can obtain information from the public and how the public can obtain information from the government. All administrative law courses and casebooks deal with the first six of these subjects; most also deal to some extent with information issues—how the government gets information (and the limits on its ability to get information) and how persons can get information from the government (in particular through the Freedom of Information Act). However, neither courses nor casebooks are consistent in the order in which they treat any of these subjects. Some begin the course with the structural constitutional issues underlying administrative law, whereas others begin directly with agency activity—either rulemaking or adjudication.

This book is arranged so that it can either be read through in the order presented or be referred to in the midst of an administrative law course, no matter how the course is organized.

CHAPTER 2

How Agencies Fit into Our System of Separated Powers

> The accumulation of all powers legislative, executive and judiciary in the same hands, whether of one, a few or many, and whether hereditary, self appointed, or elective, may justly be pronounced the very definition of tyranny.
>
> —*James Madison, The Federalist No. 47* (1788)

I. INTRODUCTION

The Constitution establishes a national government of three branches, each with a different type of power. Article I vests legislative power in Congress; Article II vests executive power in the President; and Article III vests judicial power in the federal courts. Roughly speaking, this means that Congress has the power to make laws; the President has the power to enforce the laws; and the Judiciary has the power to decide how the laws apply in particular cases. The purpose of this separation of different types of powers was to prevent tyranny and thereby protect individual liberty. This purpose is clear from James Madison's warning, quoted above, that an accumulation of these separate powers would produce tyranny.

The existence of federal agencies seems to be in tension with the separation-of-powers scheme in two ways. First, many agencies seem to combine legislative, executive, and judicial powers. Specifically, an agency may have (1) the "quasi-legislative" power to adopt regulations that control people's everyday conduct; (2) the executive power to enforce those regulations and other laws that the agency is responsible for administering; and (3) the "quasi-judicial" power to apply those regulations and laws in individual cases. The EPA, for example, can adopt a rule that prohibits people from destroying wetlands; it can investigate suspected violations of that rule; and, if the EPA decides that someone has violated that rule, it can issue an injunctive-style cease and desist order to that person (subject to judicial review). In a sense, the EPA acts like a legislature, a police officer, and a court all rolled into one.

Second, some agencies not only combine powers resembling those of the three separate branches but also are somewhat insulated from presidential control. These are called "independent agencies," as discussed in Chapter 1. Though insulated from presidential control, most independent agencies serve the executive function of enforcing the laws, often using the combination of powers described in the last paragraph. For example, the Federal Trade Commission enforces the statutes governing unfair trade by promulgating rules defining unfair trade practices, investigating suspected violations of the unfair trade practice rules and statutes, and issuing cease-and-desist orders in individual cases where it has decided a violation has occurred. The FTC thus executes the unfair trade laws, yet, in the ways discussed in Chapter 1, it is independent of control by the President, the head of the Executive Branch. This raises an important question: how can the execution of laws by independent agencies be squared with the fact that Article II specifically vests executive power in the President and obligates him or her to "take care" that the laws are faithfully executed? *See* U.S. Const. art. II, § 3.

These two features of many modern agencies—the combination of different types of powers that many have and the independence from presidential control that some have—have provoked a long-running debate over how agencies fit into the scheme of separated powers established by the Constitution. Indeed, some legal scholars have argued that the modern administrative state violates the Constitution. That is a minority view, however. Most important, that view is not shared by the U.S. Supreme Court. The Court has generally accepted the combination of powers found in many agencies and the independence of some of those agencies. That acceptance stems in part from the text of the Constitution and in part from pragmatism.

Two constitutional provisions are especially relevant to the Court's acceptance of the modern administrative state. First, the Constitution not only prescribes a scheme of separated powers; it also authorizes Congress to make all laws "necessary and proper" for ensuring that all of these powers, including the executive power, are exercised effectively. U.S. Const. art. I, § 8, cl. 18. The Court has often recognized that, in light of the complexity and rapidly changing nature of society, it is "necessary and proper" for Congress to give quasi-legislative and quasi-judicial powers to administrative agencies. Second, the Constitution prescribes a system of checks and balances that precludes a complete separation of powers. For example, the President's power to veto legislation gives him or her a role in the legislative process. On the flip side, the Senate has the power of "advice and consent" with respect to the President's selection of the most important officers in the executive branch. The system of checks and balances implies that some overlap among the branches is necessary to the effective functioning of the government, and the Necessary and Proper Clause empowers Congress to enact statutes to ensure its proper functioning.

In light of these provisions, the Supreme Court sometimes takes what academics call a "functional"—and what the Court itself often calls a "practical"—approach in separation-of-powers cases. This approach emphasizes that the Constitution was designed to create a "workable" government. *See, e.g., Loving v. United States*, 517 U.S. 748, 756 (1996) ("While the Constitution diffuses power the better to secure liberty, it also contemplates that practice will integrate the dispersed powers into a workable government." (quoting *Youngstown Sheet & Tube Co. v. Sawyer*, 343 U.S. 579 (1952) (Jackson, J., concurring))). When the Court adopts that emphasis, it usually focuses on whether an administrative scheme undermines the proper functioning of any of the three branches. Sometimes the Court adopts a different emphasis, one that stresses the seemingly sharp separation of the branches established in Articles I, II, and III. When the Court adopts that emphasis, it usually takes what academics call a "formalistic" approach in reviewing separation-of-powers challenges. It looks for clear lines, and tries to announce clear-cut rules, dividing the powers of the three branches. These two approaches—one functional (practical), the other formalistic—are much debated among scholars of administrative law. You will find evidence of each approach in the case law that we discuss in this chapter.

This chapter discusses how agencies fit into the structure of government established by the Constitution. First, we discuss precedent on Congress's power to delegate quasi-legislative and quasi-judicial powers to administrative agencies. After discussing those limits in Section II, we turn in Section III.A to constitutional limits that apply when, having invested an agency with power, Congress tries to control the agency's exercise of that power. You are no doubt familiar with the most prevalent and well-established form of congressional control: congressional oversight, which is done primarily by congressional committees—in oversight hearings, for example. Congress has also used other ways to control agency action, some of which the Supreme Court has held unconstitutional.

After discussing congressional means of controlling agency action, we explore executive means of controlling agency action. The primary means available to the President are the powers to appoint and to remove executive officers. These powers, as we will see, are subject to some limits. In addition to the "life and death" powers of appointment and removal, the President has less drastic means of control over administrative action, many of which he or she exercises through subordinates. These executive controls on agency action are explored in Section III.B.

Before wading in, we warn you. The constitutional limits on the creation and control of agencies is an incredibly rich (some would say dense) subject, like a triple-layer, chocolate-fudge cake, with cream-cheese icing and cherries on top. You may have an administrative-law sweet tooth, or you may prefer the meat-and-potatoes subjects, such as agency rulemaking and adjudication, discussed in other chapters. Either way, you may find the material in this chapter more digestible if you realize its fundamental importance to the practice of administrative law.

The material in this chapter is all about power. Agencies wield enormous power over almost every aspect of modern life. Agencies have the power to do great harm to someone (by penalizing a polluter, for example) or to confer great benefits on someone (by awarding a lucrative telecommunications license, for example). Furthermore, many agency actions affect not only individuals, such as polluters and license applicants, but also millions of members of the public. Those who seek to avoid agency harms, those who seek to gain agency benefits, and those who assert the public interest need lawyers. So do the agencies themselves. For a lawyer to help her client effectively (whether the client is a private person, a public interest organization, or a government agency), the lawyer must understand how agencies fit into the structure of government. That structure, as we hope this introduction has begun to show, differs from the simple, three-branch system that most people learn about in school.

Example

Some people describe federal agencies, especially the independent agencies, as collectively constituting the "headless fourth branch of government." *City of Arlington, Texas v. FCC*, 569 U.S. 290, 314 (2013) (Roberts, C.J., dissenting). In what sense do federal agencies make up a "fourth" branch? In what sense is that fourth branch "headless"? Were our high school civics teachers lying to us when they said that our national government has only three branches?

Explanation

Some have described federal agencies as making up a fourth branch of government because so many of those agencies combine powers resembling those separately associated with the legislative, executive, and judicial branches. This combination feature makes agencies seem distinct from the three branches established in the Constitution. Indeed, the designation "fourth branch" is sometimes used pejoratively, to imply that the combination of powers in the typical federal agency violates the separation-of-powers scheme of the Constitution.

This fourth branch has been called "headless" to imply that agencies are not subject to any central control. The implication is not limited to independent agencies, though they have been singled out for particular criticism by some. Even traditional executive branch agencies are, some would say, too large and powerful to be effectively controlled by the President. Moreover, officials in many agencies are the specific recipients of congressional grants of power that apparently can be exercised without presidential interference.

Nonetheless, our high school civics teachers were not lying to us; at worst, they were just simplifying. The term "headless fourth branch" is a figure of speech. It has a kernel of truth, but it is not entirely accurate.

For one thing, agencies do not literally exercise the powers of the three separate branches. In particular, although many agencies have the power to make rules that have a legal effect similar to that of legislation, an agency's rulemaking power, unlike Congress's legislative power, comes from a statute, not the Constitution. Thus, Congress gets to decide the scope of the agency's rulemaking powers. Moreover, most agency rules are subject to judicial review to determine whether they fall within the statutory grant of rulemaking power. For these reasons, the rulemaking power of agencies is only "quasi"-legislative. Similarly, an agency's power to adjudicate cases is only "quasi"-judicial because it comes from a statute, rather than the Constitution, and the agency's exercise of that power in individual cases is ordinarily subject to judicial review. Here is how the Court has explained the point that executive branch agencies do not literally exercise legislative or judicial power:

> Agencies make rules ("Private cattle may be grazed on public lands X, Y, and Z subject to certain conditions") and conduct adjudications ("This rancher's grazing permit is revoked for violation of the conditions") and have done so since the beginning of the Republic. These activities take "legislative" and "judicial" forms, but they are exercises of—indeed, under our constitutional structure they *must be* exercises of—the "executive Power." Art. II, § 1, cl. 1.

City of Arlington, Texas v. FCC, 569 U.S. 290, 304 n.4 (2013).

For another thing, even "independent" agencies are not beyond the control of officials in the three branches. Most independent agencies are considered part of the executive branch; for example, the statute creating the Social Security Administration states, "There is hereby established, as an independent agency in the executive branch of the Government, a Social Security Administration." 42 U.S.C. § 901(a). Independent agencies in the executive branch are subject to many of the same laws, including the Administrative Procedure Act (APA), as are other executive branch agencies. Moreover, as a practical matter, independent agencies depend on, and are therefore subject to control by, the three branches. Congress has to fund the agency; the Executive Branch must (if nothing else) create office space for the agency; and the federal courts will usually be able to review most actions by the agency affecting private rights. Other means of congressional and executive control are discussed later in this chapter.

II. DELEGATION DOCTRINE

In general, administrative agencies are creatures of statute. The typical federal agency exists only because Congress has created it to deal with a particular problem. In addition to creating the agency and assigning it a problem, Congress "delegates" powers to the agency for it to use in dealing with the assigned problem. The constitutional limits on Congress's authority to delegate certain types of power to administrative agencies make up what is called the "delegation" (or, interchangeably, the "nondelegation") doctrine. The Court's cases on the delegation doctrine divide into two lines.

One line of cases concerns federal statutes that delegate "quasi-legislative" power, meaning the power to make rules that have a legal effect on people's everyday conduct. The central issue in those cases is whether Congress has given an agency so much rulemaking discretion that Congress has abdicated its responsibility to exercise "[a]ll legislative Powers" granted in the Constitution. U.S. Const. art. I, § 1.

The other line of cases concerns federal statutes that delegate "quasi-judicial" power, meaning the power (typically subject to judicial review) to apply the law to particular cases and issue orders that affect the legal rights of identified parties. The central issue in these cases is whether Congress has given so much adjudicatory power to an agency that Congress has undermined the federal courts' authority to exercise "[t]he judicial Power of the United States." U.S. Const. art. III, § 1.

Unlike Congress's delegation of quasi-legislative or quasi-judicial powers, Congress's delegation of executive powers to an executive agency does not implicate the delegation doctrine. Constitutional issues do arise when Congress delegates executive power to an agency or official who is independent of presidential control. These issues are not the subject of the delegation doctrine, however, and so we defer discussion of them for now.

A note on terminology before we start: You will often hear the terms "delegation doctrine" or "nondelegation doctrine" used to refer to precedent on statutes that delegate quasi-legislative power to agencies. Those terms are not often used to refer to precedent on statutes that delegate quasi-*judicial* power to agencies. And indeed, in the latter context, the term "delegation" is not entirely accurate. Congress cannot "delegate"—i.e., transfer—judicial power because Congress has no judicial power to begin with. But the more important point is that both congressional grants of quasi-legislative power and congressional quasi-judicial power to executive agencies raise separation-of-powers concerns. The constitutional limits on such grants differ, however, as we shall now see.

A. Legislative Powers

Congress gives many agencies the power to make rules that create legal duties. One question that can arise when Congress has done so is whether a particular agency rule falls within the scope of that agency's statutory grant of rulemaking power. Does the EPA's statutory power to make rules controlling the pollution of "navigable waters," for example, allow it to make rules for wetlands? The issue of whether a regulation falls within an agency's statutory grant of rulemaking power is discussed in Chapter 5 (Rulemaking) and Chapter 7 (The Scope of Judicial Review). We raise the issue here just to distinguish it from the issue that we discuss in this section.

Distinct from the issue of whether a rule falls within the agency's statutory grant of rulemaking power is the issue of whether the statute granting that power is too broad. For example, does the Federal Trade Commission's statutory power to make rules defining "unfair or deceptive" trade practices impermissibly delegate legislative power to the Commission? That issue is the subject of the delegation doctrine, and that doctrine is the subject of this section.

The constitutional test for Congress's delegation of quasi-legislative power to an agency or official is easily stated: Congress can delegate quasi-legislative power as long as it gives the agency (or official) an "intelligible principle" to follow in exercising that power. The Supreme Court has generally interpreted the "intelligible principle" test to allow Congress to give very broad rulemaking powers to federal agencies. To understand the test and the Court's current interpretation of it, you need a bit of history.

The earliest relevant cases of the Court actually did not involve grants of rulemaking power to agencies; they involved, instead, statutes that gave some control over foreign trade to the President. The first such case was *Brig Aurora*, 11 U.S. (7 Cranch) 382 (1813). That case involved a statute that authorized the President to suspend a statutory trade embargo against France and England when the President determined that those countries had stopped violating the "neutral commerce" of the United States. One of the parties in *Brig Aurora* argued that the statute improperly delegated "legislative" power to the President by allowing him to decide when the statute imposing the embargo would be suspended. *Id.* at 386. The Court rejected that argument with little discussion. *See id.* at 388. In a later case involving a similar statute, the Court explained that Congress can enact legislation the effect of which depends on the President's determination that a "named contingency" exists. *See Field v. Clark*, 143 U.S. 649, 693 (1892). These cases are relevant to the delegation of quasi-legislative power because they upheld executive action that had a legislative effect.

In other early cases, the Court upheld federal statutes that gave executive agencies the power to adopt regulations. In *United States v. Grimaud*, 220 U.S. 506 (1911), for example, the Court affirmed the conviction of the defendants for grazing sheep in a national forest without getting the permits required under a regulation promulgated by the Secretary of Agriculture. The Court rejected the defendants' argument that the statute authorizing the regulation impermissibly delegated legislative authority to an executive official. The Court emphasized that the statute did not empower the Secretary to make rules "for any and every purpose." *Id.* at 522. Instead, the statute required those rules to serve the purpose of preserving national forests. The statute thus drew a "circle" within which the Secretary was to regulate. *Id.* at 518. This reasoning went further than the "named contingency" cases. Those cases had upheld only executive action that triggered rules that Congress itself had enacted. In contrast, cases such as *Grimaud* allowed the executive to make the rules.

In *J.W. Hampton, Jr., & Co. v. United States*, 276 U.S. 394 (1928), the Court adopted the test for legislative delegations that is still used today. *J.W. Hampton* concerned a federal statute that authorized the President to increase statutorily prescribed duties on certain foreign goods. The statute allowed him to increase the duties on a certain type of goods when he determined that an increase was necessary to equalize the costs of production between the United States and the foreign country that produced the goods. In upholding the statute, the Court said, "If Congress shall lay down by legislative act an intelligible principle to which the person or body authorized [to exercise delegated authority] is directed to conform, such legislative action is not a forbidden delegation of legislative power." *J.W. Hampton*, 276 U.S. at 409. This "intelligible principle" test seemed to allow executive agencies and officials to take actions that had legislative effect and that were based on their own policy judgments, as long as Congress gave them an overarching policy within which to act.

Despite the apparent breadth of the intelligible principle test articulated in *J.W. Hampton* in 1928, the Court struck down two federal statutes on delegation grounds in 1935. The first case was *Panama Refining Co. v. Ryan*, 293 U.S. 388 (1935), which is often called the *Hot Oil Case*. There, the Court invalidated a provision in the National Industrial Recovery Act (NIRA) that authorized the President to ban interstate shipments of oil produced in violation of state law. The Court found no intelligible principle for the President to follow in determining when to ban an interstate shipment of "hot oil." *See id.* at 252-253 ("As to the transportation of oil production in excess of state permission, the Congress has declared no policy, has established no standard, has laid down no rule. There is no requirement, no definition of circumstances and conditions in which the transportation is to be allowed or prohibited."). The second case was *A.L.A. Schechter Poultry Corp. v. United States*, 295 U.S. 495 (1935), which is known as the *Sick Chicken Case*. There, the Court struck down a provision of the NIRA that authorized the President to approve "codes of fair competition" for the poultry industry and other industries. The Court was particularly concerned that the Act did not prescribe adequate administrative procedures for approval of the codes.[1]

This pair of 1935 delegation cases may have reflected a broad skepticism by the Court at that time toward statutes that attempted ambitious economic regulation. At around the same time, the Court struck down other economic regulation statutes as violating substantive due process or exceeding Congress's power under the Commerce Clause. The period is thought to have ended in the late 1930s and early 1940s. In that later period, the Court overruled some of its earlier decisions that had been based on substantive due process and the Commerce Clause. The Court has never disavowed its delegation rulings in *Panama Refining* and *Schechter Poultry*, however.

Nonetheless, since 1936, the Court has upheld all of the many federal statutes that it has reviewed under the delegation doctrine. Many of those statutes delegated rulemaking authority to federal agencies under quite broad standards. For example, the Court upheld a wartime statute that authorized a federal Price Administrator to set "generally fair and equitable" prices. *Yakus v. United States*, 321 U.S. 414 (1944). The Court upheld a statute authorizing the Federal Communications Commission to issue regulations "as public convenience, interest, or necessity requires." *United States v. Southwestern Cable Co.*, 392 U.S. 157 (1968). *See also National Broadcasting Co. v. United States*, 319 U.S. 190 (1943) (upholding statute empowering FCC to regulate broadcasters in the "public interest."). The Court upheld a statute authorizing the Federal Power Commission to set "just and reasonable" rates for power. *FPC v. Hope Natural Gas Co.*, 320 U.S. 591 (1944). More recently, the Court upheld a statute authorizing EPA to set standards for certain air pollutants at a level "requisite to protect the public health" with

---

1. In a third case from the same period, *Carter v. Carter Coal Co.*, 298 U.S. 238 (1936), the Court struck down a statute that, in effect, delegated regulatory authority to members of the coal industry. The Court said that delegation "to private persons whose interests may be and often are adverse to the interests of others in the same business" is "legislative delegation in its most obnoxious form." *Id.* at 311. The Court invalidated the statute on the ground that it violated the Due Process Clause of the Fifth Amendment. Because *Carter Coal* involved delegation to private parties, rather than government officials, and rested on due process instead of separation of powers, it is usually not counted as a case invalidating a legislative delegation. *See, e.g., Loving v. United States*, 517 U.S. 748, 771 (1996) ("Though in 1935 we struck down two statutes for lack of an intelligible principle [citing *Panama Refining* and *Schechter Poultry*], we have since upheld, without exception, delegations under standards phrased in sweeping terms.").

an "adequate margin of safety." *Whitman v. American Trucking Assns.*, 531 U.S. 457, 474 (2001).

The most recent case by the Court on the nondelegation doctrine reaffirms that the doctrine will seldom invalidate a statute delegating quasi-legislative power to a federal agency. At the same time, this recent case shows that some Justices think the doctrine should be more restrictive of Congress's delegation of quasi-legislative power.

The case is *Gundy v. United States*, 588 U.S. 128 (2019). *Gundy* concerned the Sexual Offender Registration and Notification Act (SORNA). SORNA requires sex offenders to register their addresses with local law enforcement agencies or face criminal penalties of up to ten years in prison. Gundy challenged a provision in SORNA that authorized the Attorney General to issue rules specifying how and to what extent SORNA's requirements applied to people, like Gundy, who were convicted of sex offenses before SORNA's enactment. The Court held that the provision did not violate the nondelegation doctrine. A plurality of four Justices held that the provision supplied an "intelligible principle" for the Attorney General to follow because it required pre-Act offenders to be subject to SORNA's registration requirements "as soon as feasible." *Id.* at 132 (opinion of Kagan, J., joined by Ginsburg, Breyer, and Sotomayor, JJ.). A fifth Justice concurred in the judgment but stated that he would support an effort "to reconsider the approach we have taken for the past 84 years." *Id.* at 149 (Alito, J., concurring in the judgment). Three Justices dissented, arguing that the current version of the "intelligible principle" test "has no basis in the original meaning of the Constitution, in history, or even in the decision from which it was plucked" (*J.W. Hampton, supra*). *Id.* at 164 (Gorsuch, J., joined by Roberts, C.J., and Thomas, J., dissenting). One Justice (Kavanaugh) did not participate. Overall, *Gundy* is significant in showing a level of dissatisfaction with the "intelligible principle" standard that we have not seen in other modern precedent.[2]

The primary rationale for the Court decisions upholding broad delegations is pragmatic (or, to use the scholarly term, "functional"). The plurality in *Gundy* explained that the Court's intelligible principle test and the Court's lenient application of it reflect that "in our increasingly complex society, replete with ever changing and more technical problems . . . Congress

---

2. An increased willingness to consider nondelegation challenges to statutes is reflected in a recent *en banc* Fifth Circuit decision. *Consumers Research v. FCC*, 109 F.4th 743 (5th Cir. 2024) (*en banc*). There, the court said that as a result of the lack of intelligible principle it had "grave concerns" about the constitutionality of the congressional delegation to the Federal Communications Commission to fund the Universal Service Program. Ultimately, the court held the program unconstitutional because it relied on two questionable delegations, one from Congress to the FCC and one from the FCC to a private organization. Because two courts of appeals had upheld the program against such challenges, this case is sure to go to the Supreme Court and provide further elucidation of the limits of delegation.

simply cannot do its job absent an ability to delegate power under broad general directives." *Gundy*, 588 U.S. at 135 (plurality opinion) (quoting *Mistretta v. United States*, 488 U.S. 361, 372 (1989)). This reasoning emphasizes that, for Congress to fulfill its legislative function effectively, it must be able to leave details to the agencies.

While consistently upholding broad delegations, the Court has also suggested that the delegation doctrine still has teeth. The Court has sometimes emphasized that a broad statutory standard was informed by practices in the regulated industry. *See, e.g., Fahey v. Mallonee*, 332 U.S. 245, 250 (1947) (statute delegating regulatory authority to banking agencies was informed by "well-known and generally acceptable standards" in banking industry). In other cases, the Court has determined that an agency's exercise of delegated authority would be curbed by administrative procedures prescribed by statute. *See, e.g., Yakus, supra* (Price Administrator had to follow public procedures and issue a written explanation in fixing prices). These cases stress the importance of circumstances that control the exercise of broad delegations, rather than the breadth of the delegation itself.

Moreover, although the Court has not used the nondelegation doctrine to invalidate a federal statute since 1936, the Court has used it to justify interpreting a federal statute narrowly. The most important such case is *Industrial Union Dept., AFL-CIO v. American Petroleum Institute*, 448 U.S. 607 (1980), which is known as the *Benzene Case*. In that case, a plurality of the Court narrowly construed statutes that authorized the Occupational Safety and Health Administration (OSHA) to regulate benzene and other toxic chemicals in the workplace. The plurality rejected OSHA's broad interpretation of those statutes partly because the plurality believed that, so interpreted, the statutes "might" violate the delegation doctrine. *Id.* at 646. A fifth Justice concluded that the statutes themselves violated the delegation doctrine, however they were interpreted. *Id.* at 672 (Rehnquist, J., concurring in the judgment). *See also National Cable Television Assn. v. United States*, 415 U.S. 336 (1974) (narrowly interpreting an FCC statute to avoid delegation problem).

In sum, the delegation doctrine permits Congress to delegate broad regulatory authority to administrative agencies and officials. These delegations do not violate the doctrine as long as Congress articulates an "intelligible principle" for the agency or official to follow. The principle may be as general as one that directs the agency or official to regulate "in the public interest." Although the Court has expressed concern that such broad delegations be accompanied by procedural or other abuse-curbing safeguards, those safeguards typically will be supplied by the APA. Accordingly, unless the Court changes the doctrine, it will apply only rarely, and even then will usually result, not in the invalidation of a statute, but in a narrow interpretation.

Example

A federal statute lists the types and amounts of nutrients that infant formulas must contain. The statute also provides, however, that the Secretary of the Food and Drug Administration "may by regulation" revise the list so as to add or delete nutrients or to change the amounts prescribed in the statute. The statute does not expressly provide any standard for these revisions. Does the statute violate the delegation doctrine?

Explanation

The infant-formula statute probably does not violate the delegation doctrine. The statute does grant quasi-legislative authority to the Secretary of the FDA. Congress engaged in legislative action when it enacted the list of required nutrients for infant formula, and, when the Secretary revises that list by promulgating a regulation, she engages in quasi-legislative action. The statutory grant of power to the Secretary to make such a revision therefore implicates the delegation doctrine. To decide whether the statute violates that doctrine, a court would determine whether it supplies an "intelligible principle" for the Secretary to follow when she undertakes a revision. Although the statute does not explicitly prescribe any principle to guide the Secretary, a court would probably construe the statute to do so implicitly. In particular, the court would probably reason that the statute requires the Secretary to make revisions to ensure that infant formulas are "nutritious." This implicit "nutritiousness" standard would almost certainly be intelligible enough to withstand constitutional challenge. *See* 21 U.S.C. § 350a.

Example

A federal statute authorizes the Secretary of Interior to issue regulations "for the use and management" of the national parks. The statute requires the regulations to "conform to the fundamental purpose[s]" of having national parks, which are "to conserve the scenery, natural and historic objects, and wild life . . . and to provide for the enjoyment of [the same] in such manner and by such means as will leave them unimpaired for the enjoyment of future generations." The statute provides that violations of the Secretary's regulations can be punished with imprisonment for up to 6 months and fines.

The Secretary has issued regulations establishing speed limits and prohibiting drunk driving on roads in national parks. Sammi is convicted of violating those regulations and receives a $500 fine and a three-month prison sentence. He challenges his conviction on the ground that the statute authorizing the regulations violates the delegation doctrine. Evaluate his challenge.

Explanation

Sammi's delegation challenge to the Secretary's traffic regulations for national parks will almost certainly fail. The statute does delegate quasi-legislative power to the Secretary. Indeed, these regulations operate much like criminal statutes since a violation of them triggers the criminal penalties prescribed in the statute. Thus, the statute implicates the delegation doctrine. The statute, however, satisfies the requirements of the delegation doctrine. In the case on which this example is based, the court made two determinations in rejecting a delegation challenge. *See United States v. Brown*, 364 F.3d 1266 (11th Cir. 2004). First, the court determined that the statute, though broadly worded, provides an "intelligible principle" for the Secretary to follow when issuing regulations for the national parks. As relevant to the regulations that Sammi was convicted of violating, the statute allows the Secretary to design a system of roads as well as a system of road regulation that permits safe use and enjoyment of the national parks. Second, the court emphasized that although violations of the regulations carry criminal penalties, that is true only because Congress has authorized those criminal penalties and specified what the penalties could be. The court's second determination reflects Supreme Court case law. The Supreme Court has held that Congress can delegate to administrative agencies the power to issue regulations the violation of which carries criminal penalties. *See United States v. Grimaud*, 220 U.S. 506 (1911). In so holding, however, the Court has made clear that Congress must specifically authorize criminal penalties for regulatory violations. *See Loving v. United States*, 517 U.S. 748, 768 (1996). Thus, for example, a statutory grant of power merely to issue "such regulations as may be necessary and proper" for the use and enjoyment of the national parks probably would not be sufficient authority for the Secretary to issue regulations that carried criminal penalties. Courts would hold that Congress must make the fundamental policy decision of whether violations of a particular body of regulations should be a crime.

B. Adjudicative Powers

In addition to delegating quasi-legislative power to administrative agencies and officials, Congress can delegate quasi-judicial powers to them. The Supreme Court has treated such adjudicative delegations differently from legislative delegations, however. Whereas the test for a legislative delegation is whether it prescribes an intelligible principle, the test for an adjudicative delegation cannot be encapsulated so easily. The Court's main concern about an adjudicative delegation to an agency or other non-Article III entity is that the delegation not undermine the Article III branch. That concern, like the concern limiting legislative delegations, is best understood through a brief history of the Court's major decisions.

In early cases, the Court approved federal laws that delegated adjudicatory power to non-Article III entities in three main situations. Non-Article III entities could serve as military courts, as territorial courts, and as tribunals for adjudicating "public rights." *Northern Pipeline Construction Co. v. Marathon Pipe Line Co.*, 458 U.S. 50, 67-68 (1982).

Of these three situations, the most important one for administrative law purposes is the one authorizing non-Article III entities to adjudicate public rights. *See Crowell v. Benson*, 285 U.S. 22 (1932). The "public rights exception" not only authorizes administrative agencies to adjudicate matters without violating Article III, the exception also allows them to adjudicate matters without a jury, including matters as to which the Seventh Amendment would require a jury trial if the matter were tried in a federal court. *Oil States Energy Servs., LLC v. Greene's Energy Grp.*, 584 U.S. 325, 345 (2018) ("[W]hen Congress properly assigns a matter to adjudication in a non-Article III tribunal, the Seventh Amendment poses no independent bar to the adjudication of that action by a nonjury factfinder.") (internal quotation marks omitted).[3] The public rights exception functions as an exception to both Article III's and the Seventh Amendment's requirements.

In early cases, the Court defined "public rights" to mean noncriminal, statutory claims by or against the federal government. Examples of claims *by* the government were agency enforcement proceedings for regulatory violations. Examples of claims *against* the government were claims for government benefits. *See, e.g., Granfinanciera, S.A. v. Nordberg*, 492 U.S. 33, 68 (1989) (Scalia, J., concurring in part) (public rights were long understood to include "rights *of the public*—that is, rights pertaining to claims brought by or against the United States").

The Court later extended "public rights" to include disputes between *private* parties that were "closely intertwined with a federal regulatory program Congress ha[d] power to enact." *Granfinanciera*, 492 U.S. at 55 & n.10. In *Commodity Futures Trading Commission v. Schor*, 478 U.S. 833 (1986), for example, the Court upheld federal agency adjudication of claims and counterclaims between commodity brokers and their customers under a statute comprehensively regulating the sale of commodity futures. In *Thomas v. Union Carbide Agricultural Products Co.*, 473 U.S. 568 (1985), the Court upheld agency adjudication of claims by one pesticide manufacturer against another under a comprehensive statutory scheme regulating pesticides and other chemical products used in agriculture.

A still more recent case by the Court, however, has restricted the scope of the public rights exception, at least with respect to claims by the federal government. The case is *Securities and Exchange Commission v. Jarkesy*, 144 S. Ct. 2117 (2024).

---

3. The Seventh Amendment says in relevant part, "In suits at common law, where the value in controversy shall exceed twenty dollars, the right of trial by jury shall be preserved. . . ."

In *Jarkesy*, the SEC brought an administrative enforcement proceeding for securities fraud against George Jarkesy, Jr., and his company. In that enforcement proceeding, the SEC obtained civil penalties of $300,000 against Jarkesy and the company. Jarkesy argued that the proceeding violated the Seventh Amendment because the administrative proceeding did not (and could not) include a jury trial. *See Pernell v. Southall Realty*, 416 U.S. 363, 383 (1974) ("[T]he Seventh Amendment is generally inapplicable in administrative proceedings, where jury trials would be incompatible with the whole concept of administrative adjudication.").

The Court in *Jarkesy* agreed that the SEC's use of an administrative adjudication to impose civil penalties violated the Seventh Amendment. The Court used a two-step analysis.

It held, first, that the SEC's claims for civil penalties implicated the Seventh Amendment. The Court explained that the Seventh Amendment's preservation of the right to a jury trial in "[s]uits at common law" referred to suits "which are not of equity or admiralty jurisprudence"—i.e., suits that are "legal in nature." *Jarkesy*, 144 S. Ct. at 2128 (internal quotation marks omitted). The Court determined that the SEC's claims for civil penalties were "legal in nature." *Id.* at 2129. They were legal, rather than equitable, because they were "designed to punish or deter the wrongdoer," rather than to "restore the status quo." *Id.* (second quoted phrase quoting *Tull v. United States*, 481 U.S. 412, 422 (1987)). Thus, the Seventh Amendment applied to the SEC's claims.

Second, the Court held that the SEC's claims did not fall into the "'public rights' exception" to the Seventh Amendment. *Id.* at 2131. For one thing, the SEC's claims did not fall into any of the categories of cases that "historically could have been determined exclusively by the executive and legislative branches." *Id.* at 2132 (internal quotation marks and brackets omitted). Those "historic categories" included the federal government's collection of revenue, certain immigration and tariff matters, relations with Indian tribes, administration of the public lands, and granting of government benefits, like payments to veterans, pensions, and patent rights. *Id.* at 2132-2133. For another thing, the SEC's claims "replicated common law fraud," a type of claim that the Court had held must be tried by a federal court, where a jury trial is available. *Id.* at 2134-2136 (discussing *Granfinanciera, S.A. v. Nordberg*, 492 U.S. 33 (1989) (creditors' claims against bankrupt debtor for fraudulent conveyance had to be brought in Article III court rather than in non-Article III bankruptcy court)).

The *Jarkesy* Court distinguished *Atlas Roofing Co. v. Occupational Safety & Health Review Commission*, 430 U.S. 443 (1977), on which the SEC relied in arguing that its claims for civil penalties could be adjudicated by the agency. In *Atlas Roofing*, the Court held that a federal agency could adjudicate the government's claim for civil penalties against a roofing company for violating workplace safety laws. But *Atlas Roofing* differed materially from the case before it, said the *Jarkesy* Court, because the government's claims for civil penalties in *Atlas Roofing* involved "a new cause of action . . . unknown to the common law." *Jarkesy*, 144 S. Ct. at 2137 (quoting *Atlas Roofing*, 430 U.S. at 461). "Rather than reiterate common law terms of art," like the securities-fraud provisions in *Jarkesy* did, the workplace safety standards for which civil penalties were sought in *Atlas Roofing* "instead resembled a detailed building code." *Id.* at 2138. Thus, they did not replicate any common law cause of action.

As a result of *Jarkesy*, the SEC must now go to federal court to recover civil penalties for securities fraud. In addition, *Jarkesy* will likely bar other federal agencies' use of administrative proceedings to impose civil penalties. The dissent observed that Congress has "enacted more than 200 statutes authorizing dozens of agencies to impose civil penalties for violations of statutory obligations." 144 S. Ct. at 2155 (Sotomayor, J., joined by Kagan and Jackson, JJ., dissenting). Those statutes had generally been thought to be constitutional under *Atlas Roofing*. *Jarkesy*, however, suggests that civil penalties can be imposed in an agency adjudication only if they either (1) fall into one of the "historic categories" of public rights, several of which the Court identified in *Jarkesy* (while emphasizing that it did not intend to be exhaustive) (*id.* at 2133) or (2) involve "a new cause of action . . . unknown to the common law," *id.* at 2137 (quoting *Atlas Roofing*, 430 U.S. at 461).

Although the *Jarkesy* dissent accused the majority of "tak[ing] a wrecking ball to . . . settled law," the majority addressed only agency adjudication of civil penalties and other remedies that are "legal in nature." *Jarkesy*, 144 S. Ct. at 2128. It did not address remedies that are equitable in nature. *Id.* at 2139 (civil penalties sought by SEC in that case "can make no pretense of being equitable"). The administrative adjudication in *Jarkesy* imposed not only civil monetary penalties but also nonmonetary remedies that would probably qualify as equitable in nature. Specifically, the SEC directed Jarkesy and his company to cease and desist violating the laws against securities fraud; it ordered Jarkesy's company to disgorge earnings; and it barred Jarkesy from participating in the securities industry. *Id.* at 2127; *see also Liu v. SEC*, 591 U.S. 71 (2020) (holding that disgorgement award in SEC civil enforcement action that did not exceed wrongdoer's net profits, and that was awarded for victims, was equitable relief). *Jarkesy* does not disturb the use of agency adjudication to impose remedies that are equitable in nature.

Nor did the majority in *Jarkesy* address its past decisions upholding agency adjudication of disputes between private parties: namely, *Commodity Futures Trading Commn. v. Schor*, 478 U.S. 833 (1986) (upholding agency adjudication of claims and counterclaims between commodity brokers and their customers); and *Thomas v. Union Carbide Agricultural Products*, 473 U.S. 568 (1985) (upholding agency adjudication of claims by one pesticide manufacturer against another). The majority's silence on *Schor* and *Thomas* contrasts with the concurring opinion, which criticized *Schor* and *Thomas* for departing from "a traditional understanding of public rights." *Jarkesy*, 144 S. Ct. at 2149 (Gorsuch, J., joined by Thomas, J., concurring); *see also id.* at 2165 (Sotomayor, J., joined by Kagan and Jackson, JJ., dissenting) (criticizing majority for "failing to account for" *Schor* and *Thomas*). While the Court might revisit *Schor* and *Thomas* in a future case, in the meantime *Jarkesy* will cast doubt on the many federal statutes authorizing agencies to impose civil penalties in administrative adjudications.

Example

The EPA requires companies that incinerate hazardous waste to get a permit. To get a permit, a company initially applies to EPA staff for the Region in which the incinerator is located. If the Region denies the permit, the company can appeal to an "Environmental Appeals Board," an administrative tribunal in EPA. If the Board upholds the denial of the permit, the company can seek review by the EPA Administrator. If the Administrator's decision is adverse to the company, the company can get judicial review under the APA.

Invincerator, Inc., is denied an incinerator permit at all levels of the EPA. In the lawsuit challenging the EPA's denial of the permit, Invincerator argues that the permitting scheme violates Article III because it improperly delegates adjudicatory powers to non-Article III entities (namely, the Region, the Board, and the Administrator). Is Invincerator right?

Explanation

An incinerator company's delegation argument went up in flames in the case on which this example was based. *See Marine Shale Processors, Inc. v. EPA*, 81 F.3d 1371 (5th Cir. 1996). The EPA is, indeed, exercising adjudicatory power when it rules on the company's application for a permit. The court held, however, that the statute granting the EPA adjudicatory power did not violate Article III. The court observed that the EPA adjudication involved public rights; it was a dispute to which the government was a party. The other factors cited by the court were that (1) the permit process was part of a broad regulatory program designed to protect the public health; (2) the scientific and technical nature of the dispute made it well-suited for initial adjudication by administrative bodies; (3) the class of disputes adjudicated under the statute was small; (4) the right at stake was not analogous to ones considered to be at the core of those traditionally adjudicated by Article III courts; (5) the EPA did not have a wide range of judicial powers, such as the power to issue writs or hold jury trials; and (6) the EPA's decision was subject to judicial review.

The factors cited by the court in *Marine Shale Processors* come from the Court's decision in *Commodity Futures Trading Commission v. Schor*. As discussed above, *Schor* involved a dispute between private parties. After *Jarkesy*, it is unclear whether *Schor*'s multi-factor test will continue to govern analysis of disputes between the government and a private party, like the permit proceeding in *Marine Shale Processors*. *Jarkesy* suggests that if a permit proceeding involves public rights, the public rights nature of the proceeding, standing alone, obviates Article III and Seventh Amendment concerns.

The Fifth Circuit in *Marine Shale Processors* held that the permit proceeding there did involve public rights. That decision likely remains correct after *Jarkesy*. Although *Jarkesy* did not mention the issuance of government permits among the "historic categories" of public rights, the granting or denial of a permit is somewhat like a category that the Court did mention in *Jarkesy*: the granting or denial of a government benefit. And, as mentioned above, the Court in *Jarkesy* did not intend to be exhaustive in its discussion of the historic categories of public rights.

Example

Federal immigration statutes authorize the Immigration and Naturalization Service (INS) to impose fines on people who violate the immigration laws. Under those statutes, INS filed an administrative complaint against Umberto seeking $96,000 in fines for falsifying immigration documents. The complaint was filed with the Executive Office for Immigration Review, which is in the Department of Justice, and a hearing was held on the complaint by an administrative law judge (ALJ). As we discuss in greater detail in Chapter 3, ALJs are not Article III judges; they are employed by federal agencies to hold hearings in certain adjudications. The ALJ in Umberto's case upheld the fine, and her decision became the final decision of the Attorney General. On judicial review, Umberto argued that the imposition of a fine by the ALJ violated Article III. Is he right?

Explanation

This is a harder example than the last one, because this example involves a large fine. That feature makes the proceeding seem somewhat like a criminal proceeding. It is doubtful that Congress could delegate the adjudication of an entire criminal case to a non-Article III entity. Nonetheless, a divided court of appeals rejected an Article III challenge to the agency's imposition of a fine in the case upon which this example is based. *See Noriega-Perez v. United States*, 179 F.3d 1166 (9th Cir. 1999). The majority in *Noriega-Perez* initially determined that the proceeding was civil, not criminal. It then relied in part on the public rights exception to hold that agency adjudication of the matter complied with Article III. The majority observed that "the field of immigration—with which we are concerned here—has remained solidly within 'public rights' and the statutory delegation to agencies of the power to adjudicate immigration issues has been consistently upheld by the courts." *Id.* at 1175. The dissent disagreed with the majority on almost all points, beginning with whether the fine was civil or criminal. Based in part on its conclusion that the fine was criminal, the dissent also disagreed that the case involved public, as distinguished from private, rights. *See id.* at 1178-1187 (Ferguson, J., dissenting).

The case on which this example is based, *Noriega-Perez*, pre-dated *Jarkesy*, and today *Jarkesy* would play a central role in the analysis. In particular, the Court in *Jarkesy* classified immigration matters as involving public rights. Relevant to this example, the Court said that under the public rights exception, Congress could "prohibit immigration by certain classes of persons and enforce those prohibitions with administrative penalties assessed without a jury." *Jarkesy*, 144 S. Ct. at 2132-2133. Although the Court was addressing the inapplicability of the Seventh Amendment, its statement applies equally to the issue of whether a matter can be adjudicated by a non-Article III entity consistently with Article III. As discussed above, the public rights exception is an exception to both Article III and the Seventh Amendment.

III. DIFFERENT BRANCHES' ROLES

A. Congress

The delegation doctrine addresses Congress's authority to *grant* power to administrative agencies and officials. We now turn to Congress's authority to *retain* power over administrative agencies and officials.

Congress's authority to retain control over the exercise of administrative power, like its authority to delegate that power in the first place, raises separation-of-powers concerns. The separation-of-powers concerns differ in the two settings, however. When Congress delegates quasi-legislative power, we worry that it may be abdicating its responsibility to exercise the powers conferred by Article I. When Congress delegates quasi-judicial power, we worry that it may be undermining the powers conferred on the federal courts by Article III. In contrast, when Congress retains power for itself over administrative matters, we worry that Congress may be "aggrandizing" itself at the expense of the other branches. That "aggrandizement" concern is essentially the opposite of the "abdication" concern, and it differs, as well, from a concern that Congress is undermining the judicial branch.

The U.S. Supreme Court has invalidated five ways that Congress has tried to retain control of administrative action: (1) by appointing administrative officials; (2) by having members of Congress themselves serve on administrative bodies; (3) by controlling the removal of administrative officials; and (4) by exercising a "legislative veto" over administrative action. The major means of congressional control that remains intact, the validity of which is beyond dispute, is (5) the oversight power. We next discuss each of these congressional means of retaining control over administrative action.

1. Congressional Appointment

Although Congress can create administrative agencies, Congress generally cannot appoint the officials who fill those agencies. Most agency officials are "officers of the United States" whose appointment is governed by the Appointments Clause of Article II.[4] The Appointments Clause does not give Congress any power to appoint "officers of the United States." Instead, Article II provides for some officers of the United States, called "principal" officers in the case law, to be appointed by the President with the advice and consent of the Senate. Article II allows other, "inferior" officers to be appointed by the President alone, the Courts of Law, or the Heads of the Departments. The Appointments Clause conspicuously fails to vest any appointment power in Congress or members of Congress.

This omission was deliberate. As the Court explained in *Buckley v. Valeo*, 424 U.S. 1 (1976), it reflects another way in which the Constitution separates powers to avoid tyranny. The Framers generally did not want Congress to have both the power to create offices and the power to fill them. The Framers feared that such a combination of powers would permit Congress not only to make laws but also to control their enforcement. Based on that fear, the Court in *Buckley* struck down a federal statute that authorized members of Congress to appoint officials to serve on the Federal Election Commission, an agency that administers laws on campaign financing.[5]

The Court in *Buckley* was careful to say that Congress does have some appointment power. Specifically, Congress can appoint officials to help it exercise its legislative powers. These officials can, for example, gather information relevant to determining whether Congress should enact a new law. You may be familiar with one such group of officials, who make up the Congressional Research Service in the Library of Congress. The Court in

4. The Appointments Clause says: "The President . . . shall nominate, and by and with the Advice and Consent of the Senate, shall appoint Ambassadors, other public Ministers and Consuls, Judges of the Supreme Court, and all other Officers of the United States, whose Appointments are not herein otherwise provided for, and which shall be established by Law; but the Congress may by Law vest the Appointment of such inferior Officers, as they think proper, in the President alone, in the Courts of Law, or in the Heads of Departments." U.S. Const. art. II, § 2, cl. 2.

5. The Federal Election Commission still exists. After *Buckley v. Valeo*, however, Congress amended the statute establishing the Commission. As amended, the Commission consists of two Members of Congress who are not permitted to vote on Commission matters and six other people appointed by the President with the advice and consent of the Senate. 52 U.S.C. § 30106(a)(1). The D.C. Circuit held that the amended version of the statute still violates the separation-of-powers doctrine. *See Federal Election Commn. v. NRA Political Victory Fund*, 6 F.3d 821 (D.C. Cir. 1993), *cert. dismissed*, 513 U.S. 88 (1994). The Commission cured the violation by excluding the two non-voting members of Congress from its future proceedings.

Buckley said that such legislative officials are officers "in the generic sense," but they are not "[o]fficers of the United States" within the meaning of the Appointments Clause. 424 U.S. at 138. Congress has the power to appoint legislative officers, not under the Appointments Clause of Article II, but, instead, as an "incident" of its legislative powers under Article I.

Although Congress cannot appoint "officers of the United States," one chamber of Congress, namely the Senate, can check the President's appointment power by withholding its consent to presidential appointments. For example, the Senate can, and has, used this power to prevent the President from appointing people whom the Senate finds objectionable to head federal agencies. In turn, Presidents can, and have, sometimes circumvented Senate obstructionism by making appointments under the Recess Appointments Clause, which does not require senatorial "advice and consent."[6]

The U.S. Supreme Court interpreted the Recess Appointments Clause in *NLRB v. Noel Canning*, 573 U.S. 513 (2014). There, the Court invalidated the President's recess appointment of three members of the National Labor Relations Board. The President made the appointments during a three-day period when the Senate was not in formal session. The Court held that, because of its brevity, this three-day period did not qualify as "the recess of the Senate," which is the only period during which the President can make a recess appointment. *Supra* note 4. In so holding, the Court relied partly on a "background consideration" that requires avoiding interpretations of the Recess Appointments Clause that would allow the President to use the Clause "routinely to avoid the need for Senate confirmation." *Id.* at 522-524. After *Noel Canning*, the Senate retains a strong check on presidential appointments, even though neither it nor Congress as a whole can wield the appointment power.

Example

The Congressional Budget Office (CBO) is, according to the statute that creates it, "an office of the Congress." 2 U.S.C. § 601(a). The "primary function" of the CBO is to give the House and Senate Committees on the Budget information that "will assist such committees in the discharge of all matters within their jurisdictions." 2 U.S.C. § 602(a). The CBO also has additional duties, all of which relate to giving Congress information on budget matters. The CBO is headed by a Director. The Director is appointed for a four-year term by the Speaker of the House of Representatives and the

6. The Recess Appointments Clause says, "The President shall have to fill up all Vacancies that may happen during the Recess of the Senate, by granting Commissions which shall expire at the End of their next Session." U.S. Const. art. II, § 2, cl. 3. In addition to the discussion in the text above, *see infra* Section III.B.1.

President Pro Tempore of the Senate. Does this appointment scheme violate the Appointments Clause?

Explanation

It does not violate the Appointments Clause for the Director of the CBO to be appointed by two members of Congress. The Director is an officer whose sole job is to aid the legislative function. The Director is therefore not an "officer of the United States" within the meaning of the Appointments Clause. The statute should have been a tip-off. It calls the CBO an "office of Congress," indicating that it is an office "in the generic sense" (to quote *Buckley v. Valeo*), not an office "of the United States" subject to the Appointments Clause.

2. Legislative Membership on Administrative Bodies

"Never give a job to someone else that you can do better yourself." This saying may have prompted the unique means of congressional control over administrative action that was struck down in *Metropolitan Washington Airports Authority v. Citizens for the Abatement of Aircraft Noise, Inc.*, 501 U.S. 252 (1991) (*MWAA*).

In a way, *MWAA* involved a variation on the scheme struck down in *Buckley*. *MWAA* concerned a federal statute governing the operation of two airports that serve Washington, D.C. The federal statute authorized the airports to be run by an Airport Authority that was to be created under the laws of Virginia and the District of Columbia. The federal statute also, however, subjected major decisions of the Airport Authority to the veto of a Board of Review. The Board of Review was also to be created under the laws of Virginia and D.C. The federal statute dictated, however, that the Board be composed exclusively of Members of Congress. Thus, instead of appointing non-Members of Congress to serve on an administrative body (as in *Buckley*), under the statute at issue in *MWAA* Congress selected its own Members to serve on such a body.

In striking down this scheme, the Court identified "two basic and related constraints" that the separation-of-powers doctrine puts on Congress. *MWAA*, 501 U.S. at 274. First, Congress "may not invest itself or its Members with either executive or judicial power." Second, "when [Congress] exercises its legislative power, it must follow the single, finely wrought and exhaustively considered, procedures specified in Article I." *Id.* The procedures to which the Court was referring come from the Bicameralism and the Presentment Clauses. Those Clauses require every bill, before it becomes law, to pass both Houses of Congress and to be presented to the President for approval or veto. In light of the prohibition on Congress's exercise of executive or judicial power and the requirement that legislative power comport with the bicameralism and presentment requirements, the Court found it unnecessary to decide whether the power exercised by the Board of Review was executive power or legislative power. "If the power is executive, the Constitution does not permit an agent of Congress to exercise it. If the power is legislative, Congress must exercise it in conformity with the bicameralism and presentment requirements of Article I." *Id.* at 276. Because the Board of Review was an "agent of Congress" and did not exercise its powers in accordance with the bicameralism and presentment requirements, the statute creating it was unconstitutional whether those powers were executive or legislative.

Compare the statutory delegation struck down in *MWAA* to the statutory delegations of quasi-legislative (rulemaking) authority that the Court has upheld. Delegations of rulemaking authority give power to agencies whose heads are not Members of Congress and not subject to removal by Congress. When Congress delegates authority to an agency over which it retains little direct control, it is transferring power away from itself. In contrast, when Congress delegates authority to an "agent of Congress," which is what the Board of Review was found to be, Congress is effectively keeping the power for itself. That situation poses a risk that Congress will "aggrandize" itself at the expense of the other branches. The risk is particularly acute because, in transferring power to its agent, Congress is not only keeping the power for itself; it is making the power easier to exercise. That is because Congress's transfer of power to its agent removes that power from the bicameralism and presentment requirements of Article I that Congress itself must follow.

Example

Why didn't the scheme in *MWAA* violate the Incompatibility or Ineligibility Clauses? Those Clauses prohibit any Member of Congress, while serving in Congress, from being appointed "to any civil Office under the Authority of the United States, which shall have been created, or the Emoluments whereof shall have been [i]ncreased during such time," and they provide that "no Person holding any Office under the United States, shall be a Member of either House during his Continuance in Office." U.S. Const. art. I, § 6, cl. 2.

Explanation

The Incompatibility and Ineligibility Clauses did not apply in *MWAA* because membership on the Board of Review was not an "Office under the Authority of the United States" or "an Office under the United States," which is what those Clauses cover. At least as a formal matter, the Board was a creation, not of federal law, but of the laws of Virginia and D.C.

3. Congressional Removal of Officers

The Constitution prescribes only one way for Congress to remove "officers of the United States": by impeachment. *See* U.S. Const. art. II, § 4. The impeachment process, however, does not give Congress a particularly effective means of controlling administrative action. For one thing, the impeachment process is cumbersome. For another thing, the grounds for impeachment are limited to "Treason, Bribery, or other high Crimes and Misdemeanors." U.S. Const. art. II, § 4. It is not a "high Crime or Misdemeanor" for an officer of the United States to make decisions that Congress does not like. Can Congress remove such an officer without going through the impeachment process?

The answer is no as to officers who exercise executive power. In *Bowsher v. Synar*, 478 U.S. 714 (1986), the Court struck down a federal law that gave budget-cutting authority to the Comptroller General, who heads the General Accounting Office. The Court determined that the budget-cutting authority conferred under the law was an executive power. The Comptroller General, however, is removable by Congress. The Court held that "Congress cannot reserve for itself the power of removal of an officer charged with the execution of the laws except by impeachment." To conclude otherwise, the Court believed, "would . . . reserve in Congress control over the execution of the laws," a result at odds with the separation of powers.

Not only the holding in *Bowsher* but also the aftermath of *Bowsher* tells you something about Congress's removal power. The office of the Comptroller General still exists. Moreover, the Comptroller General is still subject to removal by Congress. *See* 31 U.S.C. § 703(e). Congress's power to remove the Comptroller General no longer violates the Constitution, though. That is because the Comptroller General's remaining duties are all in aid of the legislative process. The Comptroller General gives Congress information about how federal money is being spent. He or she is therefore no longer an executive officer whom the President must have the power to remove.

Although Congress cannot reserve for itself the power to remove executive officials, Congress can *restrict* the President's power to remove certain officers. The extent of Congress's powers to restrict the President in this regard will be discussed below in Section III.B.2. For now, recognize that it is one thing for Congress to restrict the President's power to remove officers; it is quite a different thing for Congress to remove those officials itself.

Here is the bottom line: Congress cannot remove executive officials except by impeachment. Congress can, however, restrict the President's power to remove certain officers. Furthermore, Congress can remove officials who exclusively serve the legislative function.

4. Legislative Veto

In *Immigration & Naturalization Service v. Chadha*, 462 U.S. 919 (1983), the Court invalidated what had become a popular means for congressional control of administrative action: the "legislative veto." The legislative veto is dead. *Chadha* remains an important case, however, because of its relevance for other means of congressional control.

The facts of *Chadha* illustrate how a legislative veto worked in one setting. Mr. Chadha overstayed his student visa and for that reason was subject to deportation. When the Immigration and Naturalization Service (INS) started to deport him, Mr. Chadha applied for a suspension of deportation. The INS had authority to suspend deportations for humanitarian reasons. The INS got that authority from a federal statute that delegated the suspension power to the Attorney General, who, in turn, had subdelegated it to the INS. That same federal statute, however, contained a legislative veto provision. Under that provision, the Attorney General had to report to Congress all cases in which the INS suspended deportation; each House of Congress then had a certain amount of time to pass a resolution disapproving the suspension in any particular case. If either House passed such a resolution, the INS's decision to suspend deportation was invalidated, and the person had to leave the United States.

That is what happened to Mr. Chadha. The INS determined that his deportation should be suspended; the Attorney General reported the suspension to Congress; the House of Representatives, however, passed a resolution disapproving the suspension, rendering Mr. Chadha deportable. Mr. Chadha challenged the legislative veto provision as unconstitutional.

The Supreme Court agreed, holding that the provision violated the Bicameralism Clause and the Presentment Clause. As discussed earlier, those Clauses require every bill, before it becomes law, to pass both Houses of Congress and to be presented to the President for approval or veto. The Court first determined that the House's disapproval of the suspension of Mr. Chadha's deportation was "essentially legislative in purpose and effect." 462 U.S. at 952. That was because the House's disapproval "had the purpose and effect of altering the legal rights, duties and relations of persons . . . outside the legislative branch." *Id.* The Court continued that, when Congress or part of Congress wants to take legislative action, it generally must comply with the Bicameralism and Presentment Clauses. The Constitution makes some exceptions to that rule (for impeachments, for example), but the legislative veto did not fall within any of them. The Court emphasized that the care with which the Constitution describes the legislative process "represents the Framers' decision that the legislative power of the Federal government be exercised in accord with a single, finely wrought and exhaustively considered, procedure." *Id.* at 951.

Although *Chadha* involved an esoteric type of administrative action—the suspension of someone's deportation—it had a huge impact on administrative law. According to Justice Byron White's dissent in *Chadha*, at the time of *Chadha* more than 200 statutes contained legislative veto provisions. As Justice White observed, many of those provisions authorized legislative vetoes of agency regulations and other types of agency action. Justice White believed that Congress needed the legislative veto to control federal agencies' exercise of their delegated powers. He worried, "Without the legislative veto, Congress is faced with a Hobson's choice: either to refrain from delegating the necessary authority, leaving itself with a hopeless task of writing laws with the requisite specificity to cover endless special circumstances across the entire policy landscape, or in the alternative, to abdicate its law-making function to the executive branch and independent agencies." 462 U.S. at 968. Whether or not his worry was justified, the decision in *Chadha* invalidated the legislative vetoes in more than 200 existing statutes. This meant that Congress lost an important form of control over many types of agency actions.

Chadha is an important case not only because it eliminated a popular and effective means for Congress to control agencies, but also because the Court's opinion in *Chadha* shows that it can be hard to tell whether a power is legislative, executive, or judicial. As mentioned, the majority held that the House's disapproval of the suspension of Mr. Chadha's deportation was "essentially legislative." In contrast, Justice Powell argued in his concurring opinion in *Chadha* that the House's disapproval was judicial. 462 U.S. at 960. To complicate matters further, while the majority labeled the House's disapproval of the suspension "legislative," it considered the INS's suspension itself to be executive. 462 U.S. at 953 n.16. As Justice John Paul Stevens wrote in a later case, *Chadha* shows that "governmental power cannot always be readily characterized" as legislative, executive, or judicial; rather, a governmental power, "like a chameleon, will often take on the aspect of the office to which it is assigned." *Bowsher*, 478 U.S. at 749 (Stevens, J., concurring in the judgment).

Example

A federal statute enacted in 1996, the Congressional Review Act (CRA), requires every federal agency to make a report to Congress every time the agency wants to adopt a major new rule. *See* 5 U.S.C. §§ 801-808; *see also* Chapter 5, Section III.H.6. The CRA then generally gives Congress 60 days to introduce a "joint resolution of disapproval" that, if passed, must be presented to the President. Until that 60-day period expires, the agency rule cannot take effect. If Congress passes a joint resolution disapproving the rule, and the President either approves it or has his or her veto overridden, the rule cannot take effect at all. Why doesn't the CRA violate the Constitution under *Chadha*?

Explanation

The CRA does not violate either the bicameralism or presentment requirements that the Court relied upon in *Chadha* to strike down legislation authorizing a legislative veto. Under the CRA, Congress can invalidate a rule only by passing a joint resolution, thus meeting the bicameralism requirement. The resolution must be presented to the President for approval or veto, in accordance with the presentment requirement.

5. Legislative Review and Oversight

The tried-and-true way for Congress to control the agencies that it has created is through oversight. Much more politics than law is involved in the oversight process. Nonetheless, congressional oversight is well worth learning about in a course on administrative law. That is because congressional oversight affects the way agencies administer the law.

Congressional oversight of administrative agencies is usually carried out, not by Congress as a whole, but by congressional committees (or subcommittees). Most federal agencies are overseen by at least six congressional committees. A typical agency will be subject to oversight by (1) an appropriations committee, which oversees how the agency spends its budget; (2) a "substantive" committee, which oversees the substance of the agency's work; and (3) some sort of "government operations" committee, which is concerned with the agency's efficiency and its coordination with other parts of the government. One of each of these three types of committees will exist in both the Senate and the House. As you might guess, the heads of federal agencies spend much of their time "on the Hill," testifying before, and producing written information for, one of these many committees.

This is just the formal oversight process. In addition, an informal oversight process goes on outside the committee hearing room. The informal process includes all types of contacts (telephone calls, e-mails, and so on) between individual Members of Congress or their staffs, or a committee's staff, and agency officials. Many of these informal contacts relate to discrete agency actions affecting specific constituents. Members of Congress enjoy the same right as their constituents to "petition" their government, including the relevant agency, about some grievance of their own or of their constituents. As a practical matter, however, inquiries and complaints from Members of Congress tend to get prompter, fuller, and higher-level attention in the agency than those from other citizens.

Most, but not all, of the power exercised in both the formal and informal congressional oversight process is the power of persuasion. The oversight process may of course lead to legislation that gives an agency additional or different duties or powers. Of particular relevance to administrative law, congressional committee review of agency rules under the CRA, a federal statute discussed in the last Example and Explanation, may lead to legislation in the form of a joint resolution of disapproval (subject to presidential veto). Alternatively, new agency duties or powers may be alluded to in the substatutory (though still influential) form of committee reports or testimony in the *Congressional Record*. The appropriation committee's report that accompanies the legislation funding the agency, for example, may describe the committee's expectation of how the agency will spend its money. Most of the time, however, the oversight process affects agency action merely through the power of personal contact between legislators and administrators.

Legal limits determine how far Congress can go to influence agency action during the oversight process. *Chadha*, for example, makes clear that a congressional committee could not "veto" agency regulations or orders (any more than could a House of Congress). Moreover, if a committee or member of Congress persuaded an agency to adopt a regulation or order for a reason that was legally irrelevant, the agency action might be struck down by a court as "arbitrary" and "capricious" within the meaning of the APA. *See* 5 U.S.C. § 706(2)(A). Finally, due process concerns would arise from congressional interference with agency adjudications that involve someone's life, liberty, or property.

Nonetheless, congressional oversight undoubtedly affects how agencies administer the law. Legal scholars and political scientists debate the nature and extent of the effect. In any event, the oversight process is all the more important in light of the Supreme Court cases, such as *Chadha*, that have invalidated other means of congressional control. To be effective, an administrative lawyer therefore must be aware of how congressional oversight could influence the lawyer's own matters before the agency. Indeed, many lawyers end up taking part in the oversight process so they can protect or further their clients' interests in agency matters. Lawyers do this, for example, by testifying or making written submissions to the relevant oversight committees. This can be an exciting part of legal practice, but you should be aware that it is subject to detailed federal laws and regulations governing lobbying. *See, e.g.*, 2 U.S.C. §§ 1601-1614.

Example

Congress enacts a statute that appropriates a lump sum of $10 million for the Indian Health Service (IHS), a federal agency in the U.S. Department of Health and Human Services. The appropriations statute is accompanied by a report from the appropriations committee. The report says that IHS should use part of the $10 million to continue operating an existing medical clinic located on a reservation in New Mexico. The appropriations statute itself, however, does not refer to the clinic. Nor does IHS's organic statute. The organic statute broadly authorizes IHS to spend its appropriation "for the benefit, care, and assistance of the Indians."

1. Ignoring the statement in the committee report for now, does IHS's organic statute violate the nondelegation doctrine by giving the agency too much discretion over its appropriation?

2. Now consider the statement in the committee report. Suppose that IHS decides to close the clinic and use its $10 million appropriation for other things. Also suppose that this decision prompts a lawsuit against IHS by patients of the clinic. Should the court in that action enjoin IHS from closing the clinic and force it to use its appropriation to keep the clinic open?

Explanations

1. We hope you felt nostalgic when you saw this delegation question and that you may even have revisited the earlier part of this chapter where the delegation doctrine was discussed. In any event, IHS's organic statute does not violate the delegation doctrine, for two reasons. First, the statute provides an intelligible principle: it tells IHS to use its money to help Indians. True, it leaves IHS with much discretion. Still, IHS's discretion seems no greater than that of agencies that have been authorized to regulate "in the public interest" by statutes that the Court has upheld against delegation challenges. Second, it is doubtful that IHS's organic statute even implicates the delegation doctrine. The delegation doctrine applies to statutes that delegate quasi-legislative or quasi-judicial power to an administrative official or entity. The power to spend money—which is what IHS's statute delegates—is probably not quasi-legislative or quasi-judicial. At least when money is spent by the executive branch, the spending is probably best characterized as an executive power. The delegation of executive power to an executive agency does not implicate the delegation doctrine.

2. A court should not enforce the statement in the appropriation committee report that tells IHS to use part of its appropriation to operate the clinic. In the case on which this example is based, the Supreme Court drew a sharp distinction between spending requirements imposed by a statute and spending expectations expressed in legislative history. *See Lincoln v. Vigil*, 508 U.S. 182 (1993). As the Court put it, an agency's defiance of the latter may "expose [the agency] to grave political consequences," but they are not judicially enforceable. Instead, the Court held, an agency's decision about the allocation of funds from a lump-sum appropriation is "committed to agency discretion by law" and therefore not subject to review under the APA.

B. The President

You should keep two constitutional provisions and one theme in mind as you learn about the President's control over administrative action. The two provisions are the Vesting and the Take Care Clauses of Article II. The theme is that of the "unitary executive." These provisions and this theme underlie many of the issues that we discuss in this section.

The Vesting Clause of Article II says, "The executive Power shall be vested in a President of the United States of America." U.S. Const. art. II, § 1. This Vesting Clause differs in wording from the Vesting Clause in Article I, which says, "All legislative Powers herein granted shall be vested" in Congress. The differences in wording raise questions. For example, does Article II's failure to refer to powers "herein granted" suggest that "[t]he executive power" includes powers besides those enumerated in Article II? Put another way, does Article II's Vesting Clause, of its own force, give the President unenumerated executive powers? The Court found it unnecessary to decide this question in its most recent opinion on presidential power. *See Zivotofsky v. Kerry*, 576 U.S. 1, 14 (2015) (holding that President's power to recognize foreign governments rests on several expressly enumerated powers, and thus it was unnecessary to determine whether Article II's Vesting Clause provided further support); *cf. id.* at 33 (Thomas, J., concurring in the judgment in part and dissenting in part) (tracing President's "residual foreign affairs powers" to Article II's Vesting Clause). In addition to differences in wording, Article II differs from Article I in vesting power, not in a multimember body, but in a single person: the President.

This difference has generated a big debate about the "unitary executive." There is no question that we have only one President. Questions do arise about the significance of this, however. For example, Congress has delegated rulemaking power to many specific executive officials, such as the Administrator of EPA. If the Administrator promulgates a rule that the President believes will improperly execute the statute that the rule is supposed to implement, can the President "veto" the rule? The same question can arise when Congress delegates adjudicatory power to specific officials. For example, recall that a federal statute specifically authorizes the Attorney General to suspend the deportation of an individual. *See supra* Section III.A.4 of this chapter (discussing *INS v. Chadha*). Can the President, as the sole recipient of executive power, "veto" a decision by the Attorney General to suspend deportation in a particular case? (Most people would agree that this second example not only implicates the "unitary executive" scheme but also raises due process concerns.) These questions have a flip side: given Article II's vesting of executive power in the President, and only the President, to what extent can Congress delegate executive power to administrative officials or agencies that are insulated from presidential control?

Questions like this concern not only the significance of the Vesting Clause but also the other constitutional provision that you should keep in mind—the Take Care Clause. Article II says that the President, specifically, "shall take Care that the Laws be faithfully executed." Art. II, § 3. That obligation suggests that the President should have a say in the execution of all federal laws. Yet Congress has delegated the execution of many federal laws to officials or agencies that have varying degrees of independence from presidential control. Does the "faithful" execution of the laws require the President to respect laws that delegate the execution of laws to someone else? Presumably not, if the law delegating that executive authority to someone else is unconstitutional.

If your head is spinning now, you are ready for the following discussion of presidential control of administrative action. Actually, although there are mind-dizzying questions in the background of this subject, the subject itself breaks down into several fairly straightforward means of executive control. Two of the chief means of presidential control are the powers to appoint and remove administrative officials, which we discuss first. Next we discuss a less obvious but nonetheless important means of control: presidential coordination and oversight of administrative action. Today, that coordination and oversight is carried on to a large extent by the subordinates of the President. Finally, we discuss a long-debated but ultimately invalidated means of presidential control: the line item veto.

1. Appointment

Article II empowers the President to appoint "Officers of the United States" with the advice and consent of the Senate. Article II then creates an exception for "inferior Officers." Inferior officers do not have to be appointed by the President with the advice and consent of the Senate. Instead, Congress can "by law" vest the appointment of inferior officers "in the President alone, in the Courts of Law, or in the Heads of Departments." The Constitution permits Congress to provide for this alternative way of appointing inferior officers, but it does not compel Congress to do so. Indeed, Congress may well prefer to retain a say (through Senate confirmation) in the appointment of even inferior officers. In any event, the officers who fall outside of the "inferior officer" exception—and who can therefore be appointed only by the President with the advice and consent of the Senate—are called "principal" officers in the case law. The President is entitled to appoint all principal officers of the United States (with the advice and consent of the Senate) as well as all inferior officers that Congress designates for presidential appointment. The President thus has the lion's share of the appointment power.[7]

By now you may be wondering how to distinguish between principal and inferior officers. The Supreme Court has developed criteria for identifying them, to which we will turn shortly. Before we do, though, we must mention a third category of executive-branch actors, whom the Court often calls "mere employees." Mere employees are not "officers of the United States" and therefore not subject to the Appointments Clause. They can be hired, for example, through the competitive civil service system. Roughly speaking, then, if you think of the executive branch as a pyramid, "mere employees" make up the massive base; "inferior officers" occupy a slice of the pyramid near the top; and "principal officers" are at the top of the pyramid, directly under the President, who occupies the apex.

Perhaps you can guess why it matters whether an executive-branch official is an employee, an inferior officer, or a principal officer (aside from its relevance to the official's self-esteem). One reason the distinctions matter is that they bear on how the official can be appointed, and appointments, in turn, bear on the balance of power among the three branches. In addition, the distinctions can matter to members of the public. Suppose your client is harmed by some action taken by an official who was not selected in accordance with the Appointments Clause. You may be able to get a court to invalidate that official's action if you can prove that the official is an officer of the United States. Such proof would mean that the official's selection for federal employment was defective. Similarly, you can challenge action taken by an inferior officer who was not appointed by one of the appointing authorities named in Article II (i.e., the President, a Court of Law, or the Head of a Department). *See Ryder v. United States*, 515 U.S. 177 (1995) (setting aside court martial conviction because military judges were appointed in violation of Appointments Clause).

To start from the bottom of the federal executive pyramid, "mere employees" are executive-branch officials who do *not* "exercise[] significant authority pursuant to the laws of the United States." *Lucia v. SEC*,

7. We focus in this section on the President's power under the Appointments Clause, which is in clause 2 of Article II, § 2. In addition to the power granted in Clause 2, Clause 3 empowers the President—without having to get the Senate's "advice and consent"—to "fill up all Vacancies that may happen during the Recess of the Senate." As discussed earlier in this chapter, many Presidents can, and have, used Clause 3, which is known as the Recess Appointments Clause, to circumvent the need for senatorial consent, including when filling vacancies in federal agencies. *Supra* Section III.A.1. The Court interpreted the Recess Appointments Clause in *NLRB v. Noel Canning*, 573 U.S. 513 (2014). Although the Court interpreted the Clause broadly in some respects, the Court also emphasized that the Clause should not be interpreted to allow the President "routinely to avoid the need for Senate confirmation." *Id.* at 524. The Court explained that the Recess Appointments Clause "*sets forth a subsidiary, not a primary, method for appointing officers of the United States.*" *Id.* at 522 (emphasis in original). The Appointments Clause "provides the primary method of appointment." *Id.*

585 U.S. 237, 245 (2018) (quoting *Buckley v. Valeo*, 424 U.S. 1, 126 (1976) (per curiam)). These employees include, for example, the kindly agents of the Transportation Security Administration who screen you at the airport and the park rangers who collect your entrance fee at national parks. More importantly for our purposes, many administrative law scholars and practitioners, as well as lower court judges, used to believe that federal ALJs are likewise "mere employees" and, as such, fall outside the Appointments Clause.

The Court concluded otherwise, however, in *Lucia v. SEC*, *supra*. The Court in *Lucia* held that the ALJs who conduct formal adjudications for the SEC are "officers of the United States," not mere employees. The Court relied on its earlier decision in *Freytag v. Commissioner*, 501 U.S. 868 (1991), to determine that SEC ALJs exercise significant authority pursuant to laws of the United States. The Court explained that, like the special trial judges at issue in *Freytag*, SEC ALJs "take testimony, conduct trials, rule on the admissibility of evidence, and have the power to enforce compliance with discovery orders"; in carrying out these functions, they exercise significant discretion. *Lucia*, 585 U.S. at 247 (quoting *Freytag*, 501 U.S. at 881-882). They are therefore officers who must be appointed in accordance with the Appointments Clause.

The Court's explanation applies to all federal ALJs, not just those employed by the SEC. Indeed, after *Lucia* the heads of federal agencies scrambled to appoint the ALJs they employed. It has been assumed, probably correctly, that ALJs are inferior officers, not principal officers. The Appointments Clause accordingly allows Congress "by law" to vest their appointment in, among other entities, "Heads of Departments." Congress did provide in the federal APA for agencies to appoint their ALJs. 5 U.S.C. § 3105. As long as a federal agency qualifies as a "Department[]," the person or multi-person group that heads the agency can validly appoint the agency's ALJs. Thus, the APA will enable most federal agencies to comply with *Lucia* pretty easily.

Still, the *Lucia* decision raises important questions that need answers for the vast amount of federal agency adjudication to continue. One question, for example, concerns the validity of the law that entitles ALJs to a formal adjudication before they can be fired, which we discuss in Chapter 3, Section III.D. Laws like that, which restrict removal of officers of the United States, raise separation of powers concerns as discussed below in the next subsection. Another question concerns the status of other executive branch officials who, though not ALJs, have adjudicatory authority and discretion comparable to ALJs. These officials, often collectively called "Administrative Judges" or "AJs," might be officers of the United States under *Lucia* but have not in all cases been appointed in accordance with the Appointments Clause.

We put those questions aside for now, though. Having discussed how to distinguish mere employees from officers of the United States, we turn to the question of how to distinguish principal officers from inferior officers.

We warn you up front that the Court has not provided a single, coherent way to draw the principal/inferior officer distinction.

In the modern era, an early leading case was *Morrison v. Olson*, 487 U.S. 654 (1988). *Morrison v. Olson* involved a federal statute that authorized "independent counsels" to investigate and prosecute crimes by high-level federal officials. Under the statute, an independent counsel was not appointed by the President with the advice and consent of the Senate. Instead, she was appointed by a panel of three federal judges. Once appointed, the independent counsel had "full power and independent authority to exercise all investigative and prosecutorial functions" of the U.S. Department of Justice and the Attorney General. The Attorney General could remove an independent counsel, but only for good cause. *Morrison* arose when the target of an investigation by Independent Counsel Alexia Morrison challenged the method of Morrison's appointment on the ground that she was a principal officer and, as such, could be appointed only by the President with the consent of the Senate.

The Court in *Morrison v. Olson* rejected that argument, holding that independent counsels were inferior officers. The Court cited four factors in holding that independent counsels were inferior officers. First, independent counsels could be removed (though only for good cause) by a higher executive branch official, (*i.e.*, the Attorney General). Second, independent counsels had only certain, limited duties: namely, those of investigation and prosecution. Third, their offices were limited in jurisdiction, reaching only certain serious federal crimes by certain high-level federal officials. Finally, their offices were limited in tenure; once a particular investigation and any related prosecutions were finished, the independent counsel's office ended. Thus, the Court classified independent counsels as inferior officers based on the nature and scope of their duties and the fact that they were removable by a higher executive official.

The Court again addressed how to distinguish principal from inferior officers in *Edmond v. United States*, 520 U.S. 651 (1997). Whereas *Morrison* involved the status of an officer with investigative and prosecutorial powers and duties, *Edmond* involved officers with adjudicatory duties: namely, judges on the Coast Guard Court of Criminal Appeals, a non-Article III entity that reviews the decisions of courts-martial. The judges on that court included civilians appointed by the Secretary of Transportation. That method of appointment, as discussed above, is constitutional only for inferior officers.

The Court in *Edmond* upheld that method of appointment, holding that the judges on the Coast Guard Court of Criminal Appeals were inferior officers. The Court did not rely on a multi-factor test, as it had in *Morrison*. Instead, it said, "'[I]nferior officers' are officers whose work is directed and supervised at some level by others who were appointed by Presidential nomination with the Senate's advice and consent." *Id.* at 663. The Court determined that the judges at issue satisfied that condition. Their work was adequately supervised by two executive-branch entities: the Judge Advocate General of the Coast Guard and the Court of Appeals for the Armed Forces. Even though each of these supervisory entities lacked complete control over the judges' work, the Court explained, "What is significant is that the judges of the Court of Criminal Appeals have no power to render a final decision on behalf of the United States unless permitted to do so by other Executive officers." *Id.* at 665.

This significant feature was missing in the Court's latest Appointments Clause decision, *United States v. Arthrex, Inc.*, 594 U.S. 1 (2021). *Arthrex* involved Administrative Patent Judges (APJs), who sat on an executive-branch adjudicative entity called the Patent Trial and Appeals Board (PTAB). APJs were appointed by the Secretary of Commerce, a method of appointment that is constitutional only for inferior officers. A panel of three APJs issued a decision for the PTAB invalidating Arthrex's patent on a surgical device. The relevant statutes made the PTAB's decision final for the executive branch. Review of PTAB decisions occurred only outside the executive branch: in the United States Court of Appeals for the Federal Circuit, an Article III court.

The Court in *Arthrex* held that that "the unreviewable executive power exercised by APJs is incompatible with their status as inferior officers." 594 U.S. at 18. The Court said, "An inferior office must be 'directed and supervised at some level by others who were appointed by Presidential nomination with the advice and consent of the Senate.'" *Arthrex*, 594 U.S. at 13 (quoting *Edmond*, 520 U.S. at 663)) The Court acknowledged that APJs were subject to some control by the Director of the Patent and Trademark Office, who in turn answered to the Secretary of Commerce—but concluded that "[i]n all the ways that matter to the parties who appear before the PTAB, the buck stops with APJs, not with the Secretary or Director." *Id.* at 17.

Having found that the APJs' final decision-making authority created a "violation of the Appointments Clause," the Court in *Arthrex* had to decide on a remedy. *Id.* at 23. While Chief Justice Roberts wrote for the Court in finding the violation, his opinion on the appropriate remedy was joined by only three other Justices. He concluded that, to remedy the violation, the APJs' decisions had to be reviewable by the PTO director. *Id.* at 24. Additional support for this remedy came from Justices Breyer, Sotomayor and Kagan, who supported the remedy while disagreeing that there was a need for it! They concluded, in an opinion by Justice Breyer, that the APJs' authority did *not* violate of the Appointments Clause. *Id.* at 44 (Breyer, J., joined by Sotomayor and Kagan, JJ., concurring in the judgment in part and dissenting in part).

Chief Justice Roberts' opinion for the Court in *Arthrex* relied solely on the *Edmonds* test in concluding that APJs' appointment as inferior officers violated the Appointments Clause. The opinion did not mention *Morrison's* multi-factor approach to distinguishing principal officers from inferior officers. At the same time, the *Arthrex* Court did not overrule the *Morrison* approach. Indeed, the *Arthrex* Court emphasized that it did not "attempt to 'set forth an exclusive criterion for distinguishing between principal officers for Appointments Clause purposes.'" *Arthrex*, 594 U.S. at 23 (quoting *Edmond*, 520 U.S. at 661). From this, it's safe to say that the law on distinguishing principal from inferior officers remains less than clearcut.

Example

Your client, a farmer, applied to the U.S. Department of Agriculture (USDA) for an emergency loan and was turned down. Your research reveals that the loan application was denied by a USDA official whose job consists solely of determining whether loan applications meet the financial-need requirements prescribed in a regulation. Research also reveals that the Secretary of Agriculture played no role in the hiring of the loan official who denied your client's application. Can you successfully challenge the denial of the loan on the ground that the loan official was hired in violation of the Appointments Clause?

Explanation

Your client the farmer does not have a viable Appointments Clause argument. The Appointments Clause only prescribes the method for appointing "officers of the United States." If the loan official were a principal officer, she would have to be appointed by the President with the advice and consent of the Senate. If she were an inferior officer, Congress could have provided for her, instead, to be appointed by the President, or a court of law, or the head of a Department (for example, the Secretary of Agriculture). Unfortunately, the loan official who turned down your client's application almost certainly was not either kind of officer. Instead, the official was only an employee, considering the official's limited authority and discretion. Most people who work for the federal government are mere employees, not "officers of the United States" subject to the Appointments Clause. *See Buckley v. Valeo*, 424 U.S. 1, 126 & n.162 (1976) (officers of the United States "exercise significant authority pursuant to the laws of the United States," whereas employees are "lesser functionaries"). The appointment of a federal employee who is not an officer of the United States simply is not addressed by the Appointments Clause.

Example

As mentioned in Chapter 1, historically the most important agencies are "departments," the heads of which make up the President's Cabinet. One of the newer departments is the Department of Veterans Affairs (the VA), which is headed by the Secretary of Veterans Affairs. The chief lawyer for the VA is called the General Counsel. The General Counsel is responsible for giving legal advice to the Secretary of the VA. In that role, the General Counsel issues legal opinions binding the VA on issues related to various veterans benefits programs. The General Counsel is also responsible to the Secretary for all litigation arising out of the VA's activities. Is the General Counsel an employee, an inferior officer, or a principal officer?

Explanation

The General Counsel clearly is not an employee. Unlike the loan official described in the last example, the General Counsel exercises significant authority on behalf of the VA. She renders opinions on legal issues that bind the entire department and oversees all of its litigation. Because she is an officer, rather than an employee, her appointment is governed by the Appointments Clause.

The hard question is whether the General Counsel is a principal officer or an inferior officer. The Court has not stated a bright-line rule for distinguishing between these two types of officers. The Court has instead identified several relevant factors. The Court in *Morrison v. Olson* considered the scope of the officer's duties and powers and the fact that the officer was subject to removal by a higher-level executive official. The Court in *Edmond* and *Arthrex*, in contrast, considered one factor determinative of an officer's inferior status: namely, whether the officer was directed and supervised by officers appointed by the President with the consent of the Senate. *See also Free Enter. Fund v. Public Co. Acct. Bd.*, 561 U.S. 477 (2010). *See generally Intercollegiate Broadcasting Syst., Inc. v. Copyright Royalty Bd.*, 684 F.3d 1332, 1337 (D.C. 2012) (stating that there is "some conflict" between Court's varying approaches to distinguishing principal from inferior officers).

Under these factors, the General Counsel might qualify as a principal officer. Although the General Counsel is responsible to the Secretary of the VA for various legal matters, the General Counsel is probably not closely supervised by the Secretary. This distinguishes the General Counsel from the judges on the Coast Guard Court of Criminal Appeals, who were found to be inferior officers in *Edmond*. The General Counsel is appointed for an indefinite period, not for a period necessarily limited as the independent counsel in *Morrison v. Olson*.

A good argument can be made to the contrary, however. The General Counsel, even if not closely supervised by the Secretary, is still clearly subordinate to the Secretary. In this respect, the General Counsel's position is analogous to the position of the independent counsel in *Morrison v. Olson*. Moreover, the General Counsel's duties and responsibilities are limited to giving legal opinions on matters relevant to veterans' affairs; the General Counsel does not make rules or adjudicate cases for the department.

If the statute creating the General Counsel position provided for her appointment by the President with the advice and consent of the Senate, this might suggest that Congress thought the General Counsel should be a principal officer. Then again it might not; it might indicate only that Congress wanted the Senate to have a say in the appointment of this officer, whether or not she was a principal officer. In short, you cannot assume that an officer is a principal officer merely because Congress has provided for that officer to be appointed by the President with the advice and consent of the Senate. You must look for clearer evidence that Congress considered this method of appointment to be constitutionally required before you can conclude that Congress considered the officer to be a principal officer, rather than an inferior officer. Nevertheless, if the statute provided for this means of appointment, the legal question whether the General Counsel was a principal officer would be moot, because she would be appointed in an appropriate manner whether or not she was a principal officer.

If, on the other hand, the statute creating the General Counsel position provided that the Secretary (the head of the department) appointed the General Counsel, this would definitively indicate Congress's intent that the position be that of an inferior officer, because only an inferior officer can be so appointed. We can expect the courts to accord Congress some deference in the determination of whether an office it creates should be filled by a principal or inferior officer. Indeed, until *Arthrex* the Supreme Court had never ruled an appointment unconstitutional because an officer was appointed in the manner provided for inferior officers. *See Arthrex*, 594 U.S. at 44 (Thomas, J., joined by Breyer, Sotomayor, and Kagan, JJ., dissenting) ("For the very first time, this Court holds that Congress violated the Constitution by vesting the appointment of a federal officer in the head of a department."). Moreover, if the Secretary could appoint the General Counsel, the implication would be that the Secretary could remove the General Counsel, further suggesting that the General Counsel should be considered an inferior officer. (Recall that, in concluding that the independent counsel was an inferior officer, the Court in *Morrison v. Olson* relied on, among other factors, the fact that she could be removed by the Attorney General.)

In short, it is not clear that the General Counsel by reason of her duties and responsibilities and the lack of close supervision over her is necessarily a principal officer. It seems unlikely that a court will find that a subordinate officer that Congress has specified for appointment as an inferior officer must be appointed as a principal officer. The more difficult question arises when Congress has not specified a method of appointment, which would require the person to be a mere employee, not an officer at all. In these circumstances it is entirely possible that Congress, while settling responsibilities or powers on the person, simply did not focus on the question whether the person needed to be an officer.

If you have followed this explanation of the General Counsel's status (and even if you have not been able to follow it), you should now understand why the Court has so often said that it is hard to draw a clear line between principal officers and inferior officers.

2. Removal

After an officer has been appointed, he or she can be removed. As discussed earlier, the only method of removal prescribed in the Constitution is impeachment. Since the grounds for impeachment are limited and the impeachment process is cumbersome, officers are seldom impeached. They are removed all the time, however. Indeed, the power to remove an official is an important means of control.

The Supreme Court has often addressed the respective powers of the President and Congress to remove administrative officials. Most of the cases have involved congressional restrictions on the President's power to remove officials involved in executing the law. The law governing congressional restrictions on the President's removal power has evolved. As we will see, recent decisions by the Court in this area seem to expand the President's removal power and diminish Congress's ability to restrict that power.

A rule that emerged from the early cases on the subject was simple. Congress could not restrict the President's power to remove an officer whom the President had appointed with the advice and consent of the Senate, if that officer exercised "purely executive" powers. But Congress *could* restrict the President's power to remove a presidential appointee who exercised quasi-legislative or quasi-judicial powers.

The early rule came from two Supreme Court cases. In *Myers v. United States*, 272 U.S. 52 (1926), the Court struck down a federal statute that required the President to get Senate approval to remove a postmaster. The Court held that Congress could not interfere with the President's removal of an executive officer whom the President had appointed with the Senate's advice and consent. In *Humphrey's Executor v. United States*, 295 U.S. 602 (1935), however, the Court upheld a federal statute restricting the President's ability to remove a member of the Federal Trade Commission (FTC), who had been appointed by the President with the Senate's advice and consent. The Court in *Humphrey's Executor* explained the different result in terms of the different powers exercised by the two removed officers. The Court said that the postmaster involved in *Myers* was a "purely executive officer." *Humphrey's Executor*, 295 U.S. at 628. In contrast, the Court determined that the FTC and its Commissioners exercised "no part of the executive power"; rather, they exercised "quasi-legislative or quasi-judicial powers" to carry out "specified duties as a legislative or as a judicial aid." *Id.* (The FTC made investigations and reports for Congress, and, in cases involving antitrust violations, it proposed judicial decrees for the courts.) Taken together, *Myers* and *Humphrey's Executor* established a rule: the President had to have unrestricted discretion to remove "purely executive" officers whom he had appointed with the Senate's advice and consent; in contrast, Congress could restrict the President's power to remove presidential appointees who exercised quasi-legislative or quasi-judicial powers. *See also Wiener v. United States*, 357 U.S. 349 (1958).

The Court modified this rule, at least with respect to inferior officers, in *Morrison v. Olson*. (See Section III.B.1 for a description of this case.) Under the statute at issue in *Morrison*, an independent counsel could be removed by the President's subordinate, the Attorney General. The Attorney General could effect that removal, however, only "for good cause." The Court in *Olson* upheld this statutory "for cause" restriction on the Executive's removal power. The Court did not dispute that independent counsels were purely executive officials because they exercised powers traditionally associated with the Executive Branch: the investigation and prosecution of crime. Rather, the Court held that "the determination of whether the Constitution allows Congress to impose a 'good cause'-type restriction on the President's power to remove an official cannot be made to turn on whether or not that official is classified as 'purely executive.'" *Morrison*, 487 U.S. at 689. The Court identified "the real question" as whether the restrictions on removal "impede[d] the President's ability to perform his constitutional duty." *Id.* at 691. The Court determined that no such impediment was posed by the statutory restrictions on the removal of independent counsels. The Court based that determination on the facts that the independent counsel was "an inferior officer . . ., with limited jurisdiction and tenure and lacking policymaking or significant administrative authority." *Id.* The Court thus took a functional approach in upholding a for-cause restriction on the President's power to remove a purely executive officer.

In *Morrison*, the official involved in executing the laws had only one layer of protection from presidential control: the independent counsel could be removed by the Attorney General only for good cause, but the Attorney General was removable by the President "at will." As a result, the President could remove the Attorney General if the President concluded that the Attorney General was wrong in removing—or in failing to remove—the independent counsel. In effect, then, it was really the President, not the Attorney General, who determined whether there was "good cause" for removing the independent counsel. And so the restriction on the Attorney General's removal power was really a restriction on the *President's* removal power.

In a case after *Morrison*, the Court addressed whether Congress can give an executive officer multiple layers of protection from removal. The Court said no, in *Free Enterprise Fund v. Public Company Accounting Oversight Board*, 561 U.S. 477 (2010).

Free Enterprise Fund concerned the Public Company Accounting Oversight Board. The Board is a government entity created by Congress in the Sarbanes-Oxley Act of 2002 to regulate accounting firms that audit public companies under the federal securities laws. Under the Act, members of the Board could be removed by the SEC only for good cause. The SEC Commissioners, in turn, were themselves subject to removal by the President only for good cause. The Board members thus enjoyed "two layers of good-cause tenure." *Free Enterprise Fund*, 561 U.S. at 497.

The Court held that "the dual for-cause limitations on the removal of Board members contravene the Constitution's separation of powers." *Id.* at 492. The limitations prevented the President from holding members of the Board accountable for their actions. This, in turn, hampered the President's ability to carry out his or her duty to "take care" that the laws are faithfully executed. The Court held that the Board could continue to exist, however, because the for-cause restrictions on removal of Board members were severable from the rest of the Sarbanes-Oxley Act.

The next major case is *Seila Law LLC v. Consumer Financial Protection Bureau*, 591 U.S. 197 (2020). *Seila Law* concerned the Consumer Financial Protection Bureau (CFPB), an independent agency that regulates companies that provide financial services to consumers, like credit card companies, mortgage companies, and banks that make consumer loans and student loans. Congress gave the CFPB broad rulemaking, executive, and adjudicatory powers over these companies.

The CFPB's structure was distinctive. As the Court explained, "In organizing the CFPB, Congress deviated from the structure of nearly every other independent administrative agency in our history. Instead of placing the agency under the leadership of a board with multiple members, Congress provided that the CFPB would be led by a single Director." *Id.* at 202. The Director was appointed by the President with the advice and consent of the Senate for a five-year term, and could be removed from office by the President only for good cause. It was the CFPB's single-Director feature that ultimately led the Court to strike down the good-cause restriction on the President's removal power. But we are getting ahead of ourselves.

The case arose when the CFPB issued a "civil investigative demand"—i.e., an administrative subpoena—against Seila Law, a law firm. The CFPB was investigating whether, in providing debt-relief services to its clients, Seila Law had violated the CFPB's telemarketing rules. *Id.* at 208. Seila Law refused to comply with the civil investigative demand, so the CFPB went to court to enforce it. In that enforcement proceeding, Seila Law argued that the good-cause restriction on the President's power to remove the CFPB Director was unconstitutional.

The Court agreed, holding that "the CFPB's leadership by a single individual removable only for inefficiency, neglect, or malfeasance violates the separation of powers." *Id.* at 213. The Court explained that "[t]he entire 'executive Power' belongs to the President alone," who must "'take Care that the Laws be faithfully executed.'" *Id.* (quoting Art. II, § 1, cl. 1). To carry out that duty, the President needs help from "lesser executive officers," who "must remain accountable to the President." *Id.* The removal power was a way to ensure their accountability, the Court said, and for that reason, the "President's removal power has long been confirmed by history and precedent." *Id.* at 214.

The Court identified "two exceptions" to this rule of unrestricted presidential removal power. *Id.* at 204. First, the Court read *Humphrey's Executor* to allow for-cause restrictions on removing the heads of "multimember expert agencies that do not wield substantial executive power." *Id.* at 218. Second, the Court read *Morrison v. Olson* (and a second case, *United States v. Perkins*, 116 U.S. 483 (1886)), to allow good-cause restrictions on the removal of "inferior officers with limited duties and no policymaking or administrative authority." *Seila Law*, 591 U.S. at 218. Aside from these "two limited exceptions," the Court repeated, its precedents "establish that the President's removal power is the rule, not the exception." *Id.* at 228.

The Court determined in *Seila Law* that the good-cause restriction on the President's removal of the CFPB Director did not fall into either exception. It did not fall into the *Humphrey's Executor* exception because the CFPB was not a multimember body of experts and because the CFPB wielded substantial executive power. It did not fall into the *Morrison v. Olson* exception because "[e]veryone agrees the CFPB Director is not an inferior officer, and her duties are far from limited." *Seila Law*, 591 U.S. at 219. The Court declined to "extend" the exceptions to the CFPB because in its view, "such an agency has no basis in history and no place in our constitutional structure." *Id.* at 220. The CFPB did not fit into our constitutional structure, according to the Court, because "that structure scrupulously avoids concentrating power in the hands of any single individual." *Id.* at 223. Thus, the CFPB's single-Director feature made it an unconstitutional misfit. The Court held that this defect could be remedied only by invalidating the statutory for-cause restriction on the Director's removal. The CFPB thus survives, but the President can now remove its Director at will.

The Court applied its decision in *Seila Law* to an agency structured like the CFPB in *Collins v. Yellen*, 594 U.S. 220 (2021). The agency at issue in *Collins* was the Federal Housing Finance Agency (FHFA). Congress created the FHFA after a financial crisis in the housing market. The FHFA had power to regulate two major sources of mortgage financing, the congressionally chartered corporations known as Fannie Mae and Freddie Mac. Like the CFPB, the FHFA was created as an independent agency headed by a single Director. And similar to the CFPB's Director, the FHFA's Director was appointed by the President with the advice and consent of the Senate, and could be removed only "for cause." The Court held that this for-cause restriction on the President's removal power violated the separation of powers, finding *Seila Law* "all but dispositive." *Id.* at 250.

So far, we have focused on cases involving congressional restrictions on the President's removal of officials involved in executing the laws. The President's removal power, however, is not limited to officials who serve an executive function. Instead, just as the President can appoint "officers of the

United States" who are outside the Executive Branch, the President can also remove some nonexecutive officers.

The President cannot, of course, remove Article III judges, for the Constitution gives them life tenure (assuming "good Behaviour"). U.S. Const. art. III, § 1. It is an open question whether Congress could by statute provide a mechanism for removal of judges when they were found not in good behavior. It has never done so. The Constitution imposes the standard for removal—lack of good behavior—not the procedure by which the removal takes place. So far, Article III judges have only been removed by impeachment, usually after their conviction of federal crimes in federal court.

Other officers of the United States are not so lucky. For them, the rule of thumb seems to be that, if the President appointed them, he or she can also remove them. *Cf. Ex parte Hennen*, 38 U.S. (13 Pet.) 230 (1839) (upholding court's removal of court clerk on the theory that, in the absence of a constitutional or statutory provision to the contrary, the power to remove is incidental to the power to appoint). For example, an early case indicated that the President could remove Article I judges whom he had appointed. *See McAllister v. United States*, 141 U.S. 174 (1891). Moreover, in *Mistretta v. United States*, 488 U.S. 361, 408-411 (1989), the Court upheld a statute authorizing the President, for cause, to remove from the U.S. Sentencing Commission Article III judges whom the President has appointed to the Commission. The holding in *Mistretta* is significant because the Commission is not part of the executive branch. Rather, it is "an independent commission in the judicial branch," 28 U.S.C. § 991(a). Despite the Commission's connection with the judicial function, and despite its being composed of Article III judges, the Court "s[aw] no risk that the President's limited removal power will compromise the impartiality of Article III judges serving on the Commission and, consequently, no risk that the Act's removal provision will prevent the Judicial Branch from performing its constitutionally assigned function of fairly adjudicating cases and controversies." *Mistretta*, 488 U.S. at 411. Notice in the passage just quoted that the Court takes the same functional approach as it did in *Morrison*, focusing on whether one branch's particular exercise of power over another branch undermines that other branch's ability to perform its constitutional function.

Example

Congress created the Federal Reserve System to conduct the nation's monetary policy. The System is headed by a Board of Governors. Various federal statutes characterize the Board as an independent agency. It is made up of seven members, who are appointed by the President with the advice and consent of the Senate. The statute establishing the Board provides that each member serves a term of 14 years, "unless sooner removed for cause by the President." Does this statutory restriction on the President's power to remove members of the Board violate the Constitution?

Explanation

Probably not. The question posed by this example, however, is harder to answer definitively after the Court's decision in *Seila Law.*

This example involves the same type of statutory restriction—a "for cause" restriction—and the same type of agency—an independent agency that is headed by a multimember body and involved in executing the law—as were involved in *Humphrey's Executor*. The Court in *Humphrey's Executor* upheld the for-cause restriction against the argument that it impermissibly intruded on executive power. *Humphrey's Executor* seems to support upholding the for-cause restriction on removal of Governors of the Board of "the Fed."

Seila Law muddies the waters, however. The Court in *Seila Law* described *Humphrey's Executor* as allowing for-cause restrictions on removal of the heads of "multimember expert agencies *that do not wield substantial executive power*." 591 U.S. at 218 (emphasis added). The Court based this description on the portion of *Humphrey's Executor* that characterized the agency there, the FTC, "as exercising 'no part of the executive power.'" *Id.* at 215 (quoting *Humphrey's Executor*, 295 U.S. at 628). The Fed arguably *does* wield "substantial executive power." Whereas the FTC was seen by the Court in *Humphrey's Executor* "as a legislative or as a judicial aid," the Fed has significant executive powers like the power to investigate and supervise banks. These powers might take the Fed out of the *Humprey's Executor* exception and cast doubt on the constitutionality of the for-cause restriction on the President's power to remove the Governors of the Fed Board.

On the other hand, *Seila Law* contains hints that the Fed presents a special case. The dissent in *Seila Law* argued that the agency there, the CFPB, was justified by the fact that "Congress has historically given—with this Court's permission—a measure of independence to financial regulators like the Federal Reserve Board." 591 U.S. at 285 (Kagan, J., joined by Ginsburg, Breyer, and Sotomayor, JJ., concurring in the judgment with respect to severability and dissenting in part). The majority responded, "[E]ven assuming financial institutions like . . . the Federal Reserve can claim a special historical status, the CFPB is in an entirely different league." *Id.* at 222 n.8. In short, the 4-Justice dissent in *Seila Law* endorsed the constitutionality of the for-cause restriction on the removal of the Fed Board's Governors, and the majority made clear it was not suggesting otherwise.

Example

Congress created a workers' compensation scheme for longshoremen and harbor workers in the Longshoremen's and Harbor Workers' Compensation Act of 1927 (the Act). Claims under the Act are initially adjudicated by an ALJ, who holds a formal hearing. If a claimant does not like the ALJ's decision, the claimant can appeal to an entity called "the

Benefits Review Board" and thereafter to a federal court. The Act says that the Board should consist of three people selected by the Secretary of Labor. The Act does not say anything, however, about how long these people can serve or how they can be removed. Your client is a Board member who was removed by the Secretary of Labor for no apparent reason. Is there any basis for arguing that the Secretary can remove a member of the Board only for cause?

Explanation

This example asks whether the Secretary of Labor could remove your client from the Benefits Review Board only for cause. That question actually divides into two issues. One is an issue of statutory interpretation: should the Act be construed to impose a for-cause restriction on the Secretary of Labor's removal power? The second issue is constitutional: is the Act, properly construed, constitutional? Your client can win in either of two situations: (1) if the Act does implicitly impose a for-cause restriction (and such a restriction is constitutional); or (2) if the Act does not impose a for-cause restriction, but the Constitution does impose such a restriction.

In the case on which this example is based, the D.C. Circuit held that, properly interpreted, the Act does not impose a for-cause restriction. *See Kalaris v. Donovan*, 697 F.2d 376 (D.C. Cir.), *cert. denied*, 462 U.S. 1119 (1983). The court determined "[t]he general and long-standing rule" to be that "in the face of statutory silence, the power of removal presumptively is incident to the power of appointment." Since the Secretary of Labor could appoint the members of the Board, the Secretary also could presumptively remove them at will. The court observed that a contrary result would, in effect, give members of the Board life tenure, since the Act did not give them a limited term. The court did not believe that Congress intended inferior officers in the executive branch to have that much job protection. *See also Shurtleff v. United States*, 189 U.S. 311 (1903) (rejecting claim of general appraiser whose term was not fixed by statute that he could not be removed at the pleasure of the appointing authority).

The court in *Kalaris* further held that the Constitution did not impose a for-cause restriction on the Secretary's power to remove members of the Board. There was no dispute that members of the Board were inferior officers, whose appointment was properly made by the Secretary of Labor, as the "Head of a Department." The question was whether the quasi-judicial powers of the Board made the at-will removal of its members unconstitutional. The court observed that this question was not addressed in *Humphrey's Executor*. *Humphrey's Executor* addressed whether the Constitution permitted Congress, by statute, to impose a for-cause restriction on executive removal of quasi-judicial officers. *Humphrey's Executor* did not address whether the

Constitution itself imposed a for-cause restriction. The court also observed that there are many federal statutes that permit the Executive to remove quasi-judicial officers at will. In the court's view, the prevalence of such statutes strongly supported their constitutionality.

We have included this difficult example for two reasons. First, it shows that removal cases may raise statutory interpretation issues as well as constitutional issues. Second, it raises a constitutional issue that is distinct from the ones that the Supreme Court has addressed in its modern cases: whether the Constitution permits the Executive to remove at will an inferior officer in the executive branch who has quasi-judicial powers. Cf. *Reagan v. United States*, 182 U.S. 419 (1901) (upholding at-will removal of commissioners of Indian Territory, who performed judicial functions). That is an important issue because, as the court in *Kalaris* noted, there are many such officers who are subject to at-will removal.

3. Supervision

Much of the control that the President has over the executive branch is exercised informally. This informal control is possible because the President personally appoints all of the principal officers in the Executive Branch, and the President can remove them (with the notable exception of the heads of independent agencies) at will. Accordingly, these appointees make it their business to know and follow the President's policies. Most of their deviations from those policies can be corrected by a phone call from, or meeting with, the President or White House staff.

In addition to these informal methods of control, the President uses a formal method: the executive order. You will not find any statute that defines executive orders or prescribes their legal effect or the procedures for promulgating them. Nonetheless, Presidents have been issuing them for a long time for many different purposes, some of which have been controversial. *See Youngstown Sheet & Tube Co. v. Sawyer*, 343 U.S. 579 (1952) (holding unconstitutional an executive order providing for the government takeover of private steel mills). Most executive orders, however, concern the internal workings of the executive branch. These executive orders help the President control the executive branch.

Of particular importance to administrative law is a series of executive orders dealing with the process for promulgating regulations. The primary current order addressing the regulatory process is E.O. 12866. *See* 3 C.F.R., 1993 Comp., at 638. Its history and major provisions, along with other executive orders on the regulatory process, are described in Chapter 5, Section III.H.1. We mention E.O. 12866 in this chapter because of its importance as a means of presidential control of the executive branch.

4. Line Item Veto

One of Congress's most important powers is the power of the purse. The Constitution says, "No Money shall be drawn from the Treasury, but in Consequence of Appropriations made by Law." U.S. Const. art. I, § 9, cl. 7. This means that Congress must authorize all federal spending in bills that pass each House and are presented to the President for approval or veto. To curb federal spending, Congress enacted the Line Item Veto Act in 1994. The Act authorized the President, after signing an appropriation bill into law, to "cancel" certain, discrete spending provisions in the law. The Supreme Court struck down the Act in *Clinton v. City of New York*, 524 U.S. 417 (1998). The Court's decision may be important more because of the statutory practices that it left standing than because of the statutory innovation that it struck down.

The Court in *Clinton* found that the legal and practical effect of the Act was to allow the President to amend Acts of Congress by repealing parts of them. The Court held that the Constitution, however, withholds from the President the power to amend or repeal an Act of Congress. The amendment or repeal of a federal statute, the Court said, has to comport with Article I, § 7: each House of Congress has to pass an identical bill amending or repealing prior law and present that bill to the President to either approve or return in its entirety. The Line Item Veto Act violated the Constitution by allowing laws to be made without following these bicameralism and presentment procedures.

In finding this violation, the Court emphasized that it was not addressing "the scope of Congress' power to delegate law-making authority, or its functional equivalent, to the President." *Id.* at 448. The Court explained that statutes delegating lawmaking authority differ from the Line Item Veto Act. When Congress delegates lawmaking authority to the President (or other executive-branch entity), Congress must prescribe a policy (an intelligible principle) for the President to follow. In contrast, the Line Item Veto Act allowed the President to reject congressional policy decisions on spending matters. *Id.* at 443-444. Thus, the Court seemed to go out of its way to avoid casting doubt on statutes in which Congress delegates broad rulemaking authority to federal agencies.

Example

An appropriation statute authorizes the Secretary of the Navy to spend an "amount not exceeding $500 million" to build a new warship. On the instructions of the President, the Secretary decides not to spend any money on building the new warship. Assume that the statute permits the Secretary to make that decision. Does the statute violate the Constitution under *Clinton v. City of New York*?

Explanation

The appropriation statute that permits the Secretary to spend nothing on a new warship would not violate the Constitution under *Clinton v. City of New York*. The Court in *Clinton v. City of New York* observed that appropriation provisions like the one in our example have been enacted since 1789. The Court said that the "critical difference" between these provisions and the Line Item Veto Act was that the Act gave the President "the unilateral power to change the text of duly enacted statutes." 524 U.S. at 447. The appropriation statute in our example does not give the President or the Secretary any such power; instead, it merely gives them discretion to spend less than $500 million on the ship. By exercising that discretion, these executive officials are acting consistently with the congressional policy prescribed in the statute. In contrast, the Line Item Veto Act allowed the President to contradict the spending policy underlying the provisions that the President cancelled.

CHAPTER 3

Adjudication

> Every new tribunal, erected for the decision of facts, without the intervention of jury, . . . is a step towards establishing . . . the most oppressive of absolute governments.
>
> —3 *Blackstone's Commentaries* 380

This quotation reflects the long-standing view of Anglo-American jurisprudence that a jury trial of facts is the sine qua non of justice and freedom. The importance of the jury trial is further reflected in the Sixth and Seventh Amendments of our Bill of Rights. As Chapter 2 indicated, however, the right to a jury trial in civil cases involving the government can be greatly restricted, and the trial of facts usually can be delegated to an administrative agency, without even the protection of an independent judge appointed for life and usually with only deferential judicial review of the agency's factual determinations. This chapter covers the procedures and protections involved in adjudications conducted by agencies, which today vastly outnumber the adjudications made by courts. It begins by describing the nature of the matters that may be decided by agency adjudication. It then distinguishes between those adjudications that must be conducted pursuant to the procedures of the APA and those that are not subject to those procedures. The chapter continues by explaining at length the procedures and protections provided by the APA and concludes with descriptions of procedures applicable to other types of adjudicatory proceedings.

I. THE SUBJECT MATTER OF ADJUDICATION

Under the APA, *adjudication* is defined as the agency process for issuing an "order." *Order* is then defined as a final disposition of an agency in a matter other than rulemaking but including licensing. What this means is that adjudication is the term used to describe the process by which agencies make final decisions on matters except for rulemaking. This is clearly a broad concept, covering a vast array of different types of agency actions. What the concept envisions, and what the different types of agency actions have in common, is a decision by an agency about a particular person or persons that requires the application of law to the particular facts of the person's situation. Nevertheless, this can extend from the ordinary and mundane determination of qualifications for government benefits, for example, to the extraordinary and important determination of national policy on a variety of matters. A few examples can illustrate the variety of adjudications.

Example

A person applies for a federal Stafford student loan. She must fill out a form and send it to the Department of Education for processing. The Department of Education reviews the information provided in the form and determines the Expected Family Contribution, which provides the basis for determining the approved amount of financial aid.

Explanation

Although this process does not bear any resemblance to a judicial proceeding, and indeed seems like any other form of bureaucratic decision making, this is technically adjudication. The Department of Education, a federal agency, has taken the facts provided to it and determined if a person qualifies for a Stafford loan and for what amount.

Example

A person applies for disability insurance benefits from the Commissioner of Social Security, stating that he is unable to perform work because of back pain. Under the Social Security Act, persons who have worked enough to qualify for Social Security benefits, but who because of disability are now unable to perform work in the national economy for an extended period, can receive monthly benefits for their disability. The person files information on his or her work history, income, and medical history with the Social Security Administration (through a state agency under contract with the Social Security Administration). The agency reviews medical records and determines whether the person qualifies for disability benefits. If the agency finds the person unqualified, it sends the applicant a notice to this effect, giving the reason for the denial of benefits. The applicant may seek reconsideration, which means the agency reviews the file again; however, the applicant may request a face-to-face hearing if the denial is based on medical reasons.

If the agency still denies the benefits, the applicant may seek a *de novo* hearing before an Administrative Law Judge (ALJ).[1] If the ALJ denies the benefits, the applicant may appeal to the Social Security Administration's Appeals Council. One judge may determine that the case should not be further heard, but if the initial judge decides the case should be heard, it is considered by a panel of three judges, generally on the basis of the record in the prior proceedings. If the Appeals Council affirms the denial of benefits, then the applicant may seek judicial review.

Explanation

The Social Security Disability example begins like the Federal Student Aid example, with a bureaucratic decision that bears none of the hallmarks of judicial adjudication. This is not surprising when one considers the volume of applications received. There are over 4 million recipients of Social Security Disability benefits. Nevertheless, again, the initial determination and determination on reconsideration are technically adjudications: the agency is ascertaining the facts and determining whether the legal standard for benefits is met.

When the applicant seeks a *de novo* hearing before the ALJ, however, the process takes on more of the characteristics we identify with adjudication: a judge, the possibility of testimony by the applicant and witnesses on his behalf, the possibility of cross-examination of persons providing evidence detrimental to the applicant, a decision based on the record in the proceeding, and a written decision explaining the outcome. The fact that this decision can then be appealed to an appellate body further reinforces the quasi-judicial nature of the ALJ hearing. At the same time, there are features of the ALJ hearing that are decidedly unlike a judicial adjudication. First, there is no adverse party. The applicant is the only party to the hearing; no one appears on behalf of the Social Security Administration to defend its

---

1. A *de novo* hearing is one in which the decision maker does not review the decision of someone else but makes the determination himself. Thus, while the ALJ may use the record compiled earlier as part of the evidence in the case, he may receive additional evidence and decide the issues without regard to the decisions made by the agency denying the benefits.

denial of the benefits. Second, an ALJ in the Social Security Disability case, unlike a judge in the judicial context, has a duty to assist the applicant in making his case.

Example

The Federal Trade Commission Act prohibits unfair competition, including restraints on trade. The Act authorizes the Federal Trade Commission (FTC) to initiate administrative proceedings against persons the Commission believes are violating the Act. Under this provision the Commission served a complaint on the California Dental Association (CDA), alleging that its ethical rules restricting price advertising were prohibited restraints on trade. In a hearing before an ALJ, the Commission, acting through its General Counsel, presented its evidence through documents and witnesses' testimony. The CDA defended, cross-examining the FTC's witnesses, calling its own, and introducing its own documentary evidence. At the conclusion of the proceeding, in a decision setting forth findings of fact and conclusions of law, the ALJ held that the CDA had violated the FTC Act. The CDA appealed to the full Commission, which, after briefing from the CDA and the FTC General Counsel, reached the same conclusion, issuing a cease-and-desist order to the CDA. The CDA then appealed to the Ninth Circuit Court of Appeals.

Explanation

This is an example of an adjudication making national policy. The FTC Act prohibits unreasonable restraints on trade, but this broad language can be made concrete in particular adjudications brought by the FTC alleging the existence of the prohibited conduct. Professional organizations historically believed that price advertising was unethical—after all, it was a profession, not a trade. Until relatively recently this was true of lawyers. The FTC, by proceeding against the California Dental Association, was bringing a precedent-setting case to try to facilitate price advertising by dentists, in the hope that it would result in price competition and lower prices for consumers.

This is also an example of adjudication in the enforcement context. Unlike the first two examples, here the agency comes after the private entity, issuing a complaint that forces the private entity to submit to the administrative process.

Finally, this is also an example of adjudication that looks very much like judicial adjudication. There are adverse parties, trial-like procedure, lawyers, a judge, and a final decision based on the evidence presented, complete with findings of fact and conclusions of law. Moreover, there is the opportunity for an appellate-like appeal of the ALJ's decision to the full Commission. But there are still some important differences between even this type of formal adjudication and a trial in a federal district court. Most importantly, an ALJ is not an Article III, lifetime-tenured, federal judge. He or she is technically an employee of the agency involved, here the FTC, but with protections designed to ensure independence of judgment. In addition, the Federal Rules of Evidence applicable in federal district court are not required to be applicable in administrative adjudications. Also, the appeal of the ALJ's decision to the full Commission is unlike the appeal of a federal district court decision to a court of appeals; the Commission, while bound by the record created in the ALJ proceeding, is allowed to make a *de novo* decision based on that record. It is not reviewing the ALJ's decision; it is making its own decision. When a court of appeals reviews a district court's decision, it can make a *de novo* decision on questions of law, but it is bound to accept the district court's decision as to the facts unless that decision is clearly erroneous. In other words, it is easier for the FTC to reach a different decision from the ALJ than it is for a court of appeals to reach a different decision on appeal from a district court judge.

Example

A developer wishes to develop some property for residential housing, but some of the property is a wetland. Under the Clean Water Act, a person cannot fill certain wetlands without a permit from the United States Army Corps of Engineers. The person must complete a form and supply information on the nature of the wetlands, the purpose of the development project, and the extent of feasible alternatives to the wetlands site. In addition, the person must demonstrate that the activity does not violate state water quality standards. The Corps provides public notice of the application and allows for public comment on the requested permit. In addition, the Corps provides other relevant federal agencies—notably the Fish and Wildlife Service of the Department of the Interior and the Environmental Protection Agency (EPA)—notice of the request. If the Corps proposes to grant the permit, it must allow the EPA an opportunity to override its determination. If it denies the permit, the applicant may appeal the denial administratively within the Corps. If that appeal is denied, the applicant may seek judicial review under the APA.

Explanation

Again, this is adjudication, although it is the particular subset of adjudication known as licensing. *Licensing*, as defined in the APA, includes any agency permit, certificate, approval, registration, charter, exemption, or other form of permission. Thus, environmental permits issued by agencies authorizing particular levels of pollution, broadcast licenses granted to television or radio stations by the Federal Communications Commission, pilot licenses issued by the Federal Aviation Administration, and grazing permits given by the Bureau of Land Management, for example, would all involve licensing.

Licensing is like the application for government benefits in that normally there is no adverse party; there is just the applicant applying to the government agency. However, when licensing involves issues that may interest persons other than the applicant, as it often does, others may wish to participate in the adjudication, just as persons may wish to intervene in judicial proceedings. In our example, environmentalists in the vicinity of the area to be developed (or persons who simply do not want the development and want to use environmental laws to help block it) may wish to participate in the proceeding.

Licensing is also like the application for government benefits in that normally the procedures used in the adjudication do not mimic judicial procedures.

The above examples all involve federal agencies, but the concept of adjudication (and licensing) is the same in the states. That is, the term covers a wide range of different kinds of determinations, some of which look like judicial adjudications and some of which do not. As in the federal system, adjudication in the states shares the characteristics of applying law to particular facts with respect to particular persons.

II. FORMAL AND INFORMAL ADJUDICATION

While the APA broadly defines "adjudication," the APA prescribes particular adjudicatory procedures for only certain adjudications. Section 554, entitled Adjudications, which contains certain procedural requirements, only applies to cases of adjudication "required by statute to be determined on the record after opportunity for an agency hearing."[2] Sections 556 and 557, which specify a number of additional required procedures, apply whenever Section 554 applies. Together, these sections prescribe a fairly formal, trial-type adjudication that bears substantial similarity to trials in courts. Adjudication carried out under these provisions is generally called "formal adjudication"; adjudication not subject to these sections is called "informal adjudication." These terms, however, are somewhat misleading. While all adjudication under Sections 554, 556, and 557 is fairly formal, inasmuch as it is presided over by ALJs and can involve oral testimony and cross-examination, these adjudications can range from the relatively less formal Social Security Disability hearings before ALJs, often without lawyers and always without adverse parties, to the large-scale and very formal hearings, such as the FTC adjudication described above. Similarly, "informal adjudication" can extend

2. Even these adjudications may be excepted from the requirements of Section 554, but these exceptions are relatively rare. *See* 5 U.S.C. § 554(a)(1)-(6).

from the bureaucratic decision making involved in the Federal Student Financial Aid and initial Social Security Disability determinations to proceedings that appear virtually indistinguishable from the most formal adjudications under the APA. Nevertheless, despite their lack of descriptive accuracy, these terms are well established in administrative law. Thus, when you read about "formal adjudication" in the federal system, it almost invariably refers to adjudication conducted under Sections 554, 556, and 557 of the APA. A more accurate way to describe these adjudications would be to call them "APA adjudications" and to call all the other adjudications "non-APA adjudications." While these terms have not caught on in administrative law, some commentators use them.

However they are styled, it is important to be able to distinguish those adjudications that must be conducted under Sections 554, 556, and 557 from those that need not be. Primarily, this is because the failure to follow the required procedures normally would result in the reversal of the agency decision. In addition, the Equal Access to Justice Act provides attorneys' fees to certain types of prevailing parties in adjudications under these sections of the APA, but not in other adjudications.

As described above, Section 554 applies to adjudications "required by statute to be determined on the record after opportunity for an agency hearing." This language directs the reader to look to a different statute to determine whether Section 554 applies. For example, if we wanted to know whether Clean Water Act permits could be issued only after a formal adjudication, we would look to the Clean Water Act to see if it referred to Section 554 or otherwise indicated that the permit proceeding was to be one determined on the record after an opportunity for an agency hearing. Some statutes clearly enunciate such a requirement. For example, under the Consumer Product Safety Act, the Consumer Product Safety Commission can order a manufacturer to recall a product that constitutes a substantial hazard "only after an opportunity for a hearing in accordance with section 554 of Title 5." *See* 15 U.S.C. § 2064(f). The National Endowment for the Arts can order the repayment of grant funds if they were used to produce an "obscene" work, but only "after reasonable notice and opportunity for a hearing on the record." *See* 20 U.S.C. § 954(l)(1). Unfortunately, many statutes are less explicit. For example, the Secretary of Agriculture can revoke a grain inspector's license for knowingly or carelessly mischaracterizing grain, "after the licensee has been afforded an opportunity for a hearing." Although the Secretary of Agriculture probably would concede that his decision ultimately must be based on the record of the hearing, nothing in the statute specifically requires a hearing "on the record." Does the absence of words mentioning that the decision must be "on the record" mean this statute does not require the use of Section 554?

In the 70 years since the APA was enacted, the Supreme Court has not addressed this issue with respect to adjudication, so there is no clear and definitive answer.

3. Adjudication

Some courts relied upon a pair of cases the Supreme Court decided with respect to formal rulemaking. Formal rulemaking is triggered by identical language to that which triggers formal adjudication, although it is found in a different statutory provision, 5 U.S.C. § 553 (c). In *United States v. Allegheny-Ludlum Steel Corp.*, 406 U.S. 742 (1972), and *United States v. Florida East Coast R.R. Co.*, 410 U.S. 224 (1973), the Court held that this language, at least in the rulemaking context, triggers the APA formal procedures only when the statute in question contains the precise language or other clear expression of congressional intent to require formal procedures. The Court made clear that the presumption was against the APA formal procedures in rulemaking. Because the language applicable to formal adjudication and formal rulemaking was the same, some courts applied the presumption against formal adjudication. Other courts, however, noted that the Supreme Court's justification for the presumption against a trial-type hearing in a rulemaking relied on the difference between legislation and adjudication. Legislation is not adopted after a trial-type hearing, while judicial orders do follow a trial-type proceeding. Thus, because rulemaking mimics legislating and administrative adjudication mimics judicial decisionmaking, some courts read a presumption in favor of formal adjudication—a trial-type proceeding. Later, the Supreme Court decided *Chevron, U.S.A., Inc. v. N.R.D.C.*, 467 U.S. 837 (1984), in which the Court held that when a statute is ambiguous, courts should defer to a reasonable interpretation of the statute contained in a rule adopted by the agency responsible for administering it. As a result, most courts then decided that this was the correct way to determine whether an ambiguous statute required formal adjudication—defer to the agency's reasonable interpretation of the statute. Because agencies invariably prefer informal adjudication, agencies routinely adopted rules providing for informal adjudication, rather than formal adjudication, whenever the language of the statute was ambiguous regarding what type of procedures is required. In 2024, however, the Supreme Court overruled *Chevron* in *Loper Bright Enterprises v. Raimondo*, 144 S.Ct. 2244 (2024). In that case, the Court said that its decision did not affect past decisions that relied on *Chevron*, so the particular adjudications that in reliance on *Chevron* had been deemed informal in the past cases should not be affected. However, with respect to adjudications about which courts have not yet decided whether they are formal or informal, we are left with the split between the two earlier lines of cases.

This is all very confusing, as the law often is when there is no agreed-upon rule to be applied. What is a lawyer to do? A lawyer must know the several rules that have been used in the various cases. Then depending on which side of the case she is on (is she claiming that an agency's order is unlawful because the agency failed to follow formal adjudication requirements, or is she defending the agency's action?), she should argue in favor of the precedents that help her case and try to distinguish or disparage the precedents that do not.

Example

Earlier we asked if the hearing required before revoking a grain inspector's license must be subject to the formal procedures of the APA. The statute states the license can be revoked "after the licensee has been afforded an opportunity for a hearing." Moreover, a person can pursuant to the APA obtain judicial review of a revocation, and the court's review will be on the basis of the record in the adjudicatory proceeding. Assume the Department of Agriculture has adopted procedural regulations applicable to revocations that provide only for informal revocation proceedings, rather than formal adjudications under the APA. Now imagine that the Department of Agriculture has revoked the license of a grain inspector because it determined that he had on several occasions carelessly mischaracterized the grain he was inspecting. The Department had received complaints from several grain buyers that the grain they received was not the type it was supposed to be. In each case the inspector was the same person. The Department gave this information to the inspector and offered him the opportunity for a "hearing" at which he could provide his own evidence or try to rebut the evidence against him, but the Department would not call any witnesses, instead relying on the written complaints, nor allow him to subpoena the complainants. Also, a deputy director of the Plant Inspection Service, not an ALJ, would preside over the "hearing." Objecting that this procedure was not sufficient under the APA, the inspector did not seek the hearing. He now seeks judicial review of his license revocation, arguing that the proceeding was unlawful because it did not follow the procedures of the APA.

You are the attorney for the grain inspector. What arguments do you make to support your claim?

Explanation

As the lawyer for the grain inspector, the person challenging the agency action, the burden is on you to show that the APA procedures are required in these license revocation cases. The statute does not clearly indicate on its face that the APA procedures are required, because it does not combine the terms "hearing" and "on the record." Rather, it only uses the term "hearing," and there are other types of hearings besides those under the APA. You would, of course, look at more of the statute than just the language requiring a hearing. Perhaps there are other indications in the statute that the hearing is supposed to be "on the record." For example, some courts have thought it noteworthy that the statute specifically provides for judicial review of the result of the hearing, implying that there would be a record for judicial review and therefore that the hearing was "on the record." You would also look to the legislative history to see if there is evidence of congressional intent on the subject. Assuming neither of these sources contains significant support, you are left with the different tests announced by the courts.

However, the cases in which courts relied on the now overruled *Chevron* as a basis for deferring to the agency's interpretation are no longer good law in terms of precedent for a new case. Later, you will learn about *Skidmore* deference, which continues to be good law. That might provide an argument for the government here, but the bottom line is that the court will have to decide itself what is the best reading of the statute.

A. Formal and Informal Adjudication in the States

Following the various Model State APAs, states likewise distinguish adjudication into two different categories that mirror the federal formal/ informal adjudication categories. In the states, the formal adjudication mode is known as a Contested Case proceeding. Informal adjudications are Other than Contested Case proceedings. And like the federal model, states generally follow the Model State APAs by specifying the procedure for Contested Cases but leaving the procedures for Other than Contested Cases unspecified. Usually, however, states are clearer about when Contested Case proceedings are required.

III. THE APA PROCEDURES FOR ADJUDICATION

Assuming that the APA's procedures in Sections 554, 556, and 557 apply to an adjudication, what precisely do they require? For the most part, the procedures are straightforward and are detailed in the sections of the APA and can be read there. As a general matter, if you think of the procedures used in a judicial trial, you will have a fairly good sense of the procedures involved in most formal adjudications. Originally, the conception was that administrative adjudications would be much less formal than judicial procedures, and the core requirements of Sections 554, 556, and 557 reflect this by imposing only the most skeletal framework for adjudications. Over time, however, agencies have tended to introduce further procedural requirements, even while judicial procedures have evolved a number of techniques to reduce the cost and time of the proceedings, so that the two have become quite similar. For example, the Department of Labor's procedural rules and rules of evidence are based on the Federal Rules of Civil Procedure and the Federal Rules of Evidence. *See* 29 C.F.R. pt. 18. Remember, however, that agencies may repeal those procedures that they have added by regulation to those required by the APA. *See Citizens Awareness Network, Inc. v. United States*, 391 F.3d 338 (1st Cir. 2004) (upholding agency repeal of discovery provisions and limitation of cross-examination to where "necessary to ensure an adequate record for decision.").

What follows highlights some of the most important APA requirements and those aspects of APA adjudication that differ from a judicial proceeding.

A. Notice Requirements

The initial requirement for an APA adjudication is that a person who is being brought before the agency (as opposed to the person who invokes the agency process, such as to obtain a benefit) must be provided with notice of the time, place, and nature of the hearing; the legal authority and jurisdiction under which the hearing is to be held; and the matters of fact and law asserted. 5 U.S.C. § 554(b). Thus, the notice under the APA serves essentially as both the notice and the complaint in a judicial proceeding. Indeed, in many agency proceedings, the notice is given in a document called a "complaint." In addition, the APA usually requires the defendant in the case to give notice of controverted issues of fact and law; this mirrors the requirement in a judicial civil case for an answer by the defendant.

The adequacy of the notice provided to a defendant is sometimes an issue in an administrative adjudication brought by an agency in its enforcement capacity. The purpose of the notice is to inform the defendant as to the nature of the charges against him and the facts supporting those charges, so that he may mount a defense. To the extent that the notice provided does not fully inform the defendant of the charges and relevant facts, the defendant may be able to claim to a reviewing court that he was not provided adequate notice. Courts take a pragmatic approach to such claims, looking to see whether as a practical matter the defendant has been provided a fair understanding of the charges and a fair opportunity to address them.

B. The Burden of Proof

The APA states that in an APA adjudication the "proponent of a[n] order has the burden of proof." This is equivalent to the general rule in civil proceedings that the plaintiff has the burden of proof. In administrative proceedings, however, the person who is the proponent of the order is not always the person who initiates the proceeding.

Example

The Social Security Administration determines on the basis of recent medical reports supplied to it that a person is no longer disabled. The agency sends the person a notice to that effect, informing him that his benefits will be terminated. The person can obtain an informal hearing on the subject prior to the benefits being stopped. If that informal hearing results in a determination that he is no longer disabled, his benefits are stopped, but he can demand a formal, APA hearing to contest this determination further. In that APA proceeding, the Social Security Administration has the burden of proof to show that he is no longer disabled.

Explanation

Although the person is in one sense the initiating party, because he is demanding the APA hearing, he is not the "proponent of the order." The order in question is an order terminating his benefits. The agency is the entity trying to terminate his benefits, so it is the proponent of the order. It therefore has the burden of proof.

Example

The Federal Trade Commission institutes an administrative action against the California Dental Association asserting it has engaged in a restraint of trade by restricting price advertising by member dentists. The Commission is seeking an order declaring the activity a restraint of trade and ordering the Association to cease and desist the activity.

Explanation

Here the agency both initiates the adjudication, by filing the notice and complaint against the Association, and seeks an order. Because the agency is the proponent of the order, it has the burden of proving that the Association is unlawfully restraining trade.

As is usually the case in the judicial context, the "burden of proof" is the same as the "burden of persuasion," not the burden of going forward or the burden of production.

C. Rules of Evidence

The APA states that "any oral or documentary evidence may be received," but it says that agencies should provide for exclusion of irrelevant, immaterial, or unduly repetitious evidence. This language makes clear that normal rules of evidence need not apply in formal administrative adjudications the way they do in court cases. Originally it was thought that this "informality" would make administrative proceedings faster and easier than judicial proceedings. In practice, however, some agencies have adopted their own rules of evidence for administrative proceedings. For example, the Department of Labor has published rules of evidence governing its formal adjudications that extend over 25 double-column pages of the Code of Federal Regulations. This is another reflection of formal administrative adjudication tending toward the attributes of judicial adjudication.

Nevertheless, one area in which formal administrative adjudication has generally strayed from the judicial model is in the treatment of hearsay evidence. If you have not studied evidence yet, think of hearsay as when a witness testifies to something on the basis of what someone told him or her, rather than on the basis of his or her own observation. This is not precisely correct, but it is close enough for our purposes. For example, if a witness is asked, "Did your boss sexually harass your co-worker?," and the witness answers, "She told me that he did," that would be hearsay.

Generally, hearsay evidence is not admissible in judicial proceedings. *See, e.g.*, Rule 801, Federal Rules of Evidence. The APA, however, does not preclude the admission of hearsay, and generally it is admitted in formal adjudications.

For a while, courts in policing administrative adjudications applied something called the Residuum Rule. It held that while hearsay was admissible evidence, the decision in an administrative adjudication could not rely *solely* on hearsay evidence; there had to be at least a residuum of non-hearsay evidence supporting the decision. Today, although the Supreme Court has never directly addressed the issue, it is generally conceded that federal courts will no longer use the Residuum Rule. This is also true of most states.

Nevertheless, under the APA (and the Model State APA that many states follow), no order in a formal adjudication may be issued that is not supported by "reliable, probative, and substantial evidence." 5 U.S.C. § 556(d). Thus, while hearsay evidence may be admissible, to the extent that it is not reliable, probative, and substantial, the decision cannot rely on it. Some hearsay evidence is more reliable and substantial than other hearsay evidence. The various rules of evidence recognize this by creating a number of exceptions to the Hearsay Rule excluding hearsay evidence. Even in the absence of a rule, however, ALJs need to decide whether admissible hearsay is still sufficiently reliable and substantial to be the basis for a decision.

Example

An ALJ was notified that his employment was to be terminated because of his sexual harassment of a secretary. He requests a hearing, triggering the need for a formal adjudication under the personnel laws protecting the independence of ALJs. At the hearing, the only evidence presented against him is the testimony of a friend of the secretary. She testifies that the secretary told her that she was quitting because the ALJ had continually pressured her for sexual favors. The ALJ testifies, denying that he ever engaged in any such conduct. Is there reliable, probative, and substantial evidence that the ALJ engaged in sexual harassment?

Explanation

The agency has the burden of proof, because it is the proponent of the order to terminate the employment of the ALJ. It must satisfy that burden by a preponderance of the evidence. Had the secretary testified, saying that the supervisor had continually pressured her for sexual favors, and the supervisor had testified denying it, the fact-finder could find sexual harassment if it found the secretary's testimony credible. As it is, however, the testimony by the friend is hearsay. She is testifying as to what someone told her. Even if she is credible, so that the fact-finder believes the secretary told her friend about the alleged sexual harassment, the fact-finder cannot determine whether the secretary was telling her friend the truth. There is no way to tell if the secretary may have lied to her friend. She is not present as a witness subject to cross-examination. This is the reason why in a judicial proceeding the hearsay would not be admissible. In an administrative adjudication, however, the friend's testimony generally would be admissible, because there is generally no bar to the admissibility of hearsay evidence. If the Residuum Rule were applicable, it would bar a decision against the ALJ because there would be no non-hearsay evidence against him. Because the Residuum Rule no longer applies in federal cases, however, it will not bar a decision against the ALJ. Nevertheless, the requirement for an order to be based on reliable, probative, and substantial evidence would preclude a decision against the ALJ here. This is not *because* the evidence is hearsay, but because this one hearsay statement is not sufficiently reliable or substantial on which to base a decision. Imagine, however, that there were several additional witnesses who testified that the secretary had told them over a period of years of numerous times that the ALJ tried to pressure her into sex, and if he did not stop she would have to quit some day. All these statements are equally hearsay, but together they probably would constitute sufficiently reliable, probative, and substantial evidence on which to justify an order terminating the employment of the ALJ for sexual harassment.

D. The Role of the ALJ

The APA provides that the "agency," one or more members of the body comprising the agency (remember those multi-member agencies?), or an ALJ can preside at a formal adjudication. *See* 5 U.S.C. § 556(b). As a practical matter, an ALJ almost always presides. When the APA was passed in 1946, ALJs were called Hearing Examiners. This reflected the view at the time that their function was generally ministerial, presiding over the hearing and assembling the record. As time passed and formal adjudications tended to take on many of the characteristics of judicial proceedings, their name was changed to reflect that development.

In 1946 there were only 196 Hearing Examiners; today there are approximately 2,000 ALJs. This would suggest it is a growth industry, but in fact the growth is only in one area—Social Security Disability determinations. When the APA was passed, Social Security Hearing Examiners made up only 7 percent of all the Hearing Examiners; most Hearing Examiners (64 percent) worked for one of the independent regulatory agencies involved in economic regulation. Today, Social Security ALJs make up more than 80 percent of all ALJs, while only 5 percent work in economic regulation.

In the federal system, an ALJ is technically an employee of the agency over whose adjudications he will preside. Nevertheless, he is supposed to be neutral and impartial in deciding the cases before him, even though in many, if not all of them, the agency will be a party to the proceeding. In order to preserve that independence, despite his employee status, the personnel laws applicable to ALJs have historically been special. First, until the Trump administration, agencies had little control over who was hired. The hiring process was performed by the Office of Personnel Management, a separate executive agency, which engaged in a rigorous selection process, that included tests and interviews, that ended up ranking the candidates for an ALJ position. The agency then could choose only from the top three candidates for each vacancy, and could not pass over a veteran.[3] By executive order, President Trump provided that all new ALJs would be placed in the "excepted" (as opposed to the competitive) service and would be hired simply by the head of the agency on the basis of whatever standard the

3. While veterans receive a preference under all the civil service laws, their preference in the ALJ selection process results in a disproportionate number of veterans being selected and, because most veterans are men, a disproportionate number of men being hired as ALJs.

agency chose to use. President Biden did not end this arrangement. Second, agencies can neither reward nor punish ALJs, and they are exempt from the annual performance ratings that normal employees must undergo. Third, unlike other federal civil servants, they have a right to a formal adjudication before they may be fired for cause, and this adjudication is heard not within the agency but by the Merit Systems Protection Board, another independent agency.[4] Of course, this means a hearing before another ALJ. In fact, ALJs think of themselves as independent and strive to maintain or enhance that independence from their employing agency. Private litigants should have no fear that ALJs are biased in favor of the agency because of their employment status. The practical independence of ALJs is further confirmed by agencies' attempts to have formal adjudications downgraded to informal adjudications for the primary purpose of avoiding the use of ALJs as judges. That said, the change in the way ALJs are hired means that it will be even easier for agencies to hire ALJs likely to share some of the views of the agency, such as a former employee of the agency.

E. The Course of the Proceeding

A formal adjudication proceeds much like a trial in a federal court. While the APA does not require the provision of discovery, many agencies have provided for it by regulation, but even if discovery is afforded, it is likely to be less extensive than in a court case. If there are adverse parties (as there are not, for example, in a Social Security Disability case), there are likely to be pre-hearing conferences, alternative dispute resolution alternatives, and motions of various sorts; private parties have the right to have the agency issue subpoenas on their behalf to compel witnesses to attend or bring documents. A case can be decided on a summary basis without a hearing in appropriate circumstances, like summary judgment decisions in court. Otherwise, the trial proceeds with the introduction of evidence and the examination and cross-examination of witnesses. At the conclusion of the case, the parties have an opportunity to submit proposed findings of fact and conclusions of law, along with supporting reasons, to the ALJ. The ALJ then makes a decision in which he makes findings of fact, conclusions of law, and the reasons therefore, together with the applicable order.

---

4. There are currently challenges to the "for cause" protection from removal for ALJs in light of the fact that members of the Merit Systems Protection Board themselves are protected from removal except for cause, thereby creating a dual for-cause removal protection situation. In *Free Enterprise Fund v. Public Company Accounting Oversight Board*, 561 U.S. 477 (2010), the Supreme Court found a dual for-cause removal protection unconstitutional with respect to persons who have not only adjudicatory authority but also policy making and enforcement authority. ALJs, of course, only have adjudicatory authority.

F. The Role of the Agency

Until the ALJ renders his decision, a formal adjudicatory proceeding, as has been said often, looks a lot like a trial in a federal court. After the ALJ makes his decision, however, most of the analogy ends. Recall the original notion of ALJs being Hearing Examiners for the agency, creating the record and assisting the agency in reaching a final decision. This concept continues in the APA in its treatment of the role of the agency.

Under the APA, the decision that the ALJ makes, including findings of fact, conclusions of law, and the reasons therefore, may be either an *initial* decision or a *recommended* decision. *See* 5 U.S.C. § 557(b). If it is an initial decision, then it becomes the decision of the agency automatically, unless there is an appeal to the agency or the agency decides on its own motion to review the decision. If it is a recommended decision, then the decision goes to the agency for final determination. Whether a case before an ALJ will result in an initial decision or only a recommended decision is up to the agency. Moreover, the agency can make this determination either on a general basis or on a particular basis.

Example

Before 1992, the EPA provided by regulation that initial decisions by EPA ALJs should become the final order of the Administrator within 45 days of service unless an appeal to the Administrator was taken or the Administrator elected, *sua sponte*, to review the initial decision. In 1992, the Administrator delegated all of his functions with respect to formal adjudications to the Environmental Appeals Board (the EAB), then a board of three members chosen by the Administrator, now expanded to four. Consequently, the regulations provide that initial decisions by EPA ALJs become the final order of the EPA within 45 days of service unless an appeal to the EAB is taken or the EAB decides on its own to review the initial decision.

Explanation

When the APA speaks about an "agency" making a decision, it really means the head of the agency making a decision. In agencies headed by a single figure, such as the EPA, the Department of Labor, and the Social Security Administration, that person acts for the "agency." In agencies headed by a multi-member board, such as the FCC, NLRB, and FTC, it takes a majority vote of that board or commission to act for the "agency." Therefore, under the APA, originally the EPA ALJ's initial decisions would have been appealed to the Administrator or recommended decisions would have gone directly to the Administrator. Moreover, whether ALJ decisions would be initial decisions or only recommended decisions would have been determined by the Administrator.

In its pre-1992 regulations, the EPA (the Administrator) had decided as a general rule that ALJs should actually make the initial decision, with the Administrator only becoming involved if someone chose to appeal the initial decision, unless it was a case of such importance that the Administrator thought he should actually be involved in the decision, in which case he could elevate the initial decision for review on his own motion.

In creating the EAB in 1992, the Administrator decided that not only did he not need to be involved in the initial decision of formal adjudication cases, he did not need to be involved in them at all. As a simple matter of time management, he was too busy doing other things that were more important. As a result, he delegated all his functions with respect to adjudication to the newly created EAB, although the Administrator has retained the authority to review an EAB decision *sua sponte*. The EAB thus becomes the "agency" with respect to adjudications.

As a general matter, the trend has been toward having ALJs make initial rather than recommended decisions, and there have been some other examples of agencies creating appellate bodies to handle the appeals of the initial decisions, rather than bothering the head of the agency with that responsibility.

When, or if, an ALJ decision goes to the agency (or a designated appellate body) for final decision, whether on appeal or otherwise, the procedure mimics the procedure in judicial appellate litigation. That is, the decision must be based upon the record created below in the ALJ proceeding. New evidence is not taken. The parties file briefs and often are provided an opportunity for oral argument. This procedure is followed whether or not the ALJ decision was an initial decision or a recommended decision. When the ALJ's decision is only a recommended decision, which automatically goes to the agency for the actual decision, it is understandable that the agency is free to accept or reject the ALJ's recommended findings of fact and conclusions of law. This, of course, is different from ordinary judicial appellate practice. A trial court's decision is not a recommendation to the appellate court. When an ALJ's decision is an initial decision that is appealed to the agency, *the same rule applies as with recommended decisions; that is, the agency is free to accept or reject the ALJ's findings of fact and conclusions of law.* As the APA states: "[o]n appeal from or review of the initial decision, the agency has all the powers which it would have in making the initial decision." Again, this is very different from ordinary judicial appellate practice. There, while an appellate court reviews questions of law *de novo* (i.e., without regard to the lower court's decision), it reviews questions of fact with deference to the findings of the trial court, which actually presided over the presentation of evidence and actually saw and heard any witnesses. In short, the agency has more power to reject ALJ decisions than appellate courts have to reject trial court decisions.

This lodging of final decisional powers in the agency, rather than in the ALJ, reflects the history of the APA and its original understanding of ALJs as hearing officers engaged in a ministerial function assisting the agency in making actual decisions.

G. Ex Parte Communications—5 U.S.C. § 557(d)

The term *ex parte communication* generally means a communication to a judge by a party to a proceeding outside the presence of all the other parties. In the judicial context ex parte communications usually are prohibited because they appear to undermine the fundamental fairness of a proceeding that rests upon adversary presentations. In 1966, as part of the trend toward the increased judicialization of formal adjudication, Congress amended the APA to add what is called the "ex parte communication provision," prohibiting such communications in certain circumstances. Congress defined ex parte communications as oral or written communications not on the public record with respect to which reasonable prior notice to all parties is not given. Ex parte communications limited to requests for a status report of a proceeding are exempted from the definition.

The provision prohibits ex parte communications "relevant to the merits of the proceeding" between any "interested person outside the agency" and a member of the body comprising the agency (e.g., a commissioner of the FCC), an ALJ, or any other employee who may reasonably be expected to be involved in the decision-making process. *See* 5 U.S.C. § 557(d)(1). The limitation of the prohibition to communications relevant to the merits of the proceeding merely means that it is not a violation for a person to communicate socially with an ALJ who is hearing a case the person is involved in. The prohibition extends beyond ex parte communications by a "party" to include ex parte communications by any "interested person." For example, if the EPA were proceeding administratively against an oil refiner for Clean Air Act violations, an environmental group such as the Natural Resources Defense Council would be barred from ex parte communications with the ALJ or the EAB, because it would be a person interested in the outcome of the proceeding. Similarly, the American Petroleum Institute, a trade group representing oil companies, even though not itself a party, would also be prohibited from ex parte communications with the ALJ and the EAB.

The prohibition runs not just to the outside interested person but also to the inside person—whether it be the ALJ, a member of the agency, or any employee who may be involved in the decisional process. That is, if the insider speaks to an outside interested person about something relevant to the merits of the proceeding, that too is a prohibited ex parte communication. If any one of these persons, outsider or insider, makes a prohibited communication to the other, the provision requires the insider to place on the public record any such written communications, memoranda describing the substance of any oral communications, and any written responses and memoranda describing the substance of any oral responses to prohibited communications. *See* 5 U.S.C. § 557(d)(1)(C). In other words, if there is a communication of which all the parties were not given notice, the first line of response is to give all the parties notice and the opportunity to respond to the ex parte communications. It may be, however, that the ex parte communication is not discovered until after the proceeding is concluded, which would make it impossible to use the curative step of giving the uninformed parties notice and an opportunity to respond before decision. In this circumstance, a court would reverse the agency decision unless the court believed that the ex parte communication did not affect the agency decision.

If the ex parte communication is "knowingly made" by a "party," the provision allows the ALJ or the agency to find against the party on the grounds of having knowingly violated the prohibition. *See* 5 U.S.C. § 557(d)(1)(D). This is an extreme remedy, and so it is reserved for situations where the party making the ex parte communication does it "knowingly"—that is, knowing that it is making an ex parte communication on the merits, which it ought to know is prohibited. Moreover, it is not to be used unless to do so would be consistent with the interests of justice and the policy of the underlying statutes involved in the proceeding. Although the ex parte prohibition generally applies to any interested person outside the agency, not just parties, the remedy of finding against a party can only be used when the party itself is the offender. As an extreme remedy, it is rarely used.

Finally, note that because the ex parte communication prohibition only applies to communications with interested persons *outside the agency*, this provision does not stop agency personnel, even the agency personnel litigating the case before the ALJ, from communicating off the record, out of the presence of all the parties to the proceedings. This is a serious loophole, but it is largely filled by another provision discussed below.

H. Separation of Functions—5 U.S.C. § 554(d)

Another provision of the APA that further protects the independence of ALJs and their decisions is known as the "separation of functions provision." This provision has essentially two parts.

The first part is a separate ex parte communication prohibition, barring the ALJ from consulting a person "on a fact in issue," unless on notice to and with an opportunity for all parties to participate. Recall that while the ex parte communication provision (5 U.S.C. § 557(d)) bars ex parte communications "relevant to the merits of the proceeding"—a broad ban—it is limited to persons outside the agency. The prohibition in the Separation of

Functions provision, on the other hand, extends to all persons, but only as to facts in issue in the proceeding. This partly closes the loophole in the ex parte communication provision discussed in the preceding section.

The second part of this provision is designed to insulate the ALJ and the ALJ's decision from the part of the agency likely to be involved in litigating the issue before the ALJ. This part prohibits any employee or agent of the agency, who is involved in the investigative or prosecuting functions of the agency, from being in a position of authority over the ALJ or from participating or advising in either the ALJ's decision or its review by the agency, except as counsel or witness in a public proceeding. This effectively bars anyone involved in the investigating or prosecuting function in the agency from engaging in ex parte communications relevant to an agency formal adjudication. This further closes the loophole in the ex parte communication provision.

The combination of these two prohibitions still allows an ALJ (and the agency upon review of the ALJ's decision) to communicate ex parte with persons in the agency not involved in the prosecution or investigative function with respect to questions of law. As a result, it also has the effect of requiring agencies that engage in such adjudications to have two separate groups of lawyers—one that is involved in investigating and prosecuting the cases and one that is involved in advising the agency. For example, in the Consumer Product Safety Commission, the General Counsel is responsible for giving legal advice to the agency and the Commissioners. The Associate Executive Director for Compliance and Administrative Litigation is responsible for bringing enforcement cases. In this way, the General Counsel can advise the Commission and Commissioners about a case before them without running afoul of the Separation of Functions provision, but the Associate Director is barred from participating in or advising the Commission about a decision, except as witness or counsel in public proceedings.

The Separation of Functions provision, however, has some exceptions. First, it does not apply to formal adjudications that involve applications for initial licenses or the validity or application of rates, facilities, or practices of public utilities or carriers. In other words, if the adjudication does involve these matters, then under this provision the ALJ *may* consult off the record on a fact at issue with a person. Because the ex parte communication bar in 5 U.S.C. § 557(d) would still apply to communications with outside persons, this exception effectively allows ex parte communications with inside persons in these kinds of cases. The theory behind this exception is that the agency is not really in an adversary relationship with the outside party in these kinds of cases. Accordingly, the safeguards appropriate to an adversary proceeding are not necessary to protect fairness to the outside party. For example, a person applying to the FCC for a broadcast license is not in an adversary relationship with the FCC. Accordingly, the applicant is not disadvantaged by the ALJ communicating off the record with other persons in the FCC. This can be contrasted with an agency proceeding to revoke someone's license, which is not subject to this exception. Here the agency is the "enemy," the prosecutor, with an agenda and goal in bringing the action. This is clearly an adversary relationship and requires safeguards to assure fairness.

Second, the Separation of Functions provision does not apply to "the agency or a member or members of the body comprising the agency." Initially, recall that a "member" is *not* simply an employee of an agency; it is a member of the board or commission that constitutes the ultimate decision-making body in the agency. For example, a Commissioner of the Federal Communications Commission is a "member" of the body comprising the agency. When an agency is not an agency headed by a collegial board, then "the agency" is the single person who is the head of the agency. The effect of this exception is to exempt the head of the agency or the members of the board that run the agency from the prohibitions on consulting with the ALJ on a fact at issue, on having authority over the ALJ, and on participating in the ALJ's decision or the agency review of that decision. The theory behind this exception is essentially one of necessity. The head of the agency or members of the board that run the agency are necessarily involved in the prosecutorial and investigative functions of the agency, since those functions ultimately occur under their authorization or direction. However, the Separation of Functions provision bars ALJs from being subject to the authority of anyone involved in prosecutorial or investigative functions. Yet ALJs are technically employees of the agency and therefore must in some sense be considered subject to the authority of the head of the agency or the members of the board that runs the agency. Thus, an exception is required. Moreover, applied according to its terms without this exception, the head of the agency would not be able to participate in the agency review of the ALJ's decision, which he or she must be able to do, because again the head of the agency is involved in the prosecuting and investigative function.

Here are some examples to apply the above rules on ex parte communications and separation of functions.

Example

The EPA is using formal adjudication under the APA to consider revoking a permit to market a particular pesticide because the pesticide may be unsafe. A key issue is the health hazards of the pesticide, because the applicable statute authorizes the EPA to cancel the registration of a pesticide if it "generally causes unreasonable adverse effects on the environment" when used in accordance with widespread and commonly recognized practice. The ALJ hearing the case has heard testimony and received evidence on the subject, but he wants help in understanding some of the technical scientific issues. Can he consult with an EPA scientist to get help?

He is also a little unclear as to the meaning of the phrase "generally causes unreasonable adverse effects," because the pesticide in question seems to be "generally" safe, but sometimes it has very serious adverse effects. Can he consult with an EPA lawyer as to the meaning of the statutory language?

Finally, he realizes that the evidence is scanty as to how the pesticide is applied in practice. Can he contact a person from the company that manufactures the pesticide to find out how the pesticide is used by farmers in practice?

Explanation

With respect to consulting with the EPA scientist, because he is not outside the agency, 5 U.S.C. § 557(d) does not apply. Moreover, because the EPA scientist is not involved in the prosecuting or investigating functions of the agency, the prohibitions on participating in or advising on the decision except as a witness or counsel in public proceedings would not apply. *See* 5 U.S.C. § 554(d). However, to the extent that the "technical scientific issues" involve "facts in issue," which they apparently would, the prohibition against an ALJ consulting any person on a fact in issue would preclude the ALJ from consulting with the EPA scientist unless on notice to and with an opportunity for all parties to participate. *See id*. None of the exceptions apply, but if this had been a proceeding for the initial registration of the pesticide, rather than a proceeding to cancel the registration, it would have been subject to the exception for initial licensing. If that exception applied, then the ALJ could consult the EPA scientist.

With respect to consulting with the EPA lawyer, again 5 U.S.C. § 557(d) does not apply because she is not outside the agency. Moreover, assuming that this lawyer is not one of the lawyers involved in the prosecuting or investigating functions of the agency, then the prohibition on such persons participating in or advising the decision would not apply. Finally, because the ALJ is consulting about a legal question, not a factual question, the bar on an ALJ consulting about a fact in issue does not apply. Consequently, the ALJ can consult with the lawyer.

With respect to consulting with a person from the chemical company, 5 U.S.C. § 557(d) *does* apply. This individual is an interested person outside the EPA, so the ALJ cannot engage in ex parte communications with him. It does not matter for Section 557 purposes whether the communication is factual or legal.

Example

The Consumer Product Safety Commission authorized the Associate Director for Compliance and Administrative Litigation to bring an administrative action against a toy manufacturer, because an investigation indicated that one of the manufacturer's crib toys is unreasonably dangerous and should be banned. The Associate Director prosecuted the case, and the ALJ issued an initial decision in favor of the Commission. The toy manufacturer then appealed the decision to the Commission.

Each of the five Commissioners receives briefs from the manufacturer and the Associate Director, and oral argument is heard before the whole Commission.

Thereafter, Commissioner A discusses the case with his personal staff assistant, who had participated in advising the Commissioner as to the decision to bring the case against the manufacturer in the first place.

In addition, Commissioner A communicates with the Associate Director about possible future actions against other toy manufacturers. Later, Commissioner A talks to the executive director of the National Association of Toy Manufacturers about possible actions against other toy manufacturers.

Finally, Commissioner A talks in private with Commissioner B about how they should rule in this case.

Which, if any, of these communications runs afoul of the APA, and if it does, what should be done?

Explanation

As to the discussion with the personal staff member, 5 U.S.C. § 557(d) does not apply because no person outside the agency is involved. The exception to the Separation of Functions provision for members of the body comprising the agency means that 5 U.S.C. § 554(d) does not apply to the Commissioner. But what about the staff assistant? He was and is involved in the prosecuting functions of the agency to the extent that he assisted the Commissioner in the decision to prosecute the toy manufacturer, and therefore he should be barred by Section 554(d) from participating or advising in the decision of the case except as witness or counsel in public proceedings. However, the case law recognizes that personal staff to members of the body comprising the agency are the alter egos of the members themselves and to the extent that their activities are limited to assisting the member, the personal staff should be considered like the member—exempt from the prohibition. Accordingly, there is no violation in Commissioner A talking with his personal staff.

As to Commissioner A's communications with the Associate Director for Compliance and Administrative Litigation, again there is no person outside the agency, so 5 U.S.C. § 557(d) does not apply. Moreover, under the Separation of Functions provision, the Commissioner is exempt. However, the Associate Director, because he is the person in charge of investigating and prosecuting actions, would violate Section 554 if he participates or advises in the decision of the case against the crib toy manufacturer. Here, though, the communication is not about the administrative proceeding against the crib toy manufacturer. Instead, it is about other toy manufacturers. Therefore, the communication might not be viewed as participating in or advising on the decision concerning the crib toy manufacturer. On the other hand, if the communication is to the effect that the Associate Director has evidence similar to that against the crib toy manufacturer with respect to other toy manufacturers, the communication could come dangerously close to being viewed as advising on the decision of the present proceeding.

What if the communication did go to the merits of the present proceeding, so that it would appear to be advising in the decision? Although the corrective procedures in 5 U.S.C. § 557(d)(1)(C), which provide for putting on the public record a memorandum stating the substance of the communication and allowing parties to respond to whatever information was communicated, would not literally apply (because they only apply to Section 557 violations), the agency would be well advised to use them anyway. Why? Because the Commission may be able to cure the error, making the original violation "harmless error." Otherwise, on judicial review, if the court believes the communication may have affected the Commission's decision, the court should reverse and remand the case to the Commission for fresh consideration. The appellant need not show that the communication did, or probably did, affect the decision. Rather, the burden is on the defending agency to prove that the communication did not affect the decision.

As to the Commissioner's communication with the executive director of the National Association of Toy Manufacturers, 5 U.S.C. § 557(d) *would* apply, if the communication was relevant to the merits of the proceeding against the crib toy manufacturer. The executive director would be an interested person outside the agency with respect to that proceeding. Whether the communication in fact was relevant to the merits of the proceeding would depend on what exactly was said. It might only relate to possible future prosecutions without any mention of the pending case.

But could this communication be an ex parte communication with respect to future prosecutions, instead of with respect to the pending proceeding? Even though there is not yet any proceeding with respect to the other manufacturers, the answer is yes, it could be a prohibited ex parte communication with respect to any future prosecution. Section 557(d)(1)(E) states that the prohibition on ex parte communications begins not later than the time at which a proceeding is noticed for hearing (which from the facts here does not appear to have happened for the possible future prosecutions), *or* when the person making the communication has knowledge that the proceeding will be noticed for hearing. Here, it is not clear whether the future prosecutions are certain to occur or that the Commissioner knows that they will be noticed for a hearing, but if he does, even if it is a secret to the world, known only within the Commission, it would be a prohibited ex parte communication by a person with that information.

Here, if this were a prohibited ex parte communication, the remedial measures listed in Section 557(d)(1)(C) would be directly applicable, and because the violation occurs before the public proceeding even begins, the curative aspects of those measures should be fully effective.

Finally, with respect to the communication between Commissioner A and Commissioner B about how to rule on the case, 5 U.S.C. § 557(d) would not apply because there is no outside person. Moreover, 5 U.S.C. § 554(d) would not apply because the only persons involved are both members of the board constituting the agency and therefore are exempt from that provision's prohibitions.

The above discussion has related to the prohibitions and requirements of the APA. Many agencies, however, have supplemented the terms of the APA with regulations that impose greater restrictions. This reflects the trend toward greater judicialization of the formal administrative adjudication process. What it also means is that a lawyer must always check the agency's regulations and not rely solely on the terms of the APA. While the APA establishes the minimum requirements for agencies, agencies may add to them. For example, an agency may by regulation eliminate the limitation of Section 557(d) to outside persons and apply its terms even to insiders. If an agency did that, the requirement could then be enforced against the agency in court, even though it was not required by the APA, and even though the agency could eliminate the requirement if it wanted to. One of the fundamental propositions of administrative law is that an agency is required to follow its own regulations, even if it never had to adopt them and could repeal them, until the agency, following the required procedures, does formally rescind them.

I. Formal Adjudication in the States

The procedures applicable to Contested Cases in the states are generally specified in the state APA. The most notable difference between the states and the federal government in this area is in the treatment of ALJs. Many states have created so-called Central Panels of ALJs to hear cases, rather than have the ALJs be even titular employees of the agency involved in the adjudication. The ALJs are employees of an independent agency whose duty it is to hear cases arising in various different agencies. This has been one of the ways that states have responded to concerns about ALJ independence. However, even in states with Central Panels, not all ALJs or adjudications may fall under the Central Panel. Often, particular agencies in a state have been able to convince the legislature to exempt their proceedings from the Central Panel jurisdiction.

IV. PROCEDURES FOR INFORMAL ADJUDICATION

As discussed earlier, the APA really does not prescribe any specific procedures for informal adjudication, although Section 555 contains provisions applicable to all agency proceedings, including both formal and informal adjudications. The particular substantive statutes under which the informal adjudications take place may themselves specify certain procedures. For example, the Clean Water Act creates certain administrative penalties that are to be assessed through informal adjudication, and it specifies a notice requirement and the opportunity for a hearing at which the person is entitled to a "reasonable opportunity to be heard and to present evidence." 42 U.S.C. § 1319(g)(2)(A).

Typically, agencies will adopt regulations specifying the procedures for their informal adjudications. For example, both the EPA and the U.S. Army Corps of Engineers (both of whom are authorized to assess the administrative penalties under the Clean Water Act) have extensive regulations governing the procedures for those proceedings. *See* 33 C.F.R. § 326.6 (Corps of Engineers); 40 C.F.R. pt. 22 (EPA). Often the procedures adopted by the agencies come very close to the procedures required for formal adjudications. For example, the EPA, after experimenting with using different procedures for its formal adjudications and its informal administrative penalty proceedings, eventually decided to merge the two different sets of procedures and essentially use the same formal procedures required by the APA for its informal administrative penalty proceedings.

One notable difference between formal and informal adjudications, however, is that only an ALJ may hear an APA adjudication, and ALJs almost never preside over non-APA adjudications. Persons who preside over non-APA adjudications go under a variety of names, but commentators refer to them generically as Administrative Judges (or AJs), to distinguish them from Administrative Law Judges. The AJs, of course, do not have any of the formal protections possessed by ALJs to preserve their independence from the agency that employs them. Nevertheless, as an empirical matter, the vast majority of AJs consider themselves to be independent of the agency when they render decisions.

The Due Process Clause of the Fifth Amendment to the U.S. Constitution imposes probably the most important requirements on informal adjudication. While the Due Process Clause applies to adjudications regardless of whether they are formal or informal, the procedural requirements of the APA applicable to formal adjudication fully meet due process requirements. The due process requirements applicable to informal adjudication, however, which apply in both the federal and state informal adjudications, are of sufficient complexity that they deserve a chapter of their own—Chapter 4 in this book.

V. PROCEDURES APPLICABLE TO ALL PROCEEDINGS

Section 555 applies to all agency proceedings. It provides that persons required to appear before an agency or entitled to appear before an agency may be represented by counsel. Of course, this means the person has to supply his own counsel. There is no provision for supplying counsel to indigents in agency proceedings. Section 555 also provides that a *party* has a right to appear in person or by counsel in an agency proceeding. As a practical matter, however, many agency proceedings are "paper proceedings," so the right to "appear in person" would not apply there.

"Interested persons," who are not parties, are also allowed to "appear" before an agency "for the presentation, adjustment, or determination of an issue, request, or controversy in a proceeding or in connection with an agency function." It is not clear what it means for an interested person to "appear before an agency." If there is a proceeding in which there are parties, does it mean that the interested person may intervene in the proceeding, as a person can intervene under certain circumstances in a judicial proceeding? If so, it would mean the interested person would become a party to the proceeding. But the only limitation on interested persons appearing before the agency is that it be "so far as the orderly conduct of public business permits." This is inconsistent with the standard for intervention in a court. The general case law response has been to distinguish between an interested person appearing before an agency in a proceeding and a person intervening in an agency proceeding. As such, it is clear that the ability to appear is largely at the discretion of the agency, because of its almost unchallengeable ability to determine what the orderly conduct of the agency's public business permits. Courts have not been clear as to the standard for intervention. There are few cases on the subject, but the leading case suggests that intervention in an agency proceeding should be allowed whenever the person seeking intervention would satisfy the constitutional requirements for standing. *See Office of Communication of United Church of Christ v. FCC*, 359 F.2d 994 (D.C. Cir. 1966). This case, however, was decided during the period when courts were playing an activist role in policing agency action, and the rationale for the case appeared largely driven by the desire to facilitate intervention by public interest groups into licensing proceedings that historically had been limited to the party seeking the license. While this case has never been overruled, it has been limited in certain circumstances. Thus, when an agency pursuant to its statutory mandate or organic act adopts procedural rules for its adjudications that do not grant intervention so broadly, courts now tend to defer to the agency's interpretation of the agency law. *See, e.g., Envirocare of Utah, Inc. v. Nuclear Regulatory Commission.*, 194 F.3d 72 (D.C. Cir. 1999).

This is especially true when the person wanting to intervene does not represent a public interest group, but merely a competitor of the person seeking the license. *See id.*

Section 555 also requires agencies to conclude matters "within a reasonable time" and to give "prompt notice" of the denial of any application, petition, or other request by an interested person made with regard to an agency proceeding. Moreover, a "brief statement of the grounds for denial" must accompany any such notice of denial.

Finally, and perhaps most importantly, Section 555 provides a party to an adjudication with the right to have the agency issue a subpoena on the party's behalf, if the agency itself has the authority to issue subpoenas. Under Section 555, this right is subject only to the limitation that the agency may require the party to show general relevance and how the scope of the evidence sought is reasonable.

VI. ALTERNATIVE DISPUTE RESOLUTION (ADR) AND ADMINISTRATIVE LAW

In the section describing the procedures applicable to APA adjudication, it was mentioned that specific provision is made for pre-hearing conferences, settlement discussions, and resolution of such issues as possible. In short, even the original APA allowed for what today we would call ADR procedures. In the 1980s, however, there was increased emphasis on ADR measures in both courts and agencies because of the high cost in dollars and time of traditional litigation or adjudication.

One of the fruits of that emphasis was the passage of the Administrative Dispute Resolution Act, 5 U.S.C. §§ 571-584. This Act does not mandate that agencies use any form of alternative dispute resolution; rather, its purpose is to facilitate the ability to use the various forms of ADR. For example, prior to the Act there had been some question whether federal agencies were even authorized to use arbitration; hence the Act's explicit authorization for agencies to use arbitration under the procedures of the Act. In addition, there had been questions concerning the confidentiality of settlement discussions, especially when third parties were present, as would be the case with mediation. Again, the Act resolved these doubts by providing generally for the confidentiality of communications made in the presence of a conciliator, facilitator, or mediator. *See* 5 U.S.C. § 574.

It is not clear to what extent agencies are in fact making use of ADR under the Act, but there has been virtually no litigation under it.

VII. LICENSING

As defined in the APA, *licensing* is the agency process for doing anything with respect to a license, including granting, denying, conditioning, and revoking a license. 5 U.S.C. § 551(9). A *license* is defined as an agency permit, certificate, approval, registration, charter, membership, statutory exception, or other form of permission. In other words, a license includes a broadcast license from the FCC, whether it is for broadcast television or ham radio; a permit from the EPA to discharge pollutants into the waters of the United States; permission from the Nuclear Regulatory Commission to close a nuclear power plant; permission from the National Park Service to have a rally on the mall in Washington, D.C.; and it includes many other things as well. 5 U.S.C. § 551(8). In short, licensing is the process by which someone obtains, is denied, or has revoked any form of federal agency permission.

Moreover, licensing is one subset of adjudication. Recall that the definition of *adjudication* in the APA is "the agency process for the formulation of an order." 5 U.S.C. § 551(7). *Order* is then defined expressly to include a final disposition "in a matter . . . including licensing." 5 U.S.C. § 551(6). Because licensing is a subset of adjudication, everything in this chapter relating to adjudication applies to licensing, with some exceptions. Several concern initial licensing—that is, when someone first applies for a license, permit, or permission.

First, recall the Separation of Functions provisions applicable to formal adjudications. *See* 5 U.S.C. § 554(d). They both insulate those who make adjudicatory decisions from those who investigate or prosecute the cases and prohibit ALJs from consulting a person on a fact at issue except on notice to and with opportunity for all the parties to participate. One of the exceptions from these prohibitions, however, involves initial licensing. Thus, if the formal adjudication involves an application for initial licensing, there is no separation of functions prohibition. The theory is that the separation of functions prohibition is only necessary when the agency and a party before it are in an adversarial relationship. If, however, the agency has no stake or interest in the adjudication, but is merely the neutral decision maker, these safeguards are not necessary. In an application for an initial license, the agency is not a party to the proceeding; it has no interest or stake in the outcome. If, however, the formal adjudication is for the removal of a license, the agency is the prosecutor; it has a stake and interest in the outcome, so safeguards are necessary, and the Separation of Functions provisions do apply.

Second, under the APA persons generally have the right in a formal adjudication to present their case or defense "by oral or documentary evidence, to submit rebuttal evidence, and to conduct such cross-examination as may be required for a full and true disclosure of the facts." 5 U.S.C. § 556(d). However, if the formal adjudication involves an application for an initial license, the APA specifically authorizes agencies to adopt procedures "for submission of all or part of the evidence in written form." *Id.* This provision really does not mean much, because it conditions the limitation to written materials to circumstances "when a party will not be prejudiced thereby." *Id.* Moreover, the use of summary judgment-type procedures is commonplace in formal adjudications generally.

Third, the APA specifies that when the agency makes the decision in a formal adjudication without having presided at the hearing, the ALJ must at least recommend a decision. 5 U.S.C. § 557(b). This requirement does not apply, however, if the adjudication was the determination of an application for an initial license. *Id.*

Section 558 of Title 5 contains three specific provisions relating to licensing. First, it provides that when a person seeks a license required by law, an agency shall begin and complete proceedings "within a reasonable time." 5 U.S.C. § 558(c).

The second provision relates to the revocation or suspension of a license. It provides that, except in cases of willfulness or where the public health or safety may be compromised, an agency may not revoke or suspend a person's license unless, prior to the institution of any proceedings against the person, the agency gives notice to the person in writing of the facts or conduct that might warrant revocation or suspension of the license, *and* the agency gives the person an opportunity to demonstrate or achieve compliance with all requirements. *Id.* In other words, the agency must give the alleged violator an opportunity to cure his ways, and if he does, he can keep his license—subject to the exception for willfulness or health and safety requirements.

The third provision relates to license renewals. It provides that when a person makes timely application for renewal of a license, a license for a continuing activity does not expire until the application has been finally determined by the agency. *Id.* In other words, if a person who holds a renewable license that expires at a particular time seeks renewal by the time required by the agency, the person's license will not run out because the agency delays in acting upon his renewal application.

Both these latter two provisions are also found in the 1961 Model State APA, which many states have adopted in part. In state administrative law, these provisions are frequently invoked because of the large number of licensing systems subject to state administrative law and the frequent lack of attention to legal detail by the commissions administering the licensing systems, in part because the commissions are often made up of part-time, volunteer employees from the profession subject to the licensing system.

CHAPTER 4 Due Process

> Whatever disagreement there may be as to the scope of the phrase "due process of law," there can be no doubt that it embraces the fundamental conception of a fair trial, with opportunity to be heard.
>
> —*Oliver Wendell Holmes,* Frank v. Mangum, 237 U.S. 309, 347 (1915)

In Chapter 3, Adjudication, we noted that the APA does not provide any particular procedures with respect to informal adjudications, although other statutes and agency regulations may. We also noted, however, that the Due Process Clause often does provide certain procedural safeguards in both federal and state informal adjudications. This chapter begins by describing when due process applies and when it does not. The chapter then goes on to analyze what due process requires, when it applies.

The federal government and federal agencies are subject to the Fifth Amendment to the Constitution, which provides that no person shall be deprived of life, liberty, or property without due process of law. State agencies and other state governmental institutions are subject to an identical due process requirement under the Due Process Clause of the Fourteenth Amendment. As a result, the case law under the Due Process Clauses of the Fifth and Fourteenth Amendments is interchangeable, and the requirements of those clauses apply equally to federal, state, and local government entities.

There are two different types of "due process" law: Substantive Due Process and Procedural Due Process. Substantive Due Process refers to limits on *what* government can regulate; Procedural Due Process refers to the procedures by which government may affect individuals' rights. For example, restrictions on the ability of government to order persons to be locked up in a mental institution is a question of Substantive Due Process, but to the extent that some persons may be committed against their will to a mental institution, the procedure by which a person is determined to be one of those persons is a question of Procedural Due Process. In law school courses and casebooks, Substantive Due Process is almost always taught in the constitutional law course, and Procedural Due Process is almost always taught in the administrative law course. Here we will limit the discussion to Procedural Due Process.

I. IS DUE PROCESS REQUIRED AT ALL?

The Constitution states that no person is to be deprived of life, liberty, or property without due process of law. Capital punishment, by which a person is deprived of life, is the culmination of the criminal law process; in administrative law, no one is deprived of life. The criminal law process can also result in incarceration in prison (a deprivation of liberty) and criminal fines (a deprivation of property). The safeguards of the Constitution applicable to the criminal process generally ensure due process of law in those circumstances.

Persons may also be deprived of liberty and property civilly. This can occur in judicial proceedings (e.g., civil fines and civil commitment of persons who are a threat to themselves or the community by reason of mental disease). The Due Process Clause is certainly applicable to these judicial proceedings, but the procedures incident to normal judicial proceedings satisfy due process.

It is also possible for government actors to deprive a person of liberty or property (or even life) by accident. For example, if a U.S. Postal Service employee drives a mail truck through a red light and hits a pedestrian or another car, the person hit might be deprived of life, liberty (freedom from physical harm), or property. If a U.S. Forest Service employee sets a fire for a controlled burn, but it gets out of hand and burns down a person's home, that person has been deprived of property. Although it took the Supreme Court a long time to decide the issue, finally in 1986, in *Daniels v. Williams*, 474 U.S. 327 (1986), it decided that only "deliberate decisions of government officials" trigger due process concerns. Citizens' relief for such accidental deprivations would be restricted to tort actions.

Statutes and government regulations may be said to be deliberate decisions to deprive persons of property or liberty. For example, if a government assesses a new tax applicable to a class of persons, those persons are likely to feel that the law has deprived them of property. Similarly, a statute or regulation might set a standard for entering a certain profession. For example, a state statute might require a person to graduate from an American Bar Association accredited law school in order to be a lawyer. This would deprive a person without such a credential of the liberty to engage in that profession. Neither of these situations, however, implicates the Due Process Clauses. Early in the twentieth century, in an opinion by Justice Oliver Wendell Holmes, the Supreme Court made clear that the concept of due process simply does not apply to general lawmaking. *See Bi-Metallic Investment Co. v. State Board of Equalization*, 239 U.S. 441 (1915). The procedural safeguard of liberty and property in general lawmaking is the political process. The Court said that due process was required only when "a relatively small number of persons was concerned, who were exceptionally affected, in each case upon individual grounds." Here the Court was contrasting the situation in *Bi-Metallic* with that in an earlier case, *Londoner v. Denver*, 210 U.S. 373 (1908), in which the Court had found that a tax levied on a property owner for the improvement of his street required due process. Today we interpret these cases as meaning that due process is required when the proceeding is functionally an adjudication, as opposed to rulemaking. Thus, an administrative adjudication that deprives someone of liberty or property must provide due process.

The issue, however, often is whether something qualifies as either property or liberty.

A. History

Historically, the concepts of property and liberty were relatively easy to understand. Property was the traditional common-law concept of property; and liberty was freedom from government restrictions on your traditional common-law rights. In other words, before government could fine you and take your money or lock you up and deprive you of liberty, government would have to provide due process of law. However, if all government did was deprive you of a "privilege" or a benefit, it did not need to provide due process.

Example

In 1940, a city fires a policeman because the police chief heard a rumor that the policeman had accepted free coffee and doughnuts from a shop on his beat. The policeman denies it. He wants to face his accuser and call the shop owner as a witness. The city is not interested. He sues the city, alleging that he has been deprived of his job without due process of law.

Explanation

In an era of employment-at-will (meaning the employer can hire and fire at will), employment was a privilege, and government employment was certainly not a property or liberty right. Accordingly, the government could fire the policeman without providing any due process rights. This is still the rule to the extent that the employment relationship is at-will, but most public employees today after a probationary period enjoy certain employment protections, which, we will see, changes the analysis.

Example

At the turn of the last century a state limited the prices warehouses could charge so that they would not receive more than a reasonable rate of return on their investment. If a warehouse charged more than necessary to obtain a reasonable rate of return, the state public utility commission could order it to refund the excess to the person charged. Was the public utility commission required to provide due process in making that determination?

Explanation

In an era of laissez-faire capitalism, the liberty to use your property and capital as you saw fit was recognized as a type of liberty protected by the Due Process Clause. This did not foreclose government regulation of business, but it assured businesses that determinations that might deprive them of liberty required government to afford them due process. This is as true today as it was then.

B. Modern Due Process

Sometime between 1950 and 1970 the concept of what could be considered "liberty" and "property" under the Due Process Clause evolved into a somewhat broader form. There is no one date to mark this development, because there was no one case in which the Supreme Court declared the doctrine. By 1970, however, in the celebrated case of *Goldberg v. Kelly*, 397 U.S. 254 (1970), the Supreme Court made clear that a new order was in place.

In *Goldberg*, New York had terminated welfare assistance to Ms. Kelly because her landlady had reported that she had a live-in male friend (at a time when only single parents could qualify for welfare). New York provided a two-step administrative procedure for the termination of welfare. The first step was an informal hearing procedure in which the welfare recipient could tell her side of the story. If the state determined that the person no longer qualified for welfare as a result of the evidence after that hearing, the state would immediately terminate welfare. The recipient, however, then could seek a *de novo*, formal administrative hearing, with retroactive payments if the person's benefits were found to have been erroneously terminated.

Under traditional due process analysis, the receipt of welfare was a "privilege," not a right, so no process would be due. By the time of *Goldberg*, however, this traditional analysis was no longer in vogue, so that New York did not even argue that the welfare recipient was not entitled to any due process; its argument was simply that the state's procedures satisfied due process. The Court took the occasion, however, to make clear that in modern society the loss of a government entitlement such as a welfare benefit has the same impact as when government deprives someone of traditional private property. What it did not make clear was how to determine when a personal interest one has in a government benefit or "privilege" would rise to the level of becoming a personal right protected by the Due Process Clause. At this point, the Court and lower courts seemed to be making ad hoc determinations based on a largely subjective determination as to how important the personal interest appeared to be.

1. Modern Concept of "Property"

In a pair of cases two years after *Goldberg*, however, the Court provided a rule for deciding when an interest became a protectable right. The cases were *Board of Regents v. Roth*, 408 U.S. 564 (1972), and *Perry v. Sindermann*, 408 U.S. 593 (1972). In *Roth*, a person hired for a year as an Assistant Professor at a state university was informed that he would not be rehired the next year. In *Sindermann*, the teacher was a full professor who had taught at a state junior college for ten years, but the college did not have an explicit tenure system and the professor was hired each year on a one-year contract. In both cases the person was not rehired, allegedly because the person had alienated the authorities by speaking on political issues. In both cases, the teacher was not afforded a hearing at which to challenge the actual cause and basis for the failure to rehire. The Court said: "To have a property interest in a benefit, a person clearly must have more than an abstract need or desire for it. He must have more than a unilateral expectation of it. He must instead have a legitimate claim of entitlement to it." The Court noted that in *Goldberg* the welfare recipient had a statutory right to continued benefits, so long as she remained eligible, and this constituted a legitimate claim of entitlement. Similarly, if the teachers had been enrolled in a formal tenure system, they would have had a legitimate claim of entitlement to continued employment under state law, which would entail due process protections. In fact, however, Roth had no tenure whatsoever. He had nothing but a unilateral expectation of being rehired, an expectation arising only because that is what normally occurred to teachers in his position. Accordingly, the Court held that Roth had no protectable property interest under the Due Process Clause.

Sindermann was in a slightly different situation. Although the junior college where he had worked for ten years did not have a formal tenure system, the official faculty handbook stated that "The Administration of the College wishes the faculty member to feel that he has permanent tenure as long as his teaching services are satisfactory and as long as he displays a cooperative attitude toward his co-workers and superiors, and as long as he is happy in his work." This official suggestion of an informal tenure system meant that Sindermann had more than just a unilateral expectation of continued employment. The question still was whether it was enough to constitute a legitimate claim of entitlement. The Court said: "'[P]roperty' denotes a broad range of interests that are secured by 'existing rules or understandings.' A person's interest in a benefit is a 'property' interest for due process purposes if there are such rules or mutually explicit understandings that support his claim of entitlement to the benefit and that he may invoke at a hearing." In other words, the answer to the question was: "maybe"; the fact that the tenure system was not formalized, written into contract, regulations, or statute was not necessarily dispositive. Contractual rights could be implied as well as explicit. The Court, therefore, remanded the case to the lower courts to determine whether under all the facts and circumstances state law would interpret Sindermann as having a legal claim for continued employment, which in turn would be a legitimate claim of entitlement to a "property" right protected by the Due Process Clause.

Example

Melissa was admitted to her state university law school[1] and given a full scholarship. In her second semester, her legal writing instructor reported to the Dean that Melissa had committed plagiarism in a legal writing paper. Expulsion is a possible penalty for plagiarism. Does Melissa have a due process right to contest whether she committed plagiarism? Could they take away her scholarship instead and avoid due process requirements?

1. The Due Process Clauses only limit governmental entities, not private entities. Thus, the Due Process Clauses impose no requirements on a private law school. Even private entities that include as members certain governmental institutions, such as the NCAA, remain outside the purview of the Due Process Clauses.

Explanation

Yes, she probably does have a due process right to some sort of hearing to contest whether she committed plagiarism before the school may expel her. The issue is whether she has a legitimate claim of entitlement to remain in law school. She would look to university documents to try to establish an explicit policy that students remain in good standing so long as they maintain certain grade point averages and do not violate the honor code. Such documents would imply a legitimate claim of entitlement to remain. Even in the absence of explicit documents, it would be highly likely that Melissa could establish that there were mutual understandings to the same effect.

No, they probably cannot take away her scholarship without affording her due process. Again, the issue is whether the terms of the scholarship, either express or implied, provided that she would retain it unless she violated some term of the scholarship or school rules. If so, then a procedure meeting the requirements of due process would be needed before the school could determine that Melissa no longer qualified for the scholarship. The fact that no one has a right to obtain a scholarship in the first place is not important.

The purpose of finding documents that establish a policy, or of confirming that there were mutual understandings, is to establish the existence of a legal right to continued enrollment and receipt of the scholarship. When a statute or regulation establishes a legal right—for example, civil service protections for many government employees or qualifications for obtaining Social Security benefits—the issue is simple. Similarly, where there are written contracts with the government, those contracts establish a legal right under the terms of the contract. The more difficult situation occurs where there are no such express materials, as in *Sindermann* or our example. Here there must be a finding of some sort of implied contract arising out of the mutual understandings and relevant documents. The Supreme Court has made clear that *state law* governs in making that determination. That is, as a matter of state law, do the mutual understandings suffice to make an implied contract? Thus, even though due process is a federal constitutional right, the existence of the "property" interest that triggers the right depends upon state law.

Example

In this example, Melissa did plagiarize, and she admits it. However, she claims there were extremely extenuating circumstances. She wants an opportunity to explain to the law school authorities the pressure she was under and why she plagiarized. Her hope is that if the school learns of the circumstances in which it happened, the school will excuse her and not expel her. The school refuses even to listen to her. Is it denying her due process rights?

Explanation

The answer is not entirely clear. There are two lines of cases, one of which suggests that in the absence of disputed facts there is no right to any due process procedure, the other of which suggests that there is a due process right with respect to how the decision maker will exercise his or her discretion. For example, in *Codd v. Velger*, 429 U.S. 624 (1977), a policeman was fired for holding a service revolver to his head in an apparent suicide attempt. The department had not provided him any hearing with respect to the allegations or to its possible responses. The policeman did not contest that he had made the apparent suicide attempt. The Court, in a 5-4 decision, said that the purpose of due process protections was to provide "an opportunity to refute the charge," and if those protections are to "serve any useful purpose, there must be some factual dispute between an employer and discharged employee."

Similarly, in *Connecticut Dept. of Public Safety v. Doe*, 538 U.S. 1 (2003), the Court reiterated this point in the context of Connecticut's law requiring a public registry of convicted sex offenders. The plaintiff sought to require a due process hearing to determine whether he was currently dangerous before his name could be included on the registry. The Supreme Court held that he was not entitled to any hearing because the fact of his current dangerousness was not relevant to the basis for his inclusion on the registry—the simple fact that he had been convicted of sexually violent offense.

Likewise, Melissa is not denying that she committed plagiarism. There are no facts in dispute. And she is not trying to refute the charge; she is merely trying to ameliorate the effects of the determination that she committed plagiarism.

More helpful to Melissa is *Cleveland Bd. of Ed. v. Loudermill*, 470 U.S. 532, 542-544 (1985). There, the Court seemed to recognize a due process right to present facts relevant to the determination of the appropriate punishment:

> An essential principle of due process is that a deprivation of life, liberty, or property be preceded by notice and opportunity for hearing appropriate to the nature of the case. . . . [S]ome opportunity for the employee to present his side of the case is recurringly of obvious value in reaching an accurate decision. Dismissals for cause will often involve factual disputes. Even where the facts are clear, the appropriateness or necessity of the discharge may not be; in such cases, the only meaningful opportunity to invoke the discretion of the decisionmaker is likely to be before the termination takes effect.

Even in *Connecticut Dept. of Public Safety* the Court concluded by saying: "Plaintiffs who assert a right to a hearing under the Due Process Clause must show that the facts they seek to establish in that hearing are relevant under the statutory scheme." There, continued dangerousness was not relevant to the requirement to list sex offenders. But, here, with regard to

Melissa's expulsion, as opposed to a lesser penalty, the facts she presents in mitigation might well be relevant to the final decision.

If, however, the school's rules *require* expulsion for plagiarism, then the Court's opinions are consistent: she would have no due process right to plead for an exception to the rules.

2. Modern Concept of "Liberty"

The above discussion has related to what constitutes "property" under modern due process analysis. But, in addition to property, deprivations of liberty are also protected by the Due Process Clause. Historical notions of liberty continue, so due process protections apply when government would restrict your physical freedom or your freedom to pursue your profession. For example, if the government wants to commit someone to a mental institution, that would interfere with that person's personal liberty. Similarly, if a state wanted to take away a person's license to practice law, that would interfere with the person's liberty to practice her chosen profession. These historical concepts of liberty continue today, but as with the concept of property, the concept of liberty has become broader too.

a. Liberty and Reputation

Although grounded in older roots, modern cases have recognized a liberty interest in a person's reputation.[2] For example, in *Wisconsin v. Constantineau*, 400 U.S. 433 (1971), a state law required the posting of the names of "public drunkards" at places where alcoholic beverages were purchased. Constantineau's name was so posted, but he denied he was a "public drunkard," and the state had provided no procedure for him to contest that label before it posted his name. The Court held that he was deprived of due process because "[w]here a person's good name, reputation, honor, or integrity is at stake because of what the government is doing to him, [due process is] essential." In *Roth*, the Court similarly recognized a person's liberty interest in his good reputation, saying that he would be entitled to due process if the state had, by not rehiring him, "imposed on him a stigma or other disability that foreclosed his freedom to take advantage of other employment opportunities." As it was, the Court found that the state had simply not rehired him, without giving any reason, so that there was no impact on his reputation.

2. Although the protection of one's reputation is usually classified as a liberty interest, it has sometimes been characterized as a property interest—as in a person's reputation is his or her property. For due process purposes, we do not care whether it is a liberty interest or a property interest, so long as it is one or the other.

In *Paul v. Davis*, 424 U.S. 693 (1976), a few years later, however, the Court seemed to cut back on its willingness to find reputation a liberty interest. There, the chief of police in Louisville, Kentucky, decided that it would reduce the incidence of shoplifting by alerting the local merchants as to persons who might be possible shoplifters. Accordingly, he distributed a five-page flyer with the names and pictures of persons identified as "active shoplifters." Davis had once been arrested for shoplifting, but he had pleaded not guilty and the case had never been brought forward by prosecutors. He alleged that the distribution of the flyer damaged his reputation and therefore implicated the Due Process Clause. In a 6-3 decision, then-Justice William Rehnquist conceded that distributing such information about a person would damage his reputation and would give rise to an action at tort for defamation, but he denied that the Court's cases stood for "the proposition that reputation alone, apart from some more tangible interests such as employment, is either 'liberty' or 'property' by itself sufficient to invoke the procedural protection of the Due Process Clause." He noted that in *Roth* the Court had only said that stigma that denied Roth of other employment opportunities would implicate due process. And in *Constantineau* the effect of being included on the list of "public drunkards" was to deprive Constantineau of the ability to purchase alcoholic beverages. As a result of *Paul*, therefore, we have what is known as the "stigma-plus" test.

The question still remained: plus what? *Paul*, and its reference to *Roth*, suggested that the plus must be some other effect in addition to mere effect on reputation, such as precluding a person's ability to obtain another job because of his damaged reputation. However, in *Siegert v. Gilley*, 500 U.S. 226 (1991), the Court rejected just such a suggestion. In *Siegert*, a psychologist at St. Elizabeth's Hospital, a federal government facility, was offered the opportunity to resign, rather than be fired, because of his poor performance. He resigned and later sought and obtained employment at a military hospital. A check of his previous employers resulted in a letter from the psychologist's supervisor at St. Elizabeth's to the effect that the psychologist was "both inept and unethical." As a result the psychologist was fired from the military hospital he was working at and denied a new job he had been seeking at a different military hospital. The psychologist sued the supervisor for $4 million, alleging a violation of his constitutional right not to be deprived of liberty without due process. The Court, in an opinion by *Paul*'s author, now Chief Justice Rehnquist, held there was no deprivation of liberty because the letter had only damaged his reputation. The psychologist's loss of his job at the military hospital and his inability to obtain further employment at military hospitals was merely the effect of his damaged reputation. The psychologist's recourse was a suit under state tort law for defamation, not a suit for a constitutional violation. In order to qualify as "stigma plus," the Court said, the damage to reputation must be "incident to the termination of . . . employment"—for example, if the hospital had fired the psychologist and issued a public statement that it was firing him because he was inept and unethical.

Example

In a previous example, Melissa was charged with plagiarism but was not provided any due process protections. Fearful of a lawsuit, the state law school did not expel her, but upon her graduation it sent a letter to the State Board of Bar Examiners informing the Board that Melissa had "engaged in plagiarism in Legal Writing during her first year." Have her due process rights been violated?

Explanation

Not under the Court's analysis in *Siegert*. In order to be admitted to the bar of any state a person must demonstrate sufficient character and fitness to practice law. A person with unsuitable character may be denied admission to the bar, and state bars are concerned about possible unethical conduct by future lawyers. Plagiarism in the academic environment is unethical and may be viewed as predictive of future unethical conduct. Consequently, a report by the law school to the bar that a student has engaged in plagiarism is likely to be viewed as not only harming her reputation but also seriously impeding her ability to become a lawyer. Nevertheless, under the analysis in *Siegert*, these hurdles to her becoming a lawyer are merely the effects of her damaged reputation. If the letter is false, she may sue under state tort law for defamation, but she cannot allege a deprivation of her liberty. Had the school expelled her and made a public statement about her plagiarism, this would probably meet the *Siegert* requirements, because she would have suffered another injury (her expulsion) in addition to the damage to her reputation, and the injury would not have been a result of her damaged reputation.

Example

In this example, the school expels her and puts an entry on her transcript that she "engaged in plagiarism in Legal Writing during her first year." Has Melissa been deprived of liberty by the damage to her reputation?

The law school maintains that she has not. It says that the law school has not harmed her reputation, because it has not publicized its finding. In fact, her transcript is confidential and cannot be released to anyone without Melissa's permission. Thus, only if Melissa herself chooses to make the transcript public will her reputation be harmed. Is the law school correct?

Explanation

Here there is "stigma plus" within the meaning of *Siegert*. Not only was Melissa defamed, but she was also expelled.

However, one of the requirements for making out a case for the deprivation of liberty by damage to reputation is that the government publicize the defamatory information. In *Bishop v. Wood*, 426 U.S. 341 (1976), a policeman who held his job on an employment-at-will basis was fired. He was told that the reason was his poor attendance at training sessions, his failure to follow certain orders, and conduct unsuited to an officer. The police department did not inform anyone else of the reasons. The Court held that this failed to make out a deprivation of liberty because there was no effect on his reputation if the defamatory claims were not made public. Here too, the school is not making the reasons for Melissa's expulsion public.

At this point, it would appear Melissa would lose on the deprivation of liberty claim, but there is an argument that to put such a notation on a person's transcript is the equivalent of making the information public. The school knows that the person will have to provide a copy of that transcript if she wishes to attend a different law school or other graduate school, and perhaps if she seeks employment. The Supreme Court was once faced with an analogous question but did not answer it, deciding the case on other grounds. *See Codd v. Velger*, 429 U.S. 624 (1977). There a police department fired a probationary policeman because he had apparently threatened suicide using his service revolver. Because he was a probationary employee, he had no property interest in continued employment, but he claimed that the inclusion of this allegation in his personnel file damaged his reputation and made it impossible for him to find other employment as a policeman. The district court held that there was no due process violation because the "information about his Police Department service was [not] publicized or circulated by defendants in any way that might reach his prospective employers." The court of appeals reversed, however, finding that "the mere act of making available personnel files with the employee's consent was enough to place responsibility for the stigma on the employer, since former employees had no practical alternative but to consent to the release of such information if they wished to be seriously considered for other employment."

Melissa's case seems directly on point. If she seeks admission to another law school, she will be required to furnish a copy of the transcript of the former law school. If she seeks admission to another graduate program, they will likely ask to see her law school transcript. Even possible employers may wish to see her law school transcript. The obvious and predictable consequence of including a notation on a transcript is that the person will need to reveal it to potential future employers or educational institutions. Thus, if the court of appeals' analysis is correct, Melissa should win. On the other hand, the Supreme Court has evidenced a distinct hostility to claims of a deprivation of liberty through damage to reputation, and the lack of a clear publication of the defamatory information might provide a court an excuse for denying Melissa's claim.

b. Liberty and Correctional Facilities

As mentioned before, liberty has always meant freedom from physical restraint (and by implication freedom from physical injury). Consequently, there is little question that a person who is to be locked away involuntarily must be afforded due process. In the criminal context, a trial meeting the requirements of the Fifth and Sixth Amendments is understood to provide due process. Consequently, a person incarcerated in prison as a lawful sentence from an otherwise unobjectionable conviction has already been afforded due process for the deprivation of liberty.

Sometimes, however, instead of a prison sentence, a person may receive probation—a sentence that says that if he complies with the terms of the probation for a period of time, he will not have to go to prison. Now, if he is alleged to have violated the terms of his probation, does he have a due process right before he is sent to prison for violating his probation? The Supreme Court has said yes. *See Gagnon v. Scarpelli*, 411 U.S. 778 (1973). Similarly, if the state creates a parole system or "good time credit" system, in which persons may earn early release from prison if they comply with certain requirements, the state may not deprive them of the early release by alleging they have failed to comply with the requirements without affording them due process. *See Morrissey v. Brewer*, 408 U.S. 471 (1972) (parole); *Wolff v. McDonnell*, 418 U.S. 539 (1974) (good time credits).The theory is that just as government can create a property interest in a government benefit by establishing legal qualifications for it that then create a legal entitlement to it, so also can government create a protectable liberty interest in those who have already been deprived of their natural liberty, by creating a system that establishes legal qualifications for conditional or early release.

This line of cases resulted in challenges to various forms of prison discipline, from imposing solitary confinement to taking away library privileges. The prisoners' argument was that they were entitled not to be punished unless they violated some prison rule, so that their liberty interest included not being punished until after their alleged violations were proved in a due process proceeding. As a logical matter, this was a good argument from the earlier cases, but as a practical matter the Supreme Court rebelled at the judicialization of prison discipline, with its implications for undermining the security and discipline of the prison system. Accordingly, in *Sandin v. Conner*, 515 U.S. 472 (1995), the Supreme Court by a 5-4 vote "clarified" the law by holding that only when discipline "imposes atypical and significant hardship on the inmate in relation to the ordinary incidents of prison life" is due process implicated. In that case, the Court rejected a claim that punishment of solitary confinement for 30 days was enough to trigger due process requirements. Rather, such discipline "falls within the expected parameters of the sentence imposed by a court of law." On the other hand, in *Wilkinson v. Austin*, 545 U.S. 209 (2005), the Court concluded that indefinite placement in a "supermax" prison, together with a disqualification from parole, was enough to trigger due process requirements. Nevertheless, the procedure the state provided satisfied due process.

Example

Prisoner Bill is transferred from a medium security facility to a maximum security facility because the prison authorities believe he has a disruptive influence on other inmates, leading to more fights and prison disturbances. He is provided no due process protections in that determination.

Prisoner Mike is transferred from a medium security facility to a mental hospital for mandatory behavior modification because the prison authorities believe he has a similar disruptive influence. He too is provided no due process protections.

The authorities' action with respect to Bill does not violate due process, but their action with respect to Mike does.

Explanation

With respect to Bill, when he received his prison sentence, the court did not specify what level of security facility he was to be sent to. That was left to the prison authorities to determine. Accordingly, wherever Bill is sent is "within the expected parameters of the sentence imposed by a court of law." Moreover, incarceration in a prison where many other prisoners must also serve their time is not an atypical and significant hardship in relation to ordinary incidents of prison life. *See Meachum v. Fano*, 427 U.S. 215 (1976).

On the other hand, when Mike was sentenced to prison, that sentence presumed only the normal program of correctional facilities; it did not include a program of "mandatory behavior modification" in the mental health sense.[3] Therefore, to discipline Mike in this manner was beyond what was implicit in his sentence. In addition, in fact it is atypical (if not virtually unheard of) to submit prisoners to such mandatory behavior modification. *See Vitek v. Jones*, 445 U.S. 480 (1980).

3. Of course, in one sense all discipline and even prison incarceration itself might be viewed as a form of mandatory behavior modification. In the mental health sense, however, this kind of activity would involve a systematic use of rewards or punishments, such as by the use of drugs or electroshock, for example, to "teach" a person different behavior. *See* Anthony Burgess, *A Clockwork Orange* (1996).

II. WHAT PROCESS IS DUE?

Once you have decided that there is a protectable due process interest, whether liberty or property, the next question is what process is due. After all, the Fifth Amendment and Fourteenth Amendment do not prohibit the deprivation of liberty or property; so long as due process is provided, the government is allowed to deprive persons of liberty and property.

A. Historically

To the Founding Fathers, due process of law probably meant a trial in court. The deprivations of life, liberty, and property they were immediately concerned with were those that only courts could order. After all, there was little administrative state in their time. It did not take long, however, before Congress created some administrative agencies, and some of the earliest agencies engaged in the deprivation of property. For example, the fifth act of the first Congress in 1789 was to establish the Customs Service, and as early as 1853, the Supreme Court upheld a Customs-imposed, 20 percent penalty duty for an undervaluation of imported goods without requiring Customs to go to court to collect.

Historically, the exact content of due process protections was never made clear. One of the earliest cases in the twentieth century, *Londoner v. Denver*, 210 U.S. 373 (1908), suggested that due process could be satisfied by the most simple procedures:

> due process of law requires that, at some stage of the proceedings, the [person] shall have an opportunity to be heard, of which he must have notice, either personal or by publication, or by a law fixing the time and place of the hearing. . . . Many requirements essential in strictly judicial proceedings may be dispensed with in proceedings of this nature. But even here a hearing, in its very essence, demands that he who is entitled to it shall have the right to support his allegations by argument, however brief, and, if need be by proof, however informal.

Nevertheless, by the time of the passage of the APA, there was a general understanding that when due process was required, only a fairly formal adjudication would suffice to protect those interests. For example, shortly after the passage of the APA, the Supreme Court suggested that whenever due process required a hearing before a federal agency, an adjudication under the APA would be required. *See Wong Yang Sung v. McGrath*, 339 U.S. 33 (1950). In that case, Wong Yang Sung was ordered deported after a hearing before an "immigrant inspector," a person involved in the investigation and prosecution of deportable aliens, not before a relatively independent person, such as an ALJ under the APA. The Court in an earlier case had held that due process required a hearing before a person could be deported. The Court then stated that the APA "represents a long period of study and strife; it settles long-continued and hard-fought contentions, and enacts a formula upon which opposing social and political forces have come to rest." Given that formula, the Court believed that statutes that required due process hearings impliedly required use of the APA adjudicatory procedures.

This approach did not last long. Congress quickly amended the immigration law to make clear that it did not intend an APA hearing to be required, and the Court upheld that law and the procedures that it provided as satisfying due process. *See Marcello v. Bonds*, 349 U.S. 302 (1955). Despite this, however, the assumption remained that a fairly formal adjudication would be required. This was reflected in the Court's decision in *Goldberg v. Kelly*, discussed earlier. While that case might be considered a modern case, in that it recognized that government entitlements could be protected as a property interest under the Due Process Clause, in another sense *Goldberg v. Kelly* is an old-fashioned case, because after deciding that due process protections were required, the Court then required the agency to provide the functional equivalent of a formal APA adjudication,[4] even while saying that it was not requiring "any procedural requirements beyond those demanded by rudimentary due process."

Goldberg listed the following requirements as necessary to provide due process:

- Timely and adequate notice of the charges against the person;
- Confrontation and cross-examination of adverse witnesses;
- The opportunity to present her own witnesses;
- The opportunity to address the fact-finder orally;
- The right to have counsel present;
- A decision on the record;
- An explanation of the decision; and
- An impartial decision maker.

A proceeding that provided all of these procedures would be a relatively formal proceeding. The fewer of these procedures provided, the more "informal" the proceeding would be.

When the interests protected by the Due Process Clause were relatively narrow, requiring a relatively formal proceeding to protect those interests was manageable. With the expansion of protected interests to include government entitlement programs and many government employment relations, however, a formal adjudicatory system groaned under the load. This

4. Because the case arose in the context of a state agency's action, the federal Administrative Procedure Act clearly was inapplicable.

was made apparent by the effects caused by the Court's decision in *Goldberg*. The costs and delays in weeding the welfare rolls became something of a scandal.

The first reaction came in *Arnett v. Kennedy*, 416 U.S. 134 (1974). There a federal civil service employee was fired after being accused of offering a bribe. Under the civil service law, the employee was given notice of the charges and the evidence against him and allowed to respond orally and in writing and to submit affidavits on his behalf. He was not, however, afforded an evidentiary hearing with an impartial agency official before he was fired, although he did have a right to a full APA adjudication after he was fired. He brought suit alleging a violation of his due process rights in the failure to provide him with an evidentiary hearing *before* he was terminated. By a vote of 5-4, the Court rejected the claim, but it could not agree on the reason. The plurality opinion by then-Justice Rehnquist, joined by two other Justices, argued that the extent of the due process right extended no further than the property interest created; that is, Arnett had a property interest in keeping his job solely because of the civil service law that created an entitlement to it, but that law also created the very procedures for the termination of that entitlement. Consequently, under this analysis, the process due was co-extensive with the procedures provided in the law that created the entitlement in the first place. This view, however, was rejected by all six other members of the Court.

While the Rehnquist analysis did not command a majority, and in fact was rejected by the other six Justices, its presence in the plurality opinion held open the possibility that it might someday prevail. In *Cleveland Bd. of Educ. v. Loudermill*, 470 U.S. 532 (1985), however, the Court finally explicitly disavowed this analysis by an 8-1 vote over Justice Rehnquist's dissent, establishing that the process due is governed by the Due Process Clause, not by the law establishing the property interest. But how to determine what process was due was left open.

B. The Modern Rule

Finally, in *Mathews v. Eldridge*, 424 U.S. 319 (1976), the Court mustered a majority to establish the rule that governs all determinations of whether the process provided is sufficient. In *Mathews*, Mr. Eldridge had been receiving Social Security Disability payments. In the course of routine monitoring, the then Department of Health, Education, and Welfare (of which the Social Security Administration was then a part) sent Mr. Eldridge a questionnaire about his medical condition. After reviewing his response and receiving reports from his physician and a psychiatric consultant, the agency preliminarily determined that Mr. Eldridge's physical condition had improved to the point where he no longer qualified for disability payments. The agency so notified him and offered him the opportunity to submit additional information. Mr. Eldridge responded, but the agency still concluded that he was no longer disabled. It notified him that his benefits would terminate at the end of the month and informed him that he could seek reconsideration of this decision. The reconsideration proceeding would be a full evidentiary hearing, approximating what would occur in an APA adjudication, and if he prevailed there, he would receive full retroactive benefits.

This system mirrored the system in place in *Goldberg*, which the Supreme Court had said did not satisfy due process. That is, both systems provided for an informal determination based upon the exchange of written materials prior to the termination of benefits, with the opportunity for a formal, full evidentiary hearing after termination of benefits with retroactive reinstatement if the person prevailed. Nevertheless, the Supreme Court found that in this case this system did not violate due process. In so doing, the Court announced what has become the familiar three-factor test for assessing the adequacy of a proceeding under the Due Process Clause:

- First, one must consider the private interest that will be affected by the official action.
- Second, one must consider the risk of an erroneous deprivation of that interest under the required procedures and the likely reduction of that risk by requiring more or different procedures.
- Third, one must consider the government's interest in using the required procedures, as opposed to more or different procedures.

In *Mathews*, the Court found that Mr. Eldridge's interest in the uninterrupted receipt of his disability payments pending the results of a post-termination hearing was important, especially because the evidence showed that post-termination hearing decisions took almost a year. Nevertheless, the Court found that interest not as important as the welfare recipients in *Goldberg*. In *Goldberg* the welfare recipient was by definition poor and welfare was the last social safety net; even temporary wrongful termination of payments in this circumstance could have disastrous consequences. Disability recipients, however, need not be poor; their payments came as a result of disability rather than poverty. Even if they were poor (and the Court was aware that as a matter of empirical fact most disability recipients were poor), if they lost their disability payments temporarily, they might qualify for some sort of public assistance.

Turning to the second factor—the risk of error inherent in the procedures provided and the reduction in risk that might be achieved by different or additional procedures—the Court opined that in disability determinations, trial-type procedures would not be particularly useful. "[I]n most cases" the decision would turn on "routine, standard, and unbiased medical reports by physician specialists," whereas in welfare cases, such as *Goldberg*, the disputes might involve issues of witness credibility and veracity, where trial-type procedures would be useful. In addition, whereas in *Goldberg* the ability to submit information in writing would not be very helpful to persons likely to lack writing skills, in disability determinations the medical personnel were perfectly able to describe in writing the nature and extent of the disability.

Finally, the third factor—the government's interest in maintaining the procedures provided—likewise counseled in favor of upholding the existing procedures. The Court explicitly acknowledged the importance of avoiding the administrative burden and cost associated with requiring an evidentiary hearing before any termination of benefits.

It is impossible to read *Mathews v. Eldridge* and its application of the three-factor test as anything other than a significant shift from the earlier paradigm. The purportedly objective distinguishing of *Goldberg* to reach a different conclusion in disability cases is hardly convincing. Much more telling is the language with which the Court ended the case:

> But more is implicated in cases of this type than ad hoc weighing of fiscal and administrative burdens against the interests of a particular category of claimants. The ultimate balance involves a determination as to when, under our constitutional system, judicial-type procedures must be imposed upon administrative action to assure fairness. . . . The judicial model of an evidentiary hearing is neither a required, nor even the most effective, method of decisionmaking in all circumstances. The essence of due process is the requirement that "a person in jeopardy of serious loss [be given] notice of the case against him and opportunity to meet it." All that is necessary is that the procedures be tailored, in light of the decision to be made, to the "capacities and circumstances of those who are to be heard," to insure that they are given a meaningful opportunity to present their case.

In other words, no longer was there to be a presumption in favor of judicial-type procedures. Now there would be a more flexible notion of what could constitute a fair procedure, so long as the person affected had a reasonable opportunity, in light of the circumstances, to address the issues.

Nevertheless, even in *Mathews* for the termination of disability benefits, as in *Goldberg* for welfare terminations and in *Arnett* for the termination of government employment, a full, trial-type proceeding had been afforded *after* the government action. The sufficiency under the Due Process Clause of flexible, informal procedures still only applied to the pre-termination proceedings when followed by full, formal post-termination proceedings. In *Cleveland B. of Educ. v. Loudermill*, 470 U.S. 532 (1985), the Court suggested that at least in the absence of exigent circumstances, *some* pre-termination proceeding must be given.[5] How flexible and informal such pre-termination proceedings might be was suggested in the later case of *Gilbert v. Homar*, 520 U.S. 924 (1997). There, a university suspended a security guard without pay solely on the basis that he had been arrested for possession of marijuana. No pre-suspension proceeding was provided. He argued that this deprived him of due process, but a unanimous Supreme Court held that, given the university's interests in assuring that its officers enjoyed the public's trust, the fact that the officer had been arrested and charged "by an independent body" was a sufficient determination to protect against arbitrary suspension by the university. Again, however, this suspension was temporary, and ultimately he was entitled to a full hearing and, if cleared, reinstatement and retroactive pay.

Both *Goldberg* and *Mathews* involved what have come to be called "mass justice" cases. That is, they involved proceedings in types of cases that number in the millions in a year. In these types of cases in particular, because of the sheer number of such proceedings, the government's interest in expedition and conservation of resources probably should weigh relatively heavily on the scales. One of the problems, however, is that even if most of these cases can be adequately treated in informal proceedings, there may be some in which trial-type proceedings might well be important. In *Mathews*, however, the Court was explicit that the determination of what satisfied due process was a determination to be made on the basis of "the generality of the cases, not the rare exceptions." Thus, even though with respect to a particular person an informal process would *not* be fair and adequate, if the process is fair and adequate in the generality of the cases, that person is not entitled to the additional procedures necessary to make the proceeding fair and adequate as to him. This approach, while failing to tailor due process protections to the particular case, serves the purpose of reducing the need to make ad hoc judgments as to fairness and makes more predictable the adequacy of agency procedures.

The retreat from *Goldberg* and from the desirability of judicial-type procedures has been particularly strong in the educational environment. In *Goss v. Lopez*, 419 U.S. 565 (1975), a high school student was given a ten-day suspension. While the Court conceded that this invaded a protected due process interest, the Court likewise did not wish to burden schools with the need to afford judicial-type proceedings, and it approved minimal procedures: "oral or written notice of the charges against him, and if he denies them, an explanation of the evidence the authorities have and an opportunity to present his side of the story." Later, in *Ingraham v. Wright*, 430

---

5. Where there are exigent circumstances, the Court has approved immediate government action without a prior proceeding. *See Ewing v. Mytinger & Casselberry, Inc.*, 339 U.S. 594 (1950) (seizure of allegedly misbranded drugs); *North Am. Cold Storage Co. v. Chicago*, 211 U.S. 306 (1908) (seizure of allegedly spoiled food).

U.S. 651 (1977), where junior high school students had been subjected to corporal punishment, the Court applied the *Mathews v. Eldridge* three-factor test and found that *no* prior notice or proceeding was required, because after-the-fact tort actions were available for abuse. While the Court discussed all three factors in the test, it clearly was most affected by how any requirement for a pre-paddling proceeding would interfere with the swift, sure exercise of school discipline, which it felt was an important government interest. Finally, in a university case, the Court upheld the dismissal of a medical student on academic grounds, rather than disciplinary grounds, in which the university had employed traditionally academic evaluations, rather than judicial-type proceedings, in making its determinations. *See Board of Curators of the University of Missouri v. Horowitz*, 435 U.S. 78 (1978). The Court said: "Academic evaluations of a student, in contrast to disciplinary determinations, bear little resemblance to the judicial and administrative fact-finding proceedings to which we have traditionally attached a full-hearing requirement."

Example

Melissa's state law school, perhaps learning from her example, adopts an Honor Proceeding process. Under that process, if a faculty member or student becomes aware of an Honor Code Violation, they are to report it to the Assistant Dean for Student Services, who is to convene the Honor Committee. The Committee is made up of one student elected by the student body in an annual election, one faculty member selected on an annual basis by the faculty, and one faculty member selected on an annual basis by the Dean of the law school. This Committee investigates the allegation, talking to such people as it deems necessary. If on the basis of its investigation, it believes a violation has occurred, the Committee is required to meet with the alleged violator, to present him with the evidence against him (that is, to describe or provide written descriptions of the evidence against him), and to provide him an opportunity to respond to the charges. There is no provision for the examination or cross-examination of witnesses. Thereafter, if the Committee concludes that the student committed the violation, it reports that to the Dean with a recommended sanction. The Dean then imposes a sanction, but there is no provision for allowing the student to speak with the Dean before the sanction is imposed.

A professor sees Harold and Todd talking to one another and passing a paper between them during the administration of an exam. The professor approaches them and demands to see the paper, but Harold stuffs it in his mouth, chews, and swallows it. The professor reports them both to the Assistant Dean, alleging that they were cheating on the exam in violation of the Honor Code, and that the refusal by Harold to give the professor the paper was a separate violation.

The Committee interviews Harold and Todd separately. Harold says that they were talking about a female member of the class and the piece of paper had obscene comments about her, and rather than give it to the Professor he destroyed it, because he was embarrassed by what was on it. He denies cheating on the exam, but admits that he knew he was not supposed to talk to anyone during the exam. Todd, however, visibly distraught, says that Harold had asked him for the answer to one of the exam questions and Todd had written the answer on the paper. He also says that Harold had told him to tell a story corroborating Harold's story, and he had agreed, but his girlfriend convinced him he should tell the truth.

The Committee concludes that Todd is telling the truth and that Harold is lying. It reports these conclusions to the Dean, recommending that Harold be expelled and that Todd be placed on probation. The Dean accepts the recommendation as to Harold, but he suspends Todd for one year.

Harold claims that he was telling the truth and sues the school, alleging a violation of due process.

Explanation

As indicated earlier, the expulsion would appear to deprive Harold of "property," in that there were mutual agreements, probably reflected in school policy documents, that students could remain in school so long as they followed the rules and stayed in good academic standing. The question is whether the Honor Proceeding provided him with all the process due.

Applying the *Mathews v. Eldridge* three-factor test, we ask first what is the private interest involved. It is obviously substantial. An expulsion from law school for cheating will significantly delay if not defeat Harold's ability ever to become a lawyer. Moreover, unlike many of the deprivations encountered in the Supreme Court cases, this is not just a temporary deprivation of some money. This is a permanent deprivation. There will be no subsequent full hearing at which initial errors may be corrected. Nevertheless, depriving a person of the ability to become a lawyer is less than denying a person the ability to survive (e.g., the deprivation of welfare payments, at least in theory) and does not necessarily destroy his life. Many people lead productive lives without being lawyers, and many have had their career plans disrupted by the government (recall that once upon a time there was a draft to maintain the military).

The second factor is the risk of error in the procedures afforded and the likely reduced risk of error by the use of additional procedures. The challenger must identify what additional procedures would be required to meet due process concerns. Harold would probably argue that two aspects of the procedure denied him due process. First, because Todd was interviewed after Harold, Harold was never informed before the Committee's decision what Todd had said. This denied Harold's ability to respond and answer or rebut what Todd said. To the extent that Todd's testimony was evidence against Harold, Harold was never informed of that evidence or given a chance to respond to it. Second, Harold might argue that while the chance to respond to the evidence against him is necessary to due process, it is not sufficient. Where the evidence is testimonial and relies on the credibility of the witness, confrontation and cross-examination are also necessary to provide due process. The failure to provide these procedures, Harold would argue, would result in an unacceptable risk of error. After all, absent confrontation and cross-examination, no one can know what motives Todd would have for lying.

The law school would argue that its procedures do not allow a significant risk of error. Harold knew the charges against him—that he had cheated in the exam—and he had a chance to respond to those charges. While Harold did not have an opportunity to confront and cross-examine Todd, the members of the Honor Committee did question Todd closely to assess possible reasons for falsely implicating Harold. There is no reason to believe that the Committee's questioning was any less successful in ferreting out the truth than Harold's questioning would have been. Moreover, the school might argue that in most cases the credibility of witnesses (other than the accused) is not the issue. When the case involves plagiarism, the most common issue is the extent of similarity between the work submitted and the original work from which the submitted work is alleged to be plagiarized. When the case involves other forms of cheating, usually the issue is the extent of the cheating or the extenuating circumstances that led the person to engage in it, not the fact of whether there was any cheating at all. Accordingly, even if credibility is considered important in this case, the standard of due process should be set according to the generic, not the extraordinary, case.

The third factor for consideration is the government's interest in not having to alter the procedures it used. Normally, government's argument is that additional procedures would increase significantly the costs and resources necessary for adjudications. Here, however, while Harold's requested procedures might increase the costs and resources devoted to Honor Proceedings somewhat, there are probably so few of these proceedings that the dollar and resource cost would not be significant. More important here would be the law school's argument that judicializing the Honor Proceeding would undermine the academic program of the school. It is important to the effective functioning of the educational environment, the school would argue, that honor questions be resolved expeditiously and with a minimum of fuss. This serves to protect those who are found not to have been in violation by minimizing the time that they must agonize under the threat of possible expulsion, as well as facilitating the rehabilitation of those who are found in violation but not expelled, such as Todd. Moreover, were confrontation and cross-examination generally required, this would result in students confronting and cross-examining professors, the persons most likely to find students violating the Honor Code, and such proceedings would undermine academic discipline.

This is probably a close case. Harold's interest is substantial. The school's interest is also substantial, especially because courts tend to be deferential toward a school's definition of its academic environment. The question of risk of error is particularly difficult, because this case seems to present tough questions on both sides of the equation. That is, traditionally the Court has upheld the idea that where questions of credibility predominate, cross-examination is essential for ensuring due process. Even when the Court has upheld denial of cross-examination, it has distinguished the case from situations where credibility is at issue. Here, credibility is *the* issue. If Harold is telling the truth, he is not guilty of cheating; if Todd is telling the truth, Harold is guilty. There is no apparent reason why Todd would lie here; it makes him guilty as well. That, however, does not detract from the fact that the issue in the case is credibility, which is traditionally tested through cross-examination. From this perspective Harold should prevail. Nevertheless, this is a school environment, where the Court has been especially critical of attempting to force determinations into a judicial mode. Of course, this is a *law* school—should that make a difference? Moreover, if the school claims that credibility is only rarely an issue in Honor Proceedings (recall the issues in Melissa's case), this would substantially undercut the force in Harold's argument, because the school is right that due process procedures are judged on the basis of the run-of-the-mill case, not the extraordinary case. Of course, this defense is a stronger one when the government entity is involved in mass justice cases, because it would be inefficient to structure the procedure in a large number of cases when it would only be useful in a few. When, as is probably the case here, there simply are not a large number of cases, there may not be any "generic" case and the loss of efficiency from tailoring the procedure may be significantly less.

One possibility is that a court might find for Harold, not on the right to confrontation and cross-examination, but on the right to be apprised of Todd's testimony and to respond to it before the Committee. Even when the Court has criticized forcing due process into a judicial model, it has said that the essence of due process is that the person be given "notice of the case against him and an opportunity to meet it." Here, it seems that Harold did not have notice of the "case" against him, in the sense of Todd's evidence against him that was relied upon by the Committee, and he had no opportunity to meet it. Moreover, there would seem to be little adverse impact on the school's asserted interests if all it had to do was inform Harold of what Todd had said, and allow Harold to respond to Todd's statements.

The above is a lengthy, detailed analysis of the due process sufficiency of the law school's procedures. Ultimately, the conclusion is uncertain. This example and explanation reflect the reality of everyday cases asking whether particular procedures satisfy due process. First, they are very sensitive to the particular facts and context in which the questions appear. Lawyers and judges cannot avoid extensive analyses of the manner in which the proceedings take place and the nature of the cases that occur there. Second, predicting the sufficiency of any given set of procedures under the *Mathews* test is difficult. As a simple empirical matter, it is a rare case that finds existing procedures insufficient, but this is due in large part to the fact that government entities take some care to ensure that their procedures will pass muster. Thus, while there are a number of close cases, in almost all of which the courts find the procedures adequate, there are only a few egregious cases where courts will find the procedures inadequate.

Example

Assume the facts are the same as in the earlier example except that the Dean's expulsion is subject to appeal to a university hearing officer, where the student receives a full, *de novo*, trial-type hearing. However, the appeal does not stay the expulsion. Thus, Harold is expelled but can then appeal and receive a full hearing, after which, if he is cleared, he will be reinstated in the law school.

Explanation

This alteration of the facts certainly changes the analysis above and almost certainly would result in upholding this procedure. Now the private interest is only a temporary deprivation, and the cases suggesting that pretermination hearings can be informal and flexible support the procedures used by the law school.

C. Particular Requirements

The *Mathews v. Eldridge* test governs the question whether particular procedures satisfy due process. There are, however, a couple of specific "due process requirements" that courts have sometimes opined are necessary in all cases. One of these is the need for an impartial judge; the other is a prohibition on certain ex parte communications (deriving from the need for a decision based on the record created in the proceeding). Nevertheless, it is not always simple to decide how impartial an "impartial" judge must be, or what exceptions there might be to the prohibition on ex parte communications.

I. The Need for an Impartial Judge

While fundamental fairness and due process may require an impartial judge, they certainly do not require life-tenured, Article III judges, but they certainly do prohibit a judge who has a personal financial stake in the case.[6] Between these two poles, however, there is a wide range of possible lack of impartiality.

It is generally accepted that any financial interest, no matter how small, is impermissible. Persons appointed to high government positions, such as heads of agencies or members of independent regulatory agencies, often place their financial interests into a blind trust. In this way, they do not know what their financial interests are and do not have to worry whether the cases before them may or may not implicate their financial interests. It is also generally accepted that persons should not be judges in cases that directly affect their spouses and close relatives. Moreover, a person would be impermissibly partial if he or she had personal animus against a party before him or her. What counts as personal animus, however, is usually not very clear. For example, would an Administrator of the National Highway Traffic Safety Administration be disqualified from participating in a case involving General Motors if he had purchased a GM car he had not been happy with before his appointment and had written a number of intemperate letters to GM at the time? The answer is almost certainly not, if the Administrator said that it would not affect his judgment. There is a strong tendency to credit the ability of high officials to put personal considerations aside, except when it comes to a financial interest, for which the rule is clear.

One basic issue is the possible problem of institutional bias. For example, if ALJs are employees of an agency that is a party to an adjudication before them, does their identification with the agency impermissibly bias them? The clear answer is no, or else the whole APA adjudication system would be unconstitutional. Even the use of AJs, who do not have the personnel protections of ALJs, generally does not raise serious questions about bias. Moreover, ALJs are insulated by the Separation of Functions provision, 5 U.S.C. § 554(d), from being involved in or subject to the direction of persons (other than the head of the agency) who participate in the investigatory or prosecutorial process. This further protects them from possible

---

6. Actually, even this latter statement has an exception—the Doctrine of Necessity—that allows a person with a personal stake in a case to judge the case if no impartial judge is available. The prime example was a lawsuit alleging that the failure to provide inflationary, cost-of-living increases to federal judges violated the constitutional requirement not to diminish their compensation during their time in office. Article III, § 1. All federal judges would have a financial stake in the outcome, so all would be disqualified, but then the case could not be heard at all. As a result, the Doctrine of Necessity would allow any judge to hear the case; the theory is that it is better to have a potentially partial judge than no judge at all. *See United States v. Will*, 449 U.S. 200 (1980).

bias. AJs, whose proceedings are not subject to the Separation of Functions provision, potentially can be involved in or subject to those involved in the prosecutorial process. Agencies address part of this problem by routinely providing in their own regulations that an AJ cannot adjudicate any case in which he or she has been involved in a prosecutorial or investigative manner. *See, e.g.*, 40 C.F.R. 22.4(b) (EPA Regional Judicial Officers may not have performed prosecutorial or investigative functions in connection with any case in which they serve as Regional Judicial Officers).

Under the APA, however, heads of agencies, or members of independent regulatory agencies, may be involved both in directing the investigation and in prosecuting of someone, as well as having ultimate responsibility for the adjudicatory decision. The APA creates an exception from the Separation of Functions provision, 5 U.S.C. § 554(d), for these persons, but what about due process? In *Withrow v. Larkin*, 421 U.S. 35 (1975), the Supreme Court addressed this issue in the context of a state board. The state medical examining board investigated a doctor for performing illegal operations. After an investigatory hearing to review the evidence against him (at which he was allowed to be present and to speak at the end), the board formally charged him with professional violations. It then scheduled an adjudicatory hearing to try the charge, which might result in suspension of his license. Moreover, it held a further investigatory hearing resulting in a finding of probable cause that he had violated state criminal law and a referral of the matter to the local district attorney. The doctor sought and obtained an injunction against the board's scheduled adjudicatory hearing on the grounds that it violated due process for the same persons who brought the charge to decide the case against him. The Supreme Court reiterated the fundamental importance of the need for an unbiased decision maker, but it found that the mere combination of investigatory, prosecutorial, and adjudicatory functions in the same entity did not necessarily make the entity biased in adjudicating. Thus, it upheld the basic structure of federal and state administrative agencies that do combine these functions. In addition, while it conceded that particular circumstances might indicate bias by particular members of the entity, it found that nothing in this case indicated that the persons on the board were in fact biased. In reaching this latter conclusion, the Court discounted the fact that they had already concluded that the doctor should be charged with violation of professional standards and that there was "probable cause" that he had violated criminal provisions. It noted that judges routinely sit as judges in trials over persons for whom they may have issued arrest warrants based on findings of probable cause, and judges also routinely hear cases for permanent injunctions when they have already ruled on a motion for a preliminary injunction. The Court indicated that the presumption should be that when members of agencies sit as judges, they can set aside whatever determinations they made in deciding to investigate or prosecute the case.

If the presumption is that the members are not biased, what is required to overcome that presumption? The test hinted at in *Withrow* and often stated in subsequent cases is a showing that the person's mind is "irrevocably closed."[7] Another statement of the necessary showing, which is slightly more protective, is whether "a disinterested [person] could hardly fail to conclude that the [decision maker] had in some measure [already] decided [the case]."

The question then is how a person can possibly prove that the decision maker has already decided the case or has an irrevocably closed mind. The cases are unanimous that a person cannot prove this by analysis of the decision itself (unless the decision maker was so obtuse as to state that prejudgment in his or her decision). The only way to show such bias is through extrinsic evidence. As a practical matter, this has meant public statements by the decision maker. The only case in which an adjudication was overturned for such bias involved the Chair of the FTC who made a speech while a proceeding against a particular oil company was under way. In that speech he identified the oil company as one of the entities involved in unlawful practices, and he in effect promised his audience that the oil company would be found in violation. This was too much. *See Texaco, Inc. v. FTC*, 336 F.2d 754 (D.C. Cir. 1964). There are a handful of other cases, none of which reached the Supreme Court, in which claims that public statements about pending cases were evidence of prejudgment, but none went quite so far, and none resulted in findings of impermissible bias.

Example

Under its power to review and set aside mergers that may substantially lessen competition or create a monopoly, the FTC investigated the acquisition by Kennecott Copper, a large copper company, of Peabody Coal Company, a large coal company. While Kennecott was not a competitor in the coal industry, the FTC brought an administrative case against Kennecott, arguing that but for Kennecott's purchase of Peabody, Kennecott would have entered the coal industry, thereby increasing competition. While the case was pending, one of the Commissioners gave an interview to a trade reporter explaining the FTC's theory. During that interview she said:

> Perhaps it's easier to see in a case like the Kennecott Copper-Peabody Coal complaint. We have here an instance of a copper company that was actually moving into the coal industry on its own. Kennecott was experimenting with a small, previously acquired coal property. The complaint says that Kennecott, in effect,

---

7. This is clearly the test in rulemaking proceedings (where due process generally does not apply at all!). *See Association of National Advertisers, Inc. v. FTC*, 627 F.2d 1151, 1170 (D.C. Cir. 1979). But no rulemaking has ever been overturned on this basis.

> eliminated itself as a probable new entrant into the coal industry when it went out and bought a major coal company.

Kennecott argued that this demonstrated that the Commissioner had in effect already decided the case against it.

Explanation

The D.C. Circuit held that this did not evidence prejudgment. The interview, the court said, merely described what was in the complaint; it did not purport to describe how the case ultimately would or should be decided. The court went on, however, to chastise the agency:

> Public expressions with regard to pending cases cannot, of course, be approved because regardless of what is said such expressions tend not only to mar the image but to create embarrassment and to subject the proceedings to question. We do not, however, perceive any evidence of prejudging or the appearance of it.

Kennecott Copper Corp. v. FTC, 467 F.2d 67 (10th Cir. 1972).

This example demonstrates the lengths to which courts will go to avoid overturning an agency decision because of alleged prejudgment.

Nevertheless, if the court finds that even one Commissioner of five had prejudged the case, this would probably require reversing and remanding the case for reconsideration. The theory is that if one Commissioner has prejudged the case, his participation in the deliberations of the full Commission fatally taints those deliberations, requiring reversal and remand for the Commission to reconsider the case without the participation of the biased Commissioner.

As may be seen, unless the agency head or member of the independent regulatory agency speaks out in public concerning an ongoing case, there is really no basis for a claim of prejudgment. Thus, agency lawyers try to counsel the head of the agency or the members of the agency *not* to mention pending cases in public statements.

In one notable case, the FTC was engaged in an administrative proceeding against the Pillsbury Company, challenging its acquisition of competing flour mills. Rather than arguing a dramatic, per se rule against certain concentrations in industry, the Commission argued a narrow, fact-based case. The Senate Judiciary Committee was unhappy with this approach and called the Chairman of the Commission, his staff, the General Counsel, another Commissioner, and the Director of Litigation before the Committee. The Committee questioned the witnesses at length about their theory of the case and criticized the Commission for not being more forceful. The Chairman of the Commission complained about this political interference in an ongoing adjudication and removed himself from the case. Nevertheless, when the FTC decided the case against Pillsbury, two of the witnesses before the Committee were members of the Commission participating in the case. Pillsbury appealed the decision, alleging improper political coercion on the Commission. The court of appeals agreed that it was an "improper intrusion into the adjudicatory process" that deprived Pillsbury of a fair and impartial hearing. *See Pillsbury Co. v. FTC*, 354 F.2d 952 (5th Cir. 1966). The primary effect of this case—the only one of its kind—is to insulate agencies from having to discuss pending cases before congressional committees. Committees that wish to use their political power to affect an agency's adjudication are reminded of *Pillsbury* and they back off.

It should be obvious that no one should be a judge of facts of which he or she has personal knowledge. The whole purpose of adjudication is to judge facts on the basis of some sort of proceeding, whether formal or informal. If the adjudicator already knows (or thinks he knows) facts relevant to the proceeding, he would not be deciding them on the basis of the proceeding.

Finally, it is possible for an adjudicator to act in a manner in the course of the proceeding that will provide a basis for a claim of bias. For example, in *Cham v. Attorney General*, 445 F.3d 683 (3d Cir. 2006), the AJ in an immigration proceeding so bullied the applicant for asylum that the court found that this was bias by the AJ against the applicant in violation of due process.

2. Ex Parte Communications

We have already explored prohibitions on ex parte communications contained in the APA. In cases of informal adjudications—those not subject to 5 U.S.C. §§ 554(d) and 557(d)—the Due Process Clause also places limits on ex parte communications.

Recall that under 5 U.S.C. § 557(d), ex parte communications with interested persons outside the agency relevant to the merits of the proceeding were prohibited; under 5 U.S.C. § 554(d), ex parte communications by an ALJ with any person on a fact at issue were prohibited. As indicated in that discussion, these distinctions result in allowing ALJs to communicate ex parte with persons inside the agency (not involved in the investigative or prosecuting function) concerning non-factual issues.

In federal adjudications not subject to the APA, and in state adjudications, a recurring question is the extent to which decision makers, in particular AJs or state ALJs, may communicate ex parte with persons inside the agency or with lawyers for the agency (who in the states are sometimes found outside the agency).

Example

A federal bank examiner allegedly submitted false medical leave forms. His agency proposes to terminate his employment and he seeks a hearing. While this hearing is not a formal adjudication under the APA, he is entitled to review the evidence against him and to prepare an answer to it. In fact, the deciding official receives two memoranda that are not provided to the employee. One was from the official who originally recommended his dismissal and the other was from another official in the agency. Both memoranda urged that the employee be terminated and allegedly contained new and damaging information about the employee. When the agency indeed did terminate the employee, he sued, arguing that the memoranda were ex parte communications that deprived him of due process.

The agency argued that these intra-agency communications were not ex parte communications, but instead were merely advice to the deciding official. Moreover, the agency argued that the deciding official had stated in an affidavit that he would have terminated the employee even if he had never seen the memoranda, so the memoranda were at worst harmless error.

Explanation

To the extent that these communications contained new and substantial information, they can deprive the employee of due process by denying him the opportunity to respond to the evidence against him. Here it is not important where the new information comes from; what is critical is that the employee never had a chance to respond to it. Recall the curative measures in 5 U.S.C. § 557(d)—placing the ex parte communication in the record and affording the parties a chance to respond to it.

Some cases have gone further and said that ex parte advice *from those involved in the investigation or prosecution* can violate due process, even if there is no new factual information. Here it is critical *who* is making the ex parte communication, not the information itself. Here at least one of the memoranda is from the official who started the proceeding. Thus, even if it only contained advice, and not new facts, it could violate due process.

Not all prohibited ex parte communications are sufficiently serious to warrant reversing an adjudicatory decision. An ex parte communication can be harmless error. The generally accepted rule is that the test for harmless error is objective, not subjective. The agency in this example is arguing for a subjective test—how the deciding official said it affected him. The objective test asks whether a reasonable person looking at the ex parte communications would conclude that they would be likely to cause prejudice. In essence, under the objective test the focus is on the ex parte communications themselves and their likelihood of affecting a decision maker, while the subjective test focuses on the decision maker and his explanation of his decision.

It is worth noting a significant difference between judicial review of ex parte communication violations under the APA and under due process. Under the APA, once a communication is found to violate the statutory prohibition, in order to show harmless error the burden is on the government to show that it did not affect the outcome. In order to establish that an ex parte communication violates due process, however, the burden is on the person challenging the agency decision to show that a reasonable person would conclude that the communication would affect the decision maker. Once so established, though, there is no harmless error possible. The APA rule is friendlier to the challenger.

Many state agencies do not have their own lawyers. They may hire lawyers on a part-time basis from the private bar for particular purposes, or they may obtain the assistance of lawyers in the state Attorney General's office. In either situation, it is entirely possible that the lawyer who prosecutes the case (or assists the agency in prosecuting the case) before the agency may also assist the agency in its decision-making capacity. This raises a clear potential for problems, but it has not stopped some states from maintaining such a system.

CHAPTER 5

Rulemaking

> Notice and comment rulemaking is one of the greatest inventions of modern government.
>
> —*Kenneth Culp Davis,* Administrative Law Treatise § 6.15, *at* 283 *(Supp. 1970)*

This chapter deals with rulemaking, the agency process for making rules, which often look like and have the effect of laws passed by legislatures. It begins by describing the nature of rules—what they are and how they are defined. It then distinguishes between two types of rules—legislative and nonlegislative rules—a distinction that is important under the APA, because the procedures for adopting them are different and their effects are different. The chapter then discusses rulemaking procedures, first by describing the various types of rules that are exempted from those procedures and then by describing the procedures applicable to Notice-and-Comment Rulemaking. The chapter concludes with sections on the relatively unusual phenomenon of negotiated rulemaking and on the requirements applicable to rulemaking not found in the APA, particularly the hybrid rulemaking requirements found in executive orders and certain statutes.

I. THE NATURE OF RULES

As indicated in Chapter 1, normally we think of rulemaking as the agency equivalent of legislation. An agency proposes and then adopts a rule, just as a legislature proposes a bill and adopts a law. When the agency is an independent regulatory agency headed by several members, the rule is actually adopted by a majority vote, just as laws are passed in legislatures. After a rule is adopted, it usually is indistinguishable in style and format from a statute adopted by a legislature. For the most part, federal rules are published in the Code of Federal Regulations (CFR), where they are organized according to numerical title, chapter, part, subpart, and section, again just as federal statutes are organized in the United States Code.

For example, Congress established the Council on Environmental Quality (the CEQ)[1] in the National Environmental Policy Act (NEPA), which is codified at 42 U.S.C. Chapter 55. Subchapter II of Chapter 55 is the portion that establishes the CEQ and assigns its functions and duties. 42 U.S.C. § 4342, a particular section in Subchapter II, is the section that establishes the agency. The CEQ in turn has adopted rules. They can be found at 40 C.F.R. Chapter V, which contains all of the CEQ's rules. Part 1502, which is one of several parts in Chapter V, specifically addresses the requirements for an Environmental Impact Statement (EIS) required by NEPA. 40 C.F.R. § 1502.9, a specific section in Part 1502, creates the requirement for a draft and final EIS.

You will often see or hear the word *regulation* in administrative law. Regulation is simply another word for rule.

A. "Rule" Under the APA

> **5 U.S.C. § 551(4)**
>
> "Rule" means the whole or a part of an agency statement of general or particular applicability and future effect designed to implement, interpret, or prescribe law or policy or describing the organization, procedure, or practice requirements of an agency and includes the approval or prescription for the future of rates, wages, corporate or financial structures or reorganizations thereof, prices, facilities, appliances, services, or allowances therefor or of valuations, costs, or accounting, or practices bearing on the foregoing.

The definition of "rule" in the APA is difficult, but if you break it down, it gets simpler. First, almost all agency rules would fit within the words: "an agency statement of general applicability and future effect." Again, this is like legislation. While technically there may be laws and rules of "particular

1. When it was created in 1970, the CEQ was one of the rare multi-member agencies that was not an independent regulatory agency. This anomaly ended in 1998 when Congress amended the law to provide that the Council would consist of only one member who would serve as Chairman. Now the CEQ is a completely unique institution, a council of one.

applicability,"[2] almost all the laws and rules we care about are of general applicability. That is, unlike orders resulting from adjudication, rules do not name particular persons or entities at whom the rule is directed. Rather, rules contain provisions identifying the types of persons or entities subject to the rule or who would qualify for the benefits of the rule. For example, the EPA's rules dealing with the Clean Water Act specify that persons who "discharge a pollutant from a point source" are subject to the rules. The Social Security Administration's rules providing for disability benefits state that they apply to persons whose disabilities prevent them from having any job in the national economy.

Not only are virtually all rules of general applicability, they are also of future effect. That is, they govern conduct that is yet to occur. Again, this is like laws passed by Congress or a state legislature. In fact, the Supreme Court has held that a rule cannot be retroactive unless the statute authorizing the rule explicitly empowers the agency to adopt a retroactive rule. *See Bowen v. Georgetown University Hospital*, 488 U.S. 204 (1988). In that case the Department of Health and Human Services adopted a rule changing the costs for certain procedures for which it would reimburse hospitals under the Medicare program. The change applied not just to costs that would be incurred after the rule was adopted, but also retroactively to costs that had been incurred during the two-year period before the rule was adopted. In other words, costs incurred by hospitals, which the regulations in effect at the time said would be reimbursed by Medicare, were changed so that the hospitals were denied reimbursement. This, the Court said, the agency could not do without explicit statutory authorization. Explicit statutory authorization would be tantamount to an amendment to the APA's definition limiting rules to statements of future effect.

Examples

1. The National Highway Traffic Safety Administration (NHTSA) gathers data showing that most automobiles do not adequately protect persons in side impact collisions. It then adopts a rule applicable to cars sold in later years requiring automobile manufacturers either to reinforce the structural integrity of the sides of cars or to install side airbags to protect persons in side impact collisions. Is this a retroactive rule?

2. The Occupational Safety and Health Administration (OSHA) gathers data showing that automobile paint shops have been providing inadequate ventilation in painting areas so that workers have been exposed

2. In the legislative world, these laws of particular applicability are known as "private laws." Find a copy of the Public Laws and look at the very back of the book. There you will find the private laws passed by Congress.

to dangerous levels of toxic fumes. Accordingly, the agency adopts a rule declaring that such inadequate ventilation is and has been a violation of the Occupational Safety and Health Act and that any paint shop that had maintained such inadequate ventilation shall be liable for paying the expenses of workers for health screening tests. Is this a retroactive rule?

Explanations

1. No, this rule is not retroactive. Although the rule is based on information relating to the past, the rule changes prospectively the legal requirements applicable to manufacturers. No legal consequences flow from the rule with respect to any manufacturer's past conduct.

2. Yes, this rule is retroactive. Again the rule is based on information relating to the past. Here, however, the agency's rule not only has prospective effect—prohibiting inadequate ventilation in the future—it also makes the past inadequate ventilation unlawful. The legal consequences of employers' actions taken before the rule was adopted have changed. This is retroactive and prohibited unless specifically authorized by statute. The Occupational Safety and Health Act does not authorize retroactive rules, so this rule would be invalid.

   Beyond the requirement that rules be general statements of future effect, the definition of "rule" continues with a description of the kinds of matters that rules can address. The general description that rules are "designed to implement, interpret, or prescribe law or policy" covers most cases. The further description specifies a number of particular types of rules, such as procedural rules.

   Typically, a statute creating an agency or a program will authorize or require an agency to adopt rules to carry out a program. For example, the National Traffic and Motor Vehicle Safety Act of 1966 directs the Secretary of Transportation or his or her delegate (such as NHTSA) to issue motor vehicle safety standards that shall meet the need for motor vehicle safety. Similarly, the Occupational Safety and Health Act of 1970 authorizes the Secretary of Labor to establish mandatory nationwide standards governing health and safety in the workplace. Thus, these statutes direct or authorize agencies to adopt rules prescribing law—the law governing motor vehicle safety standards, such as air bag requirements and bumper protection, and workplace safety standards, such as the permissible exposure level to a workplace chemical for workers.

   So, for most purposes, rules are general statements of future effect that are designed to implement, interpret, or prescribe law or policy.

B. Legislative and Nonlegislative Rules

Now things get a little more complex. Some rules are "law," because they have binding legal effect. For example, the motor vehicle safety standards and the workplace health and safety rules are "law." That is, just like statutes passed by Congress, these rules adopted by an agency are legally binding on persons, and in many cases violations of these rules can subject a person to civil or criminal penalty. These types of rules are known as "legislative rules," because they make law.

At the same time, some rules are not "law" in this sense. These rules merely express the agency's view as to the meaning of a statute or regulation or publicize an agency's policy on a matter. In a sense they are nothing more than a glorified press release by the agency. Nevertheless, they fall within the definition of "rule" in the APA, because they "interpret law" or "prescribe policy." These rules are known as "nonlegislative rules." An example of a nonlegislative rule is the Guidelines issued by the Equal Employment Opportunity Commission (EEOC) that interpret Title VII of the Civil Rights Act of 1964, governing discrimination in employment. These Guidelines provide employers with an understanding of how the EEOC interprets that Act and therefore what actions the agency may consider discriminatory. However, the Guidelines do not actually set the standards as to what constitutes discrimination; those standards are contained in the Act and court decisions interpreting it.

In order for an agency to adopt legislative rules, a statute must give the agency the authority to adopt such rules. An agency does not have any inherent authority by reason of being an agency to adopt legislative rules. Just as Congress derives its authority to make laws from the Constitution, agencies derive their authority to make legally binding rules from Congress. NHTSA can make legislative rules governing motor vehicle safety standards, for example, because Congress has so provided.

Nonlegislative rules, however, because they do not have legal effect, do not require statutory authorization. An agency is always free to announce what its policy is or how it interprets the law, but that announcement does not make "law."

Distinguishing between these two different types of rules is important both for the agency and the public, because the effects and adoption procedures are different; however, this can sometimes be difficult, because the two types of rules do not necessarily look different, and sometimes an agency with the authority to issue legislative rules may choose only to issue a nonlegislative rule. For example, OSHA may set a workplace safety standard in a legislative rule but decide to elaborate on its meaning in a nonlegislative rule designed to inform employers of OSHA's interpretation of the standard.

C. Rules v. Orders

Chapter 3 discussed adjudication, the agency process that concludes with the issuance of an order and that often has trial-type procedures. Agencies without rulemaking authority can only make legally effective policy through decisions in adjudications. Agencies with rulemaking authority, however, often have a choice whether they wish to make policy through adjudication or rulemaking. The National Labor Relations Board is such an agency. Even agencies that are required to use rulemaking to establish certain standards are often faced with the option of clarifying ambiguities in their rules with amendments to the rules or by decisions in adjudications. Both methods of proceeding have advantages and disadvantages to the agency.

The advantages to the agency making policy by adjudication include the fact that, like common-law courts, it is sometimes easier to see what the correct policy should be in the context of a particular fact situation, rather than trying to make a policy somewhat in the abstract without the benefit of a particular case. In addition, when the agency is the initiator of the adjudication, such as in enforcement actions, the agency can choose the best defendant—for example, the worst violator—for establishing a particular enforcement policy. Also, when an agency adjudicates a case, usually only the particular parties to the case have the opportunity to participate in the decision, rather than the public at large as is the case for rulemaking. Related to this is the fact that adjudication generally proceeds less in the public and political eye, which better insulates the agency from outside pressures to adopt a particular policy.

One of the major advantages of making policy by rulemaking is that the agency can decide an issue in one proceeding that otherwise would have to be decided repeatedly in adjudications. This is true even when a statute specifically provides for an adjudication of an issue.

Example

The Federal Communications Commission (FCC) is supposed to allocate television broadcast licenses "in the public interest." This has meant that in the licensing proceeding—an adjudication—the agency decides whether it would serve the public interest for this applicant to receive a license. The Federal Communications Act provides that if an applicant is initially denied a license because the FCC cannot find that granting a license would serve the public interest, the applicant can obtain a hearing at which it may contest that finding. To ensure competition in the television broadcasting industry, the FCC believed that it was not in the public interest for individual companies to own too many stations. For years the FCC considered in each licensing case whether, because of the other stations already owned by the applicant, it would be in the public interest to grant another license to the applicant. Then the FCC adopted a rule stating that it was not in the public interest to grant a license to anyone already owning five TV stations. Thereafter, when a company that already owned five stations sought a sixth license, the FCC denied the application on the basis of the rule without holding a hearing on whether it was in the public interest to grant the license. The company challenged the rule, arguing that the agency could not decide this issue by rule, because the statute specified that an applicant could contest a "public interest" finding in an adjudicatory hearing. The Supreme Court upheld the rule. *See United States v. Storer Broadcasting Co.*, 351 U.S. 192 (1956).

Explanation

First, the Court recognized that the Act gave the FCC general rulemaking authority. Accordingly, it could make legislative rules deciding matters of policy, such as how many stations owned by individual companies would result in excessive concentration in the industry. Second, the Court held that the statutory right of persons denied licenses to have an adjudicatory hearing to contest a finding, despite the statute's apparent unqualified statement of that right, did not apply when there was essentially nothing for the adjudication to decide. One did not have a right to a hearing if there was nothing to be heard. Third, the Court held that the agency's rule had the effect of deciding the issue as to how many stations were too many, so that all the adjudication could do would be to apply the rule. Adjudications cannot overrule rules; they can only apply them.

As may be imagined, this principle can be used in a number of circumstances to limit what might be contested in adjudicatory hearings. Thus, in one rulemaking proceeding the agency can eliminate the need to consider an issue in all subsequent cases. This can both save time and resources that might be used in multiple adjudications of the issue and ensure consistent resolutions of questions likely to be repeated. This consistency, however, comes at the price of a lack of individuated consideration. For this reason, the agency often provides in such rules for exceptions. This leaves the agency with the option of making an exception to the rule when it is deemed appropriate, without requiring it to consider the issue as a routine matter.

Another advantage of rulemaking, at least historically, was that the procedures for informal rulemaking, by which almost all legislative rules are made, were much less formal than those applicable to adjudication, so that rulemaking could be done more quickly and cheaply.

Finally, rulemaking is advantageous to the agency because it establishes "law," not just precedent. A legislative rule, like a statute, becomes binding, enforceable law. Orders, however, legally bind only the parties to the particular proceeding in which the order is issued. For the rest of the world the orders become precedent, which the agency may cite in the future, but like judicial precedent it is less strictly binding than legislative rules. A party to a subsequent adjudication can always raise the validity of the precedent being employed in the case, but a party in an administrative adjudication cannot raise the validity of a legislative rule being applied in the adjudication, which is "law" binding the adjudicator.

While the advantages and disadvantages of rulemaking and adjudication result in some agencies generally using adjudication for making policy (e.g., the NLRB) and some agencies eschewing adjudication for policy making (e.g., OSHA), depending upon their experience and circumstances, courts have generally expressed a preference for making policy by rulemaking. The apparent appropriateness of making policies applicable to the public through a public process, the seeming benefit to the agency of input and comment from a wider range of persons, and the prospective nature of rules (as opposed to the retrospective effect of policy made through adjudication) have led courts to suggest, sometimes rather strongly, that agencies should generally make policy through rulemaking. Despite these judicial statements of preference, however, it is black-letter law that the decision whether to make policy by adjudication or rulemaking, assuming the agency has the statutory authority to use either, is a decision to be made by the agency in its informed discretion. *See Securities & Exchange Commission v. Chenery Corp.*, 332 U.S. 194 (1947). Although, at least theoretically, this discretion could be abused, resulting in a court overturning the agency's decision, there are no Supreme Court cases and only one circuit court decision reversing an agency's decision whether to make policy through rulemaking or adjudication. *See Ford Motor Co. v. FTC*, 673 F.2d 1008 (9th Cir. 1981).

II. BEGINNING RULEMAKING

Statutes often require agencies to adopt rules implementing programs. It is not unusual for the statute to specify a date by which the rules must be adopted, often speaking in terms of days or months following the passage of the statute or some other triggering event. For example, the Noise Control Act of 1972 required the Administrator of the EPA to adopt regulations "not later than 24 months after October 27, 1972," the date on which the Act became law. Sometimes the deadlines are quite short. For example, the Secretary of Housing and Urban Development was required to adopt regulations to implement certain amendments to public housing programs within 30 days of the passage of the amendments.

Agencies, however, are notorious for not complying with statutory deadlines for adopting rules. Sometimes the deadlines are simply too short; either the problems involved in deciding what the regulations should provide were more difficult than originally envisioned, or Congress simply set a wholly unrealistic deadline. Other times the agency's priorities are different from those suggested by a particular statutory deadline, and the agency does not devote necessary resources to fulfilling the statutory deadline. Typically, when Congress adopts legislation requiring agencies to adopt regulations, it does not at the same time provide additional funds to the agency to cope with this new workload. Moreover, the agency may receive informal signals from congressional committees with oversight or fiscal responsibility for the agency indicating that the committees do not view meeting the deadline as important.

Obviously, if an agency does not meet a statutory deadline for adopting a rule, it is violating the law that set the deadline. However, rarely does the statute setting the deadline contain any sanction for not meeting the deadline. This lack of "punishment" is another reason why agencies do not place a higher priority on meeting statutory deadlines. Finally, although someone who is injured by the failure of an agency to meet a deadline may sue the agency for violating the law, a court is not able to make the agency comply with the law (the deadline already having been missed) and is only able to order the agency to act as expeditiously as is reasonable.

While Congress often sets a statutory deadline for required rules, more often it does not. Instead, it simply requires the agency to adopt rules in certain circumstances or to meet certain needs. For example, the National Highway Traffic Safety Act requires the Secretary of Transportation simply to adopt motor vehicle safety standards (which are rules) "to reduce traffic accidents and deaths and injuries resulting from traffic accidents." That is, the Act *requires* the Secretary to adopt rules when he or she believes it would reduce traffic accidents and deaths and injuries resulting from such accidents, or in other words when the Secretary determines some rules are appropriate to achieve that end. Sometimes Congress merely *authorizes* an agency to adopt rules, rather than requiring it to adopt rules. For example, the Federal Trade Commission Act, as amended, authorizes the Federal Trade Commission (FTC) to adopt rules "which define with specificity acts or practices which are unfair or deceptive acts or practices in or affecting commerce." Thus, if the Commission believes certain acts or practices are unfair or deceptive acts or practices in or affecting commerce, it may adopt rules to prohibit them.

In the vast majority of rulemakings, the agency undertakes a rulemaking because of a statutory command compelling the rulemaking or because of internal agency determinations that a rulemaking is appropriate under one of the agency's statutory authorizations. Often, however, these internal agency deliberations are influenced by actions of those outside the agency. For example, the President may declare a new initiative or policy for his administration that suggests strongly that the agency adopt one or more rules. Or Congress holds hearings on a subject with the result that the agency feels substantial political pressure to adopt one or more rules. In addition, private or "public interest" groups may lobby an agency to adopt a rule the group desires.

Finally, the APA requires that agencies provide a person "the right to petition for the issuance, amendment, or repeal of a rule." *See* 5 U.S.C. § 553(e). Accordingly, when a person wants an agency to adopt a rule, and the informal means of influencing the agency in that direction have not succeeded, the person may file a petition with the agency asking it to adopt the rule. Of course, an agency that has not shown any interest in adopting a rule before receiving a petition for rulemaking is unlikely to change its mind merely because someone has petitioned for it. Nevertheless, another section of the APA, 5 U.S.C. § 555(e), has been interpreted as requiring an agency at least to respond to the petition in a timely fashion. *See Auer v. Robbins*, 519 U.S. 452, 459 (1997). Then, if the agency does reject the petition, the rejection is judicially reviewable, and the person bringing the action at least has a chance to prove that the agency's failure to engage in rulemaking was unreasonable.

III. RULEMAKING PROCEDURES

The APA in essence provides three different procedures for rulemaking. One, usually called "Formal Rulemaking," is rarely used today, although it was the dominant form of rulemaking when the APA was passed. Generally speaking, the procedure for Formal Rulemaking is similar to the procedure for APA, or formal, adjudication. That is, it is a trial-type procedure governed by Sections 556 and 557 of the APA. A second procedure is called "Notice-and-Comment Rulemaking" or "Informal Rulemaking."[3] This is the predominant method of rulemaking under the APA. In a sentence, the agency gives notice of the rulemaking to the public, accepts comments from the public about the proposed rule, and after consideration of the comments provides an explanation of the basis and purpose of the rule when it adopts the final rule. *See* 5 U.S.C. § 553. It has become the model procedure for many agency actions. For example, the procedure under the National Environmental Policy Act by which Environmental Impact Analyses are conducted is copied from Notice-and-Comment Rulemaking. Any rule not required to be adopted either through Formal Rulemaking or Notice-and-Comment Rulemaking

3. Unfortunately for those trying to learn the basics of administrative law, courts sometimes refer to Notice-and-Comment Rulemaking pursuant to the APA as "formal rulemaking," to distinguish it from rules that are exempt from the APA's notice-and-comment procedure and thus adopted without any particular procedure.

is subject only to the requirement that the final rule be published in the Federal Register.[4] *See* 5 U.S.C. § 552(a)(1).

While the APA provides the fundamental procedures applicable to rulemaking generally, it is not the only statute that provides general requirements. For example, the National Environmental Policy Act requires additional procedures to those in the APA if a rule would have a significant effect on the environment, and the Regulatory Flexibility Act requires additional procedures if a rule would have a significant effect on small businesses. In addition, many statutes require particular procedures applicable to rules adopted under those statutes. For example, the Department of Energy Organization Act adds a number of procedural requirements to rulemaking by the Department of Energy beyond those required by the APA, *see* 42 U.S.C. § 7191, and the Clean Air Act contains specific procedures applicable to most rules adopted under that Act, *see* 42 U.S.C. § 7607. Executive Order 12866 requires executive agencies to follow certain additional procedures if the rule will have more than $100 million impact on the economy. In fact, today probably most rulemakings are subject not only to the APA but also to one or more other procedural requirements. We refer to rulemaking under these other, additional requirements as "Hybrid Rulemaking," because they generally mix both the requirements of the APA's Notice-and-Comment Rulemaking and other procedural requirements.

Administrative law courses usually focus on the APA requirements but discuss some of the other hybrid requirements as well.

State Administrative Procedure Acts differ somewhat from the federal APA with respect to rulemaking inasmuch as states generally do not have a category of rulemaking equivalent to Formal Rulemaking. They utilize Notice-and-Comment Rulemaking exclusively, except for those rules exempt or excepted from its requirements, which like equivalent federal rules are subject only to a publication requirement. In the states, however, there are generally fewer exceptions from Notice-and-Comment Rulemaking than under the federal APA. As a result, some rules that under the federal APA would only need to be published in the Federal Register must go through notice and comment under the state APA.

4. The Federal Register is a daily publication of the Office of the Federal Register of the National Archives and Record Administration, which is intended to provide a uniform system for making available to the public regulations and legal notices issued by federal agencies, as well as Proclamations and Orders by the President. It is also available online at https://www.govinfo.gov/app/frtoc/today.

A. Rules Exempt from Section 553

Subsection (a) of Section 553, the Rulemaking Section of the APA, states that the section does not apply to rulemaking involving two different types of functions: rules involving the military or foreign affairs function of the United States; and rules involving matters relating to agency management or personnel, public property, loans, grants, benefits, and contracts. Thus, if a rule is not subject to Section 553 (and is not subject to some other specific rulemaking requirement), the only requirement is that the rule be published in the Federal Register. 5 U.S.C. § 552(a)(1).

1. The Military and Foreign Affairs Exemption

The exemption for rules involving the military and foreign affairs function has been explained as being based on a desire not to impede military operations or to interfere with the United States' conduct of foreign relations by subjecting decisions in these areas to the publicity and open dialogue otherwise applicable to rulemaking. Some matters clearly are within this exemption, such as rules governing the activities of uniformed members of the armed services and rules implementing international agreements. And some matters that are arguably within the language of the exception are nevertheless pretty clearly *not* within the exemption, such as Department of Defense regulation of civilian workers in non-combat situations, and State Department regulations involving U.S. passports. Consistent with the legislative history of the APA, courts have said that this exemption is not to be loosely interpreted. Rather, it is to be applied only as necessary to serve its purposes. One area in particular has caused problems: immigration.

Example

Under the immigration laws, if an alien is found in the United States illegally, often he or she is allowed to depart voluntarily, rather than be deported. Aliens prefer voluntary departure because it does not prejudice them to later lawful re-entry, while a deportation would. In 1979, American diplomats in Iran were seized and held hostage. In retaliation, the United States suspended diplomatic relations with Iran and took other actions in the domestic and international arena designed to pressure Iran into releasing the hostages. One of the actions was for the Immigration and Naturalization Service to adopt a rule limiting to 15 days, rather than the normal 90 days, the period in which Iranian nationals would have to complete their voluntary departure in lieu of deportation. The INS did not go through notice and comment in adopting the rule. The courts uniformly upheld this action as being within the foreign affairs exemption to Section 553. *See, e.g., Nademi v. INS*, 679 F.2d 811 (10th Cir. 1982).

Explanation

This rule was expressly adopted as part of a series of actions intended to be an expression of our foreign policy adopted by the President. Thus, the rule merely implemented our foreign policy. To submit such a rule to notice and comment might have suggested that the President and the nation were not committed to taking this action with respect to Iran; it would suggest indecision and lack of dedication. This would embarrass the United States and interfere with the successful execution of our foreign affairs; hence it should not be subject to notice and comment.

Example

Ordinarily, in order to obtain political asylum in the United States an alien must establish that he or she has a well-founded fear of persecution on account of race, religion, nationality, membership in a particular social group, or political opinion. In 1989, following the events in Tiananmen Square in China, both houses of Congress passed a bill providing in essence that any Chinese alien seeking refugee status in the United States on the basis of having refused an order for sterilization or abortion should be granted asylum. However, the President vetoed the bill, saying that he could accomplish the same end through executive action. Thereafter, the Attorney General adopted a rule, without going through notice and comment, which stated that aliens who have a well-founded fear that they will be required to abort a pregnancy or to be sterilized because of their country's family planning policies may be granted asylum. The two courts to consider this rule found that it was invalid, because it had not gone through notice and comment and the exemption for foreign affairs did not apply.

Explanation

There appear to be a number of similarities between this example and the previous one, and yet the courts reached different conclusions. Here the courts found there was no evidence that following the APA would embarrass the United States or interfere with our execution of foreign affairs. The rule to allow asylum on the basis of a fear of forced sterilization or abortion was not adopted as part of a foreign policy initiative by the United States to pressure China into changing its policy. While some may have viewed it in that way, the Attorney General did not explain the rule in that manner. Rather, the rule was explained as simply making it easier for persons to receive asylum status. Thus, the focus of the rule was on our asylum policy, which only indirectly related to our foreign affairs. In order to invoke the exception, courts have said that there should be evidence that the public rulemaking provisions would provoke definitely undesirable international consequences. The asylum policy change rule would not have had those consequences, whereas the Iranian rule arguably would have. There is also a suggestion in this case that because immigration rules all implicate foreign affairs somewhat, but there is general agreement that immigration rules do not as a general matter fall under the foreign affairs exemption, exemptions should only be found in extraordinary situations. Certainly, the Iranian hostage crisis and the reactions to it would qualify in that regard. *See Zhang v. Slattery*, 55 F.3d 732 (2d Cir. 1995).

2. The Exemption for Matters Involving Agency Management or Personnel, Public Property, Loans, Grants, Benefits, and Contracts

This exemption on its face is exceedingly broad. It would mean that Section 553 would not apply to any rulemaking involving Social Security or Medicare (public benefits), the U.S. Forest Service, Bureau of Land Management, or the Park Service (public property), subsidized housing (public loans), funding for research and the arts (public grants), or any government contracts. Much of the rulemaking today is in these areas, and it involves issues of great importance to the public. One might ask why the APA exempted such rules from the basic rulemaking requirements of Section 553.

The answer is that when the APA was passed, concern with the administrative process was expressed most vociferously by those economic actors subject to government regulation. In their view, their liberty and property should not be restricted without more procedures adequate to assure fairness and accuracy. In rulemaking this resulted in procedural requirements when rules would act as law to regulate their activities. At the same time, agencies, which opposed the APA, did not want procedures to interfere with their activities. The compromise was to exempt from Section 553 those rulemakings that did not involve regulating private behavior, leaving rules governing agencies and voluntary transactions with agencies subject to whatever procedures the agency might give.

Starting in the 1960s, however, there was increased recognition that important public policies were being determined in these rulemakings without any requirement for public participation and involvement. The Administrative Conference of the United States, a government agency that studies the administrative process government-wide, recommended that these exemptions largely be repealed by Congress and urged that agencies voluntarily waive the exemption in the absence of legislation.

Many agencies, probably to forestall legislation, adopted rules voluntarily waiving in whole or in part their exemption from Section 553. Among these were the Departments of Housing and Urban Development, Health and Human Services, Transportation, Interior, Agriculture, and Labor. The effect of this waiver was to subject these agencies' rulemakings to the requirements of Section 553, just as if there were no exemption. Some agencies thought that because they had voluntarily waived the exemption, they could invoke it again when they pleased. Courts uniformly held that, while agencies had the power to repeal the rules waiving their exemptions, so long as their rules waiving the exemption remained in place, the agencies were bound by them. *See, e.g.*, *Batterton v. Marshall*, 648 F.2d 694, 700 (D.C. Cir. 1980). This reflects one of the bedrock administrative law rules: *agencies are bound by their own regulations*.

While showing no interest in amending the exemption provision of the APA, Congress has effectively revoked one or more of the exemptions for various agencies from time to time. For example, the Department of Energy Organization Act eliminated the exemption for public property, loans, grants, and contracts for that agency. The Civil Service Reform Act eliminated the exemption for agency management and personnel rules with respect to the Office of Personnel Management's government-wide personnel regulations. A 1984 amendment to the Social Security Act requires that regulations establishing the standards for Social Security Disability determinations be subject to Section 553.

What this means for a lawyer is that he or she cannot rely on the fact that there is an exemption in Section 553 for certain types of rules. The lawyer must also establish what other statutes may say on the subject and what the agency's regulations may say.

Although much of Section 553(a)'s broad exemption has been cut back by particular statutes and regulations, there are still a number of situations in which the exemption can apply. If an exemption has not been waived by an agency or overridden by another statute, it applies so long as the rulemaking "clearly and directly" involves one of the exempted subjects.

Example

The National Park Service adopts a rule without any public procedure governing the permit process for cruise ships entering national parks, and a cruise ship line challenges the rule as violating Section 553's requirement for notice and comment. The court upholds the rule. *See Clipper Cruise Line, Inc. v. United States*, 855 F. Supp. 1 (D.D.C. 1994).

Explanation

Although the rule affects what a private economic actor can do (bringing cruise ships into national parks) and obviously has an impact on important public interests (such as the environmental effects of cruise ships in national parks and the policy regarding the proper utilization of national parks), the rule clearly and directly involves the use of public property. Consequently, absent any waiver or statutory override of the Section 553(a) exemption, the rule is exempt from Section 553's requirements.

B. Rules Excepted from Section 553's Notice-and-Comment Requirements

The previous exemptions applied to all of Section 553. Section 553(b), however, creates two additional categories of exceptions specifically from Section 553's notice-and-comment requirements:

(1) interpretative[5] rules, general statements of policy, and rules of agency organization, procedure, and practice; and
(2) rules when the agency finds for good cause that notice and public procedure are impracticable, unnecessary, or contrary to the public interest.

Section 553(b) itself only excepts these rules from the notice requirement, but Section 553(c), which requires agencies to give persons an opportunity to comment, only applies "after notice required by this section." Thus, if notice is not required because of one of the Section 553(b) exceptions, there is likewise no requirement to provide an opportunity for public comment.

The theories behind these exceptions differ. The exception for interpretative rules, general statements of policy, and rules of agency organization is justified on the basis that these rules do not have binding legal effect on the primary conduct of the public. They are not "legislative rules." They are more in the nature of formalized press releases by the agency merely informing the public of internal agency views — how the agency interprets a statute or other rule, what the agency's policy is as to a given matter, and how the agency organizes its business. Moreover, it is in the public's interest to know what the agency is thinking, so the law should

5. This is the term used in the APA, although some dictionaries do not even recognize the word. The more common word is "interpretive," which means exactly the same thing. Courts use the terms interchangeably.

not create procedural obstacles before agencies can inform the public. This theory is fine as far as it goes, but it ignores the often extreme practical, if not legal, effect of agency interpretations and general statements of policy. As we will see in Chapter 7, Judicial Review, if a court defers to an agency interpretation or policy statement as being a correct interpretation, then even the formalized press release has some sort of "legal effect," because it changes how a court views an issue. The exception for agency procedural regulations likewise is justified on the basis that they do not govern the public's primary conduct (that is, activities in the "real world" as opposed to activities in agency proceedings). However, procedural rules are legislative rules in the sense that they are law. For example, the failure of an applicant for a federal permit to comply with any pertinent procedural regulations will usually result in the agency's denial of the permit. Thus, while rules about "crossing your t's and dotting your i's" may seem trivial, they can have important effects because they establish what is legally required.

The theory behind the "good cause" exception is more apparent. If there is a good reason *not* to have public participation in the formulation of a rule, then the rule should be exempt from such participation. The only problem is determining when public rulemaking is impracticable, unnecessary, or contrary to the public interest.

Agencies generally would like to avoid the procedural requirements of Section 553, because those requirements increase the time and resources it takes to adopt a rule. Consequently, agencies have an interest in characterizing their rules as falling within the terms of these exceptions, and it is important for lawyers to be able to determine whether a rule is properly characterized as being within one of these exceptions.

1. Interpretative Rules, General Statements of Policy, and Procedural Rules

This category of exceptions can be broken down into its three different parts for better understanding.

a. Interpretative Rules

Interpretative rules, as the name suggests, interpret law. They may interpret statutes or other regulations. However, legislative rules often interpret statutes as well, and they must go through Notice-and-Comment Rulemaking, because they are intended to create legally binding norms, to make "law." Thus, the fact that a rule seems to "interpret" a statute (or a regulation) does not by itself determine whether the rule is an interpretative rule or not.

Example

EPA wants to adopt a rule under the Clean Water Act interpreting the meaning of the statutory language "waters of the United States" as applied to restrictions on filling of wetlands. The rule would state that the term "waters of the United States" (which defines the jurisdiction of EPA under the Clean Water Act) includes wetlands that potentially provide habitat to migratory birds. Is this an interpretative rule exempt from notice and comment, or is this a legislative rule required to go through notice and comment?

Explanation

We cannot tell yet. It could be either. If EPA's intent is to create "law," that is, to create a legally binding interpretation, then the rule would be legislative and would have to go through notice and comment. If EPA's intent is merely to announce what EPA thinks the statutory language means, providing guidance to persons who might be involved in filling wetlands, then the rule could be an interpretative rule exempt from notice and comment. If EPA adopts the rule as a legislative rule after notice and comment, the resulting rule will become "law," and persons will violate "the law" if they violate the regulation. If EPA adopts the rule as an interpretative rule, however, then the resulting rule is not "law," but only EPA's opinion of what the law is. A person violating the interpretative rule is not, by violating the rule itself, violating the law. Of course, if EPA is telling people what it thinks that statutory language means, *and EPA is correct as to its interpretation*, then EPA's "mere" interpretation in fact states what the law is. That is, EPA's rule reflects what the law is even if it does not make law. Thus, a person violating the interpretative rule, if the interpretation is correct, is violating the underlying law that the rule interpreted.

The difficulty in discerning between an interpretative rule that does not require notice and comment and a legislative rule that does has posed problems for courts, and the Supreme Court has not provided a definitive answer to the question how to identify an interpretative rule. As a result, there is no one good test for distinguishing between interpretative rules and legislative rules. The following describes some of the rules used by lower courts.

1. The Substantial Impact Test Prior to 1978, one line of cases had looked at each claimed interpretative rule and assessed whether it had a substantial impact on the regulated community. The courts looked to the practical effect of the rule to determine whether it had a substantial impact. If the court felt that it did, then it held that the rule required notice and comment. It was not always clear whether the court was interpreting the meaning of "interpretative rule" in Section 553 or deciding that, even if Section 553 did not require notice and comment, the court would require it as a matter of common law, because of the effect of the rule. In 1978, however, the Supreme Court decided the landmark case of Vermont Yankee Nuclear Power Corp. v. Natural Resources Defense Council, 435 U.S. 519 (1978). In that case the Court held that courts did not have the authority to require additional procedures beyond those found in the APA except as might otherwise be required by other statute or the Constitution. In short, the enactment of the APA had displaced the historic judge-made, common law of administrative procedure. Nevertheless, Vermont Yankee did not end the "substantial impact" test; instead, it transformed it to a test of what constituted an interpretative rule. That is, if a claimed interpretative rule did not have a substantial impact, it would be found to be an interpretative rule, but if it did have a substantial impact in practical terms, then the rule would be found not to be an interpretative rule.

Example

In the previous example, if EPA adopted the rule as an interpretative rule without notice and comment, the rule would not be binding on regulated entities. It would, however, still have great practical effect, because persons with wetlands that are potentially habitat for migratory birds would have to think twice about whether they could fill them without a permit under the Clean Water Act. And potential buyers might avoid purchasing such land because it might be subject to regulatory restrictions.

Explanation

Courts using the "substantial impact" test for determining whether a rule is interpretative would likely find the EPA rule not to be an interpretative rule because of its practical effect. Thus, it would be deemed invalid, because it failed to follow the required procedures—notice and comment.

2. The "Legally Binding" or "Force of Law" Test The "substantial impact" test has been criticized by commentators and several courts, and it is no longer the favored test. In its place most courts have adopted the "legally binding" or "force of law" test. In other words, if the questioned rule is legally binding on persons outside the agency, by creating rights, imposing obligations, or effecting a change in existing law, it cannot be an interpretative rule.[6] The trouble with this test is that it really just restates the conclusion that only

6. Although an interpretative rule cannot bind persons outside the agency, an agency can generally require its employees and contractors—in effect the agency—to abide by its interpretation without making the rule a legislative rule. See, e.g., Erringer v. Thompson, 371 F.3d 625, 631 (9th Cir. 2004). In some situations, however, a court might find that binding the agency will satisfy the binding effect test. See, e.g., Community Nutrition Inst. v. Young, 818 F.2d 943 (D.C. Cir. 1987).

legislative rules can be "legally binding" or have the effect of law. Moreover, if the agency is defending a rule as an interpretative rule, it always claims that the rule is not legally binding. And while a contemporaneous statement by the agency that the rule is intended to be interpretative and not legally binding may have some weight, it generally has not been found to be determinative. Instead, courts applying the "legally binding" test have looked to a number of factors to assess whether the rule really is interpretative.

a. Whether in the absence of the rule there would not be an adequate basis for enforcement action or other agency action to confer benefits or ensure the performance of duties. This factor is difficult to understand in the abstract. It refers to the concept that statutes sometimes directly create an enforceable duty or establish a right to benefits, and the agency's role could be limited to carrying out the statutory commands, which it could do even without implementing rules. Under these statutes the issuance of a non-legally binding interpretative rule does not add to the agency's legal authority. With or without the rule the agency can enforce the commands of the statute, as it interprets them. Other statutes, however, command the agency to establish the specific duty or specific qualifications for benefits. With these statutes, the agency must exercise legislative rulemaking power to establish the required legal duty or qualification. Under these statutes there is nothing to enforce or carry out with respect to the public until the agency has adopted legally binding rules. Therefore, one test to see if a rule is legislative or interpretative is to see if the agency can enforce duties or confer benefits in the absence of the questioned rule. If so, then the rule would be interpretative; if not, the rule would be an invalid legislative rule—invalid because it did not go through notice and comment.

Example

In the previous EPA example, would EPA's interpretation of "waters of the United States" as including wetlands that are potential habitat for migratory birds satisfy this factor? Yes, it would. That is, there is an adequate basis for an enforcement action in the absence of the rule.

Explanation

The Clean Water Act does not require EPA to define the ambiguous term "waters of the United States." Rather, the Act simply uses the term. In fact, the Act provides that persons filling waters of the United States without a permit violate the Act. Thus, absent any rule, legislative or interpretative, EPA would have a basis for enforcing the Act against someone it thought was violating it. Imagine that EPA never issued its interpretative rule, but agency officials believed that such wetlands were protected as waters of the United States. If a person started to fill such a wetland without a permit,

EPA could bring an enforcement action against the person, alleging that the person was violating the Act itself. If EPA is right that "waters of the United States" includes such wetlands, then the person would be violating the Act, whether or not EPA issued an interpretative rule indicating that it held such an interpretation. Consequently, when EPA does issue a rule that it claims is interpretative, announcing what it believes to be covered by the Act, that rule would meet this factor's test. Of course, this does not mean the interpretation is correct. Indeed, the Supreme Court has held that the term "waters of the United States" does not include waters merely because they provide habitat to migratory fowl. *See Solid Waste Agency of Northern Cook County v. Army Corps of Engineers*, 531 U.S. 159 (2001). Thus, this interpretative rule would be substantively invalid but not procedurally invalid. Unfortunately, courts do not always recognize this distinction.

Example

The Clean Water Act has a section aimed at protecting the waters of the United States from toxic effluents in particular. *See* 33 U.S.C. § 1317. It allows EPA to adopt a standard stricter than otherwise applicable if EPA believes a stricter standard is appropriate in light of the risk from the toxic effluent. If EPA adopted a rule without notice and comment setting a stricter effluent standard than otherwise applicable, would that rule meet the requirements of this factor? No, it would not. That is, there is not an adequate basis for enforcement in the absence of this rule.

Explanation

Here, unlike in the previous example, the Act does not directly make it unlawful to discharge a highly toxic effluent unless it meets stricter than normal standards. Rather, the Act allows EPA to create a stricter standard, the violation of which would then become a violation of the Act. But EPA must first exercise that legislative authority, through a legislative rulemaking, to create the standard before there becomes an enforceable duty on the discharger. In this example, EPA did not create a legislative rule establishing a stricter standard applicable to the toxic effluent, because it did not go through Notice-and-Comment Rulemaking. The rule that it adopted would fail this factor's test, because in the absence of the rule there would not be a basis for enforcing its command.

---

b. Whether the rule interprets a legal standard or whether it makes policy. An interpretative rule is supposed to interpret either a statute or a legislative rule; it is not supposed to make new policy. There are a number of indications suggesting an agency is interpreting something, rather than making new policy. For example, does the agency use interpretive tools? If the agency derives the meaning for its claimed interpretative rule by using traditional means of interpreting a legal document (e.g., legislative history, tools of statutory construction, grammatical inferences, etc.), this would suggest that the rule is interpretative. On the other hand, if the agency explains its rule in terms of how it will serve the general purpose of the statute or underlying regulation, then the primary thrust is on policy issues. Of course, the difficulty here is that one of the tools of statutory construction is to determine if a particular interpretation best serves the purposes of the statute, so there is some possible overlap between interpretation and policy making. If, however, the agency relies on factual information to support its conclusion that the rule supports the law's purposes, this is a further indication that the agency is making policy, rather than interpreting.

Another indication that a rule is not interpreting a legal standard but is making policy is the level of specificity of the rule compared with the standard being interpreted. For example, if a statute requires someone to file something with an agency in a reasonable period of time, and the agency issues a rule without notice and comment requiring the person to file within seven days, this would probably be considered making policy, rather than interpreting. Seven days might be *a* reasonable period of time, but it is unlikely to be the *only* reasonable period of time. Such a broad concept as "reasonable" can be applied in particular circumstances that interpret what reasonable might mean in those circumstances, but *interpreting* "reasonable" as a general matter should not result in a fixed and set number. On the other hand, it might be perfectly lawful for the agency to adopt as a legislative rule that the period to file is limited to seven days in light of the purposes of the statute and the advantages of having a clear and specified rule. Such a rule, however, would have to go through notice and comment to make that rule the law, *unless* it is a procedural rule—and this probably would be—for which there is a separate exception from notice and comment.

Example

The Animal Welfare Act requires the Department of Agriculture to set standards for the humane handling, care, treatment, and transportation of animals by dealers, including minimum requirements for handling, housing, feeding, etc. *See* 7 U.S.C. § 2143(a). Under this authority the Department of Agriculture adopts a legislative rule through notice and comment governing enclosures of animals that provides: "facilities shall be structurally sound and shall be maintained to protect the animals from injury and to contain the animals." Thereafter, the Department adopts a rule without notice and comment stating that dangerous animals must be inside a perimeter fence at least eight feet high. The Department maintains that this rule interprets the requirement to have facilities that will contain the animals. The court found that this was not an interpretative rule. *See Hoctor v. United States Dept. of Agriculture*, 82 F.3d 165, 170 (7th Cir. 1996).

Explanation

The court first said that the eight-foot-fence rule might well have been a valid legislative rule under the statute's authority to set minimum requirements for housing animals, if the rule had gone through notice and comment. Because it did not go through notice and comment, however, it could not be a valid legislative rule. The court read the legislative rule that was adopted by the Department to impose a general duty of secure containment. The decision as to eight feet, as opposed to seven and a half or eight and a half feet, however, could not be made on the basis of interpreting what is a secure containment. Such line-drawing, the court said, is uniquely legislative, not interpretive, when made on a general basis.

Example

The National Park Service adopted, after notice and comment, a legislative rule governing permits for demonstrations in national parks in the District of Columbia. That rule specified a number of limitations on permits, including length of duration, the maximum number of persons allowed, the distance from certain objects (e.g., the White House or the Vietnam Veterans Memorial). In addition, the rule also contained a section that authorized a permit to contain "additional reasonable conditions and additional time limitations, consistent with this section, in the interest of protecting park resources, the use of nearby areas by other persons, and other legitimate park value concerns." For Lafayette Park (across the street from the White House), the National Park Service announced the following additional limitation without affording notice and comment: "property may not be stored in the Park, including, but not limited to, construction materials, lumber, paint, tools, household items, food, tarps, bedding, luggage, and other personal property." The National Park Service explained that this limitation was an interpretative rule and hence did not need to go through notice and comment. The D.C. Circuit said that this limitation was not a valid interpretative rule, but an invalid legislative rule because it had not gone through notice and comment. *See United States v. Picciotto*, 875 F.2d 345 (D.C. Cir. 1989).

Explanation

The Park Service argued that the "additional" conditions and limitations provision in the original legislative rule authorized it to add any further general conditions or limitations it found reasonable without additional notice and comment, because the original provision went through notice and comment. The court, however, said that an agency cannot grant itself the power to avoid Notice-and-Comment Rulemaking by adopting a catch-all provision through Notice-and-Comment Rulemaking. In other words, again, the "law" the agency claimed to be interpreting was too broad to support the specific "interpretation" the agency gave it. Here, the term "additional 'reasonable' conditions and limitations" was too broad to mean something as specific as prohibiting food, tarps, bedding, luggage, etc. from demonstrations in Lafayette Park. Rather than interpreting the legislative rule, the agency was making policy about what it thought the additional limitations ought to be. When, as in these examples, the vague "law" being interpreted is itself a legislative rule, requiring notice and comment for further policy choices made under them creates an incentive for agencies to make clearer legislative rules in the first place. If courts were willing to accept such choices as interpretative rules, agencies could avoid public input on important policy choices by adopting only the vaguest legislative rules and then fleshing them out through so-called interpretative rules.

---

c. If the agency is interpreting a legislative rule, whether the claimed interpretative rule is consistent with the legislative rule it is supposedly interpreting. If an interpretative rule is inconsistent with the legislative rule it is supposedly interpreting, it cannot be accurately interpreting the rule. One possible response a court might make to such a circumstance would be to say that the rule is an interpretative rule, but it is invalid because it does not accurately interpret the legislative rule. In other words, the court would not be finding that the rule was invalid for procedural reasons—failure to use notice-and-comment procedures—but for substantive reasons. Another possible response, however, is to say that the rule is procedurally invalid for not going through notice and comment, because only if it went through notice and comment and became a legislative rule would it be able to amend or change the legislative rule with which it is inconsistent.

Example

The Department of Interior leases federal lands for oil exploration and development. In return, oil companies must pay royalties to the federal government on oil taken from federal lands. The Department has regulations (legislative rules) that govern the calculation of those royalties. At one point those regulations stated that the Department would consider a number of factors in arriving at the value of the oil produced to determine the royalties. Then it issued a rule without notice and comment stating that it would value production on the basis of the prices being paid on the spot market—a particular market for immediate purchase of oil, as opposed to long-term contracts. It said that it was interpreting the royalty regulations. The court held that this was an invalid legislative rule for not having gone through notice and comment. *See Phillips Petroleum Co. v. Johnson*, 22 F.3d 616 (5th Cir. 1994).

Explanation

The court said that the rule issued without notice and comment could not be an interpretative rule because it was inconsistent with the royalty regulations. Those regulations said the agency based the valuation on a number of factors, and the court believed that specifying one factor—the spot price—was inconsistent with a rule stating that the valuation would be based upon a consideration of a number of factors. In essence, the court said, the agency was simply changing the regulations without going through notice and comment. That it could not do.

---

d. Whether the agency contemporaneously indicated that it was issuing an interpretative rule. The earlier factors were determinative, meaning that whether the rule passed them determined if the rule was interpretative. There are factors, however, that are not determinative, but that can help to persuade a court whether a rule is interpretative or not. This is one of those factors. If, when an agency issues a rule, it states that the rule is interpretative, often courts will give substantial weight to that characterization. Not only may it be an accurate representation of the intent of the agency, but by announcing it as such, the agency is telling the public that the rule is not binding. On the other hand, if the agency does not say that the rule is interpretative when it is issued, then a later claim that it is interpretative may be just an excuse.

Related to this idea is simply whether the agency published the interpretative rule in the Federal Register. Although interpretative rules do not have to go through notice and comment, Section 552(a) of the APA says that they are to be published in the Federal Register. If an agency does not publish the rule in the Federal Register, it may look like the agency is doing something not quite "by the book," making suspect the agency's claim that it avoided notice and comment only because the rule was interpretative. Again, it sounds like an excuse.

e. Whether the person signing the agency document had the authority to bind the agency or make law. Some cases have considered as a factor whether the person signing the document in question had the authority to bind the agency or make law. For example, in Amoco Production Co. v. Watson, 410 F.3d 722 (D.C. Cir. 2005), the court in an opinion by then-judge John Roberts held that a letter sent by the Associate Director of the Mining and Minerals Service of the Department of Interior could not bind the Service or the department because the Associate Director had no delegated authority to make law or bind the agency. Consequently, the court found that the letter could not be a rule required to be issued after notice and comment. See also Center for Auto Safety v. NHTSA, 452 F.3d 798 (D.C. Cir. 2006).

f. Doubtful factors. From time to time courts have identified some other factors to consider that, for the most part, have been subsequently questioned, although you may see references to them.

One involves publication of the rule in the Code of Federal Regulations (CFR). The Federal Register Act describes the documents required to be published in the CFR as those agency documents having "general applicability and legal effect." Some courts have concluded that an interpretative rule should not be published in the CFR, because it is not supposed to have "legal effect." Thus, if an agency publishes a rule in the CFR, it suggests that the agency's intent is for the rule to have legal effect. Other courts have rejected (or at least severely limited the weight of) this factor, arguing that "legal effect" is not the same as "binding legal effect." Alternatively, one may argue that the Federal Register Act describes what must be published in the CFR, but it does not expressly prohibit other documents from being published there, and routinely non-legally binding documents are published in the CFR. In addition, courts have recognized the positive value of having an agency's formal statements of its interpretations published where the public may find them more easily than in some old Federal Register.

Another factor once deemed important but currently not considered so is whether the agency has adopted after notice and comment a rule like the one under consideration. For example, if an agency adopted one rule after notice and comment but did not adopt a similar one after notice and comment, one might ask why the agency acted differently. Some courts assumed that the agency believed it was required to use notice and comment in the first case and therefore its action in the second case is questionable. Other courts, however, have noted that agencies are allowed to use Notice-and-Comment Rulemaking even when it is not required, and courts should not adopt tests that penalize agencies for using Notice-and-Comment Rulemaking when not required. To require, in effect, an agency always to use Notice-and-Comment Rulemaking if it uses it once, by assuming that the agency thought its initial use was required, would create a disincentive for agencies to use Notice-and-Comment Rulemaking voluntarily.

For some time, the D.C. Circuit required agencies that had adopted an authoritative interpretation without going through notice and comment to utilize Notice-and-Comment Rulemaking to change that interpretation. In *Perez v. Mortgage Bankers Assn.*, 135 S. Ct. 1199 (2015), the Supreme Court unanimously ruled that the APA contained no such requirement, and courts had no authority to institute such a requirement on their own.

g. Conclusion. If the above seems to be a long and confusing set of factors for determining whether a rule an agency claims is interpretative really is, you should take heart in the fact that courts find this equally difficult and have characterized the distinction between interpretative and legislative rules as "fuzzy," "tenuous," "blurred," "baffling," and "enshrouded in considerable smog."[7]

b. General Statements of Policy

General statements of policy are rules; however, like interpretative rules, they do not have binding legal power and consequently do not require notice-and-comment procedures. And, again like interpretative rules, general statements of policy are often difficult to distinguish from legislative rules. Indeed, when an agency has the authority to make legislative rules, virtually any general statement of policy *could* be made into a legislative rule if notice-and-comment procedures were used. Moreover, often general statements of policy can even look like an interpretative rule, and often agencies claim both exceptions when they are challenged for not having adopted a rule after notice and comment.

While agencies may make general statements of policy to announce how they prospectively will exercise any discretionary power, there are two situations in which they are most likely to use general statements of policy. One is to indicate when the agency will take investigative or enforcement action. The other is to indicate how the agency intends to act under certain circumstances in adjudication. The agency may have either or both of two motivations for making a general statement of policy: to provide guidance to its employees or to announce its intentions to the public, especially regulated entities.

Example

Under the Federal Mine Safety and Health Act, the Secretary of Labor is responsible for setting and enforcing mine safety standards, and the Secretary has set those standards through legislative rules after Notice-and-Comment Rulemaking. Persons who operate mines ("production operators") often utilize independent contractors to perform particular functions. When there is a violation of the standards at a mine by an independent contractor,

7. See Richard J. Pierce, Jr., Distinguishing Legislative Rules from Interpretative Rules, 52 Admin. L. Rev. 547 (2000).

ordinarily the Secretary brings an action against the contractor, rather than the production operator, but sometimes the Secretary believes it is appropriate to proceed against the production operator as well. The statute and standards clearly authorize actions against either or both. In order to give guidance to production operators as to when the Secretary might proceed against them, the Secretary issued a statement of policy. It stated that:

> Enforcement action against production operators for violations involving independent contractors is ordinarily appropriate in those situations where the production operator has contributed to the existence of a violation, or the production operator's miners are exposed to the hazard, or the production operator has control over the existence of the hazard. Accordingly, as a general rule, a production operator may be properly cited for a violation involving an independent contractor: (1) when the production operator has contributed by either an act or an omission to the occurrence of a violation in the course of an independent contractor's work; or (2) when the production operator has contributed by either an act or omission to the continued existence of a violation committed by an independent contractor; or (3) when the production operator's miners are exposed to the hazard; or (4) when the production operator has control over the condition that needs abatement.

Explanation

This is an example of a general statement of policy indicating when an agency might take enforcement action against someone. It is intended both to give guidance to the agency employees responsible for bringing enforcement actions and to give notice to production operators of the Department's intent. It does not legally bind the production operator or impose any new legal duty on him. It merely informs him when the agency may proceed against him. Nevertheless, it is clear that the production operator will consider himself affected by this statement. He now should avoid these particular situations if he wishes to avoid enforcement actions. However, this policy statement does not legally restrict the agency to proceeding against the production operator *only* when these conditions are present. The agency may still proceed against the production operator in other circumstances as well. The policy statement makes clear that it only states the "general rule." *See Brock v. Cathedral Bluffs Shale Oil Co.*, 796 F.2d 533 (D.C. Cir. 1986).

Example

The Coast Guard is authorized to investigate and enforce against certain oil pollution in the waters of the United States under the Clean Water Act. To aid its officers engaged in these functions it has created a Marine Safety Manual. That Manual gives guidance as to what appropriate penalties might be for various types of pollution incidents.

Explanation

This is an example of a general statement of policy designed to provide guidance to agency personnel involved in an agency adjudication. The statute provides an upper ceiling on the amount of penalty a polluter may have to pay, but it leaves to the enforcer's discretion how much below the maximum the enforcer might seek or assess in a particular case. The Manual provides guidance to help the personnel exercise that discretion in a way that is generally consistent across the agency. While the Manual is available to the public under the Freedom of Information Act, it is not generally provided to the public, so this general statement of policy is not made to inform the public, only to help manage the agency.

As with interpretative rules, because general statements of policy may be issued without notice and comment, agencies have an incentive to save the time and resources involved in Notice-and-Comment Rulemaking by issuing rules as general statements of policy, rather than as legislative rules. While these general statements of policy cannot be used to bind persons, they may effectively coerce persons into compliance because of the fear of agency enforcement or adverse agency rulings in adjudications. Or they may provide assurance of a relatively safe harbor from enforcement to persons if they take certain actions. Thus, to an agency, if persons act on the basis of the general statements of policy, they may be almost as effective in fact as legislative rules. In fact, they may even be better than legislative rules in one regard; as we will see in the next chapter on judicial review, many courts are reluctant to review general statements of policy until after they have been applied, whereas generally the same courts would be willing to review the rule if it was legislative.

Example

Under the Clean Water Act, the U.S. Army Corps of Engineers is responsible for issuing permits to persons for adding dredged or fill material to waters of the United States, which includes certain wetlands. The Corps might issue a general statement of policy that it generally intends to grant permits to persons who want to fill wetlands if they undertake to restore wetlands twice the size of the area filled. However, the policy statement also says that a person may also obtain a permit if the person can convince the Corps that wetlands values will otherwise be preserved or restored.

A person who wants to fill a wetland and needs a permit will read this general statement of policy and understand that if he makes an application that includes provision for restoring twice the area filled, he is likely to obtain the permit. Perhaps the person does not believe that the Clean Water Act authorizes the Corps to make such a condition on issuing permits, but he knows that many courts are not likely to allow him to challenge the statement of policy on that ground until the agency has acted on it by denying a permit that does not comply with it. The person also realizes that if he does not make the undertaking to restore twice the fill area, while it may be possible for him to obtain a permit, it is likely to take longer and be more difficult, if he obtains it at all. As a result, he submits an application with the undertaking to restore twice the area filled, because he cannot take the chance of a substantial delay, greater cost, or a denial.

Explanation

This is an example of a general policy statement designed to announce how the agency will act in the future in adjudications. We presume at this point that the Corps has sufficient discretion under the Act and regulations to condition permits on the basis of restoring a certain amount of wetlands. Were it to issue a legislative rule *requiring* persons to restore twice the area filled in order to obtain a permit, it would have to go through Notice-and-Comment Rulemaking. Instead, it can avoid the cost and effort of Notice-and-Comment Rulemaking by announcing the policy of generally granting permits if the person agrees to restore twice the area filled. The Corps is not requiring the person to make a particular undertaking, and it holds open the possibility of obtaining a permit without the particular undertaking, so the general statement of policy does not have a binding legal effect. Nevertheless, most applicants will not run the risk of denial, so they will conform to the suggestion of undertaking to restore twice the area filled.

Note that even if the Corps does not have sufficient discretion under the Act to make this condition, but it issues this general statement of policy anyway, pursuant to the ripeness doctrine (explained in Chapter 6, The Availability of Judicial Review) it is possible that courts would not review it at this time, preferring to wait until the agency has actually denied a permit for failure to meet this condition. Knowing this, most applicants are likely to comply, even if they believe they might prevail in a challenge to a denial of a permit, because they cannot afford the risk of delay or ultimate denial.

Because agencies have a substantial incentive to avoid issuing legislative rules and try to achieve the same objective through the use of general statements of policy, courts have been vigilant in attempting to assure that agencies do not misuse the exception for general statements of policy. There is one agreed-upon test for whether a rule is a general statement of policy or a legislative rule: whether the rule creates a binding legal norm. This is the equivalent of the binding legal effect test used by most courts to distinguish between interpretative rules and legislative rules. Thus, many of the factors used for assessing whether there is a binding legal effect in purported interpretative rules are also used to determine if a purported policy statement actually has binding legal effect. In addition, however, there is an additional test by which courts assess whether a purported policy statement is really a legislative rule.

Courts look for evidence that the agency will not use the general statement of policy to *decide* future cases. It is allowed to influence future cases, but not to decide them. If the policy statement in effect decides future cases, then it is almost indistinguishable from a legislative rule that would legally decide future cases. Therefore, courts look for evidence that the agency's statement is tentative, not a finally decided matter, and that it is open to reconsideration.

Example

In the previous example, if the Corps' general statement of policy had said that it intended to grant permits only when applicants undertook to restore twice the area filled, and it thereafter denied a permit application, simply saying that the applicant had not agreed to restore twice the area filled, a court would probably consider the twice-the-area-filled "policy" to be a legal requirement and therefore invalid because it did not go through Notice-and-Comment Rulemaking.

Explanation

In the previous example, the Corps' general statement of policy indicated tentativeness by saying that "generally" it would grant permits if there was an undertaking to restore twice the filled area, but it also indicated that other showings could result in granting a permit. The suggestion of this language was that its new policy did not decide future cases. The change in language and the subsequent action in this example together would likely convince a court that the agency's alleged general statement was really an attempt to impose a new binding norm on regulated entities. There is no indication in the statement that it is a tentative determination or that any other possible approach is possible. Moreover, subsequently, the agency acts consistently with the perception that it has decided that all permits must be conditioned on restoring twice the area filled. It is possible that a change in just the language alone, eliminating any mention of possible alternatives to the need to restore twice the filled area, might be enough to convince a court that the statement effectively creates a legally binding norm, because it would suggest that there would be only one way to obtain a permit. Even absent a change in the language, so that the policy statement continued to hold out the possibility of alternative ways of obtaining a permit, if the Corps denied a permit simply by referring to the lack of an undertaking to restore twice the filled area, it is possible that a court might find the action more convincing as to the agency's actual intent than the words of the policy statement.

Courts have used the same vigilance when assessing alleged general statements of policy regarding when to initiate investigations or enforcement. For example, in a celebrated case, the Food and Drug Administration issued what it called a general statement of policy indicating that it would not take enforcement action with respect to food contamination unless the contamination exceeded certain "action levels." The D.C. Circuit found this to establish a binding legal norm, in the sense that it effectively made contamination below the action levels lawful. There was no evidence it was a tentative decision or that the agency might not always follow the policy, so it seemed to finally decide the issue. *See Community Nutrition Institute v. Young*, 818 F.2d 943 (D.C. Cir. 1987). This case has been heavily criticized, for it has resulted in agencies publishing enforcement policies with elaborate caveats that it is tentative, may change at any time, may not be followed in any particular case, and should not be relied upon. Taken at face value these policy statements then become useless; they do not communicate any intention at all. As a practical matter, however, the agency "winks"; that is, it is understood that, actually, you can rely on the policy statement and avoid enforcement if you act in conformance with the policy statement.

Courts have also struck down statements of policy that attempted to coerce regulated entities into actions the agencies could not mandate through legislative rules. In *Chamber of Commerce of the United States v. U.S. Dept. of Labor*, 174 F.3d 206 (D.C. Cir. 1999), OSHA had issued an alleged general statement of policy in which it stated that it would not inspect workplaces as often or as thoroughly if the employer adopted a workplace safety plan that exceeded federal requirements in certain specified ways. OSHA clearly could not have mandated this new workplace safety plan, but presumably it could have exercised its prosecutorial discretion in determining which places to inspect, and how thoroughly, to give a break to an employer that on its own adopted a workplace safety plan more protective than required by regulation. Because of the costs and burdens associated with OSHA inspections, the offer to reduce those inspections exercised substantial coercive power on employers to adopt these workplace safety plans. The court found this to exceed the agency's power to adopt statements of policy.

A last problem with respect to statements of policy is the extent to which they may bind agency employees, as opposed to the agency itself. That is, the agency decision makers may in fact be tentative about the new policy and be fully willing to reconsider it in a subsequent case, but they still may wish to assure that lower employees follow the policy until the agency decision makers have an opportunity to reconsider it. For the most part, courts have not distinguished between general statements of policy that bind only agency employees and those that are viewed as binding the agency itself, viewing both as impermissible in general statements of policy. This has been criticized by some commentators, *see, e.g.*, Kenneth Culp Davis & Richard J. Pierce, Jr., *Administrative Law Treatise* (3d ed.) 232-233 (1994), and it creates a conflict with the general understanding with respect to interpretative rules, which the agency may use to bind agency employees, *see, e.g., Splane v. West*, 216 F.3d 1058 (Fed. Cir. 2000); *Warder v. Shalala*, 149 F.3d 73 (1st Cir. 1998).

c. Rules of Agency Organization, Procedure, or Practice

While the APA phrases this exception in terms of an agency's rules of "agency organization, procedure, or practice," as a practical matter the issue is always phrased in terms of "procedural rules." Procedural rules, unlike interpretative rules and general statements of policy, are "law." They are legally binding. If a procedural rule says a permit application has to be filed in duplicate, and an applicant files only a single copy, that is grounds for denying the permit. The theory behind excepting such rules from notice-and-comment requirements is that these rules, even if they are legally binding, do not govern the primary conduct of the regulated public. Rules that govern the primary conduct of persons, such as health and safety standards, are labeled substantive rules.

Procedural rules often prescribe the procedures applicable to adjudications. For example, the agency may (and usually does) adopt procedures describing how APA adjudications will take place. Sometimes these rules look a lot like the Federal Rules of Civil Procedure or the Federal Rules of Evidence. Agencies often also publish procedures governing their non-APA adjudications. *See, e.g.*, 40 C.F.R. pt. 22—Consolidated EPA Rules of Practice Governing the Administrative Assessment of Civil Penalties and the Revocation/Termination or Suspension of Permits. With some exceptions, there has been little problem distinguishing procedural rules from substantive rules in this context. For example, a rule mandating that applications for a license need to be filed and be complete within a specified period was deemed procedural. *See, e.g., JEM Broadcasting Co. v. FCC*, 22 F.3d 320 (D.C. Cir. 1994). On the other hand, a rule that specifies the substantive criteria an applicant needs to show in order to obtain a benefit or permit would not be a procedural rule. *See, e.g., Pickus v. U.S. Board of Parole*, 507 F.2d 1107 (D.C. Cir. 1974) (parole board's rule on what prisoners had to show in order to obtain parole was not a procedural rule). One court described procedural rules as covering agency actions that do not themselves alter the rights or interests of parties, although it may alter the manner in which parties present themselves or their viewpoints to the agency.

Agency manuals and directions for when to initiate investigations or enforcement are often characterized as procedural rules rather than as statements of policy. While loosely called "procedural rules," it would probably be more accurate to call them "rules of agency organization," because they simply organize the agency's internal operations and do not directly apply to the public at all. As such, they have often been upheld. *See, e.g., American Hospital*

Assn. v. Bowen, 834 F.2d 1037 (D.C. Cir. 1987) (Department of Health and Human Services directives spelling out when and on what basis Peer Review Organizations should initiate hospital reviews held procedural rule); *United States Dept. of Labor v. Kast Metals Corp.*, 744 F.2d 1145 (5th Cir. 1984) (OSHA calculus to determine which employers to target for inspection held procedural rule).

Discerning between procedural rules, which do not require notice and comment, and substantive, legislative rules, which do, generally is not difficult, but at the margins the difference may be hard to perceive. The attempt to find the line between procedural and substantive rules recurs throughout the law, not just in administrative law.

I. Substantial Impact Test As with interpretative rules, the substantial impact test was the primary test used for deciding whether a rule was procedural or substantive. Today it continues to be used but less widely than earlier.

Application of the test is slightly different than with respect to interpretative rules. Clearly, procedural rules can have a substantial impact on persons—as in the case of denying a license for failing to file an application within a specified time. The proper application of this test asks whether the alleged procedural rule has a substantial impact on a person's conduct outside the proceeding itself.

Example

The Department of Health and Human Services changed the method by which home health providers could obtain reimbursement for expenses under the Medicare Program. In particular it required that they submit their requests in a new format and to regional intermediaries, rather than to HHS directly. This change was not done after notice and comment, and the Department argued that the change was a procedural rule. The court held that it had a substantial impact on the home health providers and therefore was not a procedural rule.

Explanation

The court explained that the change would cause home health providers great expense and inconvenience. Nationally the costs of making billing changes and training employees to comply with the new system would range from $10 million to $30 million. *See National Assn. of Home Health Agencies v. Schweiker*, 690 F.2d 932 (D.C. Cir. 1982).

Example

OSHA adopted a plan for deciding in what priority it should inspect workplaces for health and safety requirements. The plan described the steps agency employees should follow and the criteria they should apply in selecting workplace establishments for inspection pursuant to the Occupational Safety and Health Act. An employer, selected under this plan, argued that the plan was invalid for not having gone through notice and comment. It claimed that OSHA inspections imposed costs and inconvenience on employers and so the rule had a substantial impact on employers. The court held, however, that there was no substantial impact on employers, and the rule was properly a procedural rule.

Explanation

There is no doubt that OSHA inspections impose costs and inconvenience on employers. However, the court found that the inspection plan did not have a substantial impact on any legitimate interest the employer had with respect to its primary conduct. That is, the inspection plan did not alter or affect the substantive workplace health and safety requirements applicable to the employer. The idea that an employer might alter its primary conduct—maintaining a healthy and safe workplace—based on inspection schedules did not receive a sympathetic ear from the court. The fact that under one inspection plan or another an employer might be more likely to escape citation was again not a legitimate interest. *See United States Dept. of Labor v. Kast Metals Corp.*, 744 F.2d 1145 (5th Cir. 1984).

Unlike the impact in the previous example, where the alleged procedural rule directly required the regulated entity to do something new—file new and different forms with a new entity—which itself increased costs and caused inconvenience, that was not the case in this example. Here the procedural rule was aimed solely at agency employees, not at anyone outside the agency. It did not require the employers to do anything different. The fact that employers might in their own interest alter their conduct to avoid the likelihood of inspection or citation was not deemed enough to constitute a substantial impact.

The outcome in *Kast Metals* has been the general rule. Manuals and plans that direct agency employees or contractors on when and how to engage in inspections, investigations, and enforcement actions have routinely been upheld as procedural rules.

2. "Encoding a Substantive Value Judgment" Test In 1987, the D.C. Circuit announced that it was changing from a substantial impact test to a new test, which it described as asking whether an agency's rule "encodes a substantive value judgment or puts a stamp of approval or disapproval on a given type of behavior." American Hospital Assn. v. Bowen, 834 F.2d 1037 (D.C. Cir. 1987). It applied this test to a directive of the Department of Health and Human Services (HHS) that instructed Peer Review Organizations (PROs) (contractors who perform auditing and investigational services for HHS under the Medicare Program) how to determine which hospitals should be selected for 100 percent review of their admissions. The directive told PROs that they should make a 5 percent sample of admissions of all hospitals, and when a sample showed that a hospital had a "significant pattern" of unnecessary admissions, the PRO should then make a 100 percent review of all admissions to the hospital. While under the Kast Metals analysis this directive would likely be found not to have a substantial impact, the D.C. Circuit asked instead whether the directive sent any new message to hospitals as to what they should do. Existing regulations already provided that only necessary admissions were entitled to cost recovery. The directive did not attempt to define what unnecessary admissions were, which would be a substantive standard. Nor did the directive establish any presumption of invalidity based upon a sample, such as concluding that when a sample showed a significant pattern of unnecessary admissions, HHS would presume that all admissions had the same pattern. The court said that establishing such a presumption would be a substantive rule. All the directive did was to focus HHS's inspections in ways likely to be most productive. As a result, the court found that the directive did not encode a value judgment or put a stamp of disapproval on any given type of behavior.

The D.C. Circuit's new standard has not been expressly adopted in other circuits, nor has it resulted in a more consistent line of cases in the D.C. Circuit itself. It reflects, however, another attempt to articulate a principle between substantive and procedural rules.

2. When the Agency Finds for Good Cause That Notice and Public Procedures Are Impracticable, Unnecessary, or Contrary to the Public Interest

This exception from the normal requirement for Notice-and-Comment Rulemaking contains both a substantive and a procedural component. First, as a substantive matter, the APA requires the agency to find that there is a good reason (or "good cause") not to provide notice and opportunity for public participation because to do so would be either impracticable, unnecessary, or contrary to the public interest. Second, as a procedural matter, the APA requires that the agency put this finding and the reasons for it into the rule when it is adopted. In practice, this means that when the agency publishes the rule in the Federal Register, it includes the finding of good cause and reasons for it in the preamble to the rule. If the agency fails to comply with this procedural requirement, the rule will not qualify for this exception.

As with all the exceptions to notice and comment, courts have routinely held that this exception is to be narrowly construed. This is especially important with regard to this exception because an agency's incentives for avoiding notice and comment may well color its view of whether there is a need for notice and public participation. Typically a court will judge the adequacy of the agency's finding by reading its statement of reasons critically. Thus, there is no particular "test" applicable to this exception.

Clearly, a true emergency requiring immediate government action would provide good cause for finding that notice and public participation are contrary to the public interest. However, the fact that a statute requires an agency to adopt a rule by a particular date, which could not be met if the agency uses Notice-and-Comment Rulemaking, is not sufficient to find notice and public participation impracticable or contrary to the public interest. In a number of cases agencies waited until the last minute to adopt a rule required to be adopted by a certain date and invoked the good cause exception for avoiding notice and comment. Courts did not approve of this procedure.

In recent years, especially when agencies have been faced with difficult-to-meet statutory deadlines, agencies claimed good cause and adopted without notice and comment what they called "interim final rules." The agencies then invited public comment on these rules and promised to make changes in light of the comments, if convinced the changes were appropriate. In other words, the agencies were providing after-the-fact public participation in lieu of normal Notice-and-Comment Rulemaking. If an agency could not otherwise meet the good cause exception's requirements, courts generally did not accept this after-the-fact public participation to excuse the agency's failure to provide prior notice and public participation. The courts believed that agencies, having adopted a particular rule, would be less likely to be open to comments to change or to rethink its position. However, in close cases, the agency's attempt to provide some form of public participation may influence a court to accept the good cause claim.

The fact that the public's health and safety may be involved is not itself sufficient to make notice and public participation contrary to the public interest. Public participation may delay the adoption of a rule intended to protect public health or safety, but courts uniformly have not accepted such normal rulemaking delay as good cause merely because the rule addresses health and safety issues. If, however, the rule addresses a particular public health or safety crisis, courts are more likely to accept a good cause claim. For example, the Federal Aviation Administration was able to adopt emergency security procedures for airports after receiving intelligence information concerning planned terrorist activities.

Sometimes merely to announce that an agency is considering a particular rule may interfere with accomplishing the rule's goals. For example, if an agency with authority to impose price controls fears that prices are rising too swiftly, it might want to temporarily freeze prices, but if it announced that it was considering such a step, the announcement would trigger an immediate jump in prices as sellers sought to beat the freeze. This would be an example of where notice and public participation would be impracticable or contrary to the public interest.

Some rules that agencies adopt are purely ministerial. Notice and public participation on these rules is unnecessary. For example, a statute may provide that the civil penalties payable for violations of a certain act be adjusted annually by a specified measure of inflation and that an agency provide by regulation what the new civil penalty amount is. The rule specifying the inflation-adjusted civil penalties should qualify for this exception because notice and public participation are unnecessary. The statute specifies the formula the agency must use, and the agency merely carries out the statutory command. There is little or no discretion to be exercised. In this circumstance there is no role for public participation. The agency cannot change what the statute commands it to do no matter what comments or input it receives from the public.

When agencies adopt rules, there are often typographical or editorial errors in the rules. Corrections of these errors must be by rule, but the corrections usually do not raise new issues or concerns beyond what was addressed in the original rule and are not important enough to justify a further round of notice and comment. These too would qualify for the exception for rules where notice and public participation are unnecessary. And there may be other rules that the agency honestly believes are so unimportant or uncontroversial that no one is really interested in commenting on them. The agency may find notice and public participation unnecessary because of lack of public interest in these cases. If the agency is right that no one cares, and no one complains, then its finding was appropriate. However, if the agency misjudges the lack of interest in the rule and someone complains, then the complaint alone is likely to impeach the agency's finding of lack of interest. The Environmental Protection Agency initiated what is known as "direct final rulemaking" to address this situation. The agency issues the rule without providing prior notice and comment, invoking the "unnecessary" good cause exception but saying that the rule will go into effect after 30 days only if no adverse comment is received. If any adverse comment is received, the rule will be withdrawn and reissued as a notice of proposed rulemaking and go through notice-and-comment procedures.

C. The Procedures for Formal Rulemaking

If no exception applies, a rule as defined by the APA must go through either Notice-and-Comment Rulemaking or what is known as Formal Rulemaking.[8]

8. Unfortunately, courts have created unnecessary confusion by sometimes referring to Notice-and-Comment Rulemaking as "formal rulemaking" when distinguishing it from agency adoption of interpretative rules or statements of policy.

Formal rulemaking procedure looks much like formal adjudication with an ALJ presiding over an evidentiary hearing. *See* 5 U.S.C. §§ 556-557.

Historically, ratemaking was probably the primary form of rulemaking. For example, the first independent regulatory commission, the Interstate Commerce Commission (ICC), used to set the rates that railroads and interstate pipelines, buses, and trucks could charge for moving oil and gas, passengers, or freight; the Civil Aeronautics Board set the rates that airlines could charge customers for flights; and the Federal Communications Commission set the rates that the American Telephone & Telegraph Company (then the only interstate telephone company) could charge for long-distance calls. Moreover, the Supreme Court early in the twentieth century had indicated that, because ratemaking was perceived as being both highly factual in nature and affecting a small set of actors in a particular way, setting rates implicated the due process rights of those regulated, requiring that they be afforded a hearing on the record. *See Interstate Commerce Commn. v. Louisville & Nashville Railroad Co.*, 227 U.S. 88 (1913). The trial-type procedures of Formal Rulemaking were thought to be the best means to satisfy such Due Process requirements and assure fairness and accuracy. Today much has changed. The current wisdom is that government need not set rates for businesses except in rare circumstances. At the federal level ratemaking has been all but eliminated, and the agencies primarily involved in that activity abolished. At the same time, as discussed in Chapter 4, Due Process no longer is viewed as requiring a trial-type proceeding. Moreover, trial-type procedures have become identified with expense and delay, resulting in judicial sympathy for agency flexibility within statutory constraints to avoid such procedures.

The APA itself does not define which rulemakings must be conducted through the trial-type procedures of Sections 556 and 557 of the APA. Instead, it provides in Section 553 that Formal Rulemaking is required "when rules are required by statute to be made on the record after opportunity for an agency hearing." In other words, one must look to the statute governing the substance of the rulemaking to determine if it requires the rule to be made on the record after opportunity for an agency hearing.

In two cases involving the ICC, the Supreme Court interpreted the language in Section 553 very narrowly, requiring a statute either to state in terms or by reference to Sections 556 and 557 that Formal Rulemaking is required or to use language explicitly invoking the need for the rule to be made both on the record and after an opportunity for an agency hearing. The first case, *United States v. Allegheny-Ludlum Steel Corp.*, 406 U.S. 742 (1972), held that a requirement in the Interstate Commerce Act that a rule be adopted only "after [a] hearing" was not sufficient under Section 553 to trigger the requirement for Formal Rulemaking. The second and better known case, *United States v. Florida East Coast Railroad Co.*, 410 U.S. 224 (1973), raised the same issue, and the Court reaffirmed its year-earlier opinion, despite the lower court's persuasive historical analysis suggesting that when the "hearing" requirement was adopted, everyone understood a "hearing" to mean a trial-type procedure. Moreover, in *Florida East Coast Railroad*, the Court went on to hold that the "hearing" required by the Interstate Commerce Act could be a "paper hearing," involving merely the filing of papers with no oral testimony or evidence. In short, these cases essentially raise a presumption against statutes being interpreted to require Formal Rulemaking; only the clearest language indicating such an intent or the magic language requiring both a decision on the record and an opportunity for an agency hearing will suffice.

Example

An agency's statutory mandate provides that it may adopt rules only after providing a hearing at which interested persons may testify and give evidence. The statute also requires that a transcript be kept of any testimony given and that the agency take any public comment and evidence into account in its final rule. Does this require Formal Rulemaking?

Explanation

No. Although the statute requires a hearing and provides some details about the type of hearing to be given, it does not clearly require a "record proceeding," that is, a proceeding at which all the evidence on which the rule is to be based must be entered into evidence in an "on-the-record" hearing. This agency's statutory mandate would require what is called "hybrid rulemaking," because it goes beyond the requirements of Section 553's Notice-and-Comment Rulemaking, but it does not go so far as to require Formal Rulemaking.

Example

An agency's statutory mandate provides that after the head of the agency provides notice of a proposed rule, a potentially adversely affected person may file an objection, specifying with particularity the provisions of the proposed rule deemed objectionable, stating the grounds therefor, and requesting a public hearing on such objections. The statute then states:

> As soon as practicable after such request for a public hearing, the [head of the agency], after due notice, shall hold such a public hearing for the purpose of receiving evidence relevant and material to the issues raised by such objections. At the hearing, any interested person may be heard in person or by representative. As soon as practicable after completion of the hearing, the [head of the agency] shall by order act upon such objections and make such order public. Such order shall be based only on substantial evidence of record

at such hearing and shall set forth, as part of the order, detailed findings of fact on which the order is based.

Does this statute require Formal Rulemaking?

Explanation

Yes. This is the statutory language in the Food, Drug, and Cosmetic Act requiring the Food and Drug Administration to adopt certain rules through Formal Rulemaking. The difference between this example and the previous example is that this statute specifically requires that the order[9] "be based only on substantial evidence of record at such hearing." In other words, only the evidence produced in this hearing can be considered by the head of the agency in adopting the rule. This satisfies the two-part requirement of *Florida East Coast Railroad* that the statute clearly mandate a proceeding that is "on the record after an opportunity for an agency hearing."

Although Formal Rulemaking is very rare today, there remain a handful of statutes that do require Formal Rulemaking, most notably the one quoted above with respect to certain rules under the FDA's jurisdiction. *See* 21 U.S.C. § 371(e)(3). Accordingly, it is necessary to review the procedures applicable to Formal Rulemaking.

First, under Section 553(b), as in Notice-and-Comment Rulemaking, the agency generally gives notice of the proposed rule to the general public through publication in the Federal Register. When persons subject to the rule are specifically named in the rule, then the agency is supposed to personally serve notice on them, unless they already have actual notice of it. This might occur, for example, in a ratemaking proceeding where there are particular companies whose rates will be set by the rule.

The notice must contain information on the "time, place, and nature" of the rulemaking proceedings. That is, when and where will the hearing take place and what will be the rules governing the proceeding? Typically, agencies will have published rules governing their formal proceedings, much like the Federal Rules of Civil Procedure. The notice must also identify the legal authority for the proposed rule. Normally, this would merely be a citation to the agency's statutory mandate. Finally, the notice is to contain "the terms or substance of the proposed rule or a description of the subjects and issues involved." All these requirements are identical to those applicable

9. Again, unfortunately for those trying to learn the basics of administrative law, the statutory mandates for a number of agencies, in particular independent regulatory agencies, speak of the agency issuing an "order" to adopt a rule. Under the APA itself, such an appellation is a misnomer. An *order* is defined as the final disposition "in a matter other than rulemaking."

to Notice-and-Comment Rulemaking, and more will be said about them in the next section.

After the notice, however, rather than receive written comments from interested persons, the agency holds a hearing meeting the requirements of Sections 556 and 557 of the APA. These requirements were discussed and explained in Chapter 3 on Adjudication and may be summarized as providing for a trial-type hearing, typically before an Administrative Law Judge. In Formal Rulemaking, however, the agency may provide only a "paper hearing," if no party would be prejudiced by lack of an oral hearing. A paper hearing is like motion practice without the oral argument in federal district court. The parties file papers and briefs, but no testimony need be taken. A paper hearing could be appropriate when any facts at issue are technical in nature and may be better adduced through documents than a person's testimony.

The hearing usually concludes with an ALJ recommended or tentative decision, except, unlike in adjudication, the agency may take this role away from the ALJ and make its own recommended or tentative decision based on the record before the ALJ.

D. The Procedures of Notice-and-Comment Rulemaking

Notice-and-Comment Rulemaking is the bread and butter of the legislative side of administrative law, as the quotation introducing this chapter suggests. The term *Notice-and-Comment Rulemaking* refers to the procedure by which the rule is adopted. Notice-and-Comment Rulemaking is contrasted with Formal Rulemaking, the procedure for which is similar to an APA adjudication. Before the APA, much if not most rulemaking was performed using the formal procedure, but after passage of the APA and its provision for Notice-and-Comment Rulemaking, almost all rulemaking follows the notice-and-comment format, rather than the adjudicatory format.

1. The Notice

The first step in Notice-and-Comment Rulemaking is for the agency to give notice to the public of the intended rulemaking. This step is identical to the notice required in formal rulemaking.

Section 553(b)

General notice of proposed rulemaking shall be published in the Federal Register, unless persons subject thereto are named and either personally served or otherwise have actual notice thereof in accordance with law. . . .

Despite the statute's allowance of an alternative to publication in the Federal Register, today all notices of proposed rulemaking are published in the Federal Register. Moreover, there is growing use of additional means of giving notice of proposed rules, particularly the Internet, to facilitate public involvement in the rulemaking. Indeed, all executive agencies are now putting these rulemaking notices and information online. *See www.regulations.gov.*

The statute also specifies what the notice is to contain.

Section 553(b)

. . . The notice shall include—

(1) a statement of the time, place, and nature of public rulemaking proceedings;
(2) reference to the legal authority under which the rule is proposed; and
(3) either the terms or substance of the proposed rule or a description of the subjects and issues involved, and
(4) the Internet address of a summary of not more than 100 words in length of the proposed rule, in plain language, that shall be posted on the Internet website under section 206(d) of the E-Government Act of 2002 (44 U.S.C. 3501 note) (commonly known as regulations.gov).

The third of these three items is the meat of the notice of proposed rulemaking. While the APA does not require the agency to publish an actual proposed rule, allowing either a description of the "substance of the proposed rule or a description of the subject and issues involved," today virtually every notice of proposed rulemaking contains the text of the actual rule proposed to be adopted. In addition, preceding the text of the proposed rule is what is known as the "preamble." Here the agency explains what it is trying to do in the rulemaking and why, and it explains the provisions of the rule. Also included in the preamble are the other matters required to be contained in the notice.

The time of the rulemaking is the time during which comments will be received and the time of any oral hearing that may be provided.

The place of the rulemaking is the address where persons should send comments, and, if there is an oral hearing or hearings, where they will take place. Agencies also indicate the place where the rulemaking docket may be found. The rulemaking docket is a compilation of all of the agency's supporting materials for the proposed rule as well as all comments received. Today this can often be found online.

The nature of the rulemaking proceeding indicates whether it is an informal Notice-and-Comment Rulemaking or a formal rulemaking.

The reference to the legal authority for the rule is supposed to provide the public with a citation to the legal basis for the proposed rule. Agencies cite to the statutory provisions that provide the legal authority for the rule.

2. The Comment

Section 553(c)

After notice required by this section, the agency shall give interested persons an opportunity to participate in the rulemaking through submission of written data, views, or arguments with or without opportunity for oral presentation. After consideration of the relevant matter presented, the agency shall incorporate in the rules adopted a concise general statement of their basis and purpose. . . .

The APA requires agencies to provide an opportunity for written comment ("data, views, or arguments") but does not require an oral hearing for Notice-and-Comment Rulemaking. Oral hearings, however, are not unusual in controversial rulemakings. Some other statutes do require oral hearings for some rules, and some agencies will provide an oral hearing when a rule elicits substantial public interest, even if the law does not require it. These oral hearings should not be confused with the trial-type hearings provided in formal rulemakings. Instead, they are like congressional hearings. They generally involve persons giving speeches to one or more staff members of the agency involved in the rulemaking. These staff members may also ask questions of the persons presenting their views. Transcripts are normally made of the oral presentations and these become part of the rulemaking docket along with the written comments.

The APA does not specify the time period an agency must provide for persons to submit comments in writing. Presumably, if the agency did not provide adequate time for a person to receive the Federal Register, read the notice of proposed rulemaking, and then write a comment, this would be inconsistent with the APA, but what may be "adequate time" is less than crystal clear. A number of other statutes applicable to particular programs or agencies have set minimum periods, usually 30 days, for public comment. It is not unusual, however, for agencies to afford 60 or 90 days for comment on proposed rules of any complexity.

Written comments received by the agency, any transcripts of oral hearings, as well as any internal, non-privileged information or data generated inside the agency relating to the proposal are placed in the "docket." This is a publicly available repository of the information that ultimately will provide the factual underpinnings for the rule finally adopted. Agencies are increasingly creating dockets that are accessible through the Internet to facilitate public consideration of the issues involved in the rulemaking.

Today, as more and more of rulemaking is taking place on the Internet, some new problems have arisen. One is that organized groups can enlist their members to bombard the agency with emails commenting on a proposed rule. Usually, the emails are simply a repeat of whatever the group has provided to its members. This is generally not helpful to the agency and merely requires the expenditure of resources to deal with the large number of comments. In addition, the groups' members may be misled into thinking that the number of comments the agency receives supporting or opposing a proposed rule actually matters. It does not. The agency is seeking substantive comments, not votes.

The second problem is the filing of comments under false names to hide the identity of the real commenter. In 2017, the Federal Communications Commission engaged in a rulemaking to repeal the so-called "net neutrality rule." It received millions of comments, many of which were the result of public interest groups calling on their members to comment against the repeal. However, there were apparently over 9 million comments filed under stolen identities, mostly in favor of repeal. This was apparently an attempt to mask the fact that most people in fact were opposed to repeal.

3. The Final Rule

The APA does not by its terms require agencies to publish a summary of and response to the comments received, but this is standard practice today. Instead, the APA requires the agency to "incorporate in the rules adopted a concise general statement of their basis and purpose." Normally, the statement of basis and purpose, along with a summary of and response to comments, is included in the preamble published in the Federal Register preceding the actual rule adopted. The "statement of basis and purpose" in essence repeats the notice of proposed rulemaking's explanation of what the agency is attempting to do in the rule and why, as modified in light of further information and comments received during the rulemaking. However, this statement is "concise" only for the most routine rules. For example, the Research and Special Programs Administration of the Department of Transportation adopted a rule on the required qualifications for persons engaged in certain activities on pipeline facilities. This was a new rule, one of importance to those in the pipeline business, but just one of several rules relating to pipeline safety. The rule itself covered less than 2 pages in the Federal Register. The preamble, however, took up more than 12 triple-column, small-print Federal Register pages. *See* 64 Fed. Reg. 46853 (1999). The summary and response to the 41 comments received on the proposed rule comprised 3 of these pages. The description of how the rule worked involved another 5 of these pages. The introduction, a history of the rulemaking, and other matters required by other statutes filled the remainder. This is an ordinary, run-of-the-mill rule. "Big" rules are an entirely different matter. For example, the actual rule adopted by the Health Care Financing Administration to govern the prospective payment system and consolidated billing for skilled nursing facilities only filled two pages of the Federal Register, but the preamble took up no less than 37 pages. *See* 64 Fed. Reg. 41644 (1999). And then there are the blockbusters, rules whose preambles take up literally hundreds of pages.

Section 553(d)

The required publication or service of a substantive rule shall be made not later than 30 days before its effective date, except—

(1) a substantive rule which grants or recognizes an exemption or relieves a restriction;
(2) interpretative rules and statements of policy; or
(3) as otherwise provided by the agency for good cause found and published with the rule.

Section 553(d) requires that as a general matter a substantive final rule be published at least 30 days before it becomes effective. The purpose of this requirement is to provide regulated entities time to learn about any new rule and to come into compliance with it before the rule goes into effect. This general requirement applies only to "substantive" rules; that is, it does not apply to procedural rules. Because its purpose is to provide regulated entities time to come into compliance with a new rule, there is an exception for rules that do not impose new requirements but instead grant an exemption or otherwise relieve a restriction. These rules are allowed to go into effect immediately so that regulated entities can utilize them as soon as possible. Because interpretative rules and statements of policy do not impose legal obligations, as described earlier, subsection (d) provides an exception for them as well. They also may go into effect immediately. Finally, there is a general exception for when the agency finds good cause to waive the 30-day delayed effective date rule. Like the good cause exception from Notice-and-Comment Rulemaking, the agency must invoke this exception and explain why there is good cause.

4. The "Logical Outgrowth" Test

The purpose of Notice-and-Comment Rulemaking is twofold: to inform the agency so that the rules it adopts will be as accurate and fair as possible, and to involve the public so that it has a sense of participation in the rules that may affect it. Obviously, if notice and comment are to mean anything, the agency must be open to changing the proposed rule in light of the comments and information received. However, if the final rule the agency adopts differs too much from the rule proposed, members of the interested public may feel that they did not have a fair opportunity to comment on what was finally adopted. On the other hand, if the agency were required to subject each change to further notice and comment, such a requirement would both greatly lengthen an already lengthy process and create a substantial disincentive to agencies making changes in light of comments. Courts have adopted a test for determining when a final rule is within the scope of the proposed rule, so that new notice and comment are not required. It is called the "logical outgrowth" test, and it operates as the name suggests. As long as the final rule is a logical outgrowth of the proposed rule, further notice and comment on the changes made to the proposed rule are not necessary. Like some other tests, unfortunately, the test may be easy to state, but its application is less than precise and is very case specific.

Example

The Department of Agriculture administers the Special Supplemental Food Program for Women, Infants, and Children (WIC Program). This program provides federal funds to subsidize food purchases for low-income families with infants, children, and pregnant women. In order to assure that the food purchased meets the nutritional needs of these recipients, the Department specifies by rule the quality of the food that may be purchased under the program. Believing that a previous standard allowed too much sugar in the diet of these recipients, the Department proposed a rule that would restrict the sugar content in breakfast cereals. The preamble discussed the general problem with too much sugar in the diet and also discussed the sugar content in fruit juices, but the proposal related only to cereal.

Some comments on the proposed rule suggested that the Department ban flavored milk from the approved foods because of its high sugar content. In the final rule the Department adopted this suggestion and deleted flavored milk from the approved foods. This action was challenged by the Chocolate Manufacturers Association on the grounds that there had been no notice that the Department might ban chocolate milk from the approved foods. The Fourth Circuit agreed and remanded the rule to the agency for further notice and comment on the issue of banning flavored milk from the approved foods.

Explanation

The court did not believe this part of the final rule was a logical outgrowth of the proposed rule. The proposed rule had not mentioned flavored milk at all; the only proposal related to breakfast cereal, and that proposal was to limit the sugar in approved cereals, not to ban all sugar-added cereals. There was no reason for the makers of flavored milk or associations of companies making flavoring for flavored milk to comment on what might be done to flavored milk. The final rule was literally a surprise to them; they did not have adequate notice under the APA. Indeed, their first response was to petition the agency to reopen the rulemaking on the issue so that they could comment on the ban, but the agency rejected their petition.

Usually, comments made in a rulemaking are germane to the issues raised in the proposed rulemaking, so that if an agency adopts a comment made in a rulemaking, it is likely to be a logical outgrowth of the proposed rule. Here, however, commenters who were generally opposed to high sugar content in food used a rulemaking addressed to sugar in breakfast cereals to suggest a broader scope to the problem and a broader solution. Their point may have been well taken, but the broader solution involved persons and products that were not affected by the proposed rule and hence not put on notice that they might be part of the "solution." *See Chocolate Manufacturers Assn. v. Block*, 755 F.2d 1098 (4th Cir. 1985).

Example

The Clean Air Act authorizes the EPA for certain purposes to treat Indian tribes like states, so that they can administer the federal program in their respective jurisdictions. To qualify for administering the federal program, both states and Indian tribes must meet the requirements established by EPA in rules. When EPA proposed the requirements for Indian tribes, it included a provision, like one applicable to states, that tribes provide for judicial review in state court of any Clean Air Act permit action taken by a tribe. During the comment period, the tribes argued that to subject them to judicial review in state court was inconsistent with tribal sovereign immunity. EPA in its final rule agreed and eliminated any requirement for judicial review of tribal permit actions. This was challenged by persons who might be subject to tribal permit actions. They argued that they had no notice that EPA might eliminate any judicial review requirement. The D.C. Circuit disagreed and upheld EPA's rule as the logical outgrowth of the proposed rule.

Explanation

The court explained that one way to view the "logical outgrowth" test is to ask: "whether . . . [the party], ex ante, should have anticipated that such a requirement might be imposed." When the agency responds to comments elicited by the notice of proposed rulemaking, this generally is evidence that the response could have been anticipated. This was not a case where the agency's action was totally unrelated or surprisingly distant from what was proposed. When an agency proposes to do something, or to require something in particular, an unstated but understood premise is that the agency might *not* adopt that proposal. This is especially true when the matter proposed is highly controversial, as was the judicial review provision in the EPA proposed rule. *See Arizona Public Service Co. v. EPA*, 211 F.3d 1280 (D.C. Cir. 2000). *See also Long Island Care at Home, Ltd. v. Coke*, 127 S. Ct. 2339, 2351 (2007).

If a court finds that an agency has strayed too far from the proposed rule, one possible response is to hold unlawful and set aside the rule adopted. Of course, this does not prevent the agency from then providing the additional notice and comment and then adopting the same rule prospectively. This, however, could result in disruption in the regulated community, with the regulation on again, off again, then on again. As a result, often courts will only remand the rule to the agency to provide the needed notice and comment, as the court did in the *Chocolate Manufacturers* case. Thus, if the agency in fact does not change its mind, the regulatory system will have gone on uninterrupted. Sometimes, however, courts will set aside the rule, notwithstanding the disruption, believing that if the rule is left in effect, agencies may have little incentive to consider new comments seriously.

E. Procedures for Rules Not Subject to Formal Rulemaking or Notice-and-Comment Rulemaking

The Administrative Procedure Act does not provide any particular procedure for adopting rules not subject to either Formal Rulemaking or Notice-and-Comment Rulemaking. However, Section 552(a) of the APA does require that they be published in the Federal Register.

> **Section 552(a)**
>
> Each agency shall make available to the public information as follows:
>
> (1) Each agency shall separately state and currently publish in the Federal Register for the guidance of the public—. . .
> (C) rules of procedure . . . ;
> (D) substantive rules of general applicability adopted as authorized by law, and statements of general policy or interpretations of general applicability formulated and adopted by the agency; and
> (E) each amendment, revision, or repeal of the foregoing.

Except to the extent that a person has actual and timely notice of the terms thereof, a person may not in any manner be required to resort to, or be adversely affected by, a matter required to be published in the Federal Register and not so published. . . .

Despite this explicit requirement of publication, internal agency manuals and directives typically are not published in the Federal Register. Attempts to obtain judicial injunctions against such rules simply due to the lack of publication have foundered on the "except" portion of the subsection. The implication of this "except" portion is that if a person *does* have notice of the unpublished rule, the person can be adversely affected by or required to resort to the rule, and the lack of publication is harmless error. *See, e.g., United States v. F/V Alice Amanda*, 987 F.2d 1078 (4th Cir. 1993). Moreover, courts have taken a strict approach to what constitutes "adverse effect." For example, the D.C. Circuit excused the Department of Labor's failure to publish a memorandum interpreting one of its regulations, because the adverse effect came from the underlying regulation, not the interpretive rule contained in the unpublished memorandum. *See Secretary of Labor, Mine Safety & Health Administration v. Western Fuels-Utah, Inc.*, 900 F.2d 318 (D.C. Cir. 1990). *See also Splane v. West*, 216 F.3d 1058 (Fed. Cir. 2000) (interpretation issued by the General Counsel of the Department of Veterans Affairs to the Board of Veterans Appeals, and on which it relied, did not adversely affect petitioners until the Board ruled on their claim, by which time they had notice of interpretation). Consequently, the availability in the Federal Register to a vast array of internal agency rules depends more on agency good will than law.

F. Negotiated Rulemaking

In the early 1980s, a number of observers of the rulemaking process perceived what they believed to be a breakdown in the traditional notice-and-comment procedure. The process, they believed, had become too adversarial, with persons filing comments less to inform the agency than to counter the expected comments of opposing persons and to position themselves for subsequent litigation with the agency. For example, an EPA rulemaking would be dominated by industry groups subject to regulation filing comments aimed at the organized environmental groups, which in turn filed comments establishing perhaps extreme positions to counter the comments of the industry participants. At the same time, in the judicial and administrative adjudicatory worlds, there was a birth of alternative dispute resolution procedures aimed at reducing the delay and problems of the traditional adversary process.

The observers propounded the concept of regulatory negotiation as an adjunct to Notice-and-Comment Rulemaking. Under this concept, when an agency decides to undertake a rulemaking, rather than have agency staff draft a proposed rule, the agency would convene an advisory group with representatives of all the important affected interests. This advisory group would meet and attempt to reach consensus on what the rule should be. The agency itself would be one of the persons participating in these meetings, but it would act as just another interest group. The advisory group, if it could, would develop and draft a proposed rule with which all the interests could agree. That proposed rule would then be published in the Federal Register as the agency's notice of proposed rulemaking, and comments would be solicited from the public. If the advisory group truly represented all the important interests and the group had reached consensus on the proposed rule, no adverse comments would be received, and the agency could then adopt the proposed rule as its final rule. In this way, negotiated rulemaking can occur within the procedural framework of traditional Notice-and-Comment Rulemaking, even though it changes the character of that rulemaking in at least two ways. First, it puts the real onus for developing the rule on the representatives to the advisory group from the various affected interests instead of agency staff. Second, it effectively substitutes consensus among private interests as the determinate of the public interest in place of an agency's independent determination, albeit informed by the comments from the public.

Proponents of regulatory negotiation believe that rules adopted under this process are superior to rules adopted under traditional procedures because persons who actually participated in the drafting of the rule feel a greater stake in the rule and, when consensus is achieved, are more likely to comply with the rule and less likely to challenge it in court. The Administrative Conference of the United States was an early supporter of negotiated rulemaking, and with its support Congress adopted the Negotiated Rulemaking Act, 5 U.S.C. §§ 561-570, to facilitate negotiated rules.

A lively literature has developed debating the pros and cons of negotiated rulemaking. *Compare* William Funk, *Bargaining Toward the New*

Millennium: Regulatory Negotiation and the Subversion of the Public Interest, 46 Duke L.J. 1351 (1997) (arguing that negotiated rulemaking leads to the agency abandoning its responsibility to seek the public interest and instead effectively privatizes government regulation) *and* Cary Coglianese, *Assessing Consensus: The Promise and Performance of Negotiated Rulemaking*, 46 Duke L.J. 1255 (1997) (making an empirical assessment challenging the claimed benefits of negotiated rules) *with* Philip J. Harter, *Assessing the Assessors: The Actual Performance of Negotiated Rulemaking*, 9 N.Y.U. Env. L.J. 32 (2000) (taking issue with Coglianese and providing evidence of benefits) *and* Jody L. Freeman, *The Private Role in Public Governance*, 75 N.Y.U. L. Rev. 543 (2000) (arguing for a reconsideration of traditional administrative law concern for the accountability of public officers and in favor of an increased recognition of the private role in public governance). However this debate is resolved, though, the number of rules adopted through negotiated rulemaking has remained and is likely to remain small compared to those adopted through traditional notice-and-comment procedures. This is partially a result of the increased financial and personnel resources demanded by negotiated rulemaking compared to traditional rulemaking, as well as continued hostility toward the concept of negotiated rulemaking by many government agencies.

G. Constitutional and Other Judicially Created Procedural Requirements

Prior to the adoption of the Administrative Procedure Act, while a number of individual agency mandates or program statutes required the use of particular procedures for rulemaking by that agency or under that program, *general* administrative law was an amalgam of judicially declared constitutional and common law. After passage of the APA, which to a large degree codified the judicially developed common law, there was a question whether courts could still utilize common-law authority to require particular procedures in agency proceedings. The Supreme Court answered that question in the negative in the case of *Vermont Yankee Nuclear Power Corp. v. Natural Resources Defense Council*, 435 U.S. 519 (1978). There, the D.C. Circuit had held that the Nuclear Regulatory Commission should use a trial-type hearing to determine facts concerning the potential environmental effects from nuclear waste generated by civilian nuclear power plants. That court, believing that courts were better equipped to judge the efficacy of the procedures used to produce a decision than they were to assess an agency's ultimate decision, held that in this case a trial-type procedure was the best assurance that the agency's decision would be well informed. The Supreme Court unanimously reversed. The Court made clear that, while agencies were free to adopt additional procedures voluntarily, courts were not authorized to require agencies to use the courts' notions of appropriate procedures. Except to the extent that the Constitution or other statute required otherwise, generally the APA was intended to occupy the field with respect to required administrative procedure.

This decision in 1978 has generally precluded courts from adding additional procedural requirements to agency rulemaking beyond those contained in the APA or another statute. Of course, if an agency by rule voluntarily undertakes to provide additional procedures, a court can require the agency to follow its own rules until it amends or repeals them. And, if the Constitution mandates a procedure beyond that in the APA, the courts clearly can require compliance with the constitutional mandate. When *Vermont Yankee* was decided, however, there was a body of case law that seemed to require additional procedures from agencies, and it was not always clear whether the courts that had imposed these requirements were acting under the authority of the Constitution or common law. Because both were viewed as adequate authority for judicially imposed procedural requirements before *Vermont Yankee*, courts were not always clear about the authority they were exercising. After *Vermont Yankee*, though, it was important, because only constitutionally compelled procedures could be required. Today, some of these questions remain.

One of those questions, and a pretty fundamental one, is the extent to which the Constitution *ever* requires any procedures for rulemaking. The most likely candidate for the source of a constitutional requirement is the Due Process Clause, but as described in Chapter 4, Due Process, the Supreme Court's early decision in *Bi-Metallic Investment Co. v. State Board of Equalization*, 239 U.S. 441 (1915), held that due process did not require an opportunity for persons to be heard before an agency adopts a general rule of conduct for "more than a few people." The Court's explanation was that it was impractical to provide a hearing for everyone who might be affected by the rule, and the safeguard against abuse was the same as the safeguard against abuse by a legislature making laws: "their power, immediate or remote, over those who make the rule." This analysis leaves two possible situations in which rulemaking might still implicate due process concerns. First, does the rule only affect a few persons in an exceptional way? Ordinarily, if a government proceeding would only affect a few persons in an exceptional way, we would classify that type of proceeding as an adjudication rather than a rulemaking, but it is possible that Congress might by statute require rulemaking in that situation. Second, *Bi-Metallic* by its terms only said that there was no requirement for a hearing. It did not say explicitly that procedural due process did not apply at all. Of course, the right to an opportunity to be heard is probably the most fundamental aspect of due process, but there may be some other element of fundamental fairness that would still apply.

I. Ex Parte Communications

In formal adjudication and Formal Rulemaking, Section 557 of the APA prohibits ex parte communications, that is, communications relevant to an agency proceeding not on the public record between an agency employee involved in the decisional process and an interested person outside the agency. There is no comparable provision relating to Notice-and-Comment Rulemaking. However, in a celebrated case from the D.C. Circuit in 1977, a year before *Vermont Yankee*, the court held that after publication of the notice of proposed rulemaking, agencies could not engage in ex parte communications with interested persons. *See Home Box Office v. Federal Communications Commn.*, 567 F.2d 9 (D.C. Cir. 1977). If such prohibited communications did take place, the court said, the agency would have to place them on the public record and allow interested persons to respond to them. Although the court mentioned the Due Process Clause of the Constitution in passing, it did not clearly rest its decision on due process requirements. After *Vermont Yankee*, many believed that *Home Box Office's* prohibition on ex parte communications was no longer good law. Subsequent decisions of the D.C. Circuit, however, while they have limited and distinguished *Home Box Office* and have acknowledged it to be undermined by *Vermont Yankee*, have failed to overrule it, and it continues to be argued and cited in courts. More important from the perspective of administrative law practice, however, agencies today, while they might not like the idea of a strict prohibition on ex parte communications, generally do not want ex parte communications to take place. Such communications often suggest some form of corruption, even when it does not exist, making the agency look bad, a posture that may color a court's consideration in any judicial review of the rulemaking. In addition, because the agency, if the rule is challenged in court, ultimately will need to defend the rule on the basis of information on the public record, the agency has an interest in assuring that all relevant information is on the public record. As a result, many agencies have put prohibitions or limitations on ex parte communications into their own procedural regulations relating to rulemaking, so that they are bound by those regulations if nothing else.

In one class of cases, *Home Box Office* is still considered good law because the constitutional claims seem strongest. This class of cases involves rulemakings that present "conflicting claims to a valuable privilege."

Example

One of the functions of the FCC, even in an era of deregulation, is to allocate the radio spectrum to different uses, such as UHF and VHF television, radio, cellular phones, CB radio, WiFi, etc. This is done through rulemaking. In one case the FCC was considering switching a VHF channel (which has greater range and power) from Springfield, Illinois, to St. Louis, while shifting two UHF stations (with shorter range and less power) from St. Louis to Springfield in exchange. The potential broadcaster in Springfield would be the "loser" in this exchange, to the benefit of the broadcaster in St. Louis. The broadcasters engaged in ex parte communications with FCC commissioners during the rulemaking. Thereafter, the loser challenged the rule switching the channels, arguing that the ex parte communications were unlawful. The court agreed, saying ex parte communications were prohibited when there were conflicting claims to a valuable privilege. *See Sangamon Valley Television Corp. v. United States*, 269 F.2d 221 (D.C. Cir. 1959).

Explanation

This case, which was decided before *Vermont Yankee* and *Home Box Office*, technically involved rulemaking, but it was an unusual form of rulemaking—one that really decided among discrete parties who would obtain a valuable government benefit. In that unusual situation of competing parties, the proceeding appears more like adjudication than rulemaking, even if the proceeding met the definition of rulemaking under the APA. In other words, we might say that it was a rule that affected a relatively small number in an exceptional way, escaping *Bi-Metallic's* conclusion. Because it looked like adjudication, due process considerations in adjudications seemed to come into play, one of which is that a decision be made on the record. Because the ex parte communications were not on the record, one could not say that the decision was made on the record. This analysis, because it is founded on constitutional considerations, would seem to survive *Vermont Yankee*, even if *Home Box Office* generally does not. Nevertheless, such situations are exceedingly rare.

2. Decision Makers' Bias or Prejudice

Another fundamental aspect of due process is a neutral decision maker, and in adjudications if a decision maker is biased or prejudiced against (or for) a party, that is a violation of due process. The question is whether there is any comparable requirement in rulemaking. To the extent that rulemaking mimics legislation by legislators, the answer would seem to be in the negative; there is no due process requirement for legislators to be neutral decision makers in any sense. Indeed, they are often elected specifically because they have decided what legislation should be enacted. However, if the APA requires notice and comment before an agency adopts a rule, a requirement unknown to legislatures, does this imply the need (or trigger a due process requirement) for a decision maker with an open mind?

In a 1979 case, the D.C. Circuit held that the standard applicable to disqualification for bias or prejudice in adjudication—whether a disinterested observer may conclude that the decision maker has in some measure adjudged the facts as well as the law of a particular case in advance of hearing it—was *not* appropriate in rulemaking. The court recognized that rulemaking usually involves facts of a different nature from adjudication, what have been called legislative facts, as opposed to adjudicative facts—facts concerning the immediate parties who did what, where, when, how, and with what motive or intent. Assessing prejudgment of the latter has been the focus of cases involving claims of prejudice in adjudication. Legislative facts, on the other hand, are ordinarily general, without reference to specific parties, facts that help the decision maker determine the content of law and of policy and help the decision maker to exercise his judgment or discretion in determining what course of action to take. For example, the extent to which global warming is attributable to human activity would be a legislative fact. Thus, in rulemaking, the court held that there was unlawful prejudice "only when there has been a clear and convincing showing that the agency member has an unalterably closed mind on matters critical to the disposition of the proceeding." The "clear and convincing" test, it said, is necessary to rebut the presumption of administrative regularity. The "unalterably closed mind" test is necessary to permit rulemakers to carry out their proper policy-based functions while disqualifying those unable to consider meaningfully the materials produced in the rulemaking. *Association of National Advertisers, Inc. v. Federal Trade Commn.*, 627 F.2d 1151 (D.C. Cir. 1979).

Example

The FTC adopted a rule governing fair trade practices in the sale of used automobiles that included a requirement for used car dealers to post in the window of a car a list of all known mechanical defects of the car. This "known defects" portion of the rule was very controversial, and the Commission agreed to reconsider the rule. It then proposed to adopt the rule without the "known defects" portion. It took comments on the proposal and ultimately adopted the rule as proposed—that is, without the "known defects" portion.

Prior to the notice of proposed rulemaking the Chairman of the FTC had said at a press conference that he favored the rule without the "known defects" portion. After the notice was issued but before the end of the comment period, he told a reporter that the final rule would not contain the "known defects" portion, saying that "most dealers are not mechanics, anyway."

A consumers group challenged the adoption of the rule alleging that the Chairman had unlawfully prejudged the "known defects" portion of the rule before the conclusion of the rulemaking. The court held that the Chairman's statements were not clear and convincing evidence that the Chairman had an unalterably closed mind on the issue. *See Consumers Union of United States, Inc. v. FTC*, 801 F.2d 417 (D.C. Cir. 1986).

Explanation

The court said that the first statement by the Chairman may have indicated the favored deletion of the "known defect" portion, but it did not evidence that his mind was closed on the subject. His second statement, the court said, was merely a prediction of how the Commission would rule and "an announcement of [his] own considered position." This may have been inappropriate for him to announce, but it did not indicate a mind closed to evidence in the past or that would ignore new information in the future.

This outcome is typical. No rulemaking has ever been overturned on the basis that a decision maker was unlawfully prejudiced. Often the factual evidence that the decision maker had in fact made up his or her mind was fairly strong, but the courts either found the evidence less than "clear and convincing"—a higher standard than preponderance—or they found the statements, while indicating a present intention, did not rule out the possibility of a changed opinion in light of new evidence. First, past actions and statements not directly related to the particular rulemaking have not been considered adequate evidence; only statements directly relating to the subject rulemaking may provide adequate evidence of prejudgment. Second, as to those statements, even a statement indicating how the person would decide the rulemaking would not be enough, unless it also indicated the person was unwilling to change his or her mind in light of further information. In short, nothing less than a statement that the person had made up his mind irrevocably would seem to satisfy this test.

3. Undue Influence

In adjudication it is understood that it is improper to bring political pressure or influence on a decision maker to affect an outcome. The legislative process, however, is full of political pressure and influence. For better or for worse, political trade-offs and political pressures are part and parcel of the process of legislation. Again, if rulemaking mimics legislation, should such political machinations be acceptable in rulemaking? This question usually arises in one of two circumstances: presidential influence on agency rulemaking and congressional influence on agency rulemaking.

With respect to the President, the situation is further complicated because of the President's constitutional role as head of the executive branch. Thus, the President has some constitutional authority to influence, if not direct, agency decisions as to proper policy, what constitutes the public interest, or what is faithful execution of the laws. In *Sierra Club v. Costle*, 657 F.2d 298 (D.C. Cir. 1981), allegations were made that the President, through his staff, had discussed with EPA officials how an important Clean Air Act rulemaking should be resolved. The court accepted that, at least in the absence of any explicit statutory prohibition, such discussions were entirely appropriate. Acknowledging that due process might require any communications relevant to an adjudication to be recorded and docketed as part of the adjudication record, the court held that there was no such requirement in rulemakings. The safeguard is that any rule must be supported on its own record. This safeguard is not a toothless one, as will become more apparent in Chapter 7, The Scope of Judicial Review, and it deserves noting that courts have not shied away from overturning rules when they believe the basis for the rule is political influence rather than a reasonable policy decision based on the information before the agency. *See, e.g., Northern Spotted Owl v. Hodel*, 716 F. Supp. 479 (W.D. Wash. 1988) (all of the agency documentation supported listing the spotted owl as threatened, but the politically appointed decision maker refused to list the owl). *See also Motor Vehicle Manufacturers Assn. of the United States v. State Farm Mutual Automobile Insurance Co.*, 463 U.S. 29 (1983) (elimination of airbag requirement appeared to be the product of a political decision to lessen government regulation generally rather than a decision based upon analysis of the problem).

Congressional influence does not have any particular constitutional underpinnings. Under the Constitution, Congress makes laws, but once the laws are made, Congress has no role in their execution. However, Congress does have a constitutionally implied power to gather information and investigate how the laws it passed are being carried out, so that it may decide whether new laws should be passed or whether existing laws should be amended, repealed, or left alone. The power to investigate gives Congress the practical power to influence, because agencies do not like to be investigated or forced to provide reams of information at Congress's whims. Therefore, agencies may bend over backward to accede to a congressional committee's wishes, or even those of an influential member of Congress, simply to avoid being harassed by a congressional investigation. Moreover, Congress also has the explicit power to appropriate funds for agencies and programs. Again, agencies feel a great deal of pressure to accommodate the wishes of the appropriation committees in the House and Senate, which hold their purse strings. The rough-and-tumble of the legislative process and its effect on agencies has generally been accepted. Again, the safeguard is that any rule finally adopted must be supportable on the basis of the information before the agency and explained by the agency. *See, e.g., Hazardous Waste Treatment Council v. U.S. E.P.A.*, 886 F.2d 355 (D.C. Cir. 1989) (agency explanation lacking; agency merely acquiesced to comments of members of Congress).

In one case the D.C. Circuit held that a congressional committee went too far. *See District of Columbia Federation of Civic Assns. v. Volpe*, 459 F.2d 1231 (D.C. Cir. 1971). There the chairman of the House Subcommittee on the District of Columbia threatened to withhold appropriations for the construction of the D.C. subway unless the Secretary of Transportation approved a certain bridge for inclusion in the federal highway system. When the Secretary did approve the bridge, and the approval was challenged, the court held that it would be improper for the Secretary to make the decision in whole or in part on the basis of the congressional pressure. Accordingly, it remanded the case to the Secretary to provide an explanation for his decision that relied solely on the basis of relevant considerations.

While *D.C. Federation* has been much cited, it is usually distinguished rather than followed. *Sierra Club v. Costle* was one such case. In that case, in addition to the alleged presidential communications, the majority leader in the Senate, who had the power to make EPA's life miserable or comfortable, had communicated his strong views concerning the Clean Air Act regulation EPA was considering. His views tended to support the adoption of a rule that would have less impact on the hard coal industry—the leading industry in his state—than would other possible alternatives. The final rule adopted was consistent with his views. The court, however, interpreted *D.C. Federation* to require two showings: first, that the content of the pressure be irrelevant or extraneous to the issues the agency is considering, and second, that the agency actually be affected by that pressure. Here, there was no evidence that the Senator had made some extraneous threat, such as the withholding of funds for the Clean Water Act, and there was no evidence that EPA had been influenced by the Senator's pressure in adopting the final rule. Because EPA adequately explained on the merits the basis for its rule, the fact that it coincided with the Senator's views was not evidence that it was the result of congressional influence. Clearly, the court was reluctant to "find" what it might have suspected but for which there was no real evidence. So long as the agency offers an adequate and independent basis for its rule, courts are likely to excuse attempts at congressional pressure.

H. Other Administratively or Statutorily Required Procedures—Hybrid Rulemaking

Hybrid rulemaking is the term used to describe all rulemaking conducted under procedures more extensive than required by the APA and the Constitution. Since *Vermont Yankee* it is understood that all hybrid rulemaking must be a product either of administrative or statutory requirements, not judicial impositions.

A number of statutes creating particular programs require hybrid rulemaking. The Clean Air Act is an example. Section 307(d) of the Clean Air Act, 42 U.S.C. § 7607(d), substitutes its provisions for those of the APA for most rulemakings under the Act. That section requires everything the APA requires for Notice-and-Comment Rulemaking, and in addition:

- it mandates the creation of a rulemaking docket at the time a rule is proposed;

- it requires a statement of basis and purpose to accompany the proposed rule that includes a summary of the factual data on which the rule is based, the methodology used in obtaining and analyzing the data, and the major legal and policy considerations underlying the proposed rule;
- it requires that the underlying data and analysis be available for public inspection in the docket;
- it requires that documents of central relevance that become available to the agency after the publication of notice of proposed rulemaking be placed in the docket;
- it requires that drafts of rules and comments thereon involved in Office of Management and Budget review be placed in the docket;
- it requires an opportunity for an oral presentation of views, data, and arguments, which will be transcribed;
- it requires that the final rule contain a response to the written and oral comments and an explanation for any changes made in the final rule; and
- it requires that the final rule be based only on information in the docket at the time the rule is adopted.

Most of these requirements merely codify what courts had required in interpreting the provisions of the APA. Thus, most agency rulemakings would follow the same procedures under the terms of the APA alone. Nevertheless, because of the statutory specification of these details, Clean Air Act rulemakings are considered hybrid rulemakings, but they do not add much to what is today a normal APA rulemaking.

Another example of a program-specific hybrid rulemaking requirement is found in the Federal Trade Commission Act. In 1980 Congress passed a statute granting the FTC explicit powers to make rules defining unfair or deceptive acts or practices, and it required specific procedures to be followed when the FTC adopts such rules. In addition to the normal requirements for Notice-and-Comment Rulemaking, the statute requires the FTC to:

- issue an advance notice of proposed rulemaking, which describes the area of inquiry under consideration and invites comments from interested parties;
- send the advance notice and, 30 days before its publication, the notice of proposed rulemaking to certain House and Senate committees;
- hold a hearing presided over by a hearing officer at which persons may make oral presentations and in certain circumstances to conduct cross-examination of persons;
- include a statement of basis and purpose to address certain specified concerns; and

- conduct a regulatory analysis of both the proposed and final rules that describes the proposal and alternatives that would achieve the same goal and analyzes the costs and benefits of the proposal and the alternatives.

These requirements go considerably beyond the terms of the APA or what courts have interpreted the APA to require. In particular, the provision for cross-examination of persons smacks of the trial-type procedures of Formal Rulemaking, and the requirements for an advance notice of proposed rulemaking and preliminary and final regulatory analyses would add substantial costs and time to an ordinary, APA rulemaking.

Lawyers dealing with a particular agency or program must acquaint themselves with the program- and agency-specific additional procedural requirements that may be placed on rulemaking.

There are, however, other general procedural requirements that apply across agencies and programs to rulemakings with certain effects. Some are imposed by executive orders; others by statutes. These requirements have mushroomed in recent years. In 2000, Professor Mark Seidenfeld published a checklist that showed 17 different possible sources of procedural requirements applicable to rulemaking. *See* Mark Seidenfeld, *A Table of Requirements for Federal Administrative Rulemaking*, 27 Fla. St. U. L. Rev. 533 (2000). Since then, the number has only increased.

1. Executive Orders

Beginning with Richard Nixon, virtually every President has issued an executive order to reform the rulemaking process by requiring executive agencies to perform cost/benefit analyses and to coordinate certain types of rulemaking with officials in the Executive Office of the President. President Reagan's order, E.O. 12291, established the modern standard, although it was replaced and slightly changed by President Clinton's order, E.O. 12866, which in turn was generally retained by President George W. Bush and then retained in full by Presidents Obama, and Trump, and Biden. The orders have required agencies to comply with three major requirements: to engage in a regulatory planning process, to conduct cost/benefit analyses on certain significant regulatory actions, and to submit proposed and final rules that constitute significant regulatory actions to the Office of Information and Regulatory Affairs (OIRA), a subdivision of the Office of Management and Budget (OMB) in the Executive Office of the President, for review prior to publication.

Executive Order 12866 requires all agencies to engage in a regulatory planning process that includes a review mechanism of their already existing rules and annually to publish a regulatory agenda listing all the existing rules they expect to review and all the new rules they expect to adopt in the coming year. In addition, all agencies must submit to OIRA information about significant rules expected to be adopted in the coming year. This information is then reviewed by OIRA and other high-level executive advisors to determine if the planned actions are consistent with the President's policies.

The order also requires executive agencies (that is, not independent regulatory agencies) proposing rules that have a significant effect on the economy to conduct a regulatory analysis of the proposed rule that identifies and quantifies to the extent feasible the costs and benefits of the proposal and of reasonably feasible alternatives. Generally, these rules are those that have an annual effect on the economy of at least $100 million or have a material adverse effect on a particular sector of the economy, competition, jobs, the environment, public health or safety, or state or local governments.

Under E.O. 12866, agencies must send all proposed and final significant regulatory actions to OIRA for its review before they may be published. E.O. 12866 is not the only executive order agencies must be concerned with when they engage in rulemaking. As of this writing, there are at least fourteen other executive orders they must consider.

- E.O. 12630, Governmental Actions and Interference with Constitutionally Protected Property Rights—Requires agencies when they issue rules with significant takings implications to discuss and identify the takings issues in their submissions to OMB.
- E.O. 12898, Federal Actions to Address Environmental Justice in Minority Populations and Low-Income Populations—Requires agencies when practicable and appropriate to translate public documents relating to human health or the environment for limited-English-speaking populations.
- E.O. 12988, Civil Justice Reform—Requires agencies to review any rules they issue to assure that they do not unduly burden the federal court system.
- E.O. 13045, Protection of Children from Environmental Health Risks and Safety Risks—Requires agencies when they issue economically significant rules that concern health or safety risks that may disproportionately affect children to evaluate specifically the environmental or safety effects of the regulation and to explain why the planned rule is preferable to other alternatives.
- E.O. 13132, Federalism—Requires agencies when they issue rules that impose substantial costs on state and local governments to consult with state and local officials early in the process and to publish in the preamble a description of the agency's consultation, the nature of their concerns, the need for the rule, and the extent to which the officials' concerns have been met.

- E.O. 13175, Consultation and Coordination with Indian Tribal Governments—Requires agencies to coordinate and consult with Indian tribes when they issue rules that have substantial direct effects on one or more Indian tribes, on the relationship between the Federal Government and Indian tribes, or on the distribution of power and responsibilities between the Federal Government and Indian tribes.
- E.O. 13211, Actions Concerning Regulations That Significantly Affect Energy Supply, Distribution, or Use—Requires agencies to prepare a Statement of Energy Effects with regard to significant regulatory actions that are either likely to have a significant adverse effect on the supply, distribution, or use of energy or designated by the Administrator of the Office of Information and Regulatory Affairs as a significant energy action.
- E.O. 13272, Proper Consideration of Small Entities in Agency Rulemaking—Requires agencies to provide draft rules to the Chief Counsel for Advocacy in the Small Business Administration and to give "every appropriate consideration" to the Chief Counsel's comments.
- E.O. 13563, Improving Regulation and Regulatory Review—Elaborates five new principles to guide regulatory decision making. First, agencies are directed to promote public participation, in part through making relevant documents available on *regulations.gov* to promote transparency and comment. It also directs agencies to engage the public, including affected stakeholders, before rulemaking is initiated. Second, agencies are directed to attempt to reduce "redundant, inconsistent, or overlapping requirements," in part by working with one another to simplify and harmonize rules. Third, agencies are directed to identify and consider flexible approaches to regulatory problems, including warnings and disclosure requirements. Such approaches may "reduce burdens and maintain flexibility and freedom of choice for the public." Fourth, agencies are directed to promote scientific integrity. Fifth, and finally, agencies are directed to produce plans to engage in retrospective analysis of existing significant regulations to determine whether they should be modified, streamlined, expanded, or repealed.
- E.O. 13579, Regulation and Independent Regulatory Agencies—Applies E.O. 13563 to independent regulatory agencies.
- E.O. 13609, Promoting International Regulatory Cooperation—Requires agencies to include in their Regulatory Plans under E.O. 12866 a summary of international regulatory cooperation activities. All agencies must also ensure that regulations with international impacts are designated as such in the Unified Agenda of Federal Regulatory and Deregulatory Actions (Unified Agenda), on regulations.gov, and on reginfo.gov. Additionally, agencies must consider

reforming significant regulations that create "unnecessary differences" between U.S. and international regulatory systems. Agencies are also required to consider any regulatory approaches abroad that the U.S. has agreed to consider under a regulatory cooperation council work plan.

- E.O. 13610, Identifying and Reducing Regulatory Burdens— Instructs agencies to institutionalize regular reviews of their previously issued significant regulations and take additional steps to increase public participation in retrospective review of regulations. Agencies must regularly (on the second Monday of January and July of each year) report on the status of their retrospective review efforts to OIRA. Reports should contain: progress on review, anticipated accomplishments, and proposed timelines. Agencies must make available to the public the final reports within three weeks from the date of submission of the draft report to OIRA.
- E.O. 13725, Steps to Increase Competition and Better Inform Consumers and Workers to Support Continued Growth of the American Economy — Requires agencies to identify specific actions they can take to address "undue burdens" on competition, via pro-competitive rulemaking and regulations. They must also make semi-annual reports to the National Economic Council on actions meant to promote greater competition.
- E.O. 14094, Modernizing Regulatory Review — Requires agencies to affirmatively promote public participation in rulemaking and proactively engage interested parties. Regulatory analysis should recognize distributive impacts and equity.

One executive order, E.O. 12606, which required agencies to assess the effect of all proposed rules on family well-being, was revoked by E.O. 13045, but its requirements for assessing rules were subsequently enacted into statute. *See* Pub. L. No. 105-277, Div. A, § 101(h) [Title VI, § 654], Oct. 21, 1998, 112 Stat. 2681, codified as a note to 5 U.S.C. § 601.

One feature that all the executive orders have in common is a provision that states that they are not intended to create any right in any person and shall not be subject to judicial review.[10] The courts have respected these provisions, meaning that an agency could blatantly ignore the requirements in the orders and not be subject to challenge in court. The sole means of enforcing these executive orders is political; that is, at the extreme the President could instruct the agency head to comply or be fired. As a practical matter, this means that some orders, which have strong support at high levels in the administration, are taken very seriously by agencies, because the

10. Even the statute that enacted into law the repealed order on assessing rules for their possible negative effect on families continued the exemption from judicial review.

failure to comply with them will be a black mark on the agency. However, some orders seem to have been issued for little more purpose than to be able to announce to a certain constituency that something has been done, without any real intent to follow up on the requirements imposed. Agencies learn relatively quickly which orders are which. E.O. 12866 is one that the White House takes very seriously.

2. National Environmental Policy Act

The National Environmental Policy Act (NEPA) requires that agencies include in every proposal for actions that significantly affect the quality of the human environment a detailed statement on the environmental impact of the proposed action, any adverse environmental effects that cannot be avoided, and alternatives to the proposed action. *See* 42 U.S.C. § 4332(1)(C). This detailed statement today is known as an Environmental Impact Statement, or EIS, and the Council on Environmental Quality has adopted regulations instructing agencies how to comply with this requirement. In a nutshell, before an agency adopts a rule, it must determine whether the rule will have a significant impact on the environment. Generally, this is accomplished through an Environmental Assessment (EA), which if it determines there is no significant effect results in a Finding of No Significant Impact (FONSI). The agency would produce a draft EA with its proposed rule and a final EA with its final rule. If the agency finds there will be a significant impact, it creates a draft EIS to accompany the proposed rule and a final EIS with the final rule. These documents can easily run into the hundreds of pages and involve substantial expense and effort by environmental experts. The draft documents published with the proposed rule are subject to comment, and the final rule must contain a response to comments received on the draft documents. The adequacy of the agency's compliance with these procedural requirements is subject to judicial review. There is a substantial body of case law involving challenges to agency actions as not complying with this requirement.

It is well to note, however, that NEPA is a procedural statute. It requires that agencies follow certain procedures; it does not require that agencies actually take action that protects the environment.

3. Regulatory Flexibility Act

Originally enacted in 1980, the Regulatory Flexibility Act (RFA), 5 U.S.C. §§ 601-612, was styled after NEPA with its requirement for an EIS. The concern of the RFA, however, was the effect of agency action on small entities.[11]

---

11. Small entities are defined as small businesses, governmental jurisdictions with a population of less than 50,000, and nonprofit organizations not dominant in their field.

The RFA required agencies to conduct Initial Regulatory Flexibility Analyses (IRFAs) for proposed rules and Final Regulatory Flexibility Analyses (FRFAs) for final rules, unless the agency certified that the rule would not have a significant economic impact on a substantial number of small entities. Also like NEPA's EISs, the essence of these analyses was to document the effect of the proposed and final rules and to consider alternatives to the proposed action that might have lesser impacts and to subject the initial analyses to public comment, requiring an agency response. Beyond NEPA, the RFA required agencies to use particular methods of engaging small entities in rulemaking beyond ordinary notice and comment, to create semi-annually a regulatory agenda of any rules being considered for review or adoption in the next year, and to periodically review existing rules that had a significant impact on small entities. As such, RFA potentially created substantial new obstacles to rulemaking that might affect small entities, but the political compromise that produced the RFA included one significant difference from NEPA: there was to be no judicial review of any agency decision or action under the RFA. As a result, agencies largely ignored the RFA's requirements, made unsustainable certifications of no impact, or made shoddy analyses without running the risk of the agency action being set aside.

In 1996, Congress made significant amendments to the RFA. One amendment was to eliminate the exemption from judicial review with respect to the certification of no significant impact, compliance with the requirement for an FRFA, and the periodic review of existing rules. Another amendment required EPA and OSHA, prior to publishing a proposed rule that will have significant economic impact on a substantial number of small entities, to notify the Chief Counsel for Advocacy of the Small Business Administration, who is then to identify representatives of affected small entities to review and comment on the agency's current proposal. A review panel consisting of representatives of the agency, OIRA, and the Chief Counsel for Advocacy then review the comments of these small-entity representatives. The agency is to alter its proposal as appropriate. As a result, the RFA has become a significant procedural hurdle to many agencies' rules.

One limitation in the RFA lessens its coverage. Courts have consistently interpreted the RFA to require regulatory flexibility analyses only if the significant economic impact is caused by the direct regulation by the agency, not the indirect effects. For example, if EPA makes a regulation requiring manufacturers of light trucks to meet new pollution standards, EPA would only have to consider the economic impact on small businesses that are light truck manufacturers. The fact that a substantial number of small businesses may purchase or lease light trucks and that the regulation might result in increased prices for those trucks would not trigger the RFA's requirements.

4. Unfunded Mandates Reform Act

This law, passed in 1995, requires all executive agencies to perform a regulatory analysis for any proposed rule that may impose more than $100 million per year in costs on state and local governments or on the private sector. *See* 2 U.S.C. § 1532. The analysis must include "a qualitative and quantitative assessment of the anticipated costs and benefits of the Federal mandate . . . as well as the effect of the Federal mandate on health, safety, and the natural environment." In addition, the agency must "identify and consider a reasonable number of regulatory alternatives and from those alternatives, select the least costly, most cost-effective or least burdensome alternatives that achieve the objectives of the rule." 2 U.S.C. § 1535(a). The Act allows for only a limited judicial review. It forbids courts from enjoining any agency rule for failure to perform the required analyses, allowing courts only to require the analyses to be performed. If, however, the rule is already in effect, requiring the analysis to be performed after the fact is not very useful, especially to those concerned with the effects of the rule.

5. The Paperwork Reduction Act

If a rule would require ten or more persons either to report information to the government or to the public or to collect or retain information, the Paperwork Reduction Act, 44 U.S.C. §§ 3501-3520, imposes specific procedural requirements. When an agency proposes a rule with such a collection or reporting requirement, the agency, including independent regulatory agencies, must submit the proposed rule to OIRA for its comments. OIRA then has 60 days either to approve or file comments on the rule. If it files comments, the agency cannot adopt the rule until it has resubmitted the rule to OIRA and responded to OIRA's comments. Then, if OIRA finds the response unreasonable (or if it finds that the agency has not followed the correct procedures or has substantially modified the rule), OIRA is empowered to disapprove the collection or reporting requirement,[12] unlike the OIRA review under E.O. 12866, where OIRA can comment on an agency's proposed and final rules, but not disapprove them. When OIRA approves the rule, it assigns a control number that is displayed with the rule when it is published. Failure to include the control number with the rule absolves private parties of any duty to comply with the rule's collection or reporting requirement.[13] The Act limits approval to three years, so within three years an agency will have to

12. Independent regulatory agencies are authorized to override an OIRA veto by a majority vote.

13. The lack of a control number on a rule or form does not, however, absolve one from any requirement that may arise from statute. For example, a failure to have a control number on your IRS Form 1040 would absolve you from having to submit that form in reporting your taxable income, but it would not absolve you from having to submit *some* report of your taxable income, because the requirement for an annual report is contained in a statute.

go through another rulemaking. Even if the rule is otherwise exempt from notice and comment under the APA, the Paperwork Reduction Act requires public notice and opportunity to comment.

6. Congressional Review

In the act that amended the Regulatory Flexibility Act, Congress added a wholly new law, the Congressional Review Act (CRA), requiring congressional review of all agency rules. *See* 5 U.S.C. §§ 801-808. Virtually all rules, including those exempt from notice and comment under the APA, must be submitted with a report to both houses of Congress and the Government Accountability Office (GAO) before they can go into effect. The report must contain "a concise general statement relating to the rule," a copy of any cost-benefit analysis, and any other analyses under the Regulatory Flexibility Act, Unfunded Mandates Reform Act, and any executive orders. GAO must submit a report to each house within 15 days on each rule it receives. "Major" rules, which essentially are economically significant rules as determined under E.O. 12866, generally must have a 60-day delayed effective date, although there is a good cause exception similar to the APA's as to the delayed effective date. Generally, within 60 days of receiving the rule and report, a joint resolution of disapproval can be introduced into either house. Thereafter, if the resolution is passed and signed by the President, the rule is effectively repealed retroactively back to its date of adoption. Moreover, if the rule is disapproved, the CRA prohibits the agency from adopting any subsequent rule that is "substantially the same" unless Congress specifically authorizes it. The CRA explicitly precludes judicial review of any "determination, finding, action, or omission" under the Act. The courts have almost universally respected this preclusion, leaving enforcement of the CRA to the political process. Notably, that political enforcement has been remarkably successful. Early on, the executive did not believe that interpretive rules and statements of policy needed to be reported to Congress for review, although they are textually included within the CRA's ambit. Although the courts with one exception viewed this "omission" by the executive to be non-reviewable, pressure from Congress resulted in the executive changing its stance.

The purpose of this law was to enable Congress to provide additional oversight and control of the regulatory process, but it only has practical effect after an election where the administration has changed parties and both houses of Congress are controlled by the same party as the President. In the 20 years after the law was passed, only one rule was overturned under this procedure. However, with the election of Donald Trump and Republican control of both the House and Senate in 2017, 14 Obama administration rules were disapproved. And after the election of Joe Biden in 2020, three Trump administration rules were disapproved.

7. Information Quality Act

In 2001, Congress passed what has now become known as the Information Quality Act as a rider to a large appropriations act. *See* Treasury and General Government Appropriations Act for Fiscal Year 2001, Pub. L. No. 106-554, § 515, 114 Stat. 2763A-125, 2763A-153 to 2763A-154 (2001). The Act contains only one section, which requires OMB to adopt guidelines ensuring and maximizing the quality, objectivity, utility, and integrity of information (including statistical information) disseminated by federal agencies. These guidelines in turn are to require all federal agencies to do two things: to adopt their own guidelines ensuring and maximizing the quality, objectivity, utility, and integrity of information disseminated by the agencies and to provide a procedural mechanism by which affected persons may seek and obtain correction of information maintained and disseminated by an agency. Because the act applies only to information "disseminated" by the agency, OMB had to decide what information fell within this term. Because the act had been passed as a stealth rider to an appropriations act, there were no legislative hearings, committee reports, or floor statements to clarify the intent and purpose of the provision. OMB chose to give the term *dissemination* the broadest possible meaning, which includes information "disseminated" in an agency rulemaking as part of the preamble to the rule or of the supporting factual data for the rule.

It is, of course, important for information or data upon which a rule is based to be accurate, but in the past one of the purposes of the Notice-and-Comment Rulemaking process was to subject the agency's data to review and criticism. OMB's guidelines, however, establish particular peer review procedures before certain types of scientific information may be used in a rulemaking (that is, before it is disseminated). *See* Final Information Quality Bulletin for Peer Review, 70 Fed. Reg. 2664 (Jan. 14, 2005). Such peer review, however, can delay the beginning of a rulemaking for an extended period of time.

In any case, the courts have rejected, to date, every claim based on the Information Quality Act. *See, e.g., Salt Institute v. Leavitt*, 440 F.3d 156 (4th Cir. 2006) (finding agency's claimed failure to comply with Information Quality Act unreviewable).

8. Conclusion

The original conception of informal rulemaking—a simple notice with an opportunity for comment and a concise statement of basis and purpose to accompany the final rule—was to create a process that would be simple and facilitate agency rulemaking, which was viewed as preferable to making policy through adjudication. Today rulemakings are the dominant form of agency policymaking, but despite reliance on that form of policymaking, our political culture is highly ambivalent about rulemakings that can impose costs of hundreds of millions of dollars on the economy and directly affect the lives of every citizen. The result has been initiatives by all three branches of government to assure that the process is rational and based on the best information and judgment. Congress initially created the environmental analysis requirement, and both the President and Congress have created regulatory cost/benefit analysis requirements for rules viewed as particularly important because of the extent of their impact or the particular entities subject to or affected by those rules. In addition, agencies also are conducting risk analyses for health and safety rules, and various bills introduced in past and current sessions of Congress would require them by statute. These analyses are intended to rationalize agencies' approach to risk by enabling agencies to determine the actual risks posed by different activities. Agencies then, at least in theory, would be able to concentrate their rules on those activities or problems that impose the greatest risks, and combined with cost/benefit analyses, agencies would be able to target society's limited resources where they will do the most good, achieving the greatest "bang for the buck."

Attempts to rationalize rulemaking, however, have their own costs in increasing exponentially the costs and delays involved in the process. This results in fewer rules, which some believe may be the real agenda of those pushing the various analyses. A rule designed to reduce workers' exposure to airborne toxics in the workplace may be a better rule after five years of study and analysis, but it is five years in which the workers continue to be exposed to unregulated airborne toxics and five years during which employers will not have to bear the higher costs of increased workplace safety.

This chapter has perhaps provided an introduction to what is now a complicated procedure. A good graphic that captures the process involved in agency rulemaking can be found at www.reginfo.gov/public/reginfo/Regmap/index.myjsp

CHAPTER 6

The Availability of Judicial Review

> [W]hat is there in the exalted station of [an executive] officer, which shall bar a citizen from asserting, in a court of justice, his legal rights, or shall forbid a court to listen to the claim . . . ?
>
> —*Chief Justice John Marshall, Marbury v. Madison, 1 Cranch* (5 *U.S.*) 137, 166 (1803)

The famous case of *Marbury v. Madison* is generally known for its conclusion that courts can review the constitutionality of acts of Congress, but perhaps of equal importance was its conclusion that certain acts of executive officials are subject to judicial review for legality. It can hardly be overemphasized that phrases such as "the rule of law" and "a government of laws, not of men" would be virtually meaningless without an independent branch of government whose function includes assuring fidelity to law. The procedural requirements of the APA or other statutes and the substantive statutory limitations on an agency's authority found in its statutory mandate would count for little if the threat of judicial review was lacking.

Invocations of judicial review and *Marbury v. Madison*, however, would be incomplete without remembering what happened to William Marbury—he lost! He did not get judicial review of the executive's unlawful withholding of his commission, because the Court did not have jurisdiction of his case. This reminds us that the first step in judicial review is to satisfy what laypersons would call technicalities, the prerequisites to review. To a government lawyer defending government action, however, those "technicalities" are important arrows in the quiver of possible ways to avoid judicial review altogether. To the lawyer attempting to obtain judicial review of agency action for a client, therefore, it is critical to assure that each of the requirements for judicial review is satisfied.

In this chapter we will begin by addressing the jurisdictional requirements for obtaining judicial review, in particular the constitutional requirement that plaintiffs have standing. We will then consider judicial review under the APA, starting with the two provisions that create exceptions from such review. We then turn to the requirements that must be met to obtain judicial review under the APA, including the doctrines of Finality, Exhaustion, and Ripeness. Chapter 7 will then address the scope of judicial review, or the standards that courts use when they review agency action.

I. REVIEWABILITY GENERALLY

There are a number of prerequisites that must be satisfied before a person may obtain judicial review. One, the one William Marbury failed, is the requirement that a court have jurisdiction over a case. Jurisdiction, moreover, depends on both statutory and constitutional considerations. A second requirement for judicial review is a statutory cause of action, which in administrative law is usually found in the APA, but it is subject to qualifications and exceptions. In addition, there are other requirements that relate to the timing of judicial review, to assure that courts do not inappropriately interfere with agency action. Each of these will be addressed in turn below.

A. Jurisdiction — Statutory Jurisdiction

Whether a court has jurisdiction over a case is the first question every court should ask. Parties need not raise and cannot waive the issue; courts can raise it on their own (or as the law likes to say, *sua sponte*) at any time before final judgment.

Any suit in federal court must find a grant of jurisdiction in some federal statute. The APA is not such a jurisdictional statute, but 28 U.S.C. § 1331—the "federal question" statute—provides jurisdiction for suits in federal district courts raising questions under federal law. Because suits against agencies alleging that they have acted inconsistently with law invariably raise questions under federal law, this provision is always available as a jurisdictional basis unless some other statute has withdrawn it as a basis. Congress has in many situations substituted another statutory basis for jurisdiction in place of Section 1331. The most common situation is when Congress decides that review by a trial court is unnecessary and provides for direct review in a court of appeals. Review by a trial court is often deemed unnecessary because the agency action subject to review is based on a paper record, and there are no issues of disputed fact upon which testimony is necessary. Direct review eliminates one level of review for all concerned and hopefully speeds a final resolution of any judicial challenge. For example, under the Hobbs Act, 28 U.S.C. § 2342, most of the orders of the Federal Communications Commission (FCC) are reviewed directly in a court of appeals, not in a district court. Another example involves judicial review of decisions made by the Occupational Safety and Health Review Commission, which are brought directly in a court of appeals. Yet another example is found in the Clean Air Act, which provides that judicial challenges to most rules under that Act must be brought in the Court of Appeals for the District of Columbia Circuit. Here, direct review is limited to just one court of appeals, assuring that the first decision will necessarily be nationwide in effect. In fact, jurisdiction for judicial review of rulemakings and formal adjudications is very often in a court of appeals pursuant to a specific statute relating to the federal program at issue. In other words, lawyers seeking judicial review of agency action must find the appropriate jurisdictional statutes for their challenges.

Two questions have arisen under these specific statutes. One is the extent to which they limit the default jurisdiction under Section 1331 if the specific statute does not explicitly make its jurisdiction exclusive.

Example

The Occupational Safety and Health Act provides that "[a]ny person who may be adversely affected by a [safety or health] standard issued under [the Act] may at any time prior to the sixtieth day after such standard is promulgated file a petition challenging the validity of such standard with the United States court of appeals for the circuit wherein such person resides or has his principal place of business, for a judicial review of such standard." 29 U.S.C. § 655(f). While a person obviously "may" seek judicial review of an OSHA standard in the appropriate court of appeals under this provision, might a person instead obtain judicial review in the appropriate federal district court under 28 U.S.C. § 1331?

Explanation

By its terms, this provision does not say that it is the exclusive jurisdictional basis for challenging such standards. Nevertheless, courts have uniformly held that a plaintiff cannot challenge an OSHA standard in a federal district court asserting jurisdiction under 28 U.S.C. § 1331. The courts are in agreement that they should interpret specific statutes such as this one to establish exclusive jurisdiction over the cases subject to their terms. Courts have noted that there is a general canon of statutory construction that specific statutes govern over general statutes, and to allow a plaintiff to choose a suit in district court over the specific statute's provision of review in a court of appeals would thwart the purpose of the specific statute.

The other question that has arisen is how to read a statute giving exclusive jurisdiction to a court of appeals over a particular kind of challenge, when the challenge brought is not precisely within the terms of the statute. Should the court of appeals have direct review because the nature of the case is so related to the type of case over which it has exclusive jurisdiction, should the default jurisdiction of Section 1331 apply because the terms of the specific statute do not precisely apply, or should no court have jurisdiction over such a case, inferring that the exclusive direct review provision precludes any review not within its terms?

Example

Looking at the OSH Act's jurisdictional provision in the previous example, suppose that a union wishes to sue the Secretary of Labor not for a standard she has promulgated but because she has not issued a standard that the union believes she is required to issue. The provision by its terms only addresses challenges to standards after they have been adopted. Where, if anywhere, may the union bring its challenge?

Explanation

On its face, the jurisdictional provision refers only to challenges to standards that have already been issued. If, however, a person could bring a suit challenging the failure to issue a standard in a district court under the default jurisdictional provision of Section 1331, such a suit would conflict with Congress's apparent purpose to have the Secretary's decisions with respect to standards decided in courts of appeals. On the other hand, if the provision were interpreted as precluding this type of suit in district courts under Section 1331 but not allowing it in a court of appeals, this would be inconsistent with normal practice, because ordinarily persons can challenge agencies' failure to act, as well as their actions. *See* 5 U.S.C. § 706(1). Accordingly, despite the narrow language of the statute, courts have interpreted the Occupational Safety and Health Act's jurisdictional provision to allow suits challenging the failure to adopt a standard to be brought in the court of appeals. *See, e.g., Oil, Chemical & Atomic Workers Union v. Occupational Safety & Health Admin.*, 145 F.3d 120 (3d Cir. 1998).

B. Jurisdiction—Standing

Standing is another jurisdictional prerequisite. Plaintiffs must make good-faith allegations in their complaints sufficient to meet standing requirements and must be prepared, if challenged, to produce evidence to establish standing prior to a motion for summary judgment. Moreover, because standing is a jurisdictional requirement, it can be raised anytime, even by the court *sua sponte*, and if the record does not contain sufficient evidence to establish standing, the plaintiff may be in trouble.

Courts have used the term "standing" in two different contexts. One is the constitutional limitation that federal courts only decide "cases and controversies." The other is known as "prudential standing," and it constitutes a jurisdictional limitation derived by courts as a matter of judicial management. Unlike constitutional standing, prudential standing requirements can be altered or eliminated by statute. Also, as described later, this very term has become disfavored.

1. Constitutionally Required Standing

In the course on constitutional law, students learn that the Constitution limits federal court jurisdiction to "cases and controversies" and that one of the limitations of those words is to require a person to have "standing" before the person can bring a case in federal court. The Court summarized the standing requirement in *Lujan v. Defenders of Wildlife*, 504 U.S. 555, 560-561 (1992):

> the irreducible constitutional minimum of standing contains three elements: First, the plaintiff must have suffered an "injury in fact"—an invasion of a legally-protected interest which is (a) concrete and particularized[1] and (b) "actual or imminent, not 'conjectural' or 'hypothetical.'" Second, there must be a causal connection between the injury and the conduct complained of—the injury has to be "fairly . . . trace[able] to the challenged action of the defendant, and not . . . th[e] result [of] the independent action of some third party not before the court." Third, it must be "likely," as opposed to merely "speculative," that the injury will be "redressed by a favorable decision."

In short, a plaintiff must show *injury, causation*, and *redressability*. As the Court explained in *Defenders*, the role of the courts is to protect the rights of individuals; vindicating the public interest is the role of the political branches. Thus, the standing requirement is intended to distinguish between those who are individually harmed and those who only have a generalized grievance shared by the public at large. Accordingly, in the administrative law context, before a person can obtain judicial review of agency action, the person must show that the agency action has caused or is about to cause concrete injury to the person, which can be avoided or

1. By particularized, we mean that the injury must affect the plaintiff in a personal and individual way. [Court's footnote.]

redressed by a court. The easy case is when an agency takes action against someone or adopts a rule that imposes duties on or restricts the freedom of a person.

Example

The FCC adopts a rule requiring cable companies offering broadband Internet connections to allow any Internet service provider to use their facilities. This rule in effect prohibits a cable company from limiting its customers to its own Internet service provider. A cable company that wishes to restrict users to its own Internet service provider wants to sue. Does it have standing?

Explanation

Yes. This is an easy case. The FCC rule causes injury to the company. But for the FCC rule, the company would be able to restrict its cable users to the company's own Internet service provider, which would maximize its profits. Under the rule, it has been deprived of the freedom to exclude other Internet service providers from its connection, which will reduce its profits. If the company's challenge to the rule is successful, an injunction from a court to set aside the FCC rule will enable the company to avoid injury. The person's injury is palpable; it is clearly caused by the government action; and an injunction against the action will prevent the injury.

There are, however, a number of more difficult cases. In the next several sections, we will address some of the problems faced by plaintiffs and courts with respect to each of the three requirements regarding standing: injury, causation, and redressability.

Before we go there, however, it is important to point out that in a case seeking injunctive or declaratory relief, which is the norm in challenges to agency action, as long as one plaintiff has standing, the standing of other plaintiffs is irrelevant and therefore disregarded. *See Bowsher v. Synar*, 478 U.S. 714, 721 (1986).

Example

Imagine that in the previous example a member of Congress believes that the FCC's rule is unlawful. As a sponsor of the legislation under which the FCC is purportedly acting, he believes he is injured by the agency's failure to abide by what he believes are the law's requirements. If the cable company did not sue, could the member of Congress sue? Does he have standing?

Explanation

No, the member of Congress would not have standing. In *Raines v. Byrd*, 521 U.S. 811 (1997), the Supreme Court held that members of Congress do not have the requisite particularized injury to satisfy the standing requirement to challenge the constitutionality of a statute because they believe it is unconstitutional. Similarly, the D.C. Circuit has held that members of Congress do not have the particularized injury requisite to satisfy the standing requirement to challenge agency action simply because they believe the agency action deviates from laws they passed. *See, e.g., Harrington v. Bush*, 553 F.2d 190 (D.C. Cir. 1977).

Thus, if the cable company did not sue, the member of Congress could not sue either. However, if the cable company did sue, because it had standing, the court would not bother to address whether the member of Congress also had standing.

If a member of Congress were challenging an agency action or a statute that actually affected the member's congressional prerogatives, then presumably he would have standing. For example, in *Immigration and Naturalization Service v. Chadha*, 462 U.S. 919 (1983), the Supreme Court allowed the House and the Senate to intervene in a suit that challenged the ability of the House and Senate to negative agency action by means of a one-house veto.

a. Injury for Standing

There are potentially many different ways persons might view themselves as injured even if the agency action does not act upon them directly. The constitutional requirement for injury, however, is that a person must suffer (or be about to suffer) a concrete, particularized injury, an injury that is not just a generalized grievance equally shared by everyone, and an injury that is neither conjectural nor abstract. Much of the law in this area involves trying to determine whether a claimed injury meets this requirement. The discussion below addresses various types of claimed injuries.

1. Recreational, Aesthetic, or Environmental Injury A recurring problem in environmental and "animal rights" cases is the identification of the injury to a person who is concerned about the effect of a government action on the environment or on animals supposedly protected by federal statutes. In the landmark case of *Sierra Club v. Morton*, 405 U.S. 727 (1972), the Supreme Court held that a person's mere interest in a subject, no matter how real and intense, is insufficient to establish that injury to that subject qualifies as injury to the person for standing purposes. However, the Court went on, if a person uses an area for recreational purposes and the government action would harm the area, so that the person's recreational or aesthetic pleasure would be harmed, this would qualify as constitutional injury. As a result, environmental groups now must find a member who uses an area in a way that will be harmed by the government action.

Example

A government agency plans to build a dam. The dam's reservoir will inundate a scenic river valley and destroy the habitat for an endangered species of mouse. An environmental group believes this action would violate the Endangered Species Act. Two of its members are potential plaintiffs. One is a local person who regularly has walked along the river and enjoyed the scenery. Another is an active member of Defenders of Wildlife who has devoted her life to saving endangered animals. This person once visited the river valley to observe the mouse, but she lives elsewhere and has no current plans to return. Will either of these persons be "injured" sufficiently to satisfy the standing requirement?

Explanation

The first person can demonstrate injury; the second person cannot.

The first person can establish injury because he has used, and presumably would continue to use, the scenic river valley for recreation. Inundating the river valley will make it impossible for him to continue that activity. Note that even though the challenge to the government action might allege a violation of the Endangered Species Act, the injury does not necessarily have to relate to that Act. Later, we will find that although this person may satisfy the constitutional requirement for standing, there may be a question whether he can bring the case in light of statutory restrictions.

The second person, despite her interest in the mouse, has not demonstrated how destroying the habitat of the mouse and perhaps even extinguishing the mouse species will cause her a concrete, particularized injury. The fact that she once visited the valley and saw the mouse is not sufficient. The issue is not whether she has seen the mouse in the past, but whether it would injure her not to be able to see it in the future. Absent evidence that she has an immediate or ongoing intent to see the mouse or its habitat, mere interest in the mouse species, no matter how strong, would not suffice. Were she a researcher or scientist who studied the mouse, she might stand in a better situation, especially if she had an ongoing research interest that might be thwarted by destroying the mouse's habitat or the mouse species. This would not then be a recreational injury, but it could qualify as a particularized, concrete injury.

Animal rights groups have had a particularly hard time establishing standing. Suppose that a federal agency adopts a rule governing how laboratory animals are to be treated in research grants funded by the agency. A research lab with a grant would easily have standing to challenge the rule as too burdensome, because the rule limits what they can do (and presumably raises the cost of their research). However, an animal rights group that believes the rule is inadequate to protect laboratory animals from inhumane treatment would have great difficulty showing injury to it or its members. Unlike the person who walks in the woods and whose recreational experience is injured by seeing clear-cut trees or a flooded valley or the absence of wildlife, the animal rights group member does not observe the animals in the laboratory. In one case a former researcher alleged that she would need to do animal research in the future to advance her career and that she would suffer because she would have to observe the inhumane treatment of the animals during her research. The court did not decide whether such observation would constitute injury, because it decided that in any case the injury was not imminent or immediate, but rather was conjectural or hypothetical. The researcher had left laboratory research six years before the case and her affidavit to establish standing did not specify when she would return. *See Animal Legal Defense Fund, Inc. v. Espy*, 23 F.3d 496 (D.C. Cir. 1994). In order to satisfy the constitutional standing requirement, the injury must be likely to occur in the foreseeable future and not be conjectural. One of the few cases in which an animal rights group established standing involved a challenge to rules governing zoo conditions for primates, and a member of the group had repeatedly viewed primates in a zoo in lawful but allegedly inhumane conditions. The *en banc* D.C. Circuit Court of Appeals in a deeply split decision found standing, relying on the basic notion of recreational standing—the person's zoo experience was harmed by having to see the primates in their allegedly inhumane conditions, just as a person's walk in the woods might be harmed by a clear cut. *See Animal Legal Defense Fund, Inc. v. Glickman*, 154 F.3d 426 (D.C. Cir. 1998) (*en banc*).

It is worthy of note that Justices Thomas and Gorsuch have indicated their belief that an "offended observer" does not have the requisite injury for standing. While this view was expressed in a concurrence in a First Amendment Establishment Clause case, their theory would apply equally in the aesthetic or environmental context as well.

2. Risk as Injury Physical harm clearly is an injury. Thus, if a government action were to harm a person or the person's property, the person would have standing to challenge that action. The question arises, however, whether mere risk of harm qualifies as injury. For example, the Environmental Protection Agency (EPA) might adopt a rule allowing a certain amount of pollution because the EPA believes it will pose a risk of less than one in a million of anyone contracting cancer. A person exposed to such pollution might want to challenge the rule as insufficiently protective, but what is the person's injury? Contracting cancer would certainly be an injury, but it is very speculative whether the person will contract cancer because of the pollution. Nevertheless, the person is immediately subjected to an increased risk of cancer. The lower courts initially seemed willing to consider increased risk as an immediate concrete injury. See, e.g., *Dimarzo v. Cahill*, 575 F.2d 15, 18 (1st Cir. 1978) (increased risk of fire to inmates in jail); *Village of Elk Grove Village v. Evans*, 997 F.2d 328 (7th Cir. 1993) (increased risk of flooding from construction in flood plain); *Mountain States Legal Foundation v. Glickman*, 92 F.3d 1228 (D.C. Cir. 1996) (increased risk of forest fires from Forest Service management choice); *Louisiana Environmental Action Network v. U.S. E.P.A.*, 172 F.3d 65 (D.C. Cir. 1999) (increased risk of health effects from hazardous waste deposited at nearby landfill). More recently, however, some courts have begun to question this assumption. For example, the D.C. Circuit has suggested that only some substantial increased risks may constitute sufficient concrete, immediate injury to satisfy standing. In *Natural Resources Defense Council v. Environmental Protection Agency*, 464 F.3d 1 (D.C. Cir. 2006) the initial panel rejected a claim of injury from increased risk attributable to EPA's regulation of methyl bromide to comply with the Montreal Protocol relating to chemicals depleting the ozone layer. The panel concluded that the increased risk of ten deaths in the United States over 145 years was "minuscule." On rehearing, the panel expressed concern that allowing any increased risk of injury or disease to satisfy the requirement of standing would in essence eliminate the need for a concrete, immediate injury. Accordingly, the court articulated a standard that the increased risk must be a "substantial probability" of injury. Reconsidering the evidence, it concluded that two to four of the plaintiff's 500,000 members would contract cancer as a result of the agency's rule. This, the court said, satisfied the requirement of a substantial probability of injury. In *Public Citizen, Inc. v. National Highway Traffic Safety Admin.*, 489 F.3d 1279 (D.C. Cir. 2007), the court tried to further elaborate on its "substantial probability" test. Under this test, the plaintiff must show:

> at least both (i) a substantially increased risk of harm and (ii) a substantial probability of harm with that increase taken into account. . . . If the agency action causes an individual or individual members of an organization to face an increase in the risk of harm that is "substantial," and the ultimate risk of harm also is "substantial," then the individual or organization has demonstrated an injury in fact. . . . In applying the "substantial" standard, we are mindful, of course, that the constitutional requirement of imminence as articulated by the Supreme Court . . . necessarily compels a very strict understanding of what increases in risk and overall risk levels can count as "substantial."

In this case Public Citizen was attempting to challenge an automobile safety rule regarding tire pressure monitoring systems, and it provided information regarding the increased risk to automobile drivers, including members of Public Citizen, caused by NHTSA's failure to adopt a stricter rule. The court did not believe this information was sufficient to meet its test of substantial probability of injury, but it allowed the plaintiffs an opportunity to supplement the record. Although they provided expert affidavits to the effect that the increased risk of injury from NHTSA's rule compared to Public Citizen's preferred rule was higher than the increased risk of cancer in *NRDC v. EPA*, the court held that the supplemental submission was inadequate to establish the requisite "substantial probability of injury." One of the problems was that Public Citizen had computed the increased risk of injury between NHTSA's rule and Public Citizen's preferred rule, but in its comments in the rulemaking Public Citizen had suggested that it would accept something less than its preferred rule, albeit more strict than what NHTSA had adopted. As a result, the court said, there was no evidence of the increased risk between what NHTSA had adopted and what Public Citizen would have accepted, so there was no evidence of injury. As Public Citizen would tell you, trying to provide probabilistic evidence, especially in the specificity seemingly required by the D.C. Circuit, is very expensive and difficult. If plaintiffs are required to quantify the specific increased risk suffered as a result of what they believe are regulations that do not adequately protect persons' health or safety, they may be foreclosed from challenging such regulations.

For example, in *Food & Water Watch, Inc. v. Vilsack*, 808 F.3d 905 (D.C. Cir. 2015), the consumer group could not establish that a changed method of inspecting poultry would "produce significantly more adulterated, unwholesome chicken compared to the existing inspection systems." As of this writing, both the Fifth and First Circuits have followed the *Public Citizen* test.

The Supreme Court first addressed risk of harm after *Public Citizen*. In three recent cases it has given some apparent mixed messages. In *Summers v. Earth Island Institute*, 555 U.S. 488 (2009), environmental groups wanted to challenge a Forest Service regulation that allowed for certain salvage timber sales to be made without prior notice and comment, despite a statute requiring notice and comment before all timber sales. However, because they did not know to which timber sales the regulation might be applied, they could not produce a member who walked in the woods affected by the sales. They argued that, because of their several hundred thousand members and the thousands of timber sales that the Forest Service said would be subject to the regulation, it was highly probable that one of their members would be injured by a timber sale subject to the regulation. Justice Scalia, writing for the five-member majority, derided the notion of probabilistic injury, saying that it was essential for an organization to produce an identified member who would be injured by the alleged unlawful action.

The second case, *Monsanto Co. v. Geertson Seed Farms*, 561 U.S. 139 (2010), involved a challenge by organic alfalfa farmers to a Department of Agriculture decision deregulating the planting of genetically modified alfalfa. Their claim was that planting GM alfalfa would pose a risk to their organic alfalfa as a result of possible cross-pollination and contamination. Without dissent the Supreme Court found that these farmers had standing because they established a "reasonable probability" that their crops would be infected by the deregulated seed and this "substantial risk"[2] injured them by requiring them to take expensive preventive and monitoring measures.

Finally, in *Clapper v. Amnesty International USA*, 133 S. Ct. 1138 (2013), persons who alleged that their communications were likely to be intercepted by the National Security Agency were denied standing. Although the courts below had found that there was an "objectively reasonable likelihood" that the plaintiffs' communications would be intercepted, the Supreme Court by a 5-4 vote held that this was insufficient, because they had not shown that their injury was "certainly impending." The Court conceded that it had in the past sometimes found standing based upon a "substantial risk" of harm, but here it said the harm alleged by plaintiffs required an "attenuated chain of inferences," making their injury entirely speculative.

Despite their differences, these cases can be synthesized. First, in *Summers*, the probabilistic injury involved the likelihood that one unknown member of one of the environmental groups walked in a forest that would someday be subject to a timber sale exempted from public notice-and-comment under Forest Service regulations. However, in *Geertson*, it was not a question of some, unidentified member of an organization who was faced with a risk; it was particular, identified members of an organization who were faced with the risk. Second, in *Summers*, the threat was of something that would happen indefinitely in the future; in *Geertson*, the significant risk was imminent with the approval of GM alfalfa planting. The outcome in *Clapper* probably can be best explained by the Court's statements:

> [o]ur standing inquiry has been especially rigorous when reaching the merits of the dispute would force us to decide whether an action taken by one of the other two branches of the Federal Government was unconstitutional.

and:

> we have often found a lack of standing in cases in which the Judiciary has been requested to review actions of the political branches in the fields of intelligence gathering and foreign affairs.

Nevertheless, even if we can synthesize these cases, the synthesis does not tell us much about the D.C. Circuit's test or those of other circuits regarding risk of harm and standing.

---

2. Elsewhere the Court referred to it as a "significant risk."

Example

An environmental group wants to challenge an EPA regulation limiting certain hazardous air pollutants, asserting that the regulation is not protective enough. The EPA concedes that according to its studies, the level of allowed pollution will increase the lifetime risk of lung cancer by 1/100,000 by persons within 40 miles of an emitting facility compared to a zero pollution level requirement. The EPA, however, believes the level of protection provided by its regulation is sufficient, and it provides much greater protection than the previously required level. The group finds a member who lives within 40 miles of an emitting facility. Does the group have standing to challenge the regulation?

Explanation

The environmental group should not be foreclosed by the Supreme Court's decision in *Summers*. In *Summers*, one of the key problems was the lack of an identified member who would suffer any injury. Here the group has an identified member who will suffer an increased risk of lung cancer. On the other hand, the group cannot find much support in the Supreme Court's decision in *Geertson*. There the Court found a "reasonable probability" and a "significant risk" of contamination, suggesting a much higher probability of the ultimate harm occurring than is involved with the hazardous air pollutants. While *Geertson* does not provide support for the environmental group, neither does it determine that a lesser risk could not qualify as "injury" for standing purposes. *Clapper* would, of course, provide ammunition for the government, which would quote the requirement that an injury be "certainly impending."

If the case were brought in the D.C. Circuit, the question would be whether there was both a "substantially increased risk of harm" and a "substantial probability of harm with that increase taken into account." The increase here would be from a zero lifetime risk of lung cancer to a 1/100,000 risk. Is that a substantial increase? The probability to the member of contracting lung cancer as a result of the regulation allowing this level of pollution would also be 1 in 100,000. Is that a substantial probability of harm? The answer is unclear, although one could well say neither number is substantial. However, what if the environmental group has 200,000 members who live within 40 miles of an emitting facility? According to the EPA's figures, two of the group's members would contract lung cancer as a result of the allowed pollution. In the D.C. Circuit's *NRDC* case, the likelihood of two members contracting cancer was sufficient to qualify the risk as substantial. But if that is the way the case were styled, it might run afoul of the Court's decision in *Summers*, where it said that it is necessary for the group to identify a particular member who would suffer injury, and, of course, the group could not identify which of its members would contract lung cancer. In short, the answer to this question is not clear.

A case with very similar facts to the example here held that plaintiffs had not established a significant risk of harm. *See Shrimpers and Fishermen of RGV v. Texas Commn. on Env. Quality*, 968 F.3d 419 (5th Cir. 2020).

3. Fear as Injury In some situations it appears that a reasonable fear can be requisite injury for standing purposes. In *Friends of the Earth v. Laidlaw Environmental Services*, 528 U.S. 167 (2000), for example, the plaintiffs were unable to demonstrate any "health risk or environmental harm" caused by Laidlaw's discharge of mercury into a river in excess of its permitted amount. Nevertheless, they did show that Laidlaw had violated its permit limitations with respect to a very toxic substance, and they averred in affidavits that as a result of knowing this they feared using the river for various recreational purposes, such as boating, fishing, and swimming. The Court characterized those fears as "reasonable concerns" resulting in an actual injury to the plaintiffs' recreational interests. See also *Friends of the Earth v. Gaston Copper Recycling Co.*, 204 F.3d 149 (4th Cir. 2000) (en banc). One can see here an alternative to probabilistic risk injury claims in certain types of cases. That is, in *Laidlaw* the plaintiffs might have tried to show that if they swam in or ate fish from the river they would have a greater risk of some illness or injury. Under the D.C. Circuit's "substantial probability" standard, they probably would have had a very difficult time. Under *Laidlaw*'s "reasonable fear" standard, however, they were found to have sufficient injury in fact. The difficulty is in determining which fears are reasonable and which are not.

4. Procedural Injury In *Lujan v. Defenders of Wildlife*, 504 U.S. 555, 573 n.8 (1992), the Court concluded that a procedural violation by itself did not satisfy standing's injury requirement. In that case, the agency had not engaged in the required inter-agency consultation under the Endangered Species Act (ESA) before adopting a particular rule. The plaintiff, Defenders of Wildlife, having failed to provide sufficient evidence of any members whose recreational experience would be harmed by the rule, argued that the statutory requirement for inter-agency coordination created a procedural right to such coordination in the public enforceable by any person. The Court rejected this argument, perceiving it as showing nothing more than a generalized grievance with an alleged agency failure to comply with the law. In *Summers v. Earth Island Institute*, 555 U.S. 488 (2009), the Court repeated its conclusion that procedural violations do not themselves create "injury" for purposes of standing. In *Summers*, the Forest Service had adopted a regulation exempting certain salvage timber sales from the statutory requirement for prior notice and an opportunity for public comment. Environmental groups that regularly engaged in public comment on such timber sales challenged the regulation, saying that it was contrary to statute. Their injury, they said, was being denied the opportunity to comment on timber sales. The Court reaffirmed that a procedural violation such as this did not constitute "injury" for purposes of standing. If, however, the groups had a member who walked in the woods where one of these salvage timber sales was going to occur, then the member's inability to continue being able to enjoy walking in those woods would constitute injury, and the group would have representational standing to challenge the alleged procedural violation. In other words, while an agency's procedural violation leading to an agency action does not cause injury for standing purposes, if the plaintiff can show a concrete injury resulting from the agency's action itself, then the plaintiff can have standing to challenge the agency's action on the basis of the procedural violation.

Example

The Clean Water Act requires the Corps of Engineers to provide an opportunity for a public hearing before issuing a permit to discharge dredged or fill material into a water of the United States. One of the purposes of the National Wildlife Federation (NWF) is to monitor proposed government permits to assess their impact on wildlife and to comment on proposed permits to try to avoid or mitigate the issuance of permits that adversely affect wildlife. Assume the Corps proposes to issue such a permit without providing an opportunity for a public hearing. The NWF sues to enjoin the issuance of the permit because the Corps has violated the statutory requirement to provide for a public hearing. In addition, a local landowner concerned that the proposed discharge will negatively affect the value of his adjoining property also sues to enjoin the permit issuance. The NWF does not have standing; the landowner does.

Explanation

The NWF does not have standing because it has no injury. The fact that Congress wanted public interest groups to be able to comment on proposed discharge permits and that the Corps ignored that requirement does not constitute "injury in fact" for standing purposes. There may be a procedural violation—the failure to provide an opportunity for a hearing—but there is no procedural "injury." On the other hand, the adjoining landowner does have standing. His allegation is that the discharge will adversely affect the value of his land, causing him economic injury. That is injury in fact sufficient for standing purposes, even though the injury is not directly related to what he argues is the statutory violation—the failure to provide an opportunity for a hearing. Note that the NWF could have standing if it had a member who would be adversely affected by the discharge.

5. Informational Injury If a person seeks a document from an agency under the Freedom of Information Act, and the agency refuses to produce the document, the person is injured by being deprived of the document that he or she sought. It is not necessary to show that some injury will flow to the person from not having the document. The Act gives the person the right to obtain government documents, and that is sufficient. Many statutes require the government to collect information, sometimes for general publication, sometimes for internal use but available to the public through the Freedom of Information Act. If the government fails to collect the information, it will not be available to the public. The question then is whether a member of the public can challenge that government failure to collect the information. Is this an individual injury or a generalized grievance?

Example

"Political committees" under the Federal Election Campaign Act of 1971 are required to file certain reports with the Federal Election Commission, and these reports then become publicly available. The Commission did not classify a particular organization as a "political committee," and a group that wanted information about the organization that would have been in its reports sued the Commission. Does the group have standing because it suffered a particular injury, or did it suffer only a generalized grievance?

Explanation

The Supreme Court held the group did have standing. The Court recognized that the plaintiffs' claimed injury was "one which is 'shared in substantially equal measure by all or a large class of citizens.'" "The Court has sometimes determined that where large numbers of Americans suffer alike, the political process, rather than the judicial process, may provide the more appropriate remedy for a widely shared grievance." In those cases, however, "the harm at issue [invariably] is not only widely shared, but is also of an abstract and indefinite nature—for example, harm to the 'common concern for obedience to law.' The abstract nature of the harm—for example, injury to the interest in seeing that the law is obeyed—deprives the case of the concrete specificity" necessary to satisfy the "case and controversy" requirement of the Constitution. "Often the fact that an interest is abstract and the fact that it is widely shared go hand in hand. But their association is not invariable, and where the harm is concrete, though widely shared, the Court has found 'injury in fact.'" Here, Congress, by passing the Act with the disclosure requirement, had deemed the information to be important to inform voters. Consequently, when specific voters who indicated an interest in that information were deprived of the information, their injury was concrete and specific, not abstract and indefinite. *See Federal Election Commn. v. Akins*, 524 U.S. 11 (1998).

The suggestion in *Akins*, a 6-3 decision, is that if a statute (or regulation) requires the government to collect or compile information *for the purpose of disclosing it to interested persons*, persons who identify themselves as being within the class of interested persons will suffer constitutionally recognized injury by the government's failure to collect, compile, or disclose the information. What if, however, the statute or regulation requires the government to collect or compile the information for purposes other than disclosing it to certain members of the public? Does a member of the public who desires that information (and could obtain it if the government had collected it) suffer constitutionally recognized injury by the government's failure to collect or compile the information?

Example

The ESA requires an agency proposing to take an action that affects threatened or endangered species to obtain a Biological Opinion from either the United States Fish and Wildlife Service (USFWS) or the National Marine Fisheries Service (depending upon the species) indicating whether the action will jeopardize the species. This Biological Opinion is an inter-agency document, not prepared for public consumption and not subject to public comment. It is, however, available to the public like most government documents under the Freedom of Information Act. Would the failure of an agency to obtain a Biological Opinion cause informational injury to a conservation group that makes it a practice to obtain copies of Biological Opinions and to publish their results and analysis in the group's magazine, which is distributed to members, or would the failure be only a generalized grievance?

Explanation

The answer is unclear. The failure to make such a Biological Opinion was precisely the "procedural injury" that the Court in *Lujan v. Defenders of Wildlife* held would not support standing. Here, however, the plaintiff is not claiming a procedural injury—an injury to a right to a particular procedure—but an injury to one of the organization's core functions, disseminating information to its members concerning endangered species and impacts on them. Nevertheless, the case is not directly controlled by *Akins*, because the statute does not specify that the information is for the benefit of the public. At least one circuit court case since *Akins*, however, read that case more broadly, saying "the injury alleged is not that the defendants are merely failing to obey the law, it is that they are disobeying the law in failing to provide the information that plaintiffs desire and allegedly need. This is all that plaintiffs should have to allege to demonstrate informational standing where Congress has provided a broad right of action to vindicate that informational right." *American Canoe Assn. v. City of Louisa Water & Sewer Comm.*, 389 F.3d 536 (6th Cir. 2004). In that case, the court found informational standing on behalf of environmental groups who sued a city agency for violating the Clean Water Act by not filing required monthly discharge monitoring reports with the appropriate government agency. Here, unlike *Akins* but like our case, the statute did not specifically provide that the reports were to be made available to the public, but like *Akins* the statute had provided a specific cause of action to persons adversely affected by violations of the Act. Nevertheless, even this decision was not unanimous. One judge dissented, saying the panel's decision went beyond *Akins*. He read *Akins* to rest on the fact that the statute required the information to be made public, which the Clean Water Act did not require for discharge monitoring reports.

If we try to apply the majority's rationale to our case of an agency not obtaining a Biological Opinion, it seems that the conservation organization has a good case, because, even if the ESA does not specifically provide for Biological Opinions to be made public, like the discharge monitoring reports, the ESA does, like the Clean Water Act, have a broad citizen suit provision allowing it to sue agencies that violate ESA statutory requirements. Our case is perhaps even better, because the conservation organization is in the business of collecting and disseminating information of this type, unlike the environmental group in *American Canoe*, which wanted the information generally to monitor compliance with the Clean Water Act. *American Canoe*, however, is just one case, and prior to *Akins* courts were generally reluctant to allow informational standing to groups challenging agency failures to produce environmental documents. *See, e.g., Foundations on Economic Trends v. Lyng*, 943 F.2d 79 (D.C. Cir. 1991).

6. Other Widely Shared Injuries Informational injury is not the only situation in which a widely shared injury may still be a particularized injury for certain persons or entities. Challenges to government actions (or inactions) relating to global warming have particularly raised this issue. Assume a federal agency does something or fails to do something that exacerbates the emission of carbon dioxide, a greenhouse gas, into the atmosphere. Who, if anyone, may challenge that action (or inaction)? This was one of the issues in *Massachusetts v. EPA*, 549 U.S. 497 (2007). There EPA had denied a petition requesting that EPA regulate carbon dioxide emissions from automobiles under the mobile source provisions of the Clean Air Act. The nonprofit organizations that had filed the petition as well as the state of Massachusetts sought judicial review of the denial. The first question was whether any of the persons seeking review had standing. The Court focused on the state of Massachusetts, because if it had standing, the standing of the other challengers would be irrelevant.

Massachusetts argued that its injury was the loss of coastal land owned by the state as a result of rising sea levels caused by global warming. The Court split 5-4 on the standing issue with Justice Stevens writing the majority opinion finding standing, and Chief Justice Roberts writing for the dissent denying standing. Obviously the loss of land as a result of government action (or inaction) is a palpable injury that should easily satisfy the requirements for standing. The peculiarity of injuries caused by global warming, however, is that global warming causes global injuries, so that whatever injuries Massachusetts or anyone else suffers, those injuries are shared by almost everyone in the world. Nevertheless, here the majority seems clearly correct to find Massachusetts' injury sufficient for standing. It is particularized and real, assuming the sea level will rise. It may well be that many entities will also suffer the same injury—private owners of beachfront property as well as other states—but the fact that many persons suffer their own particularized, individual injuries does not deprive them all of standing.

Recall that injuries for standing must be actual or imminent. Some of the effects of global warming, however, will not be felt for decades at least. Massachusetts provided evidence, however, that it was already losing land to rising sea levels caused by global warming, so that while further injuries might continue over decades, they were also being suffered immediately.

Even granting the fact of injury, however, Massachusetts still had to show that the agency action (denying the petition) caused the injury and that a favorable court decision could avoid that injury. We will discuss that below.

7. States as Plaintiffs In *Massachusetts v. EPA*, the Court began its opinion on standing by saying that "[i]t is of considerable relevance that the party seeking review here is a sovereign State and not . . . a private individual. [The state] is entitled to special solicitude in our standing analysis" 549 U.S. at 518, 520. A footnote seemed to suggest that if a state was suing in the role of parens patriae to protect the "quasi-sovereign interests" of the state or its citizens that somehow that would affect the nature of the standing test. However, exactly what was meant is unclear, because ultimately the Court applied the normal injury, causation, and redressability tests for standing with respect to Massachusetts. Moreover, this is the first time the Court has suggested any different treatment of standing for states. It is too soon to tell if this new aspect of standing law will have much significance, but subsequent lower court cases involving global warming claims have rejected providing any "special solicitude" for either cities or foreign nations, distinguishing them from states under Massachusetts.

b. Causation for Standing

In order to satisfy standing requirements, a plaintiff must show not only injury but also that the allegedly unlawful action caused the injury or at least that the injury is "fairly traceable" to the allegedly unlawful action. If the allegedly unlawful government action itself would directly cause the injury, this requirement does not pose a problem—for example, if the Corps of Engineers denied a person permission to fill wetlands on the person's property. At least two different situations, however, raise problems with causation. One is where the unlawful government action is because of a procedural violation; the other is where the injury is proximately caused by a third person whose action was induced by the unlawful government action.

I. Procedural Violations and Causation In the discussion above under the heading of Procedural Injuries, we noted that the Court said that procedural violations do not cause sufficient injury to support standing. However, persons whose legal complaint is that an agency violated a procedural requirement can have standing if they show that they will suffer a concrete injury as a result of the agency action. For example, the Court said in *Defenders* that a person who lives adjacent to the site of a proposed federally constructed dam would have standing to challenge the agency's failure to produce an Environmental Impact Statement (EIS), a procedural requirement. The injury would be the construction of the dam, even though the violation would be of a procedural requirement. It might be argued, however, that the plaintiff cannot show that the alleged procedural violation causes the injury, because even if the agency had complied with the procedural requirement for an EIS, the agency still could have built the dam, thereby causing the injury. In *Defenders*, the Court acknowledged this inability but said that the person would still have standing, because in this regard "'procedural rights' are special." 504 U.S. at 572 n.7. A more analytical answer perhaps would be that the cause of the injury is the final agency action (here building the dam), which is itself unlawful because of a procedural violation. There should be no need to show that the procedural violation itself is responsible for causing the injury.

Example

In an earlier example, the Corps of Engineers failed to provide an opportunity for a hearing before issuing a permit authorizing the discharge of fill material into the waters of the United States, a violation of the requirements of the Clean Water Act. We concluded that an adjoining property owner whose property would be economically harmed by the discharge would suffer injury sufficient for standing purposes. Nevertheless, in order to have standing, the property owner must also show that his injury is caused by allegedly unlawful action and that a favorable court decision can avoid or redress the injury. Can he show causation here, when it may well be that after a public hearing, the Corps still can permit the fill?

Explanation

Yes. Even though the property owner cannot show that, if the Corps engages in the correct procedure, he will not be injured (that is, that the permit will not be granted), he can satisfy the causation standard for standing. He would argue that the cause of his injury would be the unlawful grant of the permit to fill the habitat and that the grant of the permit is unlawful because of the procedural violation by the Corps. He would also remind the court of the Supreme Court's statement that procedural rights are special, to avoid having to show the normal degree of causation.

This may seem simple, but courts do not always get it right. For example, in *Committee to Save the Rio Hondo v. Lucero*, 102 F.3d 445 (10th Cir. 1996), an agency failed to prepare an EIS prior to a decision to open up a ski area for summer use. Persons living downstream from the ski area alleged that its use in the summer would result in increased water consumption and water pollution, subjecting them to increased risks in the water they use. They challenged the failure to prepare an EIS. The court said, "[T]o establish causation, a plaintiff need only show its increased risk is fairly traceable to the agency's failure to comply with the National Environmental Policy Act." This was wrong. It should have said that the plaintiff need only show its increased risk is fairly traceable to the agency's action—allowing summer use of the ski resort—which is allegedly unlawful because of its failure to prepare an EIS. The court in fact did find that the summer use of the ski resort would increase the risk to plaintiffs, which should have been sufficient, and it also found that the agency's failure to prepare an EIS increased the risk that the agency would make an uninformed decision that would injure plaintiffs. This second finding should have been unnecessary to determine causation.

The confusion these courts demonstrate probably arises from the fact that the procedural violation must at least have *possibly* affected the outcome. This is not because of any aspect of standing doctrine, but because of the general legal rule of harmless error. For example, in an ordinary civil case, an appellate court will not overturn a trial court's outcome because of some procedural violation, such as sustaining an objection that should have been rejected, if there is no reasonable likelihood that the error affected the outcome. Sometimes this is phrased as there being no possibility that the error affected the outcome. The APA adopts this general rule with respect to judicial review of agency action by stating that "due account shall be taken of the rule of prejudicial error." 5 U.S.C. § 706. Thus, if it could be shown that there was no possibility or no reasonable likelihood that the information generated by the EIS would have changed the outcome, the plaintiff should lose because the violation did not affect the outcome in any way. The important difference between the rule of prejudicial error and what the courts above wrongly did (or said) is that, while a plaintiff must prove the elements of standing, including that the allegedly unlawful action caused (or will cause) his injury, the person arguing for harmless error should have the burden of proving the lack of prejudice—that there is no possibility or no reasonable likelihood that the outcome would have been different if the procedural violation had not occurred. Thus, once the plaintiff has shown that it is at least theoretically possible for the outcome to have been different had there been no procedural violation, the burden should shift to the government to show that its procedural violation was harmless error. Because proving a negative is difficult, normally the government would not be able to show this.

2. Third-Party Actions and Causation To continue further the example of the Corps permitting the fill of waters, the agency action is to issue a permit to a third party, when it is actually the third party's action—placing fill in the waters of the United States—that will cause injury to the adjoining land owner. The Corps might argue that its permit does not cause the injury; it is the action of the third party. After all, the third party, even after it has the permit, might decide not to go forward with the placement of the fill. Perhaps the reason for seeking the permit has ceased to exist; maybe the construction turned out to be too expensive. This is a potentially good argument for the Corps, but its resolution will turn on the actual facts, and it is rare for someone to go to the expense and trouble of getting such a permit without then using it.

Example

Under the Internal Revenue Code, charitable institutions are not required to pay income tax. A group representing low-income persons in a particular area complained that a hospital claiming a charitable institution exemption is refusing to treat low-income patients for free and therefore is not a charitable institution. The group petitions the IRS to withdraw the hospital's tax-exempt status, but the IRS refuses. The group sues the IRS, alleging that it is violating the Internal Revenue Code. Will the group be able to show that its injury, the inability of its members to obtain free medical care from this hospital, is caused by the agency's failure to withdraw the tax exemption?

Explanation

In *Simon v. Eastern Kentucky Welfare Rights Organization*, 426 U.S. 26 (1976), the Supreme Court held that the group lacked standing because it failed to show that the injury to the low-income persons was caused by or fairly traceable to the allegedly unlawful tax exemption. It was conceded that the low-income persons were harmed by the failure of the hospital to treat them for free. However, there was no evidence that this injury was caused by or fairly traceable to the allegedly unlawful agency action: the failure to withdraw the hospital's tax-exempt status. The Court reasoned that if the IRS withdrew the tax-exempt status of the hospital, the hospital almost surely would not begin to treat low-income persons for free. Of course, the group representing the low-income persons did not really want the hospital's tax-exempt status removed; the group wanted the hospital to begin to treat the low-income persons for free in order to retain its tax-exempt status. However, there was no evidence in the case that the hospital would in fact change its operations in order to retain tax-exempt status as opposed to becoming a for-profit institution. Thus, the plaintiff failed to show causation.

If the plaintiff had been able to show that, historically, organizations almost always altered their behavior to retain tax-exempt status, rather than opting for for-profit status, the case probably would have had a different result. As the Court recognized in a later case, where an agency's action has determinative or coercive effect on a third party, causation may be satisfied by a showing of that effect. *See Bennett v. Spear*, 520 U.S. 154 (1997). In that case, the Court found that a USFWS Biological Opinion had a "powerful coercive effect" on the recipient. Even though the recipient was technically free to reject the Opinion, which legally was only advice, it did so "at its peril," because of the potential civil and criminal penalties it would risk. As a result, the Opinion was "virtually determinative," so that the recipient's action could be fairly traceable to or caused by the Opinion.

3. Contribution as Causation In *Massachusetts v. EPA*, the government argued that its failure to regulate carbon dioxide emissions from automobiles did not cause Massachusetts' injury, the loss of land through sea level rise. The government conceded that carbon dioxide emissions contribute to global warming, and global warming causes sea level rise, but it argued that the failure to reduce carbon dioxide emissions from new automobiles in the United States would have such a slight effect on global warming that it should not be said to "cause" Massachusetts' injury. The Court rejected that argument, in essence concluding that if the allegedly unlawful government action contributes in any meaningful way to the injury, that contribution satisfies the causation requirement.

c. Redressability for Standing

Not only must a plaintiff show that he suffers (or will suffer) an injury caused by the allegedly unlawful government action, the plaintiff must also show that a favorable court decision will result in redressing or avoiding that injury. In the administrative law context, redressability and causation often are linked. If an agency action would cause injury, then usually an injunction against the agency action will provide full relief. There are, however, some circumstances when redressability becomes a question. For example, in the highly publicized case of *Juliana v. United States*, 947 F.3d 1159 (9th Cir. 2020), in which children sued the United States for failing to preserve a stable environment in light of climate change, the court ordered the case dismissed because it was not within the power of the judiciary to provide the specific relief they sought, i.e., an injunction requiring federal government not only to cease permitting, authorizing, and subsidizing fossil fuel use, but also to prepare a plan subject to judicial approval to draw down harmful emissions,

I. Third-Party Actions and Redressability Causation problems involving third parties not before the court can equally be viewed as redressability problems. Sometimes a court will focus on one, sometimes on the other. For example, in the hospital tax exemption case, the Court also spoke about the lack of redressability, saying that a favorable court decision requiring the IRS to withdraw the hospital's tax-exempt status would not relieve plaintiffs' injury—the lack of free care for low-income persons.

Example

The ESA requires an agency to consult with the USFWS whenever the agency takes an action that may adversely affect a threatened or endangered terrestrial species. The Federal Highway Administration (FHWA) gives funds to state highway agencies to help them build roads. These funds cover a significant portion but not all of the costs of the road building. A state highway agency is proposing to build a road, with FHWA financial support, that will disturb the habitat of a threatened species, and a local group that observes and studies the species wishes to challenge the road building because the FHWA did not consult with the USFWS before deciding to provide funds for the road. Is there redressability?

Explanation

If a court found in favor of the local group, it could issue an injunction directed to the FHWA prohibiting it from providing any funds for the building of the road unless and until it consulted with the USFWS, as required by the ESA. However, would this mean that the road would not be built? The state might still build the road using only its own funds, and the group's injury would not be relieved. This would suggest a lack of redressability. In fact, this was an alternative holding by a plurality in *Lujan v. Defenders of Wildlife*.

A plaintiff need not show that a favorable court decision will definitely prevent or redress the injury. The standard is that a favorable court decision will *likely* prevent or redress the injury. In this example, evidence that the state was counting on the federal funds and that the state had not set aside sufficient funds of its own to cover the entire cost of the road would probably suffice to satisfy the "likely" standard.

2. Procedural Violations and Redressability When an agency violates some procedural requirement, we have seen that a person who would be injured by the agency action can have standing to challenge the agency action for which the procedural requirement was a prerequisite, alleging the action is unlawful because there was a procedural violation. A question could arise, however, as to redressability. For example, if a person challenged an agency's grant of a permit on the grounds that an agency did not provide public notice and an opportunity for a hearing, could it be said that a favorable court decision would likely prevent or redress the person's injury? In one sense the answer would be no, because the agency would probably be equally able to grant the same permit after a new proceeding preceded by the requisite notice and opportunity for a hearing. That is, following the required procedures does not necessarily make the outcome more likely to be favorable to the complaining person. Nevertheless, the Supreme Court has held that when persons allege procedural violations, the normal rules of redressability do not apply. In *Lujan v. Defenders of Wildlife*, the Court said, "[t]he person who has been accorded a procedural right to protect his concrete interests can assert that right without meeting all the normal standards for redressability and immediacy." 504 U.S. at 572 n.7. The courts have not made clear exactly what is meant by not having to meet all the normal standards, but at least the person must be able to show that there is a possibility that a procedural remedy will redress his injury. For example, it is possible that an agency, if it provides public notice and an opportunity for public comment on a possible permit, may receive information or argument that persuades it not to grant the permit, or to grant it in a modified fashion.

This is usually not a difficult standard to meet, so when a person asserts a procedural violation, if the person can satisfy the tests for concrete injury and causation, they usually are home free. If, however, an agency lacks the discretion to take a different action, then no amount of required procedure could avoid the injury.

3. Partial Redress or Avoidance Together with its argument in *Massachusetts v. EPA* that the failure to limit carbon dioxide emissions from new automobiles did not cause Massachusetts' injury, the government likewise argued that a favorable court decision could not redress or avoid Massachusetts' injury. Again the Court rejected the argument. It was not necessary, the Court said, for the plaintiffs to allege that their injury would be completely relieved; it was sufficient if a favorable court decision would slow or reduce the injury. Presumably, the redress must be coincident with the causation. That is, just as in *Massachusetts v. EPA* the EPA's failure to regulate only contributed to Massachusetts' injury, the appropriate redress would be to eliminate that contribution. A favorable court decision resulting in EPA regulation of automobile carbon dioxide emissions would eliminate that contribution toward Massachusetts' injury.

2. Representational Standing

The preceding sections have described the constitutional requirements to establish standing. We have seen that a plaintiff must show injury, causation, and redressability. In some of the examples, the plaintiffs were organizations, for instance the National Wildlife Federation, but the analysis of injury, causation, and redressability usually related to one or more of their members, rather than to the organizations themselves.

Organizations such as the National Wildlife Federation, the National Association of Manufacturers, the Sierra Club, and the Motor Vehicle Manufacturers Association of the United States may in fact themselves suffer injury caused by agency action. For example, if the Internal Revenue Service decided to revoke the tax exemption for these nonprofit organizations, such an action would cause injury to the organizations that could be remedied by a favorable court decision. Thus, the organizations would have standing in their own right.

More common, however, is the lawsuit brought by an organization on behalf of one or more of its members. The Supreme Court has recognized the doctrine of "representational standing," or sometimes called "associational standing." This doctrine deems an organization to have standing to bring a lawsuit on behalf of one or more of its members, if the organization meets certain requirements. The first and most critical requirement is that the organization have a member who could bring the case himself; that is, it must have a member who would satisfy the constitutional requirements for standing. Second, the purpose of the organization must be relevant to the nature of the issues in the lawsuit. In other words, an environmental group could bring an environmental lawsuit on behalf of one of its members who individually has standing, but a labor union could not. A labor union, on the other hand, could bring a suit involving workplace safety standards on behalf of one of its members who would have standing, while an environmental group could not. Third, the nature of the lawsuit must not be such that the person actually injured must be a party to the suit; this means in effect that the suit must be one for an injunction or declaratory judgment rather than one for damages. The first of these requirements is often difficult for an organization to meet; the latter two are almost never a basis for finding a lack of standing.

3. Prudential Standing

Even if a plaintiff satisfies the requirements for constitutional standing, there may be another potential hurdle: prudential standing requirements. These are requirements that the Court has evolved in its discretion to assure that cases decided by courts are most appropriately decided by courts. Because these requirements are not imposed by the Constitution's limitation on federal court jurisdiction but by the Court's discretion, the Court has allowed Congress by statute effectively to overrule or alter the prudential limitations. Historically, the Court has described three or four different principles that implicated prudential standing: a requirement that a plaintiff's complaint fall within the zone of interests protected by the law involved; the rule barring adjudication of generalized grievances more appropriately addressed in the representative branches; the general prohibition on "third-party standing" (that is, a litigant raising another person's legal rights); and the requirement that a plaintiff's case be "ripe" for adjudication. More recently, however, the Court has explicitly rejected the concept of prudential standing with respect to the first two principles and placed in question the extent or continued vitality of the second two principles.

In *Lexmark International, Inc. v. Static Control Components, Inc.*, 134 S. Ct. 1377 (2014), a unanimous Court explained that the requirement for a complaint to fall within the zone of interests protected by the law involved was simply a question of statutory construction. Either the law created a cause of action for the plaintiff or it did not. This was not a question of judicial discretion. In the same case the Court further explained that the rule barring adjudication of generalized grievances was likewise not a matter of judicial discretion. Rather it was a constitutional requirement addressed under the standing requirement for a concrete, particularized injury. The Court went on to suggest that the general rule (to which there are numerous exceptions) prohibiting third-party standing is "closely related to question whether a person in the litigant's position will have a right of action on the claim"; in other words, it is simply a matter of statutory interpretation. Because *Lexmark* did not involve third-party standing issues, the Court said "that doctrine's proper place in the standing firmament [could] await another day." Nevertheless, it stated the general proposition that courts "cannot limit a cause of action that Congress has created merely because 'prudence' dictates."

In *Lexmark*, the Court did not address ripeness, but later the same year it raised the issue in *Susan B. Anthony List v. Driehaus*, 134 S. Ct. 2334 (2014). Some ripeness issues involve constitutional limitations on whether there is an actual case or controversy. Today, however, these concerns are addressed in the analysis of constitutional standing and its requirement that the injury be actual or imminent, or certainly impending. As to ripeness concerns not rising to the constitutional level, the Court in *Driehaus* quoted from its *Lexmark* opinion that non-justiciability claims based on prudential concerns, rather than constitutional concerns, are "in some tension with our recent reaffirmation of the principle that 'a federal court's obligation to hear and decide' cases within its jurisdiction 'is virtually unflagging.'" However, it concluded that "[it] need not resolve the continuing vitality of the prudential ripeness doctrine in this case," because it was clear that the traditional grounds for ripeness were met.[3]

This leaves us with the doctrine of prudential standing seemingly about to be abolished as a category of cases that courts in their discretion will not hear. Instead, we learn that much of what has been called prudential standing in the past will be considered either under constitutional requirements of standing or in construing statutes that create a cause of action. That said, lower courts still refer to prudential standing despite the Supreme Court's decisions.

II. EXCEPTIONS TO JUDICIAL REVIEW UNDER THE APA

Section 701 of the APA identifies two classes of cases that are exempt from judicial review under the APA. One class involves statutes that preclude judicial review; the other involves agency action "committed to agency discretion by law." Lawyers wishing to bring an action under the APA must assure that their cases do not fit within these exceptions. Government lawyers wishing to avoid judicial review of agency action would like the cases to be within these exceptions, thereby avoiding judicial review.

3. The doctrine of ripeness is addressed later in this chapter.

A. Statutory Preclusion

Section 701(a)(1) provides that the chapter of the APA dealing with judicial review, 5 U.S.C. ch. 7 (§§ 701-706), does not apply "to the extent" that statutes preclude judicial review. Because the APA is a general statute, providing the general rules, it makes sense that particular statutes where Congress has either precluded review or specified another form of review should govern rather than the APA. Obviously, if a statute expressly precludes review or provides another form of review than under the APA, that specific statute will govern. When a statute does not expressly preclude review, what is the test for determining whether the statute should be interpreted to preclude it?

The most famous case on this subject is *Abbott Laboratories v. Gardner*, 387 U.S. 136 (1967). In that case, the Food and Drug Administration had adopted a rule under amendments to the Federal Food, Drug, and Cosmetic Act, requiring manufacturers of prescription drugs to include the generic name (e.g., sildenafil citrate) for the drug each time the trade name (e.g., Viagra) was used on any labels or promotional materials. The purpose of the rule was to bring to the attention of doctors and patients the fact that many drugs were available in a much cheaper generic form than that sold by a particular manufacturer under a trade name. The rule was challenged under the APA by 37 drug manufacturers and their trade association. Neither the Act nor its amendments by their terms precluded judicial review of this kind of rule, but the government argued that because the Act provided specific procedures for judicial review of certain other types of rules, substituting for the APA, the Act's lack of any specific procedures for the rules in question suggested that no review should be available. The Court rejected this argument. It said that the APA "embodies a presumption of judicial review." Consequently, the burden is on the government to show a "persuasive reason to believe" that Congress intended to cut off review. The Court suggested that a statute should be read to preclude review "only upon a showing of 'clear and convincing evidence'" of such a legislative intent. The specific provision for judicial review under special procedures in certain situations was insufficient evidence of intent to preclude review elsewhere. Moreover, the special procedures were aimed at facilitating review in those situations and did not suggest review would not be available in other circumstances.

The standards of *Abbott Labs*—the "presumption of judicial review" and the need for "clear and convincing evidence" to overcome that presumption—have been much repeated, but subsequent case law has refined the meaning of that language.

In *Block v. Community Nutrition Institute*, 467 U.S. 340 (1984), the Court backed off the need for "clear and convincing evidence," saying that this phraseology "is not a rigid evidentiary test but a useful reminder to courts that, where substantial doubt about the congressional intent exists, the general presumption favoring judicial review of administrative action is controlling." However, if "congressional intent to preclude judicial review is 'fairly discernible in the statutory scheme,'" this suffices to establish preclusion.

Example

The EPA issued an "administrative compliance order" to persons who were beginning to build a home on a lot they owned, forbidding them from any further filling of alleged wetlands on the property. The owners, not believing the land contained any wetlands subject to EPA jurisdiction brought suit under the APA for a determination that the compliance order was unlawful. The government argued that the owners could not challenge the order because the Clean Water Act impliedly precluded judicial review under the APA. In support of that position, it asserted that the Act specifically provided review for penalty orders, but it was silent as to compliance orders, suggesting no review was intended for the latter. In addition, the government argued that, because the Act provided for the EPA to enforce the Act's provisions either by seeking an injunction in court or by issuing an administrative compliance order, to allow judicial review of the compliance order would in essence eliminate the option of enforcement without going to court.

Explanation

The Supreme Court unanimously held that the owners were not precluded from judicial review. *Sackett v. NEDC*, 132 S. Ct. 1367 (2012). The Court reiterated that the APA creates a presumption of judicial review, and the government arguments were inadequate to rebut that presumption. The Court did not view the purpose of the Act's options for the EPA to enforce by order or by going to court for an injunction to reflect an intent to preclude review of the enforcement order. There were other benefits that the government derived from the option of using an administrative order. Moreover, the Court said, if "the express provision of judicial review in one section of a long and complicated statute were alone enough to overcome the APA's presumption of reviewability for all final agency action, it would not be much of a presumption at all."

The above example involved review of an agency enforcement action. There is some question whether the "presumption of review" applies to "pre-enforcement" judicial review. For example, in *Shalala v. Illinois Council on Long Term Care, Inc.*, 529 U.S. 1 (2000), the Court suggested that pre-enforcement review is an "exception" to the general rule. Pre-enforcement review refers to a challenge of agency action before the agency enforces its action through adjudication or court enforcement. For example, in *Abbott Labs*, the drug manufacturers sought an injunction to prevent the rule from going into effect. This is pre-enforcement review. The government argued that the manufacturers should not be able to obtain pre-enforcement review. Instead, the government said that if the manufacturers thought the rule was unlawful, they should violate the rule and assert the alleged unlawfulness of the rule as a defense if the government attempted to enforce the rule against them in court. This would be enforcement review. We understand why the manufacturers would prefer pre-enforcement review; they do not want to endure the negative publicity of willfully violating the rule and run the risk of large fines or the loss of their licenses (capital punishment, as it were, for a drug company) if they were to lose their case. And we understand why the government dislikes pre-enforcement review. If there is no pre-enforcement review, it is likely that many if not all of the companies will feel forced to comply with the rule, because they cannot afford to run the risks associated with violating it. If some companies do violate the rule, the government will be able to choose whom to enforce against, picking the worst apple to make its case look the best. Another negative impact of pre-enforcement review from the government's perspective is that the government will have to devote resources to defending the rule that might otherwise be used to make new rules or to enforce the existing rule. Moreover, the manufacturers are likely to ask to have the effect of the rule stayed during the pendency of the pre-enforcement litigation, which if granted would delay whatever positive effects the rule might have.

The debate over the merits and demerits of pre-enforcement review goes back at least to *Abbott Labs*, in which there was a strong dissent by Justice Fortas, joined by Chief Justice Warren and Justice Clark, decrying the delay and interference with the enforcement of rules by allowing pre-enforcement review. Sometimes Congress addresses the question directly. When it does, it usually provides for pre-enforcement review. *See, e.g.*, 42 U.S.C. § 7607(b) (requiring challenges to most Clean Air Act rules to be filed in the court of appeals within 60 days of their publication in the Federal Register and barring their review in enforcement proceedings). When it does not, courts must decide whether pre-enforcement review is available, or whether only enforcement review is available. However, when the agency action requires a person or entity to do something upon the effective date of the action, as was the case in *Abbott Labs*, the rule of *Abbott Labs* governs. When, on the other hand, the agency action does not require a person or entity to do something on the effective date of the action, further scrutiny is necessary. This is usually performed under the rubric of "ripeness," discussed later, but sometimes it is discussed as statutory preclusion of pre-enforcement review. For example, in *Thunder Basin Coal Co. v. Reich*, 510 U.S. 200 (1994), a non-union employer brought suit against the Mine Safety and Health Administration (MSHA) to enjoin it from requiring the employer to allow union representatives, chosen by its employees, to accompany mine safety inspectors during their inspections. The government argued that the statute precluded pre-enforcement review because it created a detailed structure for reviewing enforcement of health and safety standards. The employer could refuse to allow the union representatives to accompany the inspectors and await a citation from MSHA. The statute then provided a system by which the employer ultimately could obtain judicial review of the citation. The Court agreed with the government and concluded that the structure of the Act evidenced a congressional intent to preclude pre-enforcement review.

B. Committed to Agency Discretion by Law

Section 701 also excludes agency action from judicial review "to the extent" that the agency action is "committed to agency discretion by law." 5 U.S.C. § 701(a)(2). This is somewhat confusing, because we will find that one of the bases for reversing agency action is that it is an "abuse of discretion." How can a court determine that something is an abuse of discretion if it cannot review actions committed to agency discretion?

The leading case interpreting this provision is *Citizens to Preserve Overton Park v. Volpe*, 401 U.S. 402 (1971). In that case two federal statutes prohibited the Secretary of Transportation from using federal funds to finance construction of highways through public parks if a "feasible and prudent" alternative existed. When the Secretary approved funds for a highway through Overton Park in Memphis, his action was challenged. He claimed that the action was not judicially reviewable because it was committed to his discretion. The Supreme Court disagreed, saying that "this is a very narrow exception," which applies "in those rare instances where 'statutes are drawn in such broad terms that in a given case there is no law to apply.'" Here, the Secretary was governed by a statutory requirement that plainly provided "law to apply."

In a later case, the Court restated the test as precluding review if "the statute is drawn so that a court would have no meaningful standard against which to judge the agency's exercise of discretion." *Heckler v. Chaney*, 470 U.S. 821 (1985). Here the challenge was to the FDA's alleged failure to enforce the requirement that approved drugs only be used for the purposes approved, and the Court held that no law applied to the exercise of the FDA's prosecutorial discretion. Accordingly, the decision whether or not to take enforcement action in a given case was committed to the FDA's discretion by law. Today it is settled law that, absent some specific statutory limitation on an agency's prosecutorial discretion, the decision whether to enforce a particular law or rule is generally committed to agency discretion by law and therefore unreviewable. However, in *Heckler*, the Court dropped a footnote leaving open the possibility of there being law to apply when the agency's exercise of prosecutorial discretion was based on a finding that it lacked jurisdiction, or when the agency has "consciously and expressly adopted a general policy" that is so extreme as to amount to an abdication of its statutory responsibilities.

Example

The CIA fired an employee when it discovered the employee was a homosexual. The employee sued, alleging the firing was unlawful under the National Security Act of 1947 and was unconstitutional. The Act stated that the Director of Central Intelligence "may, in his discretion, terminate the employment of any . . . employee of the Agency whenever he shall deem such termination necessary or advisable in the interests of the United States." The government argued that the employee's termination was not subject to judicial review because it was committed to agency discretion by law.

Explanation

The Court found that this language "fairly exudes deference" to the Director. It expressly states that the decision is in "his discretion"; it does not say termination is only allowed when termination is necessary or advisable, but allows termination when the Director "deems" it necessary or advisable. Moreover, the statute relates to national security matters in which deference to the agency is most appropriate. Therefore, the Court found that the termination decision was committed to the agency's discretion by law, so judicial review of his claim of unlawful termination under the statute was not allowed. However, the constitutional claim was allowed. After all, Congress could not grant the Director the discretion to violate the Constitution. Although the statute might not constrain the Director's discretion, the Constitution necessarily did. And Section 701 precludes review only "to the extent" that an agency action is committed to agency discretion by law. See *Webster v. Doe*, 486 U.S. 592 (1988).

Example

Congress annually passes an appropriation act appropriating funds for the Indian Health Services (IHS). The appropriation act itself does not specify what the funds are to be used for, although reports of the House and Senate appropriations committees normally do indicate how those committees expect the money to be spent. There is another law authorizing the IHS to "expend such moneys as Congress may from time to time appropriate, for the benefit, care, and assistance of the Indians" for the "relief of distress and conservation of health." Pursuant to this law and with prior appropriations, the IHS had run what was known as the Indian Children's Program, which provided clinical services to handicapped Indian children in three reservation areas. In 1985, however, the IHS terminated this program and reassigned the staff to a nationwide program for handicapped Indian children. It announced this change in a memorandum distributed to IHS offices and Program referral sources. Persons adversely affected by this change challenged it, alleging that the change was not authorized by law and that the change was an invalid rule because it had not gone through notice and comment. Was the agency's decision how to spend the appropriated funds committed to agency discretion by law?

Explanation

The Supreme Court held that the decision how to spend the funds was committed to agency discretion by law and therefore not reviewable, but the question whether notice and comment had been required was reviewable. The appropriation acts themselves did not limit how the IHS spent the money appropriated to it. Moreover, the law authorizing the IHS to spend appropriated moneys only required that they be spent for the relief of distress and conservation of health of Indians. There simply was no law, no judicially enforceable standard by which to assess the IHS decision to terminate one health program for Indians and start another. How to spend the money to protect the health of Indians was committed to agency discretion by law. Whether the agency had to make this decision through Notice-and-Comment Rulemaking or could, as the agency argued, announce it by a statement of policy exempt from notice-and-comment requirements, however, was not a matter committed to the agency's discretion. To the contrary, the APA requires Notice-and-Comment Rulemaking except in those specific circumstances where it creates an exception. Section 701(a) exempts agency actions from judicial review only "to the extent that" they are committed to agency discretion by law. Thus, an action can be exempt to some extent and subject to review to another extent. *See Lincoln v. Vigil*, 508 U.S. 182 (1993).

How should we characterize an agency's refusal to undertake a rulemaking? Is this somehow an exercise of prosecutorial discretion? Obviously, if a statute specifically requires an agency to undertake a rulemaking, the agency does not have the discretion to refuse. More typically, however, a statute authorizes, rather than requires, an agency to adopt rules for certain purposes.

Example

In the Horse Protection Act, Congress prohibited the showing or selling of "sored" horses. Soring is the practice of fastening chains or other heavy equipment on a horse's front limbs so that when it steps on its front feet it experiences intense pain. This causes it to alter its normal walking or running pattern and to make it high stepping. The Department of Agriculture was authorized to adopt such regulations as it deemed necessary to carry out the provisions of the Act. Initially, it adopted regulations specifically banning only certain devices. Several years after adopting the initial regulations and after a series of studies had shown that some non-prohibited devices were being used for soring, an organization interested in protecting horses petitioned the Secretary of Agriculture to amend the regulations to prohibit these additional devices. The Secretary, however, responded, "I believe that the most effective method of enforcing the Act is to continue the current regulations." The organization sued, saying that the Secretary's decision was arbitrary and capricious. Was the Secretary's decision not to undertake a new rulemaking committed to agency discretion by law and hence unreviewable?

Explanation

In *American Horse Protection Assn., Inc. v. Lyng*, 812 F.2d 1 (D.C. Cir. 1987), the court held the decision reviewable. The court recognized that there was some similarity between the exercise of prosecutorial discretion and a decision not to adopt a rule to enforce a statute. However, the court also saw two important differences, which it found critical. First, the exercise of enforcement discretion in the *Heckler v. Chaney* context was the traditional exercise of prosecutorial discretion in a law enforcement context—decisions that are numerous and routine and that have a solid pedigree in terms of being solely within executive discretion. A decision whether to undertake rulemaking, however, is a less routine decision and one more likely to be based on legal considerations than particularized facts, the court said. Second, normally exercises of prosecutorial discretion do not need to be explained, so that if there were to be judicial review of the decision, any explanation would be the result of the review itself. Under the APA, however, an agency is required to explain why it denies a petition for rulemaking, so that this explanation provides a basis for review.

The D.C. Circuit's decision has been widely followed, probably in part because judicial review of agency decisions not to adopt a rule was widespread before *Heckler v. Chaney* raised any question about it. Nevertheless, one can see that a substantial argument exists that there is no law to apply, when all the statute says is that rules are authorized when the Secretary deems them necessary.

Even if the failure to adopt rules may be reviewable, we will find that courts have afforded a high degree of deference to agency decisions not to adopt rules, and, as Justice Scalia noted when he was a circuit judge, often one can equally characterize an action as non-reviewable or as reviewable but the scope of review is very narrow. *See Chaney v. Heckler*, 718 F.2d 1174, 1195 n.3 (D.C. Cir. 1983) (dissent), *rev'd sub nom. Heckler v. Chaney*, 470 U.S. 821 (1985).

III. REQUIREMENTS FOR JUDICIAL REVIEW UNDER THE APA

A. Causes of Action and the Zone of Interests

In order to bring a lawsuit, there must be a law somewhere saying you can bring a lawsuit. For example, it is a federal crime for someone to engage in arson with respect to property used in interstate commerce. If someone burns down your business, can you sue them for violating that statute? No.

Section 702 of the APA provides a cause of action for any person who suffers "legal wrong" because of agency action. This means that if agency action interferes with a person's recognized legal right—usually the use of his property or the freedom to act how he wishes—the person will have a cause of action under the APA. In other words, this part of Section 702 provides a cause of action when government directly regulates you in a way you do not like.

Section 702 also creates a cause of action for persons who are "adversely affected or aggrieved by agency action within the meaning of a relevant statute." This language establishes what is known as the "zone of interests" test. That is, the question is whether the adverse effect suffered by the plaintiff from an agency violation of some statute is within the zone of interests intended to be protected by that statute. Applying the zone of interests test or the terms of Section 702 is a matter of statutory interpretation. Who did Congress mean to protect, or what interests did Congress mean to protect, when it enacted a particular statute?

Example

The EPA adopts a regulation restricting the amount of pollutants that may be emitted from major industrial sources. A company that has a factory that currently emits more pollutants than allowed under the regulation wants to sue to overturn the regulation. A homeowner who lives near the factory believes that the regulation is not strict enough in light of the fact that there are several factories in the area emitting that pollutant and to allow them all to emit the regulated amount would be dangerous to his health. He wants to sue to overturn the regulation as well.

Explanation

If the regulation is indeed unlawful, the company is suffering a "legal wrong," but the homeowner is not. The EPA regulation directly regulates the company's factory; the company's liberty to emit what pollutants it wants is restricted. The homeowner, on the other hand, is free to do as he wishes; the EPA's regulation does not regulate him or his activities.

The question then is whether the homeowner is within the zone of interests intended to be protected by the provision in the Clean Air Act that authorizes the agency to set emission limits for the pollutant in question. The answer to that question is almost certainly "yes," because one of the purposes of the Clean Air Act is to protect persons' health.

This was an easy case, but they are not always so easy.

Example

The Endangered Species Act (ESA) generally has the purpose of protecting plant and animal species from extinction. One of the tools used by the Act is the requirement that agencies consult with the USFWS before taking action that may adversely affect a threatened or endangered species. The USFWS in turn is to advise agencies whether their actions may jeopardize the existence of the species or adversely affect the species' critical habitat. In making these determinations, the Act states that the agency "shall use the best scientific and commercial data available."

The USFWS advised the Bureau of Reclamation in a Biological Opinion that drawdowns of a reservoir managed by the Bureau would jeopardize certain endangered suckers. Ranchers who relied upon those drawdowns as a source of irrigation water challenged this determination in part on the basis that the USFWS had not used the best scientific and commercial data available. Were the ranchers within the zone of interests of the ESA?

Explanation

The Court held that the ranchers had constitutional standing and were within the zone of interests of the provision of the ESA. The ranchers' injury was that they would not be able to obtain as much water as they wanted for their crops and livestock watering; this injury would be caused by the USFWS's Biological Opinion finding jeopardy in drawdowns, and a favorable court decision enjoining reliance on that opinion would likely result in their obtaining their needed water. Hence, the ranchers had constitutional standing. The lower court, however, had found that the ranchers' interest in maintaining water for their commercial purposes was not within the zone of interests of the Endangered Species Act, which seems to be about protecting endangered species. The Supreme Court held the proper "zone of interests" to be considered was not that of the ESA generally but of the specific provision of the ESA alleged to be violated. Here that provision was the statutory requirement that agencies use the best available scientific and commercial data. The Court then hypothesized that the purpose of this provision was "to ensure that the ESA not be implemented haphazardly, on the basis of speculation or surmise. While this no doubt serves to advance the ESA's overall goal of species preservation, we think it readily apparent that another objective (if not indeed the primary one) is to avoid needless economic dislocation produced by agency officials zealously but unintelligently pursuing their environmental objectives." Because the plaintiffs' claim was that they were victims of precisely such a mistake, they were within the zone of interests of the provision. *See Bennett v. Spear,* 520 U.S. 154 (1997).

Unfortunately, at least in terms of ease of application of the zone of interests test, the Supreme Court has not limited the zone of interests to only those persons whom Congress wished to protect. Indeed, in its very first "zone of interests" case, *Association of Data Processing Service Organizations, Inc. v. Camp*, 397 U.S. 150 (1970), the Court found an organization within the zone of interests of a statute despite the conclusion that Congress had *not* intended to protect that organization's interests. In that case, the agency that regulates national banks issued a ruling that banks could, as an incident to their normal banking services, provide data-processing services to other banks and their customers. The trade association representing companies that provided data processing services—companies who would now face competition from banks—challenged this ruling, arguing that it violated the provision limiting banks to "normal banking services." The purpose of this provision, however, was not to protect companies from potential competition from banks, but to ensure the financial stability of banks by ensuring that they did not stray from traditional banking services. Nevertheless, the Court found the organization "arguably" within the zone of interests of the provision. This kind of plaintiff, although not an "intended beneficiary" of the statute, is still a "suitable challenger" to vindicate the interests of the statute, because there was a close relation between the interests of the statute—limiting the economic activities in which the financial institutions could engage—and the interests of potential competitors to limit the financial institutions' economic activities. In several similar cases, the Supreme Court has reached the same conclusion. *See National Credit Union Admin. v. First National Bank & Trust Co.*, 522 U.S. 479 (1998); *Clarke v. Securities Industry Assn.*, 479 U.S. 388 (1987); *Investment Company Institute v. Camp*, 401 U.S. 617 (1971); *Arnold Tours, Inc. v. Camp*, 400 U.S. 45 (1970) (*per curiam*).

Nevertheless, the mere fact that competitors may benefit from a particular interpretation of a statute does not put them within the zone of interests for purposes of judicial review. For example, in *Hazardous Waste Treatment Council v. Thomas*, 885 F.2d 918 (D.C. Cir. 1989), the court denied review to a trade group representing firms using advanced technology to treat hazardous waste. The EPA had adopted a rule under the Resource Conservation and Recovery Act governing the treatment of certain hazardous wastes that the trade group thought was too lax. Using their advanced treatment technologies, their members could render the wastes much safer than the EPA required, and the trade group challenged the rule. The court recognized that the rule might benefit the trade group's competitors and a different rule would benefit the trade group, but this did not mean that their interests were closely related to the statute's interests. Increasing the revenues of the trade group's members did not necessarily further the environmental interests of the statute.

Discerning when a challenger's interests are sufficiently aligned with the interests of the statute can be difficult.

Example

Under Title VI of the Clean Air Act, which implements U.S. obligations under the Montreal Protocol for reducing ozone-depleting chemicals, the EPA adopts rules phasing out these chemicals and identifying substitutes for them. There are two types of ozone-depleting chemicals: Class I substances (chlorofluorocarbons or CFCs) and Class II substances (hydrochlorofluorocarbons or HCFCs), which are not quite as bad as CFCs. In 1999, the EPA identified a Honeywell product as an ozone-friendly substitute for a Class I substance due to be phased out in 2003. In 2002, however, the EPA also identified certain Class II substances manufactured by competitors of Honeywell as a substitute in certain applications for the same Class I substance, on the ground that there were technical difficulties with using Honeywell's substitute in these particular applications. Because the statute prohibits the EPA from "replac[ing] any class I or class II substance with any substitute substance which the Administrator determines may present adverse effects to human health or the environment, where the Administrator has identified an alternative to such replacement that— (1) reduces the overall risk to human health and the environment; and (2) is currently or potentially available," Honeywell challenged the rule identifying these new substitutes. Was Honeywell within the zone of interests of the statute?

Explanation

Yes. While the EPA argued that Honeywell stood in the same position as the trade group in *Hazardous Waste Treatment Council* (*HWTC*) above, the D.C. Circuit was not convinced. There the connection between the trade group's interest in increased revenues and any benefit to the environment was too indirect. Here, however, a competitor is suing to enforce a "statutory demarcation," such as an entry restriction. "Entry-like restrictions" are less subject to manipulation than the open-ended emissions standards in *HWTC*, because "the potentially limitless incentives of competitors [are] channeled by the terms of the statute into suits of a limited nature brought to enforce the statutory demarcation." Thus, Honeywell is a suitable challenger. *Honeywell International, Inc. v. EPA*, 374 F.3d 1363 (D.C. Cir. 2004). Apparently, the court is saying that when a statute presents polar approaches—the substitute is allowed or not; a bank is allowed to provide services or not—a business is within the zone of interests of the statute to challenge an agency decision to allow the competitor in. In *HWTC*, however, the possible means of treating hazardous wastes and the appropriate levels after treatment that might benefit the challengers were vast, but they would not all benefit the environment. That is, they would not all serve the interest of the statute.

Example

Suppose that a law limits nonprofit educational institutions' tax exemption to subsidiary activities related to the educational function. Historically this has meant that the university bookstore, which runs at a profit, is considered part of the nonprofit educational institution, and so its profit is not taxed. Now suppose that the IRS has ruled that university bookstores can maintain World Wide Web bookstores, selling worldwide, and still be considered a subsidiary activity related to the educational function. Other Internet book, music, and sports apparel stores sue to challenge that ruling, because they are harmed by having to compete with entities that are exempt from taxes. Are they within the zone of interests of the provision limiting nonprofit educational institutions' tax exemption to subsidiary activities related to the educational function?

Explanation

The first question would be what is the purpose of the provision? If the legislative history suggests a concern for tax-paying firms having to compete with tax-exempt educational institutions in the sale of goods and non-educational services, this would be sufficient to indicate that the other Internet stores would be intended beneficiaries of the law and therefore within the zone of interests of the provision. If, however, the only purpose for the provision was to minimize tax losses to the Treasury and to avoid tax loopholes, one would then ask whether the competitors are arguably within the zone of interests of the provision under the "suitable challengers" line of cases. This case is not on "all fours" with the bank regulatory cases, because the IRS provision is not a law limiting the economic activities nonprofit educational institutions can engage in; rather, it merely limits the tax exemption to certain types of activities. This might distinguish it from the competitor cases. On the other hand, the law does seem to fit the description of a "statutory demarcation." The purpose of the law is to limit what tax-exempt activities the universities can engage in, and one may characterize the issue as polar: either they can obtain the tax exemption or they cannot. Finally, the interests of the Internet book, music, and sports apparel firms are likewise to limit the tax-exempt activities of the universities because of their unfair advantage of not having to pay taxes. Accordingly, the relationship between their interests and the interests of the statute is fairly aligned. While the issue is too close to be certain, it would seem likely that a court would find the Internet providers within the zone of interests of the statute.

The Supreme Court's most recent foray into the zone of interests test under the APA was in *Match-E-Be-Nash-She-Wish Band of Pottawatomi Indians v. Patchak*, 132 S. Ct. 2199 (2012). There the Secretary of the Interior had purchased land for an Indian tribe to enable it to establish a casino on the land. David Patchak lived near the land where the casino was to be built, and he alleged he would suffer economic, environmental, and aesthetic harms from the casino's operation. The question was whether he was within the zone of interests of the Indian Reorganization Act's provision that authorized the Secretary to acquire property "for the purpose of providing land for Indians." The Court held that he was. It said:

> The prudential standing test Patchak must meet "is not meant to be especially demanding." We apply the test in keeping with Congress's "evident intent" when enacting the APA "to make agency action presumptively reviewable." We do not require any "indication of congressional purpose to benefit the would-be plaintiff." And we have always conspicuously included the word "arguably" in the test to indicate that the benefit of any doubt goes to the plaintiff. The test forecloses suit only when a plaintiff's "interests are so marginally related to or inconsistent with the purposes implicit in the statute that it cannot reasonably be assumed that Congress intended to permit the suit."

The Court indicated that Patchak was concerned about the use of the property, and the purpose of the statute, while by its terms limited to acquisition of land, really was to provide property for its use by Indians to further their economic well-being. And in this particular case "from start to finish" the decision hinged on the use to be made of the property.

The *Patchak* case perhaps indicates the Court's current lenient approach to the zone of interests test, but it also may be just one odd case.

B. Agency Action

As explained above, Section 702 of the APA creates a cause of action for persons suffering legal wrong because of agency action or adversely affected or aggrieved by agency action within the meaning of a relevant statute. In either case, however, the APA provides only for review of "agency action." The APA defines "agency action" as "includ[ing] the whole or a part of an agency rule, order, license, sanction, relief, or the equivalent or denial thereof, or failure to act." 5 U.S.C. § 551(13). Ordinarily, this broad definition is easily met; but there are occasions when persons might like to challenge what an agency is doing or not doing, but there is no "agency action" to review.

Example

The Bureau of Land Management (BLM) of the Department of the Interior has the authority to reclassify public lands that are not available for mining to make them available for mining in certain circumstances. An office in the BLM is responsible for doing this, and it has been considering various public lands over a period of time for possible reclassification. When the

BLM proposes to reclassify a particular area, it prepares an EIS regarding the effects of the particular reclassification. An environmental group, however, wants the BLM to undertake a programmatic EIS for the entire reclassification program, because the group believes that assessing only the effects of each area individually does not realistically represent the harm to the environment inflicted by the combined reclassification of many such areas. It wants to challenge the BLM's failure to undertake such a programmatic EIS. Is there an "agency action"?

Explanation

No. Each individual reclassification, because it is effected by means of a license to a person to mine the area, is an "agency action"; however, the "program" of considering areas for reclassification is not an "agency action" because it does not fit within any of the listed items under the definition. *See Lujan v. National Wildlife Federation*, 497 U.S. 871 (1990).

Example

The BLM also is responsible for protecting public lands that are being considered by Congress for possible inclusion in national wilderness areas. Unless they are adequately protected, they might become unsuitable for wilderness designation because of human uses that degrade the environment. In some of these areas, people use off-road vehicles for recreation, and an environmental group believes that their use is destroying the wilderness characteristics of the areas, yet BLM is taking no action to stop the off-road vehicle use. The environmental group would like to sue BLM to force it to protect the possible wilderness areas. Is there "agency action"?

Explanation

No. The environmental group argues that "agency action" includes "failure to act" and the BLM is failing to act to protect the possible wilderness areas. In *Norton v. Southern Utah Wilderness Alliance*, 542 U.S. 55 (2004), however, the Supreme Court clarified that the "failure to act" means the failure to take one of the discrete actions listed in the definition of "agency action." Here, there was no identified failure to take a discrete act. That is, there was no identified failure to adopt a particular "rule, order, license, sanction, relief, or the equivalent. . . . " Rather, the failure was the general failure to protect the possible wilderness area. This general failure was insufficient to qualify as a failure to act.

IV. PROBLEMS OF TIMING

Before the APA, courts had evolved some common-law rules designed to keep administrative law cases from coming to courts until agencies had had a full opportunity to rule on the issue. The purpose was several-fold: one was to recognize that Congress had placed the primary responsibility for deciding matters in the hands of the agency, and courts should not interfere in that process until the agency had exercised that responsibility; another purpose was to assure that the expertise and fact-finding abilities of the agencies would be capitalized on; and still another purpose was simply to limit the number of cases coming to courts by eliminating cases that could be disposed of by agencies. Three named doctrines further these purposes: *Finality, Exhaustion,* and *Ripeness.*

- The doctrine of Finality focuses on when the agency has completed an action, so as not to have courts interfere with ongoing agency activities. Only final agency actions are subject to judicial review.
- The doctrine of Exhaustion allows an agency the initial opportunity to address a challenge to its action. By requiring persons to first appeal their challenges to agency action to the agency itself, courts respect the congressional placement of responsibility for administration of the law in agency hands, enable agencies an opportunity to cure their own mistakes, and husband judicial resources by awaiting the outcome of the internal appeal, which may result in a decision favorable to the appellant, thereby avoiding judicial involvement.
- The doctrine of Ripeness assures that an issue is sufficiently developed for judicial resolution, sometimes by considering the issue in a later proceeding.

These different doctrines have much in common, so that in some circumstances it is unclear which doctrine should apply. Indeed, in one notorious case a panel of the D.C. Circuit agreed unanimously that the court should not hear the case, but the three judges could not agree on the reason. One believed the administrative case was not final; another believed it was not ripe; and the third believed that the plaintiff had failed to exhaust his administrative remedies. *See Ticor Title Insurance Co. v. Federal Trade Commn.*, 814 F.2d 731 (D.C. Cir. 1987). If judges cannot always figure it out, what are law students to do?

Some cases, we will find, are easy. Others are not. In those cases, as an advocate the best approach is to argue in the alternative and let the judges worry about which doctrine applies.

A. Final Agency Action

Prior to the APA the Supreme Court had established the doctrine that only "final" agency actions were subject to judicial review. As Justice Frankfurter (who as a law professor at Harvard was the author of the first administrative law casebook) explained it,

> judicial abstention here is merely an application of the traditional criteria for bringing judicial action into play. Partly these have been written into Article 3 of the Constitution, by what is implied from the grant of "judicial power" to determine "Cases" and "Controversies." Partly they are an aspect of the procedural philosophy pertaining to the federal courts whereby, ever since the first Judiciary Act, Congress has been loathe to authorize review of interim steps in a proceeding.

Rochester Telephone Corp. v. United States, 307 U.S. 125 (1939).

The APA codified this doctrine in Section 704, which provides that: "Agency action made reviewable by statute and final agency action for which there is no other adequate remedy in a court are subject to judicial review. A preliminary, procedural, or intermediate agency action or ruling not directly reviewable is subject to review on the review of the final agency action." This is consistent with standard practice in federal (and state) courts. For example, if an Administrative Law Judge (ALJ) excludes certain evidence offered by a party, that party may object, but he may not run to federal court seeking immediate judicial review of that evidentiary decision. Just as in a judicial proceeding an interlocutory decision by a trial judge is generally not immediately appealable to a higher court, an interlocutory administrative decision is not subject to immediate judicial review. If, however, the party offering the evidence does not ultimately prevail before the ALJ or the agency, he may seek judicial review of the final agency action on the basis that the proffered evidence in the hearing was excluded, just as the party in the judicial case could appeal an adverse decision by the trial court on the same basis.

The Supreme Court has said that there are two requirements for agency action to be "final agency action." The first requirement is that the agency's decision is final in the sense of being the culmination of the agency's consideration of the matter and not a tentative or preliminary determination. For example, suppose that the Federal Trade Commission (FTC) files a complaint against a company alleging it is engaged in unfair and deceptive trade practices. The complaint is the consummation of the agency investigation process in the sense that it is the final decision of the agency to charge the company with violating the Federal Trade Commission Act, and it is final in the sense that it is unlikely to be subject to judicial review later—either because the FTC will rule in favor of the company after the proceeding or because the company will be seeking review of the ultimate decision and order against it, not review of the complaint that started the proceeding. On the other hand, the complaint is not the consummation of a process but is really just the beginning of the administrative process, which will culminate in a final decision and order. As is true in judicial practice, where a person receiving a complaint in a civil case cannot appeal the lawfulness of the complaint to an appellate court, in administrative law an agency's filing of a complaint is not final agency action. *See, e.g., Federal Trade Commn. v. Standard Oil Co. of California*, 449 U.S. 232 (1980).

Now suppose that an agency responds in writing to a request for an interpretation from a regulated entity. Is the letter "final agency action"? That depends. It may be final in the sense that it is not interlocutory ("a preliminary, procedural, or intermediate agency action or ruling"), but it may not be final in the sense that it may only be the agency's tentative position. And it may not even be "agency" action if the letter is sent by someone without the power to render definitive agency interpretations.

Example

An association of retail stores writes to the Administrator of the Wage and Hour Division in the Department of Labor, the person in charge of enforcing the federal minimum wage and overtime laws, seeking to clarify the effect on its members of recent amendments to these laws. The Administrator responds in a lengthy letter explaining his interpretation of the effect of the amendments and the basis for his interpretation of them. Is this "final agency action"?

Explanation

In such a case, the D.C. Circuit held that the letter was final agency action. The court looked at the facts and circumstances surrounding the letter. The court concluded that a letter from the head of the agency responsible for a matter is presumptively the agency's decision, and absent any indication that his view therein was only tentative or preliminary, it could be viewed as final. His decision could, of course, be changed in the future, but that is true of agency actions that are clearly "final," such as an agency's adoption of a legislative rule after notice and comment. Moreover, the court noted that the letter was a deliberative determination of the agency's position at the highest available level on a question of importance and applicable to an entire industry, which the agency hoped would be followed by all members of the industry.

The court contrasted the letter with the myriad of informal and advisory opinions that an agency might issue to provide guidance. It did not wish to create a disincentive to agencies issuing such guidance by subjecting them all to judicial review as final agency actions. *See National Automatic Laundry & Cleaning Council v. Shultz*, 443 F.2d 689 (D.C. Cir. 1971).

However, in a similar case, the Fifth Circuit found sufficient distinguishing features to conclude that a Wage and Hour Administrator's opinion letter was not final agency action. There, one local government wanted to challenge an opinion letter given to a different local government, because it believed the interpretation in that letter, if applied to it, would result in increased employee costs. The court distinguished *National Automatic Laundry* by saying that there the opinion letter was directed to an association and was intended to apply to the whole industry based upon generalized facts. Here, in contrast, the opinion letter was directed to a particular entity with respect to the particular facts presented by that entity; it was not directed to the local government that was challenging it. Accordingly, the court found the opinion letter only one of those informal and advisory opinions that *National Automatic Laundry* had said would not be final agency action. *See Taylor-Callahan-Coleman Counties District Adult Probation Dept. v. Dole*, 948 F.2d 953 (5th Cir. 1991).

What these two cases reflect is that often the decision whether an agency action is deemed "final" may be highly dependent upon the facts and upon the court's view of whether judicial review of such actions will chill such informal actions.

Even assuming that an agency action is the consummation of an agency process, there is a second requirement for agency action to be final agency action. The Court has given two slightly different characterizations of this requirement. In *Abbott Laboratories v. Gardner*, 387 U.S. 136 (1967), and again in *Franklin v. Massachusetts*, 505 U.S. 788, 796-797 (1992), the Court phrased the second requirement as: "whether [the agency action's] impact 'is sufficiently direct and immediate' and has a 'direct effect on . . . day-to-day business.'" In *Bennett v. Spear*, 520 U.S. 154, 178 (1997), however, the Court said: "the action must be one by which 'rights or obligations have been determined,' or from which 'legal consequences will flow.'" Normally agency action that has an impact that is direct and immediate or which has a direct effect on day-to-day business will also be one which determines rights or obligations or from which legal consequences will flow. For example, the labeling rule in *Abbott Labs*, when it went into effect, would immediately place drug companies under a legal duty to change their labels and that legal duty would have a direct effect on them. However, it is not always so, because there are agency actions that have serious practical impacts on day-to-day business without technically having legal effect. For example, the interpretation in *National Automatic Laundry* was at most an interpretative rule, and interpretative rules cannot have a binding legal effect, but it clearly had a direct practical effect, because now the members of the association knew that if they did not pay their employees the overtime wages the Administrator had said they were required to, then the Administrator would likely come after them, alleging they were violating the statute. Is this enough?

Example

Under the federal wage-and-hours laws, persons who work for two employers for a combined total number of hours that exceed 40 in a week must be paid overtime wages if the employers are "joint employers." In essence, this assures that an employer cannot avoid overtime requirements simply by declaring itself two separate companies, so that when an employee reaches 40 hours of employment at one company, she immediately stops working for that company and begins working (doing the same work) for the second company. Two companies ask the Administrator of the Wage and Hour Administration whether they must be classified as "joint employers" under the law, and the Administrator responds in a letter saying they are joint employers. He indicates that willful violations of the law are punishable by fine (as opposed to non-willful violations that result only in an order for back payment of the required wages) and that in the future if the companies are found in violation they will be considered willful violators. Does this letter have legal consequences?

Explanation

A court held that this opinion letter had legal consequences. First, the court decided that the letter was not tentative or hypothetical, because it addressed a specific factual situation and spoke in absolute terms, saying, for instance, that a joint employment relationship did exist in this situation, not that it might exist in such a situation, and that the employers must pay overtime. Second, the court said that the opinion letter established the legal obligations of the two companies and legal consequences flowed from the letter, to wit, that the companies would face fines in the future for violations that they would not have faced in the absence of the letter. *See Western Illinois Home Health Care, Inc. v. Herman*, 150 F.3d 659 (7th Cir. 1998).

In this case, while the court made a finding of legal consequences flowing from the letter, its opinion really focused more on the practical consequences of a company ignoring such an opinion letter. Its finding of finality reflected the court's predilection to review an agency's final (in the sense of non-tentative) opinion to a company that would have severe and immediate direct, practical effects. Not all courts necessarily would find the same way. Another court might stress the fact that such an opinion letter cannot—legally—change the legal obligations of the recipients of the letter. All it can do is reflect the agency's view of what the statute itself requires. Therefore, the letter itself has no legal consequences.

Example

The EPA issued "final guidance" to EPA staff to ask state permitting authorities under the Clean Water Act to assess elevated conductivity in water resulting from surface coal mining and recommending that levels not exceed a specific figure. The guidance document was challenged by two states, coal mining companies, and trade associations as beyond EPA's statutory authority, but the question was whether the guidance document was final agency action.

Explanation

The D.C. Circuit concluded that, because the guidance was a "statement of policy" (and statements of policy do not have legal effect), it was not judicially reviewable. The court went to some lengths to demonstrate that the guidance did not compel or prohibit any action, and that the states and companies could ignore the guidance without suffering any legal penalties or disabilities. The fact, it said, that "regulated entities may feel pressure to voluntarily conform their behavior because the writing is on the wall about what will be needed to obtain a permit" is simply insufficient to justify a finding of final agency action. *Natl. Mining Assn. v. McCarthy*, 758 F.3d 243 (D.C. Cir. 2014).

Example

The Clean Water Act prohibits persons from discharging dredged or fill material into "waters of the United States" without a permit from the Army Corps of Engineers. Exactly what is a "water of the United States" is often unclear and highly dependent on the particular site. In this case the Corps learned that a person planned to develop certain property, and it gave notice to him of its "preliminary determination" that the property was within the waters of the United States and could not be developed without a permit designed to protect the ecological function of the property. The owner challenged the Corps preliminary determination administratively, and the Corps responded first with a "draft jurisdictional determination" and later with an "approved jurisdictional determination" that the property was indeed within the waters of the United States. The owner then appealed this decision within the Corps according to its regulations, but the determination was upheld. The owner then sought judicial review of this decision under the APA.

Explanation

The Supreme Court unanimously held that the Corps' jurisdictional determination was final agency action subject to judicial review. What it did not do was decide what kind of consequences were necessary to make an agency action final. Chief Justice Roberts wrote for the Court. He began by invoking *Bennett v. Spear* for the test that an action must be one "by which rights or obligations have been determined, or from which legal consequences flow." He then noted that there was an interagency agreement between the Corps and the EPA that if a person received a *negative* jurisdictional determination (i.e., a determination that the property was not subject to the Clean Water Act), neither the EPA nor the Corps could bring any enforcement action against the person for five years. Such a determination, the Chief Justice said, would clearly have direct and appreciable consequences—creating a five-year safe harbor for the person. It follows, he continued, that positive jurisdictional determinations likewise have legal consequences—the denial of a safe harbor that a negative determination would have. Thus, it satisfied *Bennett*'s test for final agency action. However, he did not stop there. Instead, he said that this conclusion tracked the "'pragmatic' approach we have long taken to finality," citing *Abbott Labs*. In addition, he described an earlier case in which the Court had found final agency action because it would have "an immediate and practical impact." In other words, the Court's opinion seemed to say that this was final agency action under either test.

There were three concurring opinions. Justice Kennedy, joined by Justices Alito and Thomas, did not think it was necessary for there to have been an interagency agreement between the EPA and the Corps. Instead, in their view, the fact that the agency action "cast doubt on the full use and enjoyment of private property" meant that it would raise due process issues, so that the action should be considered final. Justice Ginsburg also did not believe the interagency agreement was necessary. Instead, all that was necessary was a final definitive action that had immediate and practical effect. Justice Kagan, however, wrote a concurrence to say that in her opinion the interagency agreement was necessary here for there to be final agency action—only an action with actual *legal* consequences would suffice. So, the Court itself is of two minds on the issue.

A final problem with respect to final agency action arises when a person wants to challenge agency *inaction*. Earlier we discussed how agency inaction or an agency's failure to act can be "agency action" under the APA. Now the issue is to determine when agency inaction or a failure to act is *final* agency action.

If a statute has established a specific deadline for a particular agency action, the failure to meet that deadline can be found to be a final agency action. In the absence of a statutory deadline, if an agency concludes a process by announcing a decision not to take action, for example, by concluding a rulemaking process by announcing a decision not to adopt a rule, this clearly meets the requirement for final agency action. If, however, an agency begins a process but never announces any final decision, when, if ever, can it be said that there is final agency action? As you might imagine, courts have taken a pragmatic approach, affording agencies the benefit of the doubt, but at some point agency inaction, even without a formal decision not to take action, can qualify as final agency action. We will also see that even when courts do review this type of agency inaction, they review it very deferentially. You may recall, in the discussion regarding agency action committed to agency discretion by law, then-Judge Scalia's remark that often the question of the availability of review and the question of the scope of review run into one another. That is true here as well.

B. Exhaustion of Administrative Remedies

Like the finality requirement, before the passage of the APA the Supreme Court had established the doctrine that courts should not review agency action until after a person had exhausted his or her possible remedies from the agency itself.

This common-law doctrine continued after passage of the APA until 1993, when the Supreme Court decided *Darby v. Cisneros*, 509 U.S. 137 (1993). In that case, the Court held that the third sentence in Section 704 of the APA created a statutory exhaustion doctrine that superseded the common-law doctrine whenever a suit is brought under the APA.

5 U.S.C. § 704

. . . Except as otherwise expressly required by statute, agency action otherwise final is final for purposes of this section whether or not there has been presented or determined an application for a declaratory order, for any form of reconsideration, or, unless the agency otherwise requires by rule and provides that the action meanwhile is inoperative, for an appeal to superior agency authority.

This sentence, because it is phrased in terms of what is final agency action, was not interpreted as stating an exhaustion rule, but *Darby* concluded that it did. As written, this sentence only requires a person to exhaust administrative remedies in two circumstances: when expressly required by statute and when an agency requires it by rule and provides for an automatic stay of the agency action pending appeal.

Example

The Department of Housing and Urban Affairs can sanction persons who misuse its benefit programs by barring them from further participation in the programs. An ALJ found a person to have violated certain eligibility requirements for mortgage insurance and issued an initial decision and order barring the person from further participation in the program for 18 months. HUD's regulations stated that "[t]he hearing officer's determination shall be final unless the Secretary or the Secretary's designee, within 30 days of receipt of a request, decides as a matter of discretion to review the finding of the hearing officer. . . . Any party may request such a review in writing within 15 days of receipt of the hearing officer's determination." The person did not seek a review by the Secretary or his designee within 15 days; instead, he filed suit in district court seeking judicial review of the ALJ's decision under the APA. Did this person fail to exhaust his administrative remedies, deliberately bypassing the available administrative review mechanism?[4]

Explanation

The Supreme Court held that the person did not need to exhaust administrative remedies under the APA. Applying Section 704's language to the case, the Court noted that there was no express statutory requirement for the person to administratively appeal the ALJ's decision. HUD's regulation, moreover, had two separate flaws, either of which alone would have excused the person from having to administratively appeal the ALJ's decision before going to court. First, the regulation did not require an appeal. The agency's regulation may have required the losing party *to ask for* an appeal, but the decision whether there actually would be an appeal rested in the discretion of the Secretary (or his designee). This did not satisfy the terms of Section 704, which states that the agency must, by rule, require an administrative appeal; that is, an administrative appeal must be provided, not just the ability to request the agency to allow an appeal. Second, the regulation did not automatically stay the agency action pending decision of the appeal. The bar on the person's participation in the program would have remained in effect while the person sought appeal. Consequently, the agency action, otherwise final (an initial ALJ decision), was final for purposes of obtaining judicial

4. Note that in this case if the court dismissed the person's suit, the person could not then seek the administrative remedy because the time for filing for that review had passed. This is not unusual in "exhaustion" cases. The failure to obtain judicial review usually means the person obtains neither administrative nor judicial review.

review even though the person had not exhausted a possible opportunity for administrative review. *See Darby v. Cisneros*, 509 U.S. 137 (1993).

In non-APA cases, when the specific review statute does not require exhaustion, the common-law rule of exhaustion still remains. That rule, as suggested above, generally requires persons to avail themselves of any administrative remedy possible. The common-law rule, however, then has a number of common-law exceptions. Some have suggested that the exceptions are so numerous that they almost swallow the rule. *See* Marcia Gelpe, *Exhaustion of Administrative Remedies: Lessons from Environmental Cases*, 53 Geo. Wash. L. Rev. 1 (1984) (describing at least eight different exceptions). While that may overstate the situation somewhat, at least the number and indeterminancy of the exceptions has meant that cases in the area are often hard to predict. The Supreme Court in its latest foray into the area identified three classes of exceptions:

1. requiring resort to an administrative remedy may undermine the ability of subsequent judicial review to provide effective relief (for example, where the agency action is not stayed and there will be irreparable harm to the person);
2. an administrative remedy may be inadequate because it cannot give effective relief (for example, where the person seeks money damages but the administrative relief cannot include payment of money, or where the person wishes to challenge the constitutionality of the statute the agency is implementing, but an agency cannot declare the law unconstitutional); and
3. requiring recourse to the administrative agency would be inappropriate because of alleged bias or prejudice.

See McCarthy v. Madigan, 503 U.S. 140 (1992).

Example

An employee of a Navy Exchange (an on-base store at which persons connected to the Navy may purchase American items not available or available at a higher cost outside the base) took advantage of her position to obtain certain clothing at a doubly reduced sale price. For this she was fired. Under Navy regulations, a person may seek reconsideration from the deciding official; the person may then request a full evidentiary hearing before the local commander; the person may appeal this decision to the commander of the Naval Resale and Services Support Office; and then the person may appeal this decision to the Deputy Assistant Secretary of the Navy for Civilian Personnel Policy. The employee in fact did seek and receive decisions, all unfavorable, from the first three of these officers, but rather than seek the last review, she brought suit in federal court alleging that the decision was arbitrary and capricious. By specific statute, 5 U.S.C. § 2105(c), the APA does not apply to the termination of Navy exchange personnel. She argued that, having lost in each of the previous appeals, making the last appeal would be futile. Did she inexcusably fail to exhaust her administrative remedies?

Explanation

Because the APA does not apply, the case is governed by common-law principles of exhaustion. Under the common-law doctrine, her failure to seek the last level of administrative appeal would constitute a failure to exhaust her administrative remedies, unless her failure is excused because it falls within one of the exceptions to the need to exhaust. Futility is one of the recognized exceptions to the exhaustion doctrine and can find its justification in two of the classes of exceptions the Court described in *McCarthy*: the inability of the agency to provide effective relief and the lack of a fair consideration because of bias or prejudgment. In both situations, further administrative appeal would be futile. However, neither of these exceptions was present with regard to the Exchange employee. Her futility claim was simply that she was unlikely to win in light of her lack of success in her other appeals. The First Circuit ruled against her, saying, "[a] pessimistic prediction or a hunch that further administrative proceedings will prove unproductive is not enough to sidetrack the exhaustion rule." *Portela-Gonzalez v. Secretary of the Navy*, 109 F.3d 74 (1st Cir. 1997).

Had the case been under the APA, she would not have had to utilize any of these appeal mechanisms, because her termination was not stayed during the pendency of the administrative appeals.

The D.C. Circuit has adopted its own terminology regarding the difference between exhaustion required by statute and common law exhaustion. The D.C. Circuit calls the former "jurisdictional exhaustion" and the latter "non-jurisdictional exhaustion." The concept is that the former is mandatory, while the latter is based on prudential principles and can be subject to exceptions when the litigant's interests in immediate review outweigh the government's interests in efficiency or agency autonomy. *See, e.g., Avocados Plus, Inc. v. Veneman*, 370 F.3d 1243 (D.C. Cir. 2004). Despite the different characterization, however, the D.C. Circuit's doctrine regarding the two different types of exhaustion is the same as other circuits.

A currently unresolved issue is whether the common-law exceptions to the common-law exhaustion requirement also apply to the exhaustion requirement in Section 704.

Example

Suppose that HUD amends its regulations in light of *Darby*, requiring persons to appeal to the Secretary (or his designee) prior to going to court and providing that the agency sanction is stayed until the Secretary (or his designee) makes a decision in the appeal. Again an ALJ renders a decision barring someone from the program for misconduct. Rather than appeal to the Secretary, the person sues in court alleging the agency is biased against him and that the statute authorizing his disbarment is unconstitutional. Would a common-law exception to the need to exhaust excuse the failure to exhaust here?

Explanation

Under Section 704 the agency action is not final, because the agency has by rule required the person to administratively appeal the decision and would automatically stay the decision pending the appeal. In other words, the person has failed to meet Section 704's exhaustion requirements. However, the person has raised at least two issues that the Supreme Court has said are a basis for creating an exception to the common-law exhaustion requirement. Can these claims also provide a basis for an exception from Section 704? The only courts to have expressly addressed the issue have held that Section 704 overrides the common-law exceptions, so that the person here would lose. Nevertheless, some courts have responded to claims for exceptions in such situations without acknowledging that any conflict may exist.

What if a person attempts to utilize the existing administrative remedies but commits some procedural error so that the appeal is dismissed? Has the person exhausted his administrative remedies, allowing him now to go to court, or has he failed to exhaust his administrative remedies and therefore is precluded from ever obtaining judicial review?

Example

A prison requires prisoners to seek administrative relief first by raising a grievance informally with a staff person and then, if dissatisfied with the result, to file a form within 15 days with the warden. Prisoner X is dissatisfied with the result of a grievance after raising it informally with a staff person, but he does not file the form with the warden until six months later. His grievance is rejected as out of time. The prisoner then seeks judicial review of the underlying grievance. Has he exhausted his administrative remedies?

Explanation

First, if this was an APA case, he would not need to exhaust his remedies unless he was required to (which he apparently was) and the agency stayed the action pending the review. When a person seeks something from the agency and does not obtain it, this latter requirement does not come into play. The agency is not required to provide the sought-after benefit or redress the grievance pending administrative review. Thus, here exhaustion would be required. Second, if this were a common-law case, while there would be a requirement to exhaust, there might be possible exceptions to the requirement, or there might be some other statute applicable to exhaustion. Indeed, the Prison Litigation Reform Act, which was designed to reduce prisoner litigation, requires prisoners to exhaust all available remedies before going to court. It has been interpreted to preclude common-law exceptions to the exhaustion requirement. See *Booth v. Churner*, 532 U.S. 731, 739 (2001). However, here the prisoner attempted to exhaust his administrative remedies. Unfortunately, his attempt was unsuccessful, and the Supreme Court held that this meant he had not exhausted his administrative remedies, so his court case should also be dismissed. *See Woodford v. Ngo*, 548 U.S. 81 (2006). In the Court's view, failure to comply with the procedural requirements for the administrative review in effect meant the person had failed to exhaust his administrative remedies. In essence, to exhaust his administrative remedies he must obtain a decision on the merits. In a later case, the Court further explained the limits of this doctrine. *See Jones v. Bock*, 549 U.S. 199 (2007). First, it said that exhaustion was an affirmative defense, meaning that the government defendant had to plead it as a defense or it would be waived. Second, the Court did not require "total exhaustion." That is, in *Jones* the plaintiff had administratively appealed several claims, but his lawsuit included new claims in addition to those he had administratively appealed. The lower courts had dismissed *all* the claims, saying that the failure to administratively appeal all meant that all had to be dismissed. The Supreme Court reversed, saying only those claims that he had not appealed administratively should be dismissed.

Closely related to the doctrine of exhaustion of administrative remedies is the doctrine of issue exhaustion. This doctrine, consistent with judicial practice, states that a person must have first raised an issue before the agency as a prerequisite to obtaining judicial review of that issue. In *Sims v. Apfel*, 530 U.S. 103 (2000), a 5-4 decision, the majority expressed the view that the "requirements of administrative issue exhaustion are largely creatures of statute." *Id.* at 107. Nevertheless, the Court went on, "it is common for an agency's regulations to require issue exhaustion in administrative appeals. And when regulations do so, courts reviewing agency action regularly ensure against bypassing of that requirement by refusing to consider unexhausted issues." *Id.* Still the Court acknowledged that it had imposed an issue-exhaustion requirement even in the absence of statute or regulation. "The basis for a judicially imposed issue-exhaustion requirement is an analogy to the rule that appellate courts will not consider arguments not raised before trial courts." *Id.* Accordingly, the Court said, "the desirability of a court imposing a requirement of issue exhaustion depends on the degree to which the analogy to normal adversarial litigation applies in a particular administrative setting." *Id.* at 109. The dissent characterized the administrative issue doctrine in a slightly different manner: "Under ordinary principles of administrative law a reviewing court will not consider arguments that a party failed to raise in timely fashion before an administrative agency." *Id.* at 114. In the dissent's view, these principles only partially reflect an analogy to the rule that appellate courts will not consider arguments made before lower courts; equally, if not more important, is respect for "administrative autonomy." Where Congress has authorized or directed an agency to provide an initial proceeding, the dissent believed it important to recognize the autonomy and expertise of the agency, so that only in rare circumstances should there be an exception to the requirement of issue exhaustion.

Example

A person filed a claim for Social Security disability benefits and was denied. She appealed that decision administratively to a Social Security Administrative Law Judge, who also denied her claim. As required by Social Security Administration regulations, she then sought review of the ALJ's decision by the Social Security Appeals Council, but the Council denied review. She then brought suit to seek judicial review of her denial, arguing, among other things, that certain of the questions that the ALJ had asked were improper, but she had not raised this issue before the Social Security Appeals Council. Did she fail to comply with the requirements for issue exhaustion?

Explanation

These were the facts in *Sims v. Apfel*. The Supreme Court held that in the circumstances of this case the person did not need to have raised the issue before the Appeals Council. Under Section 704 she had exhausted her administrative remedies, because she had appealed to the Social Security Appeals Council, even though she had not raised this particular issue in that appeal. There was no statute or regulation requiring issue exhaustion in Social Security disability appeals. Moreover, for four members of the majority, because Social Security disability appeals are informal in nature, with most appellants not represented by attorneys, these appeals are not analogous to adversarial proceedings in court, and consequently issue exhaustion was inappropriate.

After *Sims v. Apfel,* where there is no statutory or regulatory requirement to raise all issues in the administrative appeal, lower courts have excused the failure to raise an issue before the agency when the proceeding has been both informal and not truly adversarial.

Some statutes contain an explicit issue exhaustion requirement applicable to certain agency decisions, which can include rulemakings. Usually, as in the Federal Power Act, for example, they include a requirement that the grounds for objection have first been raised with the agency. Thus, these statutes contain an explicit issue exhaustion requirement for rulemakings subject to these statutes. Even in the absence of such statutes, however, some courts, including the D.C. Circuit, have generally derived a doctrine of issue exhaustion in rulemaking, which they sometimes denominate as "waiver." After *Sims,* it might be questioned whether this is appropriate, inasmuch as the majority of the Court relied on the analogy between administrative adjudication and judicial proceedings to derive an administrative doctrine of issue exhaustion. Nevertheless, the lower courts have not been persuaded and have continued to impose an issue exhaustion requirement in rulemaking. *See, e.g., Advocates for Highway and Auto Safety v. Federal Motor Carrier Safety Admin.*, 429 F.3d 1136 (D.C. Cir. 2005). These courts do, however, grant an exception to the requirement if the issue was raised by someone else in the rulemaking, so that the agency had a full opportunity to consider the issue. *See, e.g., NRDC v. EPA,* 824 F.2d 1146, 1151-1152 (D.C. Cir. 1987).

C. Ripeness

Like Finality and Exhaustion, the ripeness doctrine predates the APA. Unlike the other two doctrines, however, the ripeness doctrine has not been recognized as codified in the APA. As a matter of common, or judge-made, law, it is deemed jurisdictional, so that courts may raise it on their own motion at any time. *See Reno v. Catholic Social Services, Inc.*, 509 U.S. 43, 57 n.18 (1993). As indicated earlier, the Supreme Court has put in question the continued vitality of judge-made restrictions on judicial review of agency action that otherwise qualifies for review under the APA, thereby putting in question the continued validity of common law ripeness doctrine. Nevertheless, until the Court takes the next step of eliminating or, more likely, subsuming it within the doctrine of standing, the doctrine may be followed by the lower courts. Indeed, many lower courts today are considering ripeness and the standing requirement for an injury to be immediate or certainly impending to be equivalent tests.

The most famous case explicating the requirements for ripeness is *Abbott Laboratories v. Gardner*, 387 U.S. 136 (1967), which we also addressed under statutory preclusion, and a companion case,[5] *Toilet Goods Assn. v. Gardner*, 387 U.S. 158 (1967). Recall that in *Abbott Labs* the FDA had issued a rule requiring drug manufacturers to include the generic name each time they used the trade name for a proprietary drug in their labels or advertising. In that case the Supreme Court stated that there was a presumption of judicial review of agency action, but then it went on to say:

> A further inquiry must, however, be made. The injunctive and declaratory judgment remedies are discretionary, and courts traditionally have been reluctant to apply them to administrative determinations unless these arise in the context of a controversy "ripe" for judicial resolution. . . . [I]t is fair to say that [the doctrine's] basic rationale is to prevent the courts, through avoidance of premature adjudication, from entangling themselves in abstract disagreements over administrative policies, and also to protect the agencies from judicial interference until an administrative decision has been formalized and its effects felt in a concrete way by the challenging parties.

387 U.S. at 148. The Court then announced a two-part test: "The problem is best seen in a twofold aspect, requiring us to evaluate both the fitness of the issues for judicial decision and the hardship to the parties of withholding court consideration." *Id.* In deciding whether the issues were fit for judicial decision, the Court in *Abbott Labs* looked first at the nature of the claims. Because the claims were "purely legal" (whether the rule was beyond the statutory authority of the agency), rather than factual, the case was ready for judicial resolution. The Court then asked whether there was "final agency action." As we have already learned, if there is no final agency action, the APA does not provide for judicial relief. In *Abbott Labs* the agency had issued a final, legislative rule that imposed legal duties on manufacturers. It was clearly final agency action. Accordingly, the rule was fit for judicial decision. The Court then looked to the hardship to the parties of withholding judicial review. The government argued that there would be no hardship to the companies in withholding review because they could obtain review of the rule in the defense to an enforcement action, but the Court found instead that there was significant harm in withholding review because of "the very real dilemma" the companies found themselves in: either they must comply with the regulation and forgo review of what they believed was an unlawful regulation, or they must willfully violate the rule and run the risk of serious criminal and civil penalties. In addition, the Court dismissed the government's claims that allowing review now would delay or impede effective

5. A "companion case" is a case on the same subject decided at the same time as another case, but which usually reaches an opposite conclusion. The two cases together therefore establish the parameters of the doctrine the Court is establishing.

enforcement of the statute, saying instead that a judicial decision now as to the lawfulness of the regulation would speed enforcement. Accordingly, the Court concluded that:

> Where the legal issue presented is fit for judicial resolution, and where a regulation requires an immediate and significant change in the plaintiffs' conduct of their affairs with serious penalties attached to noncompliance, access to the courts under the [APA] must be permitted, absent a statutory bar or some other unusual circumstance. . . .

Id. at 153.

In *Toilet Goods* the FDA had also issued a final legislative rule. This rule provided that if a person refused to permit duly authorized employees of the FDA free access to all manufacturing facilities, processes, and formulae involved in the manufacture of color additives, the FDA could immediately suspend certification to use the color additives and could continue such suspension until adequate corrective action had been taken. This rule was challenged by an association of manufacturers of color additives. Applying the test from *Abbott Labs,* the Court found that this challenge was *not* ripe. First, the Court said the case was not fit for judicial resolution. Although the rule was final agency action challenged on purely legal grounds—that the rule was beyond the statutory authority of the agency—the Court said that the statute authorized regulations "for the efficient enforcement" of the statute and

> deciding whether the rule furthered efficient enforcement of the statute would depend not merely on an inquiry into statutory purpose, but concurrently on an understanding of what types of enforcement problems are encountered by the FDA, the need for various sorts of supervision in order to effectuate the goals of the Act, and the safeguards devised to protect legitimate trade secrets. We believe that judicial appraisal of these factors is likely to stand on a much surer footing in the context of a specific application of this regulation than could be the case in the framework of the generalized challenge made here.[6]

387 U.S. at 163-164. Second, the Court found that the companies did not face the same hardship found in *Abbott Labs*. Here, the rule did not immediately establish a legal duty requiring them to alter their primary conduct. Rather it imposed a conditional requirement, only *if* an inspector sought access to a facility, was he to be afforded it. Moreover, the rule provided only that the FDA *might* authorize an inspector to require unlimited access. Whether this authorization would be exercised was speculative, given the

6. It should be noted that since 1967, when *Toilet Goods* was decided, judicial requirements for what information and reasoning must accompany the adoption of rules have increased substantially, so that today the preamble to the rule would be expected to describe and explain the very matters the Court felt were lacking absent an application of the rule.

already existing and normally used statutory authority for "reasonable" inspections. Even if exercised, a violation of the rule would not result in civil or criminal penalties as violation would in *Abbott Labs*. Instead, there would "at most" be a temporary suspension of certification, which could be challenged first in an administrative proceeding, which then would be subject to judicial review.

Today, challenges to legislative rules that impose duties or restrictions requiring persons immediately to change their conduct or be in violation of law are virtually always held ripe under *Abbott Labs*. Legislative rules that do not impose such duties or restrictions, however, are often found unripe under *Toilet Goods*.

Example

Under the Clean Air Act, the EPA has adopted emission standards for a variety of air pollutants. Before 1997, the EPA had specified a number of performance or compliance tests by which to determine whether a particular emitter was emitting in excess of the applicable emission standard. In 1997, the EPA adopted a rule known as the "credible evidence" rule, which in essence provided that visual observation of smoke from a smokestack could be used as evidence that a person was violating its Clean Air Act requirements. This rule was challenged by an organization representing emitters, alleging that the rule was beyond the statutory authority of the agency. Is the issue ripe for review?

Explanation

The D.C. Circuit held that the rule was not ripe for review. Using the *Abbott Labs* and *Toilet Goods* tests, the court acknowledged that the rule was final agency action and that the question of statutory authority was purely legal, but nevertheless found that the issue was not fit for judicial resolution at this time and there was no hardship to the parties by withholding review. The issue was not fit for judicial resolution at this time because how the credible evidence rule would be applied might be critical to determining whether it was statutorily authorized. The court said: "An enforcement action brought on the basis of credible evidence would, we believe, provide the factual development necessary to determine whether the new rule [exceeds statutory authority]. Until then, we have the 'classic institutional reason to postpone review: we need to wait for a rule to be applied to see what its effect will be.'" Moreover, there was no hardship to the challengers in waiting for review because the rule did not require them to change their conduct in any way. The substantive emission standard remained the same. *See Clean Air Implementation Project v. EPA*, 150 F.3d 1200 (D.C. Cir. 1998).

Ripeness challenges today arise more frequently in circumstances involving pre-enforcement challenges to agency interpretative rules and statements of policy, because by definition they cannot require persons to change their conduct. Many of the same questions that arise under "finality doctrine" reappear under ripeness doctrine. Remember that it is often difficult to distinguish between these different doctrines. In *National Automatic Laundry & Cleaning Council v. Shultz*, 443 F.2d 689 (D.C. Cir. 1971), for example, discussed above in the section on finality, the court's discussion of finality was in the course of its discussion of ripeness under *Abbott Labs*. Having decided that the agency's opinion was final, the court also determined that it was purely a legal question that would not be aided by further factual development. This was due in large part to the inclusion of various factual hypotheticals in the agency's interpretation that provided all the factual matter necessary. Finally, the court found that there would be hardship on the regulated entities if review were postponed. In making this determination, the court emphasized the practical effect of the agency's interpretation, even if it could not be legally binding. This form of analysis for ripeness purposes is still good guidance today.

For example, in *Florida Power & Light Co. v. EPA*, 145 F.3d 1414 (D.C. Cir. 1998), a power company challenged interpretations made in a preamble to a proposed rulemaking regarding the scope of EPA's authority under the Resource Conservation and Recovery Act to require "corrective action" at certain hazardous waste facilities where hazardous wastes are being released to the environment. The court assessed whether the preamble interpretations were final agency action and, if so, whether they were ripe for review. Its analysis was similar for both, finding that the interpretations were not final agency action, and, even if they were, they were not ripe for review, and the court commented on how these two issues converged. As to ripeness, the court said that although the issue was purely legal, it was not fit for review because the interpretation had not been acted upon in a concrete application, so that the scope of the interpretation was unclear. Thus, judicial review would be assisted by waiting for further concrete development. Moreover, the court found no hardship to the power company in waiting, because the interpretation did not address what the company's legal requirements were, so it did not impose any duty or burden on the company. Instead, the interpretation only addressed what the EPA's authority was to require persons to engage in corrective action. If the EPA did require a company to engage in corrective action, the company could then seek judicial review. In other words, the court found that the company would not be prejudiced by waiting for enforcement and obtaining review in that context, rather than in pre-enforcement review.

So far all the examples have involved regulated entities seeking pre-enforcement review, and often the question is whether they should be forced to wait for review in an enforcement context. However, what if the person seeking review is a beneficiary of a statutory scheme, rather than a regulated entity, and seeks review of a rule or agency action because he or she thinks the agency has failed to protect or benefit him or her sufficiently?

Example

The Food and Drug Administration (FDA) has the responsibility of regulating unavoidable contaminants in food to protect consumers' health and safety. Pursuant to its authority, the FDA issued a public notice of "action levels"—levels of contamination deemed sufficiently harmless by the FDA that it would not engage in enforcement actions so long as the level of contamination did not exceed the "action level." A consumer group believes that these levels are too high and therefore insufficiently protective of consumers' health and safety, and it wishes to sue. Similarly, a company thinks the level is too low and therefore too burdensome, and it wishes to sue. Would either of these suits be ripe?

Explanation

The consumer group's suit would likely be deemed ripe, but the company's suit might not. The consumers' group action cannot ever be riper. To deny it ripeness here would be to deny it the ability ever to challenge the FDA's determination of the harmlessness of this level of contamination. Moreover, to the extent that the consumers' group is alleging that the action level is too high, any delay in determining whether it is too high would threaten the health and safety of consumers. Thus, there would be substantial hardship in delay. The issue could be fit for resolution because the record of the agency's determination would provide the basis for review, delay would not provide more facts or information, and the group's challenge would raise a question of law, not fact.

The challenge brought by the company subject to FDA's enforcement authority, however, would likely be held unripe. The action level does not establish *the* safe level, which companies must meet. Rather, it sets a level at which companies are assured they will not be enforced against. That is, even if they exceed that level, it does not mean the FDA necessarily will proceed against them or that the level is unlawful because it is unsafe. Accordingly, though a company might wish the level were set higher, so that it could get the advantage of an assurance of no prosecution, the lack of assurance is not the same as a determination that the company's product is unsafe or illegal. Thus, the setting of the action level does not require the company to change its practices or to meet any particular requirement. Thus, there is no hardship to the company in waiting for enforcement action, which may or may not come.

Note that these tests for ripeness can result in asymmetrical availability of judicial review.

This is not to say, however, that challenges by regulatory beneficiaries are always ripe. In the above example, the effect of setting the action level was to allow unconditionally a certain level of contamination, which the FDA thought harmless but which consumer groups thought harmful. If the FDA were wrong, consumers would be harmed without any further intervening action by the FDA.

Compare this to the case in which the Nuclear Regulatory Commission (NRC) adopted a policy statement to the effect that it would grant exemptions from regulation for certain kinds of radioactive material, because the NRC believed these kinds of radioactive material were harmless and not worth regulating. This policy statement was challenged by Public Citizen, Ralph Nader's group, as being a violation of the Atomic Energy Act's requirement that the NRC regulate radioactive material. The D.C. Circuit found the challenge unripe. *See Public Citizen, Inc. v. U.S. Nuclear Regulatory Commn.*, 940 F.2d 679 (D.C. Cir. 1991). Unlike the FDA example, here the NRC's policy statement did not have immediate effect. Persons could only obtain the exemption by applying for it and having it granted in a rulemaking or adjudication. The policy statement essentially was an invitation for people to seek these exemptions. Public Citizen, the court said, could challenge the grant of a particular exemption, because until there was an actual exemption, they would not be subject to harm.

Similarly, the Supreme Court found unripe an environmental group's challenge to a U.S. Forest Service's Forest Plan.. The environmental group challenged the Forest Plan because it allowed for the possibility of clear-cutting of timber under circumstances the environmentalists believed to violate the National Forest Management Act. The Court found there was no hardship to the environmentalists in delaying review, because no timber cutting could take place until the Forest Service had actually made a timber sale, which the environmentalists could challenge. Thus, no trees could be cut before the environmentalists had had an opportunity to challenge the lawfulness of the Forest Plan in court. Adoption of the Forest Plan by itself did not authorize cutting any trees. Also, the Court found the issue not yet fit for judicial review because courts could benefit by further factual development and judicial intervention could interfere with further agency refinement of its policies. That is, the agency could in implementing the Forest Plan interpret the circumstances in which clear-cutting was allowed in a variety of ways. Such implementation could lead to a change in policy or at least place the appropriateness of clear cutting in a more concrete setting. The Court noted, however, that had the environmentalists sued under the National Environmental Policy Act and alleged that the EIS was inadequate, their suit would have been ripe, because "NEPA, unlike the NFMA, simply guarantees a particular procedure, not a particular result. Hence a person with standing who is injured by a failure to comply with the NEPA procedure may complain of that failure at the time the failure takes place, for the claim can never get riper." Moreover, had the environmentalists been objecting to the Forest Plan because of its provisions that immediately had effect, such as opening certain trails to motorized vehicles, their challenge to those provisions would also have been ripe. *See Ohio Forestry Assn., Inc. v. Sierra Club*, 523 U.S. 726 (1998).

D. The Special Case of Structural Constitutional Claims

The recent rise in constitutional challenges to agency structure has created a new twist to the traditional requirements of judicial review of agency action. Ordinarily, as we have seen, in order to challenge agency action one needs to follow the statutory review procedure, involving first a final agency action, a need to exhaust available administrative remedies, and a need to establish that the case is ripe for judicial adjudication. Now imagine that one wishes to challenge the very structure of the agency as unconstitutional, or at least that part of the agency that would be enforcing the law against the person. Must the person await an enforcement action and raise the issue before the agency pursuant to the statutory review procedures? Presumably, the agency cannot (and assuredly would not) find that its structure was unconstitutional. In the case of *Thunder Basin Coal Co. v. Reich*, 510 U.S. 200 (1994), the Court established three factors to consider to decide if a particular claim was not of the type that Congress intended to be restricted to the statutory review. First, would requiring resort to the statutory review system foreclose all meaningful judicial review; second, is the claim "wholly collateral to [the normal] review provisions"; and third, is the claim "outside the agency's expertise."

Example

The Federal Trade Commission (FTC) brought an enforcement action against a company, alleging it had engaged in an unfair method of competition. In response, the company filed an original action in federal district court arguing that the Commission's ALJs could not constitutionally exercise governmental authority because of their dual-layer protection from removal. In addition, the company claimed that the combination of prosecutorial and adjudicative functions in the Commission renders all of its enforcement actions unconstitutional. The FTC responds by saying that the company cannot bring the case, because, before it can appeal to a court, it must await a final agency action and exhaust its administrative remedies pursuant to the statutory review system for FTC enforcement actions. How should a court rule?

Explanation

The court should rule in favor of the company. These were the facts and claims in *Axon Enterprise Inc. v. Federal Trade Commission*, 598 U.S. 175 (2023). There the Court held that all three of the *Thunder Basin* factors militated in favor of allowing the claim in district court to go forward; it did not address the merits of the claim.

First, the Court said, while requiring Axon to follow the statutory review scheme would allow it to obtain judicial review of its constitutional claims, that review would not be "meaningful," because it could not cure Axon's injury — "being subjected" to "unconstitutional agency authority." It conceded that this seems a "bit abstract," but it noted the Court had previously held that such an injury qualifies for standing purposes. Second, the constitutional claim is collateral to what is intended to be reviewed pursuant to the statutory review system — whether the facts and the law support a conclusion that the defendant violated the law. Third, the constitutional claim is outside the agency's expertise.

V. PRIMARY JURISDICTION

The doctrine of Primary Jurisdiction is not really a judicial review doctrine, because it does not arise in a judicial challenge to agency action. Nevertheless, because it is closely related to the doctrines of Exhaustion, Finality, and Ripeness, it is appropriate to consider it here. The doctrine of Primary Jurisdiction holds that courts should stay their hand when the issue in a case falls within the "primary jurisdiction" of an agency. The agency should be allowed to deal with it first, and then, if the agency's resolution does not dispose of the case, the court can consider the whole case in light of the agency's determination. As you can see, this doctrine is related to the other doctrines in that it is concerned with the proper allocation of responsibilities between agencies and courts. It is not a judicial review doctrine, because it is not a defense raised by agencies to avoid judicial review of agency action. Rather, it is an issue raised in a suit between two non-federal parties.

Historically, the doctrine was used most often in industries whose rates and practices were subject to continuing federal regulation, such as airlines, railroads, trucking, and shipping, when there was a private dispute over the proper rates to be charged. Today, most of these programs have been deregulated. Nevertheless, the doctrine of Primary Jurisdiction continues to play a role in other areas as well, particularly when national uniformity is important and one court decision would have the potential to disrupt that uniformity.

Example

The Massachusetts Department of Environmental Protection adopted a regulation requiring auto manufacturers to offer a certain number of zero-emission electrically powered vehicles (ZEVs) prior to the 2003 model year. Associations of automobile manufacturers brought suit in federal court against the state agency alleging that the federal Clean Air Act preempts states from adopting such a requirement. That Act prohibits states from adopting any emission standards for automobiles, but it allows California to adopt a stricter standard if, after reviewing the standard, the EPA determines that there is a need for California to adopt a stricter standard. The Act then allows other states to adopt standards identical to California's. California adopted a requirement for ZEVs and received EPA approval for it. Thereafter, however, California entered into Memoranda of Agreement with the various auto manufacturers that changed the ZEV requirement. Massachusetts adopted a standard that it said was identical to the California Memorandum of Agreement (MOA) requirement, but the association of manufacturers said that privately negotiated MOA were not "emission standards" within the meaning of the Act. Should the court withhold judgment to allow the EPA to determine whether the MOA are "emission standards" within the meaning of the Act?

Explanation

The court held that it was in the primary jurisdiction of the EPA to determine whether MOA were "emission standards" and, if so, whether Massachusetts' standard was identical to the MOA. The court noted that "[n]o fixed formula exists for applying the doctrine of primary jurisdiction. In every case, the question is whether the reasons for the existence of the doctrine are present and whether the purposes it serves will be aided by its application in the particular litigation." Nevertheless, the court identified three factors to be considered: "(1) whether the agency determination l[ies] at the heart of the task assigned the agency by Congress; (2) whether agency expertise [i]s required to unravel intricate, technical facts; and (3) whether, though perhaps not determinative, the agency determination would materially aid the court." Here, the court believed that what constitutes an emission standard lay at the heart of EPA's mandate to regulate auto emissions. Second, it was clear that the details of the California MOA and the Massachusetts ZEV standard were highly technical and within EPA's expertise. Finally, because resolution of the issue would turn on an appreciation of the appropriate public policy, and because the EPA is the agency entrusted by Congress with administering the Clean Air Act, the court would greatly benefit from the EPA's determination. *See American Auto Manufacturers Assn. v. Massachusetts Dept. of Environmental Protection*, 163 F.3d 74 (1st Cir. 1998).

CHAPTER 7

The Scope of Judicial Review

> [T]he rules governing judicial review have no more substance at the core than a seedless grape.
>
> —*Ernest Gellhorn & Glen D. Robinson,* Perspectives on Administrative Law, *75 Colum. L. Rev.* 771, 780-781 (1975)

Chapter 6 dealt with the hurdles to obtaining judicial review of agency action. Now we move on to the scope of that review once a person obtains it. Our opening quotation is often cited because of the sense of frustration felt by many lawyers in trying to discern the different rules governing judicial review of agency action. At some level this cynicism may have its place, but as you will find in this chapter, there are rules—different rules that apply in different circumstances, and lawyers (and law students) need to know them.

The Administrative Procedure Act (APA) specifies the scope of review under that Act in Section 706.

This chapter will consider the different standards for review enumerated in Section 706. First, we will consider review of what are widely described as *questions of law*, which can occur under several of the subsections of Section 706(2). These questions involve claims as to the meaning of a constitutional, statutory, or regulatory provision. Next, the chapter discusses *substantial evidence review*, which in the purest sense is the review of a "question of fact" in formal adjudication or formal rulemaking. But courts have sometimes characterized as substantial evidence review what are mixed questions of law and facts. The next category of review is *arbitrary and capricious review*. This category includes not only review of "questions of fact" in informal adjudications and rulemaking, but also what are often called "questions of judgment." As you will see, these characterizations are not hard and fast, and you will run into another characterization—"the application of law to facts"—that does not fall neatly into any one of the categories. After considering these three basic categories of review, this section of the chapter will also consider the relatively rare circumstance of *de novo* review and the not-so-rare review of agency inaction, as opposed to agency action, which raises special problems. These will be followed by a section on remedies available to the courts when they find agency action unlawful, an area of law that is highly contested currently. Finally, the chapter will conclude with sections on equitable estoppel and the effect of judicial decisions.

Section 706. Scope of Review

To the extent necessary to decision and when presented, the reviewing court shall decide all relevant questions of law, interpret constitutional and statutory provisions, and determine the meaning or applicability of the terms of an agency action. The reviewing court shall—

(1) compel agency action unlawfully withheld or unreasonably delayed; and
(2) hold unlawful and set aside agency action, findings, and conclusions found to be—
    (A) arbitrary, capricious, an abuse of discretion, or otherwise not in accordance with law;
    (B) contrary to constitutional right, power, privilege, or immunity;
    (C) in excess of statutory jurisdiction, authority, or limitations, or short of statutory right;
    (D) without observance of procedure required by law;
    (E) unsupported by substantial evidence in a case subject to sections 556 and 557 of this title or otherwise reviewed on the record of an agency hearing provided by statute; or
    (F) unwarranted by the facts to the extent that the facts are subject to trial de novo by the reviewing court.

In making the foregoing determinations, the court shall review the whole record or those parts of it cited by a party, and due account shall be taken of the rule of prejudicial error.

I. REVIEW OF QUESTIONS OF LAW

Questions of law can arise under several different parts of Section 706. Thus, a person might argue that an agency's rule or order is unconstitutional; this could be a question of law under paragraph (B). Or a person might argue that an agency's rule or order is beyond the agency's statutory authority; this could be a question of law under paragraph (C). A person might argue that an agency's interpretation of law within a rule or order is wrong; this could be a question of law under paragraph (A). Or a person might argue that an agency did not follow all the procedures required by law, while the agency would respond that those procedures were not required by law; this too would be a question of law, under paragraph (D). Which of these provisions is actually used to raise a question of law (and typically a claimant will cite all of them) is not determinative of how courts analyze the question.

When the dispute is over the meaning or requirements of the Constitution, the court indeed interprets the Constitution. Often, however, statutes are interpreted to avoid the constitutional question. This is one of the many canons of statutory construction applicable generally but that often arise in judicial review of agency action.

A. Statutory Interpretation

The more typical question involves the meaning of a statute. Of course, how courts interpret the meaning of a statute is a general question of statutory interpretation that you probably learned about in your first year in law school. Courts first look to the statutory language, but they also may resort to legislative history and canons of statutory construction as well.

For most of the past half-century courts have accepted the important role of agencies in our structure of government and have been solicitous of agency interpretations of the laws they administer. More recently, a Supreme Court dominated by appointees by Republican Presidents have more seriously questioned the basic legitimacy of what they call the administrative state—a situation where agencies enact and enforce regulations under broad delegations of legislative authority from laws enacted decades before and without congressional consideration of the particular problems agencies presently face and try to respond to. The result of this questioning has been two-fold. On the one hand, the Supreme Court has made significant changes regarding the very structure of the agencies, as described in Chapter 2. On the other hand, the Court has cut back on its deference to agency interpretations of the law.

What is special about statutory interpretation in administrative law is how courts treat agency interpretations of statutes. Agencies, of course, interpret statutes in a number of circumstances, often in the course of rulemaking (including the making of interpretive rules and statements of policy) and adjudications. As noted in Chapter 6, courts have established various doctrines to enable agencies to have a first crack at a problem, in part because courts may wish to take account of the agencies' experience and expertise with the subject matter. Historically, when courts have then reviewed an agency action, they have often shown significant deference to the statutory interpretation made by the agency. For example, in a famous administrative law case from the 1940s, the National Labor Relations Board (NLRB) had interpreted the term "employee" in the National Labor Relations Act to include "newsboys,"[1] so that they would be able to unionize. The newspapers claimed that the "newsboys" were independent contractors, not employees. The Supreme Court, after acknowledging the NLRB's experience and expertise with respect to employment matters, upheld the NRLB's interpretation, saying:

> Undoubtedly questions of statutory interpretation, especially when arising in the first instance in judicial proceedings, are for the courts to resolve, giving appropriate weight to the judgment of those whose special duty is to administer the questioned statute. But where the question is one of specific application of a broad statutory term in a proceeding in which the agency administering the statute must determine it initially, the reviewing court's function is limited. . . . [T]he Board's determination that specified persons are "employees" under this Act is to be accepted if it has "warrant in the record" and a reasonable basis in law.

National Labor Relations Board v. Hearst Publications, Inc., 322 U.S. 111, 131 (1944). However, in a later case in the same year, without mentioning *Hearst*, the Court used a different description of how it would view an agency interpretation, this time involving an interpretation made by the Administrator of the Wage and Hour Division of the Department of Labor as to whether the time firemen spent sleeping at the firehouse constituted time on the job for purposes of overtime pay.

> We consider that the rulings, interpretations and opinions of the Administrator under this Act, while not controlling upon the courts by reason of their authority, do constitute a body of experience and informed judgment to which courts and litigants may properly resort for guidance. The weight of such a judgment in a particular case will depend upon the thoroughness evident in its consideration, the validity of its reasoning, its consistency with earlier and later pronouncements, and all those factors which give it power to persuade, if lacking power to control.

Skidmore v. Swift & Co., 323 U.S. 134, 140 (1944). Whether you can discern it in these verbal formulations, the former description has been read to

1. "Newsboys" were persons who sold newspapers in big cities on street corners. They exclusively sold one newspaper, competing with "newsboys" from other newspapers. These jobs no longer exist. They live today only in movies depicting the first half of the 20th century with a scene involving someone on a street corner selling newspapers, yelling "Extra! Extra! Read all about it!"

mandate strong deference to the agency interpretation, whereas the latter has been read as calling not for deference, but rather for respect. The reason for the different treatment appears to be that in *Hearst* the agency's interpretation occurred in the course of an adversary agency proceeding in which the agency found facts and reached conclusions of law and the court was reviewing that agency action, but in *Skidmore* the interpretation had occurred in an opinion letter to the firemen's employer, and the court's involvement was not to review the agency action but to resolve a lawsuit between the employer and the firemen over whether they were entitled to overtime pay.

Forty years later, the Supreme Court decided *Chevron, U.S.A., Inc. v. Natural Resources Defense Council, Inc.*, 467 U.S. 837 (1984), which became the most cited (and perhaps debated) administrative law decision of the time. There it said:

> When a court reviews an agency's construction of the statute which it administers, it is confronted with two questions. First, always, is the question whether Congress has directly spoken to the precise question at issue. If the intent of Congress is clear, that is the end of the matter; for the court, as well as the agency, must give effect to the unambiguously expressed intent of Congress. If, however, the court determines Congress has not directly addressed the precise question at issue, the court does not simply impose its own construction on the statute, as would be necessary in the absence of an administrative interpretation. Rather, if the statute is silent or ambiguous with respect to the specific issue, the question for the court is whether the agency's answer is based on a permissible construction of the statute.
>
> The power of an administrative agency to administer a congressionally created . . . program necessarily requires the formulation of policy and the making of rules to fill any gap left, implicitly or explicitly, by Congress. If Congress has explicitly left a gap for the agency to fill, there is an express delegation of authority to the agency to elucidate a specific provision of the statute by regulation. Such legislative regulations are given controlling weight unless they are arbitrary, capricious, or manifestly contrary to the statute. Sometimes the legislative delegation to an agency on a particular question is implicit rather than explicit. In such a case, a court may not substitute its own construction of a statutory provision for a reasonable interpretation made by the administrator of an agency.

467 U.S. at 842-844. This quotation outlines what became known as the "*Chevron* two-step." The first step is to determine whether the statutory language being interpreted is ambiguous, or whether the meaning of the provision is clear using traditional tools of statutory construction. If the meaning of the provision is clear, that is the end of the matter, and the court announces the clear meaning of the statute. If, however, after using traditional tools of statutory construction, the meaning of the provision cannot be deemed clear, but rather remains ambiguous, then the court goes to the second step. The second step is to determine whether the agency's interpretation is reasonable

or permissible, or if the interpretation is outside the range of ambiguity in the provision. If the agency's interpretation is reasonable or permissible, the court upholds the agency's interpretation, *even if the court does not believe it is the best interpretation*.

In 2024, in *Loper Bright Enterprises v. Raimondo*, the Supreme Court overruled *Chevron* but distinguished *Hearst* and cited *Skidmore* favorably. The Court alluded to Article III of the Constitution and its assignment to the judiciary of the power to decide cases and controversies, suggesting that *Chevron* was inconsistent with that assignment. However, the Court held only that *Chevron* was incompatible with the language of the APA that "the reviewing court shall decide all relevant questions of law." Under *Chevron*, courts were affirming the agency's interpretation rather than deciding themselves the meaning of the law.

Loper Bright, therefore, directs courts to find the best meaning of a statute and to resolve any ambiguities on the basis of the court's own judgment. Nevertheless, the Court said that it is entirely appropriate to give due respect to an agency's interpretation, quoting from *Skidmore*'s list of considerations that might persuade a court to agree with the agency. Ultimately, however, the agency's interpretation and its explanation therefor are merely to inform the court in making its determination. The Court distinguished *Hearst* on the basis that there the agency had been applying the statute to a particular factbound situation. Deference to the agency, accordingly, would only apply "where application of a statutory term [is] sufficiently intertwined with the agency's factfinding."

Chevron had presumed that an ambiguity in a statute administered by an agency constituted a delegation by Congress to the agency to fill in the gaps. The Court in *Loper Bright* said that such a presumption was not justified, but it acknowledged that when the best reading of a statute is that it delegates discretionary authority to an agency, the role of the reviewing court under the APA is to honor that delegation and to ensure that agency's action is within the bounds of that delegation and supported by reasoned decisionmaking.

Example

The Family and Medical Leave Act (FMLA) entitles an eligible employee to as many as 12 weeks of unpaid leave per year for "a serious health condition that makes the employee unable to perform the functions of the position of such employee." The Act defines "serious health condition" as an "illness, injury, impairment, or physical or mental condition that involves (A) inpatient care in a hospital, hospice, or residential medical care facility; or (B) continuing treatment by a health care provider." The Secretary of Labor is authorized to adopt regulations implementing the Act. Pursuant to that authority, the Secretary adopted regulations that, among other things, defined "treatment" to "include[] . . . examinations to determine if a serious health condition exists and evaluations of the condition." An employer refused to grant FMLA leave to an employee for those doctor visits in which no active treatment ensued. The employer maintained that the regulation defining "treatment" is unauthorized by the Act to the extent that it includes mere physical examinations without resulting treatment. Is the employer right?

Explanation

This was an actual case during the *Chevron* era. The majority noted that Congress had included no definition of the term in the Act. Second, it found nothing in the legislative history relevant to the question. Standing on its own, the word *treatment* might mean either actual, active treating of an injury or illness or it might refer more broadly to everything included in the course of treatment, which certainly would include diagnosis and monitoring of a condition. Under *Chevron*, the court found the term ambiguous, proceeded to Step Two, and found the agency's interpretation reasonable. Under *Loper Bright*, however, the court would need to determine what it believes to be the best meaning, notwithstanding the ambiguity. In doing so, it can give respect to the agency interpretation.

One judge in the actual case believed that the word "treatment" was clear and unambiguous, requiring active treatment of a disease or injury, not just a physical examination. In support of his conclusion, he cited definitions of *treatment* in the Random House College Dictionary and the Oxford English Dictionary. The dissent is clearly right that "treatment" *can* mean "management in the application of remedies; medical or surgical application or service," as defined in the Oxford English Dictionary, but is that the only possible, or even the best interpretation?

The majority might find the agency's interpretation the better interpretation and be persuaded by it. After all, the agency does have experience and expertise in addressing what constitutes medical treatment generally, and Congress did grant the agency rulemaking authority generally to administer the Act. Moreover, this has been the consistent interpretation of the Act by the agency, and in adopting it the agency provided a reasonable explanation for its balance of the costs and benefits of its interpretation. Even the definition cited by the dissent in the Random House Dictionary, "the systematic effort to cure illness and relieve symptoms, as with medicines, surgery, etc.," leaves open the question of whether diagnosis and aggressive medical monitoring can be part of that "systematic effort."

What do you think? Is the agency's explanation convincing? Does the general grant of rulemaking authority to the agency to implement the Act constitute the kind of delegation of discretionary authority the Court alluded to in *Loper Bright*? Given the newness of *Loper Bright*, it is not clear how courts will answer this question.

I. The Major Questions Doctrine

Before *Chevron* was overruled, the Supreme Court on occasion decided *Chevron* was simply not appropriate, leading some commentators to refer to this as *Chevron* step zero. An early example involved the Food and Drug Administration's regulation purporting to regulate cigarettes as drug delivery devices. While nicotine was clearly a "drug" under the Food, Drug, and Cosmetic Act and at least arguably a cigarette would be a "drug delivery device" under the Act, the Court found *Chevron* deference inapplicable. The Court said: "Deference under *Chevron* to an agency's construction of a statute that it administers is premised on the theory that a statute's ambiguity constitutes an implicit delegation from Congress to the agency to fill in the statutory gaps. In extraordinary cases, however, there may be reason to hesitate before concluding that Congress has intended such an implicit delegation." This, the Court said, was such an extraordinary case because of Congress's repeated acts dealing with cigarettes in one way or another. Thus, the Court concluded, "we are confident that Congress could not have intended to delegate a decision of such economic and political significance to an agency in so cryptic a fashion." *Food and Drug Admin. v. Brown & Williamson Tobacco Corp.*, 529 U.S 120 (2000).

A later case involved Oregon's physician assisted suicide law. The Attorney General issued an interpretive rule stating that Oregon's law violated the Controlled Substances Act because it allowed the use of controlled substances for a purpose other than for a "legitimate medical purpose." Here the Court said that this phrase might be "a generality, susceptible to more precise definition and open to varying constructions, and thus ambiguous in the relevant sense. *Chevron* deference, however, is not accorded merely because the statute is ambiguous and an administrative official is involved. To begin with, the rule must be promulgated pursuant to authority Congress has delegated to the official." The Court did not believe Congress in the Controlled Substances Act had given the Attorney General broad authority to define what is a legitimate medical purpose. *Gonzales v. Oregon*, 546 U.S. 243 (2006).

Finally, in *West Virginia v. Environmental Protection Agency*, 597 U.S. 697 (2022), the Court gave a name to its approach to these and similar cases: *The Major Questions Doctrine*. It applies when agencies assert highly consequential power beyond what Congress could reasonably be understood to have granted. Exactly what circumstances trigger application of this doctrine remains unclear. In *West Virginia*, as it had in *Brown & Williamson*, the Court alluded to the economic and political significance of the regulation. If the Major Questions Doctrine is triggered, then there must be "clear congressional authorization" for the regulation.

What may qualify as clear congressional authorization also remains unclear. Justices Gorsuch and Alito indicated that it constitutes a "clear statement rule." Justice Barrett, on the other hand, concurring in a later case, suggested that the doctrine does not impose such a rigid requirement. Rather it is simply a question of interpreting the statute in context.

Example

Federal law provides for various types of student loans. Following 9/11, Congress enacted the Higher Education Relief Opportunities for Students Act, which provided that the Secretary of Education "may waive or modify any statutory or regulatory provision applicable to the student financial assistance programs under title IV of the [Education Act] as the Secretary deems necessary in connection with a war or other military operation or national emergency." The Secretary could issue waivers or modifications only "as may be necessary to ensure" that "recipients of student financial aid,,, who are affected individuals are not placed in a worse position financially in relation to that financial assistance because of their status as affected individuals." An "affected individual" was defined to include someone who "suffered direct economic hardship as a direct result of a war or other military operation or national emergency, as determined by the Secretary." And a "national emergency" for the purposes of the Act was "a national emergency declared by the President of the United States." In 2022, citing this law and the national emergency resulting from the COVID 19 pandemic, the Secretary issued a notice canceling the debt students had incurred under various financial assistance programs. About 43 million borrowers qualified for relief, involving about $430 billion in debt relief. This action was immediately challenged by a number of states. Did this trigger the Major Questions Doctrine?

Explanation

In *Biden v. Nebraska*, 143 S. Ct. 2355 (2023), the Supreme Court said it did. The Court described the past temporary, limited, and targeted uses of the Act, compared to the wholesale cancellation of debt; the failure of Congress to address the cancellation of student debt specifically; and the vast economic effects of the cancellation. Moreover, the Court found no clear congressional authorization for the cancellation; the broad, but ambiguous, language of the Act was insufficient.

Loper Bright allowed for a certain level of discretionary authority granted by a statute, within which an agency's determination would only have to be the result of a reasoned decision. *West Virginia* and its Major Questions Doctrine, however, establish an outer limit of the scope of discretion a statute may give to an agency. Exactly what triggers application of the doctrine remains unclear.

Example

The Department of Labor promulgated a rule pursuant to a directive in Executive Order (E.O.) 14,026, which President Biden issued on April 27, 2021. EO 14,026 imposed the minimum wage requirement on most federal contractors, and it rescinded an exemption for recreational services outfitters that operate pursuant to permits on federal lands, which President Trump had adopted in E.O. 13,838. President Biden issued E.O. 14,026 pursuant to his authority under the Federal Property and Administrative Services Act (FPASA), which authorizes the President to "prescribe policies and directives that the President considers necessary to carry out" FPASA and that are "consistent with" FPASA. One purpose of FPASA is to "provide the Federal Government with an economical and efficient system for . . . [p]rocuring and supplying property and nonpersonal services." Two recreational services outfitters challenged the rule, arguing in part that it violated the Major Questions Doctrine because of its major economic impact—$1.7 billion over 10 years. How should the court rule?

Explanation

This is a real case, and the court held that the rule did not trigger the Major Questions Doctrine. *See Bradford v. Department of Labor*, 101 F.4th 707 (10th Cir. 2024). First, it said this was not a case in which the executive branch sought to locate expansive authority in "modest words," "vague terms or ancillary provisions." Instead, the FPASA authorizes the President to "prescribe policies and directives that the President considers necessary to carry out this subtitle," which includes "provid[ing] the Federal Government with an economical and efficient system for . . . [p]rocuring and supplying property and nonpersonal services." In employing such expansive language, "Congress chose to utilize a relatively broad delegation of authority in the [FPASA]." Second, the court believed that the Supreme Court's concern in establishing the Major Questions Doctrine was with an "enormous and transformative expansion in . . . regulatory authority without clear congressional authorization." Here, the agency is acting in a proprietary fashion, not a regulatory fashion. Finally, the court noted that the Supreme Court has typically applied the Major Questions Doctrine where an "agency claim[ed] to discover" regulatory authority for the first time "in a long-extant statute." Here, the last three Presidents had all applied the FPASA to establish minimum wages for government contractors.

B. Interpretation of Rules

The preceding sections have considered how courts should review agency decisions interpreting *statutes*. What should be the standard for how courts should review agency decisions interpreting the agency's own rules? In 1945, the Court decided *Bowles v. Seminole Rock & Sand Co.*, 325 U.S. 410 (1945). In that case the Court said that when faced with the need to interpret an administrative regulation,

> a court must necessarily look to the administrative construction of the regulation if the meaning of the words used is in doubt. The intention of Congress or the principles of the Constitution in some situations may be relevant in the first instance in choosing between various constructions. But the ultimate criterion is the administrative interpretation, which becomes of controlling weight unless it is plainly erroneous or inconsistent with the regulation.

325 U.S. at 413-414. Although phrased differently, this standard had much in common with review under *Chevron*. First, one looks to the language of the regulation itself. If it is clear, that is the end of the matter. If, however, the language is ambiguous, the court then looks to see if the Constitution or a statute makes a particular interpretation inappropriate. Finally, if there is an administrative interpretation not ruled out by the Constitution or a statute, that interpretation is controlling unless plainly erroneous or inconsistent with the regulation. This "plainly erroneous or inconsistent with the regulation" bore a striking resemblance to *Chevron* deference to an agency interpretation if reasonable or permissible. A half-century later, *Seminole Rock's* approach was reaffirmed in *Auer v. Robbins*, 519 U.S. 452 (1997).

More recently, however, some members of the Court, led by Justice Scalia and joined later by Justices Thomas and Alito, questioned whether this doctrine should be overruled. This resulted in the Court taking the case of *Kisor v. Wilkie*, 588 U.S. 558 (2019), to consider whether to overrule *Seminole Rock* and *Auer*. By a 5-4 vote the Court declined to overrule those cases. Nevertheless, the Court's opinion, per Justice Kagan, was hardly a ringing endorsement of the doctrine. The only portions of her opinion that garnered a majority of the Court (the three other "liberals" and Chief Justice Roberts), first, described the strict limitations on when deference under the doctrine would actually apply, and second, upheld the doctrine solely on the basis of *stare decisis*. The portion of Justice Kagan's opinion that argued in favor of the doctrine on its merits was only joined by Justices Ginsburg, Breyer, and Sotomayor and was explicitly rejected by Justices Gorsuch, Thomas, Kavanaugh, and Alito, all of whom believed the doctrine is incompatible with the language of the APA as well as the Constitution. They would instead apply *Skidmore* deference. All the Justices seemed to agree that, as a practical matter, the limitations the majority opinion imposed on when the *Auer* doctrine should apply would probably have the same effect as using *Skidmore* deference. Both the Chief Justice and Justice Kavanaugh wrote separately to state their view that nothing in the opinion should be read to relate to the *Chevron* doctrine, apparently suggesting that *Chevron* was open to question. As we know now, *Chevron* did not survive, and given the justification for overruling *Chevron*, one might question whether even *Kisor* will survive. Nevertheless, until such time as it too is overruled, it remains the law.

Example

There is an ambiguous statute governing an agency's regulation of certain matters. The agency adopts, after notice and comment, a rule that in part simply reproduces the statutory language. This is not uncommon. Thereafter, the agency adopts an interpretation of both the statute and the rule. In judicial review of this interpretation, what, if any, deference should the court give to the agency's interpretation?

Explanation

As discussed in the last section on statutory interpretation, it is clear that no deference will be given to the policy statement's interpretation of the *statute*. The question then is whether the court should apply *Auer* deference to the agency's interpretation of the regulation. In *Kisor*, the Court clearly signaled that *Auer* would not apply here. One requirement for using *Auer* is that the interpretation "must in some way implicate [the agency's] substantive expertise." If the agency has failed to use its expertise, by merely parroting the statute in its regulation, it will not receive *Auer* deference in its interpretation of that regulation.

Example

A veteran denied disability benefits by the Department of Veterans Affairs (VA) can have his case reopened upon new information, and any award of benefits resulting from the new information can be retroactive to the date of the original claim according to the VA regulations, if there were "relevant official service department records" that the VA had not considered in its initial denial. A veteran claimed that he had Post Traumatic Stress Disorder (PTSD) resulting from his participation in a particular military operation. The VA's participating psychiatrist recognized his involvement in the operation but concluded that he did not suffer from PTSD. Consequently, the VA's Board of Appeals denied his claim. Years later, the veteran reopened his claim in light of new psychiatric report that he did suffer from PTSD, and the VA Board granted him benefits. Although the veteran had come up with two service records not originally considered, further corroborating his participation in the military operation, the Board granted the benefits only from the time of reopening the case, not retroactive to the original denial. The VA interpreted the regulatory language as only referring to new service records relevant to the changed decision. Here, the change in the decision did not relate to his participation in the military operation, which had been accepted in the earlier decision, rather it related to the new psychiatric report. The veteran, on the other hand, argued that the records he produced were relevant to the final decision because they related to the qualifying event that caused the PTSD, even if they were not the reason why the initial decision was changed. Should the VA receive *Auer* deference for its interpretation of the regulation?

Explanation

These were the facts in the *Kisor* case. The Court of Appeals for the Federal Circuit affirmed the VA's denial of retroactive benefits, deferring under *Auer* to the VA Board's interpretation. The Supreme Court, in light of its opinion in *Kisor*, remanded the case to the Federal Circuit because of two failures. First, it said that the court had "jumped the gun in declaring the regulation ambiguous." Part of the Court's opinion restricting the applicability of *Auer* stressed the importance of using all its interpretive tools before finding ambiguity. The court "must make a conscientious effort to determine, based on indicia like text, structure, history, and purpose, whether the regulation really has more than one reasonable meaning. On remand, the Federal Circuit would have to more rigorously determine whether or not the interpretation is ambiguous. Second, another requirement before *Auer* can be used is that the interpretation be the agency's authoritative interpretation, so that informal statements or lower level interpretations would not qualify. Here, the VA Board decision was made by one of 100 members of the Board who together make some 80,000 decisions a year, none of which are precedential. The court below had not considered whether these facts disqualified this interpretation from receiving *Auer* deference. On remand, they would have to.

On remand, the Federal Circuit decided that the regulation was not really ambiguous but instead had a clear meaning—the meaning ascribed to it by the VA Board.

The *Kisor* opinion iterated a few other requirements before *Auer* deference may be afforded. The interpretation must reflect the "fair and considered judgment" of the agency. Thus, litigating positions and post hoc rationalizations to defend past agency action would not qualify. In addition, interpretations that create "unfair surprise" to regulated entities or that reverse an earlier interpretation should not receive *Auer* deference.

II. SUBSTANTIAL EVIDENCE REVIEW

The previous section addressed judicial review of "questions of law." This section addresses judicial review of "questions of fact" raised in formal proceedings. In addition, as you will find below, substantial evidence review also can include judicial review of the exercise of judgment in certain situations. By its terms Section 706(2)(E) provides that a court shall hold unlawful and set aside agency action "unsupported by substantial evidence in a case subject to Sections 556 and 557 of this title or otherwise reviewed on the record of an agency hearing provided by statute." This provision raises two questions. First, when does it apply? Second, what does "substantial evidence" mean?

A. When Does a Court Review for Substantial Evidence?

The answer to this question is relatively simple: a court reviews for substantial evidence when the agency action was formal rulemaking or formal adjudication, or more accurately rulemaking or adjudication under Sections 556 and 557 of the APA. In addition, there are some statutes that specify "substantial evidence" review although the agency action is not formal rulemaking or formal adjudication. A number of statutes passed in the 1970s provided that their hybrid rulemakings would be subject to "substantial evidence" review. For example, certain necessary findings supporting consumer product safety rules adopted by the Consumer Product Safety Commission pursuant to a hybrid rulemaking procedure are reviewed for substantial evidence. *See* 15 U.S.C. § 2060(c).

B. What Does Substantial Evidence Mean?

The term *substantial evidence* as a basis for review of agency fact-finding predates the APA by many years. In 1912, the Supreme Court upheld a decision of the Interstate Commerce Commission, saying that courts should not examine the agency's factual findings further than to determine whether they were supported by substantial evidence. In 1914 the term appeared in the Federal Trade Commission Act, which stated that the agency's findings of fact would be conclusive if supported by substantial evidence. Thus, when it was included in the APA in 1946, it was the accepted standard for judicial review of agency factual findings in trial-type adjudications. In *Universal Camera Corp. v. National Labor Relations Board*, 340 U.S. 474 (1951), a famous case after the adoption of the APA, the Supreme Court in an opinion by Justice Frankfurter, a former administrative law professor, summarized the meaning of "substantial evidence." It is more than "a mere scintilla"; it is "such relevant evidence as a reasonable mind might accept as adequate to support a conclusion"; it is evidence sufficient to withstand a motion for a directed verdict. It is a less rigorous standard than "clearly erroneous," the standard by which appellate courts review factual findings made by a trial judge. It is more rigorous than "no basis in fact." The agency's "findings are entitled to respect, but they must nonetheless be set aside when the record before a [court] clearly precludes the [agency's] decision from being justified by a fair estimate of the worth of the testimony of witnesses or its informed judgment on matters within its special competence or both. . . ."

As may be seen, "substantial evidence" review is fairly deferential. A court does not simply substitute its judgment as to the weight of the evidence. Rather, it reviews the evidence to see whether reasonable people could make the finding the agency made. In making this review, the court looks at all the relevant evidence in the record, that both support the agency's determination and undercut the determination. The "substantial evidence" standard for judicial review of the agency's finding should not be confused with the underlying requirement that a preponderance of the evidence is necessary for the agency to make a factual finding. The court asks whether a reasonable person viewing all the relevant evidence in the record could find that a preponderance of the evidence supports the agency decision. If so, the agency's decision is supported by substantial evidence.

A recurring question under "substantial evidence" review is how an Administrative Law Judge's finding of fact should be considered by a court on review of an agency decision. For example, imagine that a Federal Trade Commission ALJ finds a company did not make false representations to consumers in selling its products, but the Federal Trade Commission's General Counsel appeals that decision to the Commission. The Commission then finds that the person did make false representations. Recall that under the APA an agency reviewing an ALJ's initial or recommended decision in adjudication has all the powers it would have had if it had heard the case in the first instance. *See* 5 U.S.C. § 557(b). In other words, an agency can decide the case *de novo*, although it is limited to considering the record compiled in the proceeding before the ALJ. Unlike an appellate court reviewing a trial judge's findings of fact, the agency can simply substitute its judgment for that of the ALJ. The question then becomes: when the company seeks judicial review of the Commission's decision, how should a court consider the ALJ's finding? The ALJ's finding itself is part of the record to be considered by the court, and if it is inconsistent with the Commission's decision, it undercuts the agency's finding and therefore may affect a court's determination whether the agency's finding is supported by substantial evidence. Moreover, when an agency makes a finding inconsistent with the ALJ's finding that was based in whole or in part on demeanor evidence—that is, on what the ALJ observed from the witnesses' testimony—the agency's determination is the weakest, because the agency cannot itself assess the demeanor evidence.

Example

Under the National Labor Relations Act (NRLA), it is an unfair labor practice to retaliate against a worker because of union activity. Violations of the Act are prosecuted by the General Counsel of the National Labor Relations Board in administrative proceedings before an ALJ with the possibility of an appeal to the full Board.

In a particular case a company is accused of firing a worker because of his union activity. The foreman who actually fired the worker is called to testify. He denies firing the worker because of his union activity; he says that he was ignorant of the worker's union activity. Instead, he fired the worker because he found him alone smoking in the men's room (which is not allowed) when he should have been at work. The worker is also called to testify. He admits that he was in the men's room and that he was smoking, but he says he merely came in to use the restroom and then had one cigarette. He also says that he was with three other workers who were also smoking, but only he was fired. He states that when the foreman came in, the foreman said, "Now, you union bum, I've got an excuse to fire you." The worker also states that the foreman knew of his union activity and had privately commented negatively to him about it. This worker can only identify two of the workers he was with in the men's room. One subsequently quit and corroborates the worker's story. The other is still employed by the company and denies being there or witnessing anything.

The ALJ finds for the company. He finds as a fact that the worker was alone in the men's room. He bases that finding on the demeanor of the foreman and the workers who testified. He says that the foreman's testimony was candid, forthright, assured, and therefore credible. He says that the fired worker's testimony was evasive and self-serving and therefore not credible. He says that the testimony of the worker who quit seemed motivated by a desire to punish the company and to help his friend, and therefore not credible. He says the testimony of the worker still employed was credible. He says that he finds it incredible that the fired worker would not know the name of the third person he supposedly was smoking with and talking to in the men's room, and this further suggests that the fired worker's testimony generally is not credible.

The Board on appeal finds for the worker, reversing the ALJ. It finds as a fact that the worker was present with three others in the men's room; that the foreman expressed the sentiment that this occurrence was an excuse to fire the worker; that the foreman did know of the worker's union activity; and that firing the worker was in retaliation for his union activities. The Board finds the testimony of the foreman not credible. Given its experience with labor/

management relations, the Board believes foremen always are aware of which employees are active in a union. Moreover, the Board finds it unlikely that the company would fire someone for smoking in a non-approved area during working hours absent some other reasons, and none were given here. There was no evidence that the company had ever fired anyone else for smoking in a non-approved area. The Board finds the fired worker's testimony credible. It was consistent with what might occur in a non-union environment. The fact that the worker said there were three workers there at the time but that he could identify only two suggested truth-telling, because if he were making up a story, he could have said there were only two persons present. The Board finds the testimony of the worker still employed at the company not credible. The Board believes he probably was afraid to tell the truth because of possible retaliation from the company and foreman. On the other hand, the Board finds the testimony of the worker who quit is credible. Because he was no longer employed at the company, he had nothing to fear by telling the truth. Moreover, he had quit the company, rather than being fired, so there is no evidence that he would have any motivation to punish the company. Is the Board's decision supported by substantial evidence?

Explanation

Had there never been an ALJ decision, it is highly likely that a court would find the Board's decision to be supported by substantial evidence. There is conflicting evidence. There is corroborated testimony that, if believed, would definitely be evidence of an unfair labor practice. While there is other testimony that contradicts that evidence and that, if believed, would suggest no unfair labor practice, the Board's explanation of why it credited certain testimony and not other testimony is reasonable, especially in light of its expertise and experience. This would suffice to find that the Board's decision was supported by substantial evidence.

But there was an ALJ decision. On some matters the ALJ simply interpreted the evidence differently than the Board. For example, the Board interpreted the worker's inability to identify the claimed third person as not impeaching his credibility, even perhaps strengthening it. The ALJ, however, viewed the inability to identify the person as suggesting that the worker made the story up. Standing by itself, the ALJ is in no better position to interpret this evidence than the Board. Both are making inferences from the uncontradicted testimony that the worker cannot identify the third person. A court reviewing the Board's inference would simply ask whether the Board's inference was one that a reasonable person could make. If so, then that finding would be supported by substantial evidence, even if a different inference might also be one that a reasonable person might make. The court should not approach the question by asking what it thinks is the reason the worker cannot identify the claimed third person.

The ALJ, however, has done more than make different inferences from uncontradicted testimony. The ALJ has affirmatively made findings of credibility based largely upon the witnesses' demeanor. The ALJ characterized some of that demeanor (candid, forthright, assured, evasive), but not all of it. Even the words used to describe the impression made by the witnesses are likely to be incomplete. For better or for worse, the ALJ found some witnesses believable and others not believable on the basis of what he saw and heard when they testified, and the Board is simply unable to respond to this finding. It cannot say, "the ALJ was wrong, the witnesses' demeanor suggests a different finding." As a result, the ALJ's credibility determinations based upon demeanor are essentially unchallengeable unless all the other evidence in the case overwhelmingly supports a different conclusion. For example, if there were a videotape of the confrontation in the men's room, showing the three workers and recording the foreman's statement that this was an excuse to fire the worker, no amount of demeanor could save the credibility of the foreman. In our case, however, virtually all the evidence depends on the credibility of the witnesses and for the most part the credibility of the witnesses has been found on the basis of their demeanor by the ALJ, such that the Board cannot impeach those findings. Accordingly, it is likely that a court in this situation would reverse the Board's decision, finding it not supported by substantial evidence.

All of the above discussion regarding substantial evidence review has been what might be termed "pure" substantial evidence review—that is, substantial evidence review of the simple, basic facts. As you may have learned elsewhere in law school, one of the basic distinctions in the law is between questions of fact and questions of law. For example, juries only get to decide questions of fact; the judge instructs them as to the law. In our NLRB example above, all the dispute was over basic facts. It would have been conceded that, if what the fired worker said was true, there would have been a violation of the NLRA, and no one would have claimed that if what the foreman said was true there would still be a violation. Often, however, the area of dispute involves a mixture of fact and law. For example, in our NLRB example, what if everything the fired worker said was true, but the company also showed that it had written policies stating that smoking in the restrooms was an offense that would automatically lead to firing, and the company showed that in the past year it had fired five other persons who had no union activity for smoking in restrooms, and these were all the persons found smoking in restrooms? Thus, even if the foreman had a subjective anti-union animus that he expressed in firing this particular worker, the company can show that the person would have been fired anyway. Would the firing still qualify as an unfair labor practice? That is, does an independent basis for firing insulate an anti-union bias from being an unfair labor practice? The ALJ in first making the decision and the NLRB on appeal would have to decide that "ultimate fact." In so doing, it would be making law in the same way a court makes law when it decides such a question, by establishing precedent. Thus, if it found in favor of the company in this circumstance, it would be deciding a legal question of the meaning of "unfair labor practice" in the context of a particular fact situation that would become precedent in the future.

This kind of decision, one that mixes fact and law or applies law to fact, is not a purely factual determination or a decision of basic fact. Nevertheless, it is a decision that is often subjected to substantial evidence review. Now, however, the focus is not on the basic facts found but on the conclusions reached based on those facts. Still, a court determines whether a reasonable person could reach the conclusion the agency reached. It is still a deferential standard. Moreover, when the agency reaches a different conclusion than the ALJ, a court should give little or no weight to the ALJ's conclusion, because to the extent that the conclusion is "making law," it is the agency, not the ALJ, to whom Congress has entrusted that responsibility.

This is certainly the case with respect to those statutes that specify substantial evidence review of certain rules adopted under hybrid rulemaking procedures. Here the findings subject to substantial evidence review are often in the nature of whether a particular risk caused by a consumer product or a chemical poses a significant public safety risk. Here even the "basic facts" are of the "legislative fact" type—that is, not what one person did in the past but what will happen generally in the future. What is the risk posed by a particular chemical in the air? This is a "basic fact" question in the sense that we do not need to know anything about the law to answer this question. At the same time, this fact is one laden with probabilities, assumptions, and scientific judgments. Substantial evidence review will ask whether a reasonable person on the basis of the record before the agency could make the finding of risk made by the agency, and the court's review will focus on the agency's explanation of how it reached the decision it reached. But the substantial evidence review will not end there, because the agency's ultimate decision, when it determines how much of that chemical will be allowed to remain in the air, will also have decided what level of risk is acceptable, as not posing a significant public safety risk. This decision will necessarily entail policy judgments and interpretations of the meaning of the statutory terms, and this decision often is subjected under these statutes to substantial evidence review. Still, the formulation of the test remains the same: could a reasonable person on the basis of the record before the agency have reached the conclusion the agency reached? And again, the court's review will focus on the agency's explanation for its conclusion in making that judgment.

If the law were neat, we would be able to say that whenever an agency applies law to fact or makes an ultimate conclusion in a case subject to substantial evidence review, the court will apply substantial evidence review to the agency action. But the law is not neat. Sometimes a court will treat the question as a pure question of law; sometimes a court will treat it as an application of law to fact subject to its own review standard; and sometimes it will treat it as a substantial evidence question.

Example

The Longshoremen's and Harbor Workers' Compensation Act establishes a federal workers compensation program for certain types of workers. In essence, it provides financial compensation if a worker's injury or death "aris[es] out of and in the course of employment." An employee covered by the Act who had been brought to Guam by a government contractor to work on a government construction project drowned under the following circumstances: He had spent a Saturday afternoon at a recreation center maintained by the employer for its employees near the shoreline, along which ran a channel so dangerous for swimmers that its use was forbidden and signs to that effect were erected. While waiting for his employer's bus to take him from the area, he saw or heard two men, standing on the reefs beyond the channel, signaling for help. Followed by nearly 20 others, he plunged in to effect a rescue. In attempting to swim the channel to reach the two men, he drowned. His dependent mother filed for workers compensation benefits. The agency found as a fact that the death arose out of and was in the course of his employment, but the employer (who would have to pay the workers compensation benefit) challenged that determination in court. The Supreme Court upheld the agency decision.

Explanation

The Supreme Court found that the agency decision was supported by substantial evidence. Three members of the Court dissented, saying that the issue was not a question of fact, so that the deferential substantial evidence rule should not apply. And, of course, they were right that the real issue was not a question of fact—there were no disputed facts. The issue was how to characterize the circumstances under which the death occurred: Was the person's death so related to his employment, even though it clearly did not occur while he was actually working, that it could be said that it arose out of and was in the course of his employment? Justice Frankfurter, writing for the Court, essentially acknowledged this, saying:

> [This] only serves to illustrate once more the variety of ascertainments covered by the blanket term "fact." Here of course it does not connote a simple, external, physical event as to which there is conflicting testimony. The conclusion concerns a combination of happenings and the inferences drawn from them. In part at least, the inferences presuppose applicable standards for assessing the simple, external facts. Yet the standards are not so severable from the experience of industry nor of such a nature as to be peculiarly appropriate for independent judicial ascertainment as "questions of law."

In other words, the Court utilized substantial evidence review in this case precisely because it was deferential to the agency and because the Court thought the particular type of decision called for deference to agency expertise and experience rather than independent judicial decision. *O'Leary v. Brown-Pacific-Maxon*, 340 U.S. 504 (1951).

Recall the case of the "newsboys" in *NLRB v. Hearst Publications*, 322 U.S. 111 (1944), from the section on statutory interpretation and the *Chevron* doctrine. They wanted to unionize, but the newspapers refused to recognize them. The NLRB found this an unfair labor practice over the objection of the newspapers that these persons were independent contractors, not "employees." The Supreme Court upheld the NLRB's determination that the sellers were "employees." In an opinion that anticipated *Chevron v. NRDC* by 40 years, the Court first determined that Congress had not intended to equate the statutory term "employee" with common-law concepts of employment, leaving the term ambiguous. Then the Court concluded: "Undoubtedly questions of statutory interpretation, especially when arising in the first instance in judicial proceedings, are for the courts to resolve, giving appropriate weight to the judgment of those whose special duty is to administer the questioned statute. But where the question is one of specific application of a broad statutory term in a proceeding in which the agency administering the statute must determine it initially, the reviewing court's function is limited. . . . [T]he Board's determination that specified persons are 'employees' under this Act is to be accepted if it has 'warrant in the record' and a reasonable basis in law."

Example

Under the NLRA, "managerial employees" do not receive the protections afforded "employees," including the right to unionize. A company refused to bargain collectively with "buyers" at one of its facilities, maintaining that they were managerial employees and therefore could not be a union. The NLRB found the refusal to bargain an unfair labor practice, holding that the only managerial employees excepted from the protections of the Act were those whose alignment with management would be inconsistent with union representation. The NLRB found that "buyers" were not so aligned. The Supreme Court disagreed with the Board's interpretation of the law and held that all managerial employees are "managerial employees" under the Act. In making this decision, the Court did not refer to substantial evidence, the *Hearst* case, or the notion that "where the question is one of specific application of a broad statutory term in a proceeding in which the agency administering the statute must determine it initially, the reviewing court's function is limited." Instead, the Court just interpreted the law. However, the Court did not hold that "buyers" were "managerial employees," remanding that question to the NLRB for determination. *See National Labor Relations Board v. Bell Aerospace Co.*, 416 U.S. 267 (1974). Why did the Court act differently here compared with *Hearst*?

Explanation

This case is often contrasted with *Hearst* as an example of the Court's lack of consistency in deciding when to defer to agency decisions, because the Court reversed the agency's interpretation of the statutory term without considering whether the agency's interpretation was reasonable or supported by substantial evidence. If, however, we focus on the Court's remand of the question whether "buyers" were managerial employees, we may find consistency. In *Hearst* the Court considered the application of the broad statutory term "employee," to a specific factual situation, and the Court said courts should uphold reasonable agency interpretations. In *Bell Aerospace*, while the Court reversed the agency's broad and general interpretation of the statutory term "managerial employee," it remanded the case to the agency to apply that term to the particular factual situation of "buyers," and presumably the Court would later uphold a reasonable agency interpretation of the term applied to the buyers. Looked at carefully, we can see that *Bell Aerospace* is actually consistent with the approach in *Hearst*. That is, in *Bell Aerospace* the law was clear (to the Supreme Court at least) that all managerial employees were excepted from protection, but the law was ambiguous as to whether "buyers" in particular were managerial employees. Thus, the first question the Court answered without deference or much attention to the agency's view, just as the Court in *Hearst* had determined without deference to the agency that the statutory term "employee" did not mean the same as the common law term. It remanded the case in *Bell Aerospace* so that the agency could apply the law, as decided by the Court, to the facts.

Thus, courts may address an agency's ultimate conclusions or an agency's application of law to facts in an adjudication either as a substantial evidence question or as a *Hearst* question, if the agency's law interpretation is viewed as within the range of ambiguity in the statute.

C. Substantial Evidence Review in Hybrid Rulemaking

As mentioned earlier, a number of statutes in the 1970s began to specify that rules adopted under those statutes, even though not adopted using formal rulemaking procedures, should be upheld on judicial review if they were supported by substantial evidence. What Congress intended by these provisions was unclear. Some courts thought that Congress intended the courts to engage in a stricter scrutiny of the factual and judgmental decisions made by the agency in those rulemakings than in other rulemakings governed by the "arbitrary and capricious" review standard that will be discussed below. Justice Scalia, when he was still a judge on the D.C. Circuit, expressed a different view. In his view, substantial evidence review and "arbitrary and capricious" review involve the same level of scrutiny. *See Association of Data Processing Service Organizations, Inc. v. Board of Governors*, 745 F.2d 677 (D.C. Cir. 1984). The Supreme Court has never definitively ruled on the issue, but most observers believe that Justice Scalia's view has carried the day. In *Motor Vehicle Manufacturers Assn. v. State Farm Mutual Automobile Insurance Co.*, 463 U.S. 29 (1983), the Supreme Court stated that the scope of review was the "arbitrary and capricious" standard, even though the statute involved, the Motor Vehicle Safety Act, stated that the agency's determination was to be supported by "substantial evidence on the record considered as a whole."

III. ARBITRARY AND CAPRICIOUS REVIEW

Inasmuch as substantial evidence review only applies to formal proceedings under the APA or to certain hybrid rulemakings under particular statutes, "questions of fact" arising in informal adjudication must be reviewed under a different standard. That standard is "arbitrary and capricious" review. Moreover, as you will see, probably the most important function of "arbitrary and capricious" review is its application to questions of judgment, what we called application of law to facts in the substantial evidence discussion, but in the context of rulemaking is rarely referred to in those terms. This is probably because rulemaking deals largely with so-called legislative facts, whereas adjudication more often involves adjudicative facts. The former refers to the types of facts that legislatures rely on when they make laws, and the latter refers to the types of facts that are decided in courts. For example, when the EPA decides that a particular standard for air pollution is requisite to protect the public health with an adequate margin of safety, the factual determinations the agency is making are global in nature: what level of pollution will cause what level of risk and whether that level of risk provides an adequate margin of safety. This is a different nature of fact from what the EPA must find when it determines that a particular polluter on a given day emitted more pollution than the EPA's regulation permitted.

Section 706(2)(A) is the provision governing "arbitrary and capricious" review and states that courts shall hold unlawful and set aside agency action that is "arbitrary, capricious, [or] an abuse of discretion." As an initial matter, these three terms do not have independent significance; "arbitrary, capricious, or abuse of discretion" review is one standard.

Historically, the terms *arbitrary* and *capricious* were used in tandem to describe which laws were unconstitutional because they deprived a person of liberty or property without due process of law. If you have taken the individual rights portion of the constitutional law course, you have learned that the current test used by the Supreme Court to decide whether a law affecting economic and social interests violates substantive due process is the "rational relationship" test. This highly deferential test finds laws unconstitutional only if there is no possible rational basis to believe that they further a legitimate governmental interest. This is what the "arbitrary and capricious" test historically meant. It may be what the drafters of the APA intended.

In *Citizens to Preserve Overton Park, Inc. v. Volpe*, 401 U.S. 402 (1971), however, what some have called the first modern administrative law case, the Supreme Court described arbitrary and capricious review in a wholly new way. There, the law prohibited the Federal Highway Administration from providing funds for any highway that went through a public park "unless there is no feasible and prudent alternative to the use of such land." Tennessee sought highway funds for an interstate that would go through Overton Park, a local park in Memphis. The Secretary of Transportation approved the use of funds, saying that he concurred in the judgment of local officials that the road should go through the park, but a local group challenged that approval. The Supreme Court held that his approval should be judged according to the arbitrary and capricious standard, inasmuch as neither substantial evidence nor *de novo* review was applicable. It described arbitrary and capricious review as "a substantial inquiry," "a thorough, probing, in-depth review, and [a] searching and careful [inquiry into the facts]." More specifically, it said that "the court must consider whether the decision was based on a consideration of the relevant factors and whether there has been a clear error of judgment." "[T]he reviewing court must be able to find that the Secretary could have reasonably believed that in this case there are no feasible alternatives. . . ." Nevertheless, the Court allowed that the Secretary's decision is "entitled to a presumption of regularity" and that the "ultimate standard of review is a narrow one. The court is not empowered to substitute its judgment for that of the agency." This review was to be made on the basis of the administrative record, even though the agency decision was the product of non-adversarial, informal adjudication. That is, a formal, evidentiary record, such as is produced by a formal adjudication, was not present. The "administrative record" was simply what was before the Secretary at the time he made his decision, and it was against this record that the reasonableness of his decision was to be assessed.[2] This concept of the administrative record and the need to judge the reasonableness of the agency decision in light of that record was further developed in later cases involving informal rulemaking.

It is hornbook law today that substantive review of an agency's decision is made on the record that was before the agency at the time of the decision. If the agency proceeding was a formal APA proceeding—either rulemaking or adjudication—the record is the formal evidentiary record compiled in the trial-type hearing. If the agency proceeding was an informal proceeding—either rulemaking or adjudication—the record is simply the information that was before the decisionmaker at the time of the decision, however compiled.[3] There are probably only two exceptions to the rule of record review. One occurs in informal adjudication if the agency does not provide an opportunity for a person to provide information for the record. In this circumstance, if the person has material information that might affect the decision, he or she can challenge the adequacy of the record, essentially arguing that for the agency to decide the issue without considering all the available information would be arbitrary and capricious. In such a circumstance a court should allow the person to supplement the record and allow the agency to reconsider its decision, but occasionally courts will have the person submit the information to the court, and the court will then assess the reasonableness of the agency decision in light of the new information.

Example

Under the National Environmental Policy Act, if an agency concludes in an Environmental Assessment that the agency's action will not have a significant effect on the environment, the agency is not required to prepare the much more extensive Environmental Impact Statement. Suppose that the Army Corps of Engineers did not provide an opportunity for members of the public to comment on an Environmental Assessment, which concluded that the proposed issuance of a Section 404 permit to fill wetlands would not have a significant effect on the environment. Environmentalists who have information that they believe will demonstrate that filling the wetlands does have a significant effect on the environment sue to enjoin the issuance of the permit on the grounds that the Corps' negative finding is arbitrary

2. In *Overton Park* the Court indicated that to the extent that the administrative record was inadequate to determine the bases for the Secretary's decision, the trial court might require the Secretary to testify to make further explanations. Today, a court would always remand the case to the agency for further explanation, rather than require the head of the agency to testify.
3. The requirements of due process may place limits on how the record is compiled in informal adjudications that may deprive a person of liberty or property.

and capricious. The complaint includes an affidavit presenting the new evidence. Should the court consider the new evidence, or decide whether the agency's decision is arbitrary and capricious solely on the basis of the information before the agency when it made its decision?

Explanation

If the court is convinced that the new information is material to the Corps' decision and that it would have been available to the Corps at the time of its decision, the court should provide the Corps an opportunity to supplement its record and respond to the new information. If the Corps had provided an opportunity for the public to provide information before it made its decision, and the environmentalists had failed to come forward, then the court should not reward the environmentalists for hiding the ball by considering the new information or allowing it to come into the record.

The other circumstance in which a court should allow supplementation of the record is when a person raises a serious claim as to the integrity of the decision-making process. Such a claim, often of prejudice, bias, or wrongful influence, almost necessarily involves information not in the agency record. Typically, if the case is before a trial court, the court will take evidence to determine the facts underlying the claim and base its decision on that evidence. If the case is initially brought before a court of appeals, typically the court directs an agency to appoint an Administrative Law Judge to take evidence and make a recommended decision to the court. *See, e.g., Professional Air Traffic Controllers Organization v. Federal Labor Relations Authority*, 685 F.2d 547 (D.C. Cir. 1982). Most recently, the Supreme Court overturned the Department of Commerce's inclusion of a citizenship question on the decennial census form on a basis similar to prejudice, bias, or wrongful influence. Although the Court found that the formal decision to include the citizenship question was not arbitrary or capricious on the record, it also found that the explanation for the decision was contrived and made up to cover what was the real reason for including the question. In reaching this conclusion, the Court looked beyond the administrative record because there was a serious claim as to the integrity of the decision-making process. *Department of Commerce v. New York*, 139 S. Ct. 2551 (2019).

Overton Park was a case of informal adjudication, and arbitrary and capricious review continues to be the standard for judging the adequacy of the factual support for, as well as the reasoning in, an informal adjudication, a standard that is indistinguishable from substantial evidence review.

Nevertheless, today arbitrary and capricious review has become a staple of challenges to rules adopted after notice-and-comment or hybrid rulemaking. It is probably the most common basis for setting aside agency rules.

Subsequent to *Overton Park* and largely in the D.C. Circuit in response to a large number of rulemakings under what were then new environmental laws, the "thorough, probing, in-depth review" of *Overton Park* took on a specific appellation—the "hard look." Initially, the "hard look doctrine" meant that courts would in their review assure that the agency had taken a hard look at the problem, and if satisfied that it had, the court would defer to the agency's expertise. Later, however, the doctrine evolved into the court itself taking a hard look at the agency's decision to assure that it was reasonable. Arguably, the hard look doctrine stressed the "thorough, probing, in-depth review" aspect of *Overton Park* and deemphasized the presumption of regularity and ultimately narrow standard of review. One of the best descriptions of the judicial process, given in the context of judicial review of an environmental rule, is as follows:

> [judicial review should] evince a concern that variables be accounted for, that the representativeness of test conditions be ascertained, that the validity of tests be assured and the statistical significance of results determined. Collectively, these concerns have sometimes been expressed as a need for "reasoned decision-making." . . . However expressed, these more substantive concerns have been coupled with a requirement that assumptions be stated, that process be revealed, that the rejection of alternate theories or abandonment of alternate course of action be explained and that the rationale for the ultimate decision be set forth in a manner which permits the . . . courts to exercise their statutory responsibility upon review.

National Lime Assn. v. Environmental Protection Agency, 627 F.2d 416, 453 (D.C. Cir. 1980).

Example

When Ronald Reagan was elected President, inaugurating a period of conservative politics in the executive branch, the Secretary of Transportation undertook a new rulemaking to reconsider a rule adopted in the previous Carter administration requiring auto makers to phase in passive restraints for automobiles. At the conclusion of that rulemaking, the Department of Transportation adopted a final rule rescinding the earlier rule that would have required passive restraints. The Department stated that under the rescinded rule manufacturers could have met the standard either by installing airbags or passive seat belts (seat belts that automatically deploy and do not require a person to fasten them), and all the manufacturers indicated they would use passive belts. However, the Department reasoned, passive belts can be detached and once detached they would be no different than the already prescribed, normal seat belts. At the time only a very small percentage of people used the seat belts in their cars, and the Department reasoned that people would detach the passive belts in about the same percentage, resulting in no increased safety but substantially increased costs resulting from the mandated passive restraints. This rule was challenged by automobile insurers. Was the rule arbitrary and capricious?

Explanation

The Supreme Court found the rescission arbitrary and capricious. The Court reiterated that the scope of review under the arbitrary and capricious standard is "narrow," and the court is not to substitute its judgment for that of the agency. Nevertheless, "the agency must examine the relevant data and articulate a satisfactory explanation for its action including a 'rational connection between the facts found and the choice made.' . . . Normally, an agency rule would be arbitrary and capricious if the agency has relied on factors which Congress has not intended it to consider, entirely failed to consider an important aspect of the problem, offered an explanation for its decision that runs counter to the evidence before the agency, or is so implausible that it could not be ascribed to a difference in view or the product of agency expertise." Here, the Court found that the agency had failed to consider an important aspect of the problem: the alternative of requiring airbags instead of allowing manufacturers the option of providing passive belts. The failure to consider this alternative was viewed as arbitrary and capricious. Moreover, the Court held that the agency's conclusion that passive belts would be disconnected to the same degree that manual belts were not connected to be unsupported by the evidence in the record. The Court found that the agency ignored the difference between detaching a passive belt and attaching a manual belt—inertia. The Court reasoned that inertia caused people to fail to attach manual belts, but inertia would cause people not to detach passive belts, leading to higher passive use. The Court stopped short of saying its own reasoning was correct, but it held that the agency's failure to consider the issue rendered the agency's decision arbitrary and capricious. *See Motor Vehicle Manufacturers Assn. v. State Farm Mutual Automobile Insurance Co.*, 463 U.S. 29 (1983).

This summary should suggest that the Supreme Court engaged in a hard look at the Department's rule. The fact that the agency's preamble to the final rule contained over 12,000 words and was based on studies comprising hundreds of pages was not sufficient. The agency had failed to consider an important factor and had failed to address what the Court thought was a decent argument.

Beyond the formulations provided by the courts, it is difficult to characterize judicial applications of arbitrary and capricious review beyond the simple statement that the court is requiring reasoned decision making. Nevertheless, it is probably fair to say that courts provide a harder look if they are convinced by the challenger that there is cause to question the reasonableness of the agency's decision. Such a cause might be a suggestion in a particular case that the decision was the product of politics without close regard to the facts. Certainly, many believed that to be the case in *State Farm*. Another warning signal for courts is when agencies act inconsistently. This too was present in *State Farm*, because the agency was determining that a rule previously found to advance safety would not advance safety. Courts, as the Supreme Court did in *State Farm*, routinely note that agencies can change their views of what is in the public interest, but "an agency changing its course must supply a reasoned analysis." Absent such an explanation for the changed position, inconsistency is arbitrary and capricious. Finally, what triggers the court's close scrutiny may be only a persuasive argument made by the challenger focusing on a particular weak spot in the agency's preamble or record.

Others suggest that the Court's formulation of the arbitrary and capricious test invites judicial subjectivity. This in turn results in decisions that differ not on the basis of any objective difference but on the basis of the political proclivities of the judges on different panels. There is a significant body of scholarship that attempts to prove or disprove this hypothesis. *See, e.g.*, Richard Revesz, *Environmental Regulation, Ideology, and the D.C. Circuit*, 83 Va. L. Rev. 1717 (1997) (finding evidence of ideologically based decision making); William S. Jordan, III, *Judges, Ideology, and Policy in the Administrative State: Lessons from a Decade of Hard Look Remands of EPA Rules*, 53 Admin. L. Rev. 45 (2001) (finding little or no evidence of such decision making). There is little question, however, that there is a perception that the ideological composition of panels affects decisions.

A couple of examples will put the arbitrary and capricious standard into a little more perspective.

Example

The Energy Policy and Conservation Act required the Department of Energy (DOE) to adopt appliance efficiency standards for 13 named household appliances so as to reduce the amount of energy consumed by those appliances. According to the Act, the standards were to "be designed to achieve the maximum improvement in energy efficiency which the Secretary determines is technologically feasible and economically justified." The Act allowed DOE not to adopt a standard if it determined that a standard would "not result in significant conservation of energy or would not be technologically feasible or economically justified." The DOE after a lengthy rulemaking concluded that no standards should be adopted. The Natural Resources Defense Council (NRDC) brought suit challenging this determination on several bases, one of which was that the computer model used by DOE to estimate projected energy savings was based on faulty assumptions and thus the results were arbitrary and capricious, and another of which was that DOE's failure to perform an environmental assessment or environmental impact analysis was arbitrary and capricious.

The assumption in the model was that consumers would not only purchase more efficient appliances as energy prices rose, but that consumers would actually have a greater willingness to pay higher initial prices for an appliance that would return that higher initial cost over a period of years. In other words, when energy prices increased 10 percent, consumers would be willing to pay more for increased efficiency if they could recover the additional initial cost in three years, but when energy prices increased 20 percent, consumers would be willing to pay more for increased efficiency even if it took seven years to recover the initial increased cost. DOE supported this assumption with the results of a study, which on its face did not appear to support the assumption, but DOE explained in its preamble why despite the numerical results the study might still be read to support its assumptions. The results of the computer model with this assumption was that consumers would buy appliances that were more efficient as a result of market forces that would make any additional savings from standards insignificant.

The Act provided that whatever standard DOE adopted, even a no-standard standard, as it did, would preempt any state standard for appliance efficiency. Because California had adopted certain appliance efficiency standards that would be preempted by the DOE no-standard rule, NRDC said that DOE's rule would result in an increase in energy use in California, which would have a significant adverse effect on the environment. In its rulemaking, DOE said it was unnecessary to conduct any environmental analysis because the maximum amount of increased energy that was estimated to be used as a result of preemption was too small to have any environmental effect. It based that conclusion on an earlier study that had shown that a decrease in energy use of the same magnitude would not have any significant effect on the environment. NRDC argued that this conclusion was arbitrary and capricious.

How should the court rule?

Explanation

In *Natural Resources Defense Council, Inc. v. Herrington*, 768 F.2d 1355 (D.C. Cir. 1985), the D.C. Circuit held that DOE's assumption and model were not arbitrary and capricious, but that its conclusion that there would be no significant effect on the environment was not sufficiently explained and therefore was arbitrary and capricious. The court suggested that DOE had gone to some length to explain why the assumption was supportable, and its explanation for why the study's results were distinguishable was reasonable. The court said that its role was not to second-guess the experts but to assure that they had taken a hard look at the issues. With respect to the failure to conduct an environmental analysis, however, the court said that DOE had not explained how it could treat an increase in energy use by a certain amount to have the same lack of an environmental effect as a decrease in energy use by the same amount. Because this was not adequately explained, DOE's conclusion was arbitrary and capricious.

Example

Under the Occupational Safety and Health Act, the Occupational Safety and Health Administration (OSHA) is authorized to adopt regulations that materially reduce a significant workplace risk to human health. Pursuant to that Act, OSHA adopted the bloodborne pathogens rule for the health care industry to protect its employees from infection against the AIDS and Hepatitis B viruses, which are transmitted by blood. Among the protections required are engineering controls (such as a requirement for the location of sinks), work practice controls (such as standards of care in handling contaminated, sharp instruments), requirements for protective equipment (such as gloves, goggles, gowns), and housekeeping practices (such as requirements governing cleaning surfaces and fabrics). The rule also required employers to offer vaccination against Hepatitis B at the employer's expense to all employees at risk of exposure to blood. Although the rule was accepted by most health care industries and organizations, the rule was challenged by two groups: the American Dental Association (ADA) and the national organization representing employers of home health care professionals (such as nurses who perform their services in persons' homes rather than in a medical facility). The ADA argued that the rule was arbitrary and capricious as applied to it, because there was no "significant workplace risk" of exposure to the viruses in dental offices. The home health care professionals organization argued that the rule was arbitrary and capricious as applied to home health care employers because, unlike every other employer covered by the rule, the home health care employers do not have control over the workplace environment, which is simply persons' homes.

OSHA responded to the ADA's argument by saying that it quantified a significant risk (over 200 health care professionals die annually from Hepatitis B infections) for the health care industry generally, but it admits that it did not quantify a specific risk for dental offices. In response to the home health care organizations, OSHA states in its brief that it will not enforce any requirement against an employer with respect to a workplace over which the employer does not have control.

Is the rule arbitrary and capricious?

Explanation

In *American Dental Assn. v. Martin*, 984 F.2d 823 (7th Cir. 1993), the court found that the rule was not arbitrary and capricious as applied to dental offices, but that it was arbitrary and capricious as applied to home health care employers.

Although the statute requires as a precondition of OSHA regulation that there be a significant risk, the court noted that OSHA cannot be required to consider each individual workplace separately. OSHA must be able to aggregate similar workplaces in determining whether there is a significant risk. While hospital emergency rooms may pose a greater risk of exposure to blood than dental offices, ordinary doctors' offices may pose less of a risk of exposure to blood than dental offices. Even dental hygienists engaged in only tooth cleaning use sharp instruments and commonly are exposed to mixtures of blood and saliva. Inasmuch as OSHA's rules only apply to those health care workers actually at risk of blood exposure, the aggregation of dental offices and other medical facilities is reasonable.

This conclusion was not unanimous. The dissent believed that, while OSHA could not be expected to consider the risk in each separate workplace, it could be expected to consider separately the risk in major industry groups. With over 200,000 dental employees nationwide, the dissent believed the failure to determine the risk to this industry group separately from hospital employees and medical office employees was arbitrary and capricious. Of course, the fact that the dissent also stated its view that OSHA should not be regulating health care procedures in any case, and that the dissent called upon Congress to amend the Act to eliminate OSHA authority in this area, may give you some perspective on how this judge viewed the issue.

The court found the rule arbitrary and capricious as to home health care employers. OSHA, in its brief promising not to enforce provisions of the rule against employers to the extent the employer did not have control over the requirements in the rule, in essence recognized the problem contained in its rule. A lawyer's promise, however, the court believed, was no substitute for a provision in the rule itself establishing a defense for employers who did not have control over the workplace.

Agencies, in attempting to avoid reversal of their rules in courts under the arbitrary and capricious review, engage in elaborate studies and reviews as well as exhaustive preambles, attempting to respond to every argument and plug every hole. Of course, as described in Chapter 5, Rulemaking, other presidential and statutory requirements at the same time also require elaborate studies and explanations for agency rules. This process makes rulemaking take an exorbitant length of time, leading some commentators to decry the "ossification of rulemaking," but it is not clear to what extent any such ossification is the product of hard look judicial review or the statutory and presidential review and analysis requirements. Moreover, to the extent that it is the result of stringent judicial review, it still is not clear that such review is inadvisable. Regulations potentially affecting the health and safety of the public and potentially imposing great costs on the economy deserve close scrutiny. Moreover, as a former EPA official wrote in a famous article: "The effect of such judicial opinions within the agency reaches beyond those who were concerned with the specific regulations reviewed. They serve as a precedent for future rulewriters and give those who care about well-documented and well-reasoned decisionmaking a lever with which to move those who do not." William Pedersen, *Formal Records and Informal Rulemaking*, 85 Yale L.J. 38, 60 (1975).

IV. *DE NOVO* REVIEW

Section 706(2)(F) provides for setting aside agency action found to be "unwarranted by the facts to the extent that the facts are subject to trial de novo by the reviewing court." Unlike almost every other form of judicial review we have considered, judicial review under this provision treats the agency decision as a nullity. The court decides the case *de novo*, deciding where the preponderance of the evidence lies. The real issue under this provision is when it applies.

The original intent is clouded in obscurity. The House Report on the bill that became the APA stated that the provision reflected "the established rule . . . [that requires a judicial] trial de novo to establish the relevant facts as to the applicability of any rule and as to the propriety of adjudications where there is no statutory administrative hearing." Under this reading, this provision would apply whenever a rule was enforced in court and whenever an informal adjudication was reviewed in court. The Attorney General's Manual on the Administrative Procedure Act, however, which was issued a year after the adoption of the APA and has generally been considered a primary source for determining the original meaning of the APA, repudiates this legislative history, denies that there was any such "established rule," and asserts that the provision only applies "to those existing situations in which judicial review has consisted of a trial de novo," and those situations exist "only . . . where other statutes or the courts have prescribed such review." Under this reading, *de novo* review would only occur when some other statute or court decision specifically requires it. Commentators have suggested that the Attorney General's Manual was hardly a dispassionate exegesis of the meaning of the APA, but rather that it was an attempt to undo legislative battles that the administration had lost in the passage of the APA. *See* John Duffy, *Administrative Common Law in Judicial Review*, 77 Tex. L. Rev. 113 (1998). The Manual's reading of the *de novo* review provision would certainly be consistent with the administration's desire to limit judicial review of agency action to the extent possible.

Whatever the original meaning, the Supreme Court in *Overton Park* rendered an opinion on the subject that is the black-letter law today. In *Overton Park*, the Court said that *de novo* review only applies in two circumstances: "First, such de novo review is authorized when the action is adjudicatory in nature and the agency factfinding procedures are inadequate. And, there may be independent judicial factfinding when issues that were not before the agency are raised in a proceeding to enforce nonadjudicatory agency action." Two years later, in *Camp v. Pitts*, 411 U.S. 138 (1973), the Court found that a very informal adjudication without any oral or trial-type hearing was an adequate fact-finding procedure. Consequently, subsequent cases have failed to find inadequate fact-finding procedures except where there are serious allegations of bad faith or lack of integrity in the fact-finding process. The second circumstance mentioned in *Overton Park* is probably an attempt at a restatement of the phrase in the original legislative history that *de novo* review is appropriate "to establish the relevant facts as to the applicability of any rule." That is, if an agency attempts to enforce a regulatory requirement in court, the applicability of the regulation to the defendant is subject to *de novo* review. This is accepted practice, but it has no relation to judicial review of the underlying agency regulation. As a practical matter, today neither of these two circumstances arises frequently.

V. REVIEW OF AGENCY ACTION UNLAWFULLY WITHHELD OR UNREASONABLY DELAYED

Section 706(1) provides that a court is to compel agency action unlawfully withheld or unreasonably delayed. While the APA defines "agency action" to include the "failure to act," so that review under Section 706(2) to "hold unlawful and set aside agency action" could reach agency inaction, normally challenges to agency inaction are considered under Section 706(1).

In Chapter 6, in discussing the availability of judicial review, we described some of the difficulties of meeting this hurdle when challenging agency inaction. If these difficulties are surmounted, so review can be had, the form of review of agency inaction reflects the nature of the legal claim. That is, if the challenger asserts that the agency has withheld action in violation of the terms of a statute, for example, a requirement to adopt a rule by a specific deadline, the claim is a question of law, and a court will review it like other questions of law.

If the claim is that the agency is acting unreasonably by withholding or delaying action, the review will in effect be arbitrary and capricious review. However, the strictness of this review will depend in part upon the current status of the agency action and in part upon the agency's claimed justification for its inaction.

Example

In September 1972, an organization representing agricultural workers petitioned OSHA to promulgate a rule requiring employers of fieldworkers to provide them access to drinking water and handwashing and toilet facilities. There was no response to the petition. In December 1973, suit was brought, and OSHA referred the petition to an advisory committee. In December 1974, the advisory committee recommended a rule, but nothing happened. In October 1975, the district court ordered OSHA to promulgate a rule as soon as possible, and OSHA appealed. In April 1976, OSHA proposed a rule. In April 1977, the court of appeals reversed the district court, but ordered OSHA to make a report on the status of the rulemaking and a timetable for promulgating the rule.

In September 1977, OSHA filed a report stating that the rulemaking had very low priority because the hazards resulting from a lack of drinking water and access to handwashing and toilet facilities were not as serious as those presented by other substances or conditions for which other rulemakings had begun, nor as serious as those presented by other substances and conditions for which other rulemakings had not yet begun. In December 1979, the court of appeals upheld OSHA's decision to delay the rulemaking but held that it could not delay the rulemaking forever.

In March 1984, OSHA issued a new proposed rule but included in the proposal the option of not adopting any rule because of "a serious question whether the evidence establishes the need for a federal [rule]." In April 1985, OSHA announced that no rule would be adopted, for two reasons: first, if adopted it would receive low priority in enforcement and would not justify the diversion of resources necessary to enforce it, and second, several states had field sanitation rules, and it was preferable for them to regulate in light of the local conditions. In February 1987, the court of appeals in *Farmworker Justice Fund, Inc. v. Brock*, 811 F.2d 613 (D.C. Cir. 1987), *vacated as moot*, 817 F.2d 890 (D.C. Cir. 1987), issued an opinion finding that OSHA's decision unreasonably delayed issuance of the rule.

Explanation

In this example, the court of appeals issued three separate decisions. All of these involved the question whether the agency was acting unreasonably, not whether the agency was violating a particular statutory duty or requirement. The first two decisions upheld the agency's delay; the third did not. There are two important factors that distinguish the situations involved in the first two decisions from the situation involved in the third decision.

The first important factor is the sheer passage of time. When the court made its first decision, it was reversing a decision of the district court that there had been unreasonable delay after only three years. When it made the second decision, it upheld the agency's decision after five years to further delay the rulemaking. When it made the third decision, however, it was reviewing 13 years of past delay and indefinite future delay. Courts have been very deferential to agency justifications for delay based upon regulatory priorities, available resources, and workload issues, but at some point that deference runs out. The length of time in the *Farmworker* case is not atypical of how long it may take to demonstrate unreasonable delay.

The second important factor is that when the court made its third decision it was in effect reviewing the conclusion of a rulemaking. Thus, the judicial review could be made on a traditional rulemaking record, whereas its two previous decisions were based on information specifically generated for the judicial proceeding. If an agency is sued for unreasonable delay in beginning a rulemaking, there is likely to be little or no agency record on which a court could base a judgment. There is no record, because there has been no agency decision for which there would be a record. The whole problem is the fact that the agency has not made a decision. Consequently, in such a challenge, the judicial review cannot really be on the record, but must be based upon affidavits filed by the agency in the answer to the lawsuit. Such affidavits are usually conclusory, such as the statements in OSHA's 1977 report. The court, however, is faced with the dilemma of essentially accepting those statements or requiring the agency to provide evidence to support the statements. Imagine what kind of evidence it would have taken to show that the risks from other substances and conditions were greater than those posed by lack of field sanitation standards. The agency is already claiming that its resources are stretched thin. Should the court further strain those resources by diverting them into establishing the evidence that it does not have adequate resources to devote to the rulemaking? The result is that courts, as the D.C. Circuit did in this case, tend to accept agency statements regarding their regulatory priorities. When the agency has, however, engaged in rulemaking and reached a conclusion—here the conclusion not to adopt a rule—a court does have a record to review, one that must contain the evidence to support a reasonable conclusion and one that may be subjected to a hard look.

When an agency has adopted a rule and the normal time for challenging the rule has passed, a person may petition the agency to amend or rescind the rule and then, if the agency refuses, sue the agency for its decision refusing to amend or rescind the rule.

Example

The Clean Water Act prohibits the discharge of a pollutant into the waters of the United States unless the discharger has a permit authorizing that discharge. In 1973, the EPA adopted a regulation excluding from the permit requirement discharges from vessels "incidental to the normal operation of a vessel." This had the effect of excluding discharges of ballast water from large vessels from the prohibitions of the Clean Water Act, even though these discharges could contain invasive species that could have substantial adverse effects on the environment into which they were discharged. In 1999, an environmental group petitioned the EPA to rescind that regulation on the grounds that it was contrary to the requirements of the Clean Water Act. The EPA ultimately denied the petition, and the environmental group sued, arguing that the denial of its petition was arbitrary, capricious, and an abuse of discretion. A district court ruled in favor of the environmental group. *Northwest Environmental Advocates v. U.S. E.P.A.*, 2005 WL 756614 (N.D. Cal. 2005).

Explanation

Although the statute of limitations had expired on the ability to challenge the 1973 regulation itself, the court relied on a line of cases that enable persons to petition an agency to change a regulation, and when the agency refuses, to challenge that refusal. *See, e.g.*, *Public Citizen v. Nuclear Regulatory Commission*, 901 F.2d 147 (D.C. Cir. 1990). This makes sense in that the challenge is not to the original regulation but to the refusal to change it. Often such a challenge fails for the same reason that a suit attempting to force agency action often fails. That is, if the agency denies a petition on the ground that, in light of its resources and priorities, a revisiting of the regulation at this time is not advisable, a court is likely to defer to that answer. However, when the challenge is based on the basic legal authority for the regulation, as was the situation in this case, that kind of agency response is probably not effective. It does not take much time or resources to assess the purely legal argument that the regulation is ultra vires. Consequently, if it then denies the petition on the ground that the regulation is authorized by the statute, this is a decision that a court can review in a normal fashion.

VI. REMEDIES

A. Agency Inaction

Section 706(1) states that in the case of agency action unlawfully withheld or unreasonably delayed, the "court shall compel agency action." The difficulty in courts compelling agency action is usually in the timetable. When an agency has withheld or delayed action because of difficulties encountered in the rulemaking or perhaps resource limitations, what can a court do? For example, the Endangered Species Act contains a rather elaborate procedure with associated deadlines for the Department of the Interior to adopt rules determining whether a species is threatened or endangered. For various reasons the Department regularly fails to meet the statutory deadlines, and environmental groups are often quick to sue. Nevertheless, the determination of whether a species is threatened or endangered is a difficult undertaking, involving scientific studies and analyses. The Department only has a certain number of scientists and analysts, not enough to make all the studies and analyses required, and Congress, which imposed the statutory deadlines in the Endangered Species Act, will not provide funds adequate to meet those deadlines. As a result, courts usually ask agencies to propose a timetable for completing the action. The proposal is scrutinized by the court and the winning plaintiff, but ultimately not much more can be done but to order the agency to meet its timetable. And if it fails to meet milestones in the timetable, the court holds a hearing to find out why, but assuming the agency is acting in good faith, again little can be done but to order a change to the timetable. Essentially, the major effect of these suits is to elevate the priority of these rulemakings over other rulemakings for which there is no lawsuit—an example of the squeaky wheel getting the grease.

B. Remand Without Vacating

Section 706(2) states that the court shall "hold unlawful and set aside agency action, findings, and conclusions" that are found to run afoul of one of the standards in subsections (A) through (F) listed in the beginning of this chapter. In most cases this prescription is followed without difficulty. There is, however, a class of cases where the resolution is not quite that simple. Sometimes when a court determines that an agency's rule is invalid, it is often possible that the agency may be able to repromulgate the rule and cure the former problem. For example, if the court found the rule arbitrary and capricious or an abuse of discretion because the agency had not adequately explained its decision, the agency might be able to cure the problem by better explaining its decision. If, however, the court set aside the invalid agency rule, it might be that there would be no rule in place, or that a rule that had been amended or rescinded in the rulemaking would automatically come back into force. Either circumstance might cause practical problems.

Example

The Department of Agriculture, pursuant to a statute authorizing it to regulate enclosures of animals to protect public safety and the animals, adopts a rule setting a minimum height for fences enclosing lions and tigers. In a pre-enforcement challenge, an exotic animal farm claims that the rule is arbitrary and capricious because the agency did not consider the alternative of a lower fence combined with a moat, which is what it uses. If the court agrees with the challenger, what sort of remedy should it use?

Explanation

If the court sets aside (vacates) the rule, there will be no rule governing the enclosures of dangerous animals, and the lack of a rule may endanger the public safety. Moreover, although it may have been arbitrary and capricious for the agency not to have considered the alternative of a moat combined with a lower fence, it may be that when the agency does consider the matter, it may find good reasons not to adopt the alternative, so that the original rule will be readopted. Two different ways of dealing with this kind of problem have arisen. One is to remand the rule to the agency without vacating it. Thus, the rule stays in effect pending the agency's reconsideration. The other way is to grant a stay to the court's decision to vacate or set aside the rule. Both achieve the same end, which is to preserve the status quo pending the agency's reconsideration, but there is a substantial debate over the propriety of the first method, inasmuch as there is no statutory language authorizing it, and the standards for granting the two types of order may be said to differ. The D.C. Circuit has said that remanding without vacating is appropriate depending on "the seriousness of the [agency's] deficiencies (and thus the extent of doubt whether the agency chose correctly) and the disruptive consequences of an interim change that may itself be changed." *International Union, United Mine Workers of America v. Federal Mine Safety & Health Administration*, 920 F.2d 960, 967 (D.C. Cir. 1990). Judge Randolph, also of the D.C. Circuit, has been the leading judicial critic of this approach. He has an alternative as described here.

> Vacating an order or rule and then entertaining [a] stay motion[] has several important advantages over remanding without vacating. First, it preserves the adversary process. When we simply order a remand at the end of our merits opinion we are invariably making a remedial decision without the benefit of briefing or argument. It is quite rare for the parties even to mention the question of remedy in their merits briefs. In post-decision motions on stay applications, that will be the question they address. The court thus will have the benefit of hearing from both sides. Second, in deciding whether to allow unlawful agency action to remain in place during the remand (by way of a stay), the court will act with its eyes open and will have the information needed to assess the consequences of granting or denying a stay. Third, the existence of a stay with time limits, rather than an open-ended remand without vacatur, will give the agency an incentive to act promptly; when we simply remand, the agency has no such incentive. Fourth, there is a long-standing body of law in this circuit establishing the factors that determine whether a stay should be granted. These include the likelihood that the agency's position will prevail on remand; the likelihood that there will be irreparable harm without the stay; the prospect that others will be harmed if the court grants the stay; and the public interest in granting the stay.

Honeywell International, Inc. v. EPA, 393 F.3d 1315 (D.C. Cir. 2005) (on rehearing adopting Judge Randolph's concurring opinion at 374 F.3d 1363, 1375

(D.C. Cir. 2004)). Judge Randolph probably has the better of the argument, but at least for the time being different courts and different panels of the same court are using both methods of preserving the status quo.

C. Universal Injunctions

As noted above, Section 706(2) states that a court should "hold unlawful and set aside" agency actions found to be unlawful for any of the reasons in paragraphs (A) through (F). If the agency action in question was an adjudication, the remedy is clear, set aside the agency decision and remand the case to the agency for appropriate subsequent consideration. Almost invariably this would require the agency to issue a decision in favor of the person who appealed its original order.

If the agency action is a rulemaking, however, the answer is not so simple. What does it mean to "declare unlawful and set aside" a rule? A rule normally has nationwide effect, affecting numerous regulated persons as well as potential regulatory beneficiaries. The judicial challenge to the rule, however, will have been brought by some specific persons. For example, if Chevron challenges a Clean Air Act regulation adopted by EPA and wins in court, does that mean that the regulation is no longer in effect at all, or does it mean that the regulation is no longer effective against only Chevron, the victorious party to the suit?

In recent years plaintiffs have brought challenges to major agency rules in a district court thought by the plaintiffs to be sympathetic to their claim. For example, challenges to the Affordable Care Act, immigration, and environmental rules under the Obama Administration were brought in a district court in Texas. Similarly, states brought action against initiatives by President Trump in the Northern District of California. Typically, these cases resulted in injunctions against the agency carrying out the rule throughout the nation. Deemed "nationwide" or "universal" injunctions,[4] they have come under increasing criticism. Ordinarily in private civil litigation an injunction would only benefit the named plaintiffs who bring the action. One could argue that the injunction against the agency likewise should only enjoin the rule as to the named plaintiffs—the particular states or parties bringing the action against the agency—rather than enjoining the agency from enforcing the rule at all nationwide, especially when other states or

4. While both terms have been used to describe injunctions against enforcing the regulation against non-parties, the term *universal injunction* is probably more accurate, This is because it is unquestioned practice that an injunction prohibiting enforcement of a regulation against only the party who won the suit would apply wherever that party could be found, i.e., nationwide. That is, the questionable aspect of the universal injunction is its effect as to non-parties to the suit, rather than the geographical reach of the injunction.

persons would like the rule to remain in effect. This argument gains support from the visceral sense that a single district court judge (or even a single circuit) should not be able to stop a nationwide program. On the other hand, one must deal with the language of the APA, which directs courts to "set aside" agency action found unlawful. By its terms, it would seem to call for universal effect, not just with respect to particular parties. Despite the increased criticism of universal injunctions from some members of the Supreme Court, the Court has yet to opine on the subject, and courts continue to issue these universal injunctions.

VII. EQUITABLE ESTOPPEL

Equitable estoppel is not an administrative law concept; it refers to a rule of equity jurisprudence that when a person affirmatively misleads another person and the other person reasonably relies on the misleading information to his or her injury, a court will not consider evidence contrary to the information that the first person provided. For example, an auto salesman tells a prospective buyer that if he does not like the car for any reason in the first 30 days, he may return it and get his money back. The buyer indicates that he is unsure about a particular car, but in light of the return policy he will buy it. He buys it and tries to return it within the first 30 days but is told that he cannot get his money back. If he sues for a return of his money, the car seller will be equitably estopped from providing evidence that nothing in the contract authorizes such a return. The question in *administrative law* is to what extent this doctrine applies when the government affirmatively misleads a person, who relies on the government information and is injured thereby.

Example

A former government employee who retired on disability is considering whether to accept a job, but he does not want to jeopardize his continued receipt of disability retirement pay. He goes to the personnel office of the federal agency for which he had worked and asks whether taking a job would affect his retirement pay. He is orally assured that it will not affect his retirement pay, and he is given an official brochure of the federal Office of Personnel Management that confirms that interpretation. In reliance upon this advice, the person takes a job. Unfortunately, unknown to the agency person who spoke to the retired employee, Congress had changed the law four years before, and the brochure had not yet been updated. Under the "new" law, by taking a job the former employee loses his retirement pay. When the government stops his retirement pay, he sues to receive it, arguing equitable estoppel. How should a court rule?

Explanation

The Supreme Court ultimately denied his claim. The Court acknowledged that in the private context these facts would make out a good case of equitable estoppel, but it reiterated its long-held position that estoppel will not lie against the government on the same basis as against private parties. Underlying the Court's reluctance to countenance an equitable estoppel claim against the government is a concern with the separation of powers. Here, to order the government to pay the person the retirement pay would be to order payment not authorized by Congress. Moreover, to justify such payment on the basis of misconduct by the executive branch would enable the executive branch to undo laws passed by Congress. These concerns argue for a general rule that equitable estoppel should never lie against the government. While the Supreme Court has found this argument "substantial," it has never actually adopted it, deciding each case on a narrower ground. In this case, the Court said that it was constitutionally prohibited from finding for the plaintiff because the Constitution provides that "No Money shall be drawn from the Treasury, but in Consequence of Appropriations made by Law." Art. I, § 9, cl. 7. And there was no appropriation authorizing payments to the person in this circumstance. *See Office of Personnel Management v. Richmond*, 496 U.S. 414 (1990).

This case makes clear that suits seeking money from the government claiming equitable estoppel are bound to failure. What if, however, the government had continued payment of the retirement funds to the person for a period of time, and when it discovered his new job, it sued him for return of the money, and he argued equitable estoppel as a defense? The same separation of powers concerns would be present, but the equities perhaps seem even stronger in favor of the individual. And what if the "new" law made it a crime to take a job while receiving disability retirement pay? Could the government prosecute the former employee in these circumstances?

The answer to this latter question, at least, is clear: the government cannot punish someone who takes action in reliance upon official advice that the action is lawful. *See, e.g., United States v. Pennsylvania Industrial Chemical Corp.*, 411 U.S. 655 (1973). This rule is based upon due process, not equitable estoppel, and is closely related to the defense of entrapment and the prohibition on overly vague criminal laws. Where the government has affirmatively misled someone, the use of due process arguments in civil suits, instead of equitable estoppel arguments, may trump the separation of powers concerns. Some commentators have suggested that due process is the more appropriate argument to be made, *see* Joshua Schwartz, *The Irresistible Force Meets the Immovable Object: Estoppel Remedies for an Agency's Violation of Its Own Regulations or Other Misconduct*, 44 Admin. L. Rev. 653 (1992), and courts have overturned agency actions under the rubric of due process, without mentioning equitable estoppel even though the facts might have supported such a claim. *See, e.g., Appeal of Eno*, 126 N.H. 650 (1985) (Souter, J.).

VIII. THE EFFECT OF JUDICIAL DECISIONS

A. Res Judicata and Collateral Estoppel

1. Against Parties Suing the Government

The doctrines of res judicata (or claim preclusion) and collateral estoppel (or issue preclusion) are ones that law students learn in civil procedure courses. Res judicata in essence says that a final judgment on the merits bars further claims by the same parties based on the same cause of action. In suits against the government, this rule applies to private parties just as it does in other civil litigation. While normally res judicata requires an identity of the parties, as with most rules, this rule is subject to exceptions, one of which is that "in certain limited circumstances," a nonparty may be bound by a judgment because she was "adequately represented by someone with the same interests who [wa]s a party" to the suit. *Richards v. Jefferson County*, 517 U.S. 793 (1996). The Court, however, has narrowly construed this exception only to cases in which either the nonparty understood that the first suit was on its behalf or there were special procedures used in the first suit to protect the interests of any nonparties.

The Supreme Court has rejected a claim that this exception from the requirement for an identity of the parties should be applied liberally in "public law" litigation. In *Taylor v. Sturgell*, 553 U.S. 880 (2008), a person had sought certain documents under the Freedom of Information Act (FOIA) that were denied as containing trade secrets and therefore exempt from disclosure under the Act. The person then appealed that decision to the courts, and the agency's decision was upheld by the Tenth Circuit. Less than a month later, Taylor, a friend of the person who had been denied the documents, filed his own FOIA request seeking the exact same documents. The lower courts dismissed the case as barred by res judicata under a theory of "virtual representation," justified in part on the theory that the number of plaintiffs who might have standing is very large and the injury suffered is less particular, thereby substantially increasing the threat of "vexatious litigation." The Supreme Court was not convinced that this threat was real in light of the ability of courts to apply *stare decisis* to repetitive cases and the financial disincentives to bringing claims on matters already decided. Accordingly, the Court held that there was no exception from the identity of parties requirement on the grounds of "virtual representation."

2. Against the Government

Normally, the doctrine of collateral estoppel (or issue preclusion) states that a decision on an issue of fact or law against a party in a suit is conclusive in a subsequent suit involving that party. It does not, however, apply to the government as litigator in all cases. In *United States v. Mendoza*, 464 U.S. 154 (1984), the plaintiff sought naturalization under the immigration laws, and when the government denied it, Mendoza brought suit to challenge the government's denial. The trial court did not reach the merits of the suit, holding that the government was collaterally estopped from arguing its position, because it had lost a similar suit involving the same issue of law in an earlier case in a trial court in a different district. The Supreme Court reversed. It noted that the government is a unique litigant both in terms in the number of cases and the number of jurisdictions in which it litigates. Allowing nonmutual collateral estoppel would result in the first decision against the government on an issue becoming national law, which would force the government to appeal each decision to the highest possible court. In turn, the Supreme Court would be faced with the first decision on a subject in each circumstance and would be deprived of the benefit from allowing several courts to explore an issue first. Accordingly, the Court held that the government is not subject to nonmutual collateral estoppel, that is, collateral estoppel raised by someone who had not been a party to the earlier proceeding with the government.

A companion case to *Mendoza* involved mutual collateral estoppel. There, the EPA had tried to execute a search warrant against a chemical company in Wyoming, using private contractors as the investigators. The company refused to allow the private contractors to enter its property, arguing that the Clean Air Act did not authorize the use of such private contractors to carry out warranted inspections. The Tenth Circuit Court of Appeals ruled in favor of the company. At approximately the same time, the EPA also tried to execute a warrant against another facility of the same company in Tennessee, which is in the Fourth Circuit. Again the company resisted and in court argued that the EPA was collaterally estopped by the earlier decision of the Tenth Circuit. The Fourth Circuit agreed with the company, and the Supreme Court agreed with the Fourth Circuit, distinguishing *Mendoza*. The Court believed that requiring the EPA to abide by decisions involving the same issue *and the same party* would not seriously burden its activities or result in the negative effects that the Court had said would result from nonmutual collateral estoppel.

B. Non-Acquiescence

In *Mendoza*, the Supreme Court approved of an agency deciding not to follow the decisional rule of one district court. Is an agency equally able to ignore the decisional rule of a court of appeals?

Example

The Social Security Administration (SSA) changes its interpretation of the Social Security Disability law with the result that a large number of recipients across the country receive letters notifying them that they have been terminated from receiving benefits. One such person living in California seeks judicial review of his termination and wins in district court, as the court finds the SSA's interpretation inconsistent with the statute. The SSA appeals to the Ninth Circuit, which affirms the district court. Subsequently, persons who received termination letters on the same basis seek reinstatement but are denied by the agency. They sue. Some are in California; some are in New York. How should the courts rule?

Explanation

A federal district court in New York, much less the Second Circuit, is not bound by the prior decisions of other circuit courts. Moreover, the agency's action that raises the legal issue—the termination letter to the New York beneficiary—did not occur within the Ninth Circuit's geographic jurisdiction. Thus, Ninth Circuit law does not apply within the Second Circuit, and absent nonmutual collateral estoppel, the agency is free to ignore (or respectfully decline to follow) the Ninth Circuit's decisional rule outside of that circuit. This is called "inter-circuit non-acquiescence," and it is generally accepted as not inappropriate. The district court in New York and the Second Circuit on any appeal should decide for themselves whether the agency's interpretation is correct.

The situation is different in the Ninth Circuit. District courts in that circuit are bound by the decisional rules of the Ninth Circuit. Moreover, the agency's action that raises the legal issue—the termination letter to the California beneficiary—occurred within the geographic jurisdiction of the Ninth Circuit. Thus, although nonmutual collateral estoppel will not apply to the agency in light of *Mendoza*, we can, and the agency can, reliably predict how the suit will come out in the Ninth Circuit. On the basis of circuit precedent, the agency will lose. One can characterize the Ninth Circuit's earlier decision as "the law" in the Ninth Circuit. Why then would the agency refuse to act consistently with the circuit's decisional rule and in apparent violation of "the law"? The agency might wish to maintain one rule for the entire nation, so that recipients in California are treated the same as in New York. The agency might also realize that keeping the agency's interpretation in effect will continue to terminate recipients' benefits in accordance with the interpretation, unless and until individual participants go to the trouble of seeking judicial review. Some, perhaps many, will not challenge their termination, maybe because they do not know of the prior litigation or maybe because they are unable to find someone to handle their case, given the relatively small amount of money involved. The agency's termination strategy thus will be successful with respect to these persons even though a court has deemed it unlawful. This is called "intra-circuit non-acquiescence," and it is highly controversial.

In addition to the Social Security Administration, a number of agencies have engaged in intra-circuit non-acquiescence, including the National Labor Relations Board, the Railroad Retirement Board, the Federal Communications Commission, the Occupational Safety and Health Administration, the Postal Service, and the Immigration and Naturalization Service. Although courts have been uniformly hostile to the practice, the Supreme Court has never heard a case challenging the practice. Commentators usually recognize that there are both costs and benefits to intra-circuit non-acquiescence, but they differ among themselves on how to balance them. Generally, however, there is agreement on one point. Agencies should not engage in implacable and obstinate intra-circuit non-acquiescence. Intra-circuit non-acquiescence is justified, if at all, as a means to an end of obtaining judicially recognized national uniformity. Thus, the agency should not avoid Supreme Court review if it intends to non-acquiesce. Moreover, when the courts consistently find against the agency, and the agency has sought but been refused Supreme Court review, the agency should abandon its position, even if some circuits have not yet spoken.

CHAPTER 8

Government Acquisition of Private Information

It is a very sad thing that nowadays there is so little useless information.

—*Oscar Wilde*

I. INTRODUCTION

If you have ever filled out an income-tax return, you know about the government's penchant for collecting information. The income-tax system is just the tip of the iceberg. The government collects information from the public for many different reasons and in many different ways. Much of this information gathering is done by administrative agencies.

Some information gathering by agencies relates to agency rulemaking or adjudication, but some does not. For example, before the EPA promulgates an air pollution rule, it uses the rulemaking process discussed in Chapter 5 to gather information from the industries and other members of the public who will be affected by the proposed rule. Similarly, when the Nuclear Regulatory Commission (NRC) adjudicates an application for a permit to operate a nuclear plant, it will get information from the applicant and other interested people. In addition to collecting information for rulemaking and adjudication, agencies gather information to determine whether Congress should enact, amend, or repeal statutes. They also gather information to aid decision making by the President or other executive officials. They gather information to use in civil or criminal court proceedings. They even gather information for use by other agencies or the public. For example, the Fish and Wildlife Service advises other federal agencies on the effects their projects will have on endangered species. In short, agencies gather information for almost everything they do.

Just as there are many purposes for which agencies collect information, there are many ways in which they collect it. Much of the information that agencies collect from the public is provided voluntarily. For example, a company that applies to the NRC for a license to operate a nuclear plant will voluntarily submit the information needed to process that application; people opposed to the license will just as eagerly submit relevant information during the licensing process. Similarly, members of the public voluntarily submit information to an agency during the rulemaking process. In addition to these voluntary methods, there are ways in which agencies can collect information under legal compulsion. The three main ways are through inspections, reporting requirements, and subpoenas. For example, the NRC inspects nuclear plants; the IRS requires people to report their income at least annually; and the Federal Trade Commission issues subpoenas in the course of investigating unfair trade practices.

While the government has good reasons for collecting information, the collection process burdens the people from whom the information is collected. In the worst case scenario (from the perspective of the person who provides the information), the information can reveal that he has committed a crime. Alternatively, the information may lead to civil penalties or other civil sanctions, such as the loss of a license to do business. Furthermore, quite apart from the risk of sanctions, it can be expensive and time-consuming to provide information to the government. For these reasons, lawyers must often help their clients deal with the government's demands for information.

II. LEGAL LIMITS ON GOVERNMENT ACQUISITION OF PRIVATE INFORMATION — IN GENERAL

This chapter examines the three main ways in which government agencies collect information under legal compulsion: inspections, reporting requirements, and subpoenas. For each type of collection method, you should ask two questions. (1) What is the source of legal authority for the agency action? (2) What are the legal limits on that authority? You can then determine whether an agency has acted within the scope of that authority and those limits in a particular situation.

The relevance of these questions is reflected in the APA. Section 555(c) of the APA says, "Process, requirement of a report, inspection, or other investigative act or demand may not be issued, made, or enforced except as authorized by law." The term "authorized by law" means two things.

First, agencies need some source of legal authority to conduct any inspection, to create or enforce any reporting requirement, and to issue or enforce any investigative order, such as a subpoena (which is one type of "process" within the meaning of APA § 555(c)). The source of authority for an agency's collection of information is usually either a statute or a regulation. For example, a statute authorizes the Occupational Safety and Health Administration (OSHA) to inspect work sites for unsafe or unhealthy conditions. *See* 29 U.S.C. § 657(a). Not all agencies that do inspections or collect information in other ways have a specific statutory grant of authority like OSHA's. Instead, an agency's information gathering may fall within a statute that gives an agency broad investigatory power. *See Dow Chemical Co. v. United States*, 476 U.S. 227 (1986).

Second, an agency cannot exercise its authority in a way that violates affirmative legal limits on that authority. Those limits may come from inside or outside the statute granting the authority. To illustrate an internal limit, the statute authorizing OSHA inspections generally requires them to occur "during regular working hours [or] at other reasonable times." 29 U.S.C. § 657(a). To take an obvious example of an external limit, OSHA could not select a business for inspection based on the race of its owner. Even if the inspection were otherwise authorized under the OSHA statute, it would violate the Constitution's equal protection principle. An OSHA inspection that violated internal or external limits on OSHA's authority would not be "authorized by law" within the meaning of APA § 555(c).

The legal restrictions on information gathering by a government agency can come from the U.S. Constitution, federal statutes, and the agency's own regulations. We will focus on restrictions that are broadly applicable. Specifically, we will discuss restrictions imposed by the Paperwork Reduction Act and by the Fourth and Fifth Amendments to the Constitution. Before we get into the limits on information gathering imposed by these provisions, however, it bears repeating that these are not the only limits that may apply in a particular situation. For example, the statute that gives the IRS broad authority to compel the production of tax-related documents has been interpreted not to cover documents that fall within the attorney-client privilege. *See United States v. Euge*, 444 U.S. 707 (1980). You cannot assume, however, that other information-collection statutes incorporate other evidentiary privileges. *See, e.g., University of Pennsylvania v. EEOC*, 493 U.S. 182 (1990) (refusing to recognize academic-freedom privilege against EEOC subpoena). Instead, you must do research to identify the source of legal authority and the legal limits applicable to a given agency's particular method of gathering information.

III. ADMINISTRATIVE INSPECTIONS—FOURTH AMENDMENT LIMITS

Many government agencies, like OSHA, inspect places where regulated activities occur to ensure compliance with applicable statutes and regulations. When an agency inspects a place that is not open to the public, the inspection is a "search" subject to the Fourth Amendment.[1] The Fourth Amendment usually requires the government, before conducting a search, to get a search warrant that is based on probable cause to believe that the search will uncover evidence of a crime. Administrative inspections, however, do not focus on detecting crime, but on ensuring compliance with regulatory requirements. Because of this difference, the Supreme Court has modified the warrant and probable-cause requirements for some administrative inspections; for others, the Court has dispensed with the warrant and probable-cause requirements altogether.

The seminal cases on administrative inspections are *Camara v. Municipal Court*, 387 U.S. 523 (1967), and the companion case of *See v. City of Seattle*, 387 U.S. 541 (1967). In *Camara*, the Court held that housing inspectors had to get a warrant before they could inspect an apartment for violations of the San Francisco Housing Code. To get the warrant, however, the inspectors did not have to show probable cause that they would find violations of the Code at the particular apartment they wanted to inspect. Instead, probable cause would exist if the inspection complied with "reasonable legislative or administrative standards" for inspections under the Code. *Camara*, 387 U.S. at 538. We discuss below the criteria that courts use to judge the "reasonableness" of inspection standards; for now, the important point is that this specialized definition of probable cause allows routine administrative inspections to occur without evidence of wrongdoing.

The Court in *Camara* made this change to the meaning of probable cause because of the differences between administrative inspections and traditional law-enforcement searches. The Court observed that many of the Code violations that the inspectors wanted to search for, such as faulty electrical wiring, could not be detected from the outside of a building, so it was hard to develop probable cause in the traditional sense. In addition, the Court reasoned that, since the inspections did not involve searches of a person's

1. The Fourth Amendment says, "The right of the people to be secure in their persons, houses, papers and effects, against unreasonable searches and seizures, shall not be violated, and no Warrants shall issue, but upon probable cause, supported by Oath or affirmation, and particularly describing the place to be searched, and the persons or things to be seized." Although the Fourth Amendment, standing alone, applies only to the federal government and its officials, it is incorporated into the Due Process Clause of the Fourteenth Amendment, as a result of which it applies to state and local governments and officials as well. *See Mapp v. Ohio*, 367 U.S. 643 (1961).

body or personal effects and were not aimed to discover evidence of crime, they intruded less on personal privacy than did traditional law-enforcement searches. In *See*, the Court extended this reasoning to uphold administrative inspections of businesses in Seattle. *Camara* and *See* thus established that an administrative inspection of a home or an ordinary business would comply with the Fourth Amendment if it was conducted under a warrant based on proof that the inspection complied with "reasonable . . . standards" for inspections.

In cases after *Camara* and *See*, the Court dispensed with the warrant and probable-cause requirements altogether for administrative inspection schemes governing "closely" regulated industries. (These industries are also known as "pervasively" regulated industries.) Specifically, the Court has upheld warrantless inspection schemes for liquor dealers, gun dealers, mining companies, and auto dismantlers. *Colonnade Catering Corp. v. United States*, 397 U.S. 72 (1970) (liquor dealers); *United States v. Biswell*, 406 U.S. 311 (1972) (gun dealers); *Donovan v. Dewey*, 452 U.S. 594 (1981) (mining companies); *New York v. Burger*, 482 U.S. 691 (1987) (auto dismantlers). The Court determined that because people in these industries are so heavily regulated, they have lower expectations of privacy than the owners of ordinary businesses.

The Court has held that the Fourth Amendment still applies to inspections of closely (pervasively) regulated industries, but it does not require either a warrant or probable cause for inspections pursuant to an inspection scheme. Instead, the Court in *New York v. Burger* described three requirements for a warrantless inspection scheme covering a pervasively regulated business. First, the scheme has to be justified by a "substantial" government interest. Second, warrantless inspections must be "necessary to further the regulatory scheme." Third, the terms of the inspection scheme must provide "a constitutionally adequate substitute for a warrant." This third requirement means that the scheme has to be detailed enough (1) to put a business owner on notice that he or she is subject to periodic inspections, and (2) to limit the discretion of the inspecting officials to ensure that they act reasonably. *See New York v. Burger*, 482 U.S. at 702-703. The most important of those three requirements—because it is the hardest to meet—is the third: namely, the requirement that the scheme for inspection of closely regulated businesses be a "constitutionally adequate substitute for a warrant."

The Court's case law on administrative inspections makes two questions particularly important. First, how do you tell if an industry is closely (pervasively) regulated? Second, how do you tell whether the standards for an administrative inspection are "reasonable" (the requirement for homes and ordinary businesses) or "an adequate substitute for a warrant" (the requirement for pervasively regulated businesses)?

The Court has suggested that it does not take much for an industry to be "pervasively" regulated so as to be subject to warrantless administrative inspections. In *New York v. Burger*, the Court held that auto dismantlers were pervasively regulated because (1) they had to get a license and keep detailed records, and (2) they were like businesses (such as junkyards) that had been heavily regulated for a long time. The dissent in *New York v. Burger* argued that, under those two criteria, most businesses are pervasively regulated. Nonetheless, the Court has made clear that not all businesses are "pervasively regulated." In *Marshall v. Barlow's, Inc.*, 436 U.S. 307 (1978), the Court struck down OSHA's warrantless inspection scheme, which covered all businesses engaged in interstate commerce. The Court refused to find that businesses engaged in interstate commerce, as a whole, are pervasively regulated. Because of this holding, a routine OSHA inspection must meet the *Camara-See* requirements, meaning that it must be based on a warrant or other court order that is, in turn, based on proof that the inspection complies with "reasonable" administrative or legislative standards. *See also Los Angeles v. Patel*, 135 S. Ct. 2443 (2015) (holding that hotels and motels are not closely regulated).

In deciding whether the standards for an administrative inspection are "reasonable" and therefore satisfy the Fourth Amendment, courts generally look to the same factors regardless of whether the inspections involve a pervasively regulated business or a home or ordinary business. In either situation, the courts require the standards to be (1) objective, (2) rationally related to the purposes for the inspections, (3) fairly detailed, and (4) reasonable overall. For example, an agency can select a business for an inspection based on the passage of time since that business's last inspection. This objective criterion makes sense, given limited agency resources for doing inspections. In addition, its objective nature prevents particular businesses from being singled out for an improper purpose, such as harassment. Even so, an inspection scheme must spell out more than just the frequency of inspections. The scheme also has to address details such as who has authority to do the inspections, where on the premises the inspector can look, and what he or she can look for. These details are necessary to prevent individual inspectors from abusing their discretion during individual inspections. Finally, the details themselves must be reasonable. For example, most courts would consider it unreasonable for an inspection scheme to allow inspections to occur in the middle of the night or to authorize inspectors to destroy property for no good reason.

So far we have discussed administrative inspections that occur routinely, and without probable cause to believe that they will uncover violations of regulatory requirements. There are two other important situations in which the Fourth Amendment permits administrative inspections. First, many agencies have statutory or regulatory authority to do "emergency" inspections. In this context, an "emergency" means that an immediate inspection is reasonably thought necessary to protect life, health, or property. For example, the EPA may learn that a local company is dumping a highly toxic chemical into a stream that supplies drinking water. In that situation, the

Fourth Amendment would permit the EPA to inspect the company's premises without a warrant, even if the company were not part of a pervasively regulated industry. The inspection would have to be limited, however, to discovering and dealing with the emergency. *See, e.g., Michigan v. Tyler*, 436 U.S. 499 (1978).

Second, many agencies, such as OSHA, have statutory authority to inspect a business based on probable cause to believe that an inspection will reveal a violation of a regulatory requirement. Probable cause may be furnished, for example, by an employee's complaint about a dangerous condition at her place of employment. *See, e.g.*, 29 U.S.C. § 657(f)(1) (authorizing OSHA to do "special inspection[s]" based on employee complaints). In that situation, the Fourth Amendment allows OSHA to do a probable-cause inspection if it gets a warrant based on a showing of probable cause. Similar to emergency inspections, however, the scope of a probable-cause inspection is usually tied to its justification. This means that, during a probable-cause inspection, inspectors ordinarily can look only for evidence of the violation for which they have probable cause. *See Trinity Industries, Inc. v. OSHRC*, 16 F.3d 1455 (6th Cir. 1994). Of course, a business that has committed many violations can be routinely inspected more often than one with a clean record.

Although we have been discussing administrative inspections as if they were totally different from traditional searches by the police for evidence of crime, the reality is not so clear-cut. Indeed, many regulatory violations carry criminal penalties. Recognizing this, the Supreme Court in *New York v. Burger* said that an administrative inspection cannot be a "pretext" for a traditional law-enforcement search for evidence of crime. 482 U.S. at 716-717 n.27. The Court in *New York v. Burger* also held, however, that an administrative inspection was not pretextual merely because it revealed evidence that was used in a prosecution and it was conducted by a police officer. Because of that holding, it is rare for a court to invalidate an administrative inspection as a pretext. *See, e.g., United States v. Aukai*, 497 F.3d 955 (9th Cir. 2007) (*en banc*) (upholding screening of airport passengers for guns and bombs by Transportation Safety Agency as an administrative search).

The final important question about administrative inspections concerns the consequences of an illegal inspection. In criminal proceedings, courts usually exclude evidence obtained in violation of the Fourth Amendment. This "exclusionary rule" generally does not apply, however, to civil proceedings. Since administrative proceedings are civil in nature, the exclusionary rule usually does not apply in those proceedings. For example, the Supreme Court has held that illegally obtained evidence can be used in an administrative proceeding to deport an illegal alien. *See INS v. Lopez-Mendoza*, 468 U.S. 1032 (1984). The Court has also refused to apply the exclusionary rule in other types of administrative proceedings. *See, e.g., Pennsylvania Board of Probation & Parole v. Scott*, 524 U.S. 357 (1998) (parole revocation hearing). Nevertheless, some lower federal courts have held that the exclusionary rule applies to some administrative proceedings that impose civil fines. *See, e.g., Trinity Industries*, 16 F.3d at 1461; *see also Caracomo v. Holder*, 713 F.3d 916 (8th Cir. 2013) (noting that some circuits have held that egregious or widespread Fourth Amendment violations could require exclusion of evidence from removal proceedings). Even these courts, however, would allow illegally obtained evidence to be used in administrative proceedings intended to correct or prevent (as distinguished from punishing) regulatory violations. *See Trinity Industries*, 16 F.3d. at 1461-1462. Thus, the lawyer who seeks to exclude illegally obtained evidence from an administrative proceeding will ordinarily have an uphill battle.

In sum, an administrative inspection will not violate the Fourth Amendment if (1) it takes place in an area open to the public (in which case it is not a "search" for Fourth Amendment purposes); (2) it takes place in a residence or ordinary business under a warrant issued based on a showing that the inspection comports with reasonable administrative or legislative standards; (3) it involves a closely regulated business and occurs under an inspection program that meets the three-part test of *New York v. Burger*; (4) it is justified by probable cause to believe that an immediate, warrantless search is needed to respond to an emergency; or (5) it occurs under a warrant based on probable cause to believe that an inspection will uncover evidence of statutory or regulatory violations. Even when an inspection violates the Fourth Amendment, the Fourth Amendment will not require evidence found during the inspection to be excluded from a civil proceeding. The following example gives you practice with administrative inspections.

Example

The New Jersey Freshwater Wetlands Protection Act (FWPA) regulates freshwater wetlands in New Jersey, including wetlands on residential property. The FWPA requires a permit before a property owner can fill in or otherwise disturb a freshwater wetland on his or her property. Permits are issued by the New Jersey Department of Environmental Protection (DEP), which often attaches conditions to the permits. To ensure compliance with permit conditions, DEP can enter onto the property to inspect it and do soil and water tests. Before entering the property, however, the DEP official must present proper credentials. In that event, the FWPA says that "[t]he permittee shall allow" the official to make the entry. If the property owner refuses, DEP has three options. It can order the owner to permit entry; it can fine the owner for refusing entry; and it can go to court for a court order requiring the owner to permit entry. The FWPA does not expressly address whether a DEP official can forcibly enter onto residential property without the owner's consent or a court order.

Kim and Kendra Gruber own a home on land in New Jersey with a freshwater wetland on it. The wetland is subject to a permit issued, with conditions, by the DEP under the FWPA. The Grubers get into a dispute with the DEP that eventually presents three questions to the New Jersey Supreme Court:

1. As applied to residential property subject to FWPA permits, does the FWPA's warrantless inspection scheme fall within the warrant exception for "closely regulated" businesses?
2. Does the FWPA authorize forcible, nonconsensual entries onto residential properties without a warrant or other court order?
3. If the answer to the second question is "no," does the FWPA satisfy the Fourth Amendment as applied to residential property subject to an FWPA permit?

How should the court answer these questions?

Explanation

In the case on which this Example is based, the New Jersey Supreme Court answered these questions as follows.

1. The exception for closely regulated businesses recognized in cases such as *New York v. Burger* does not apply "to the more heightened privacy interests that are associated with a private, residential property." *New Jersey Dept. of Envtl. Protection v. Huber*, 63 A.3d 197, 211 (N.J. 2013)
2. The FWPA does not authorize "forcible, nonconsensual entry into the backyard of a residential property owner." *Id.* at 215. Instead, as in *Marshall v. Barlow's, Inc.*, 436 U.S. 307 (1978), the FWPA's regulatory scheme "represents a choice to proceed by [judicial] process when entry is refused." *Id.* Also, similar to *Barlow's*, under the FWPA, courts in New Jersey could issue orders requiring permittees to allow DEP inspections "not only on specific evidence of an existing violation but also upon a showing that reasonable legislative or administrative standards for conducting an . . . inspection are satisfied." *Id.* (internal quotation marks omitted).
3. So interpreted, the FWPA's inspection scheme could not "fairly be viewed as unreasonable as applied to a residential homeowner whose property is subject to a FWPA permit." The court reasoned that, "by seeking the permit to disturb land on or near otherwise statutorily protected wetlands, a landowner and his or her successors in title are bound to compliance with the permit. That includes compliance with the permitting scheme's mechanism that authorizes reasonable entry onto land affected by the permit to ensure compliance" with the permit. *Id.*

In short, the Fourth Amendment permitted an administrative inspection scheme under which an agency official could demand entry to private, noncommercial land without a warrant and the landowner could be civilly fined for refusing to permit entry. Significantly, however, the statutory scheme did not authorize forcible, nonconsensual entry onto private, noncommercial land without a court order.

IV. OBTAINING DOCUMENTS AND TESTIMONY

In addition to going out and getting information—by conducting an inspection, for example—an agency can have the information come to it. An agency can get much information to come to it just by asking for the information. In addition to the voluntary approach, many agencies also can compel the production of information. The two main ways in which that compulsion is exercised are through reporting requirements and subpoenas.

A. Reporting Requirements

Reporting requirements typically apply to more than one entity and require reports to be made periodically. You are no doubt familiar with the reporting requirement that compels almost everyone in this country to report income to the IRS every year. Many other agencies likewise use reporting requirements to gather the information they need to administer the law.

While some reporting requirements are imposed directly by statute, others are established by an agency regulation or order. For example, there is a statute authorizing the Secretary of Treasury to promulgate regulations requiring banks to report transactions involving large amounts of currency. *See* 31 U.S.C. § 5313. An agency does not need a specific grant of statutory authority, however, to impose reporting requirements. Often, an agency's reporting requirement will fall within a generalized statutory grant of rulemaking authority. The courts have also authorized agencies to impose reporting requirements through adjudicative orders. *See Appeal of FTC Line of Business Report Litigation*, 595 F.2d 685 (D.C. Cir. 1978), *cert. denied*, 439 U.S. 958 (1978).

Just as there are many sources of legal authority for various agencies to impose reporting requirements, there are also many laws that restrict that authority. One set of restrictions applicable to almost all agency reporting requirements is imposed by the Paperwork Reduction Act, to which we turn next. Additional restrictions on reporting requirements are imposed by the Fourth and Fifth Amendments. We defer our discussion of these constitutional restrictions until after our discussion of agency subpoenas. That is because the Fourth and Fifth Amendments impose limits on reporting requirements that are similar to the limits they impose on agency subpoenas.

1. Paperwork Reduction Act

Far be it from us to devote too much paper to discussing the Paperwork Reduction Act! Nonetheless, the Act deserves attention, for it applies to almost all reporting and recordkeeping requirements that federal agencies impose. Moreover, the aim of the Act is not just to reduce paperwork. The Act aims to make the government's collection of information more efficient and less expensive for all concerned. The Act seeks to achieve these aims primarily by requiring agencies (1) to plan carefully before they collect information, and (2) to have their proposed collections of information reviewed by a component of the Office of Management and Budget (OMB), which is part of the Executive Office of the President.[2] OMB has additional power under more recent legislation that is aimed to improve the quality of information disseminated by agencies.

Consistent with its ambitious goals, the Act casts a broad net. It applies to nearly all federal agencies, including independent agencies, with only a few exceptions.[3] Furthermore, it applies to any "collection of information" by an agency. A "collection of information" is defined to mean the imposition of identical reporting or recordkeeping requirements on, or the posing of identical questions to, ten or more people. 44 U.S.C. § 3502(3). This definition makes the Act applicable not only when an agency requires ten or more people to give information to the government but also when the agency requires them to give information to the public. For example, the Act applies when an agency requires chemical manufacturers to put warning labels on their products.[4] Moreover, the Act applies not only when an agency's collection of information is routine—for example, when an agency requires yearly reports—but also when the agency collects information during an investigation of "a category of individuals or entities such

2. The Executive Office of the President includes the President, the White House Office, the Office of the Vice President, the Council of Economic Advisors, the Council on Environmental Quality, the National Security Council, the Office of Administration, the Office of Management and Budget, the Office of National Drug Control Policy, the Office of Policy Development, the Office of Science and Technology Policy, and the Office of the United States Trade Representative. *See* U.S. Government Manual, *available at* http://www.usgovernmentmanual.gov/.

3. The Act does not apply to the Government Accountability Office (formerly known as the Government Accounting Office); the Federal Election Commission; the governments of the District of Columbia and federal territories and possessions; and government-owned, contractor-operated facilities. 44 U.S.C. § 3502(1). The courts have also held that the United States Postal Service is not an agency subject to the Paperwork Reduction Act, *see Shane v. Buck*, 817 F.2d 87 (10th Cir. 1987); *Kuzma v. United States Postal Service*, 798 F.2d 29 (2d Cir. 1986).

4. This feature of the Act supersedes the Court's decision in *Dole v. United Steelworkers*, 494 U.S. 26 (1990). The Court in *Dole* held that the Act did not apply to OSHA regulations that required the manufacturers of hazardous workplace chemicals to label their products and take other steps to advise the public of the hazards. The Court interpreted the Act, as it then existed, to apply only when the government sought information for its own use. Amendments to the Act in 1995 legislatively overruled that interpretation.

as a class of licensees or an entire industry." 44 U.S.C. § 3518(c)(2). The Act does *not* apply, however, to the collection of information in: criminal investigations or prosecutions, civil actions to which a federal official or entity is a party, or administrative actions or investigations involving specific individuals or entities (as distinguished from investigations of entire categories of individuals or entities). *Id.* § 3518(c)(1). Thus, the Act usually does not apply to an agency's issuance of subpoenas, which, by their nature, are directed to specific individuals or entities. *See United States v. Saunders*, 951 F.2d 1065, 1066-1067 (9th Cir. 1991).

The Act prescribes a detailed process for agencies to follow before they undertake a "collection of information." *See* 44 U.S.C. § 3506(b). Every agency must designate a "Chief Information Officer" to review each proposed collection of information for compliance with the Act. *Id.* § 3506(a)(2) and (c)(1). After review by the officer, the agency publishes notice of the proposed collection in the Federal Register and allows 60 days for public comment. *Id.* § 3506(c)(2)(A). When the proposed collection is contained in a proposed agency rule, the notice of proposed rulemaking serves this function. *Id.* § 3506(c)(2)(B). The agency also must certify that the proposed collection meets certain requirements, including that the collection (1) is necessary for the agency's proper performance of its functions, (2) does not unnecessarily duplicate other information reasonably accessible to the agency, and (3) is minimally burdensome. *Id.* § 3506(c)(3).

In addition to providing for public comment, the agency must submit a description of the proposed collection, together with supporting documents, to the Office of Management and Budget. The submission is reviewed by a component of OMB: the Office of Information and Regulatory Affairs (OIRA). When the agency makes its submission, it notifies the public of the submission in the Federal Register. The public then gets 30 days to submit comments to OIRA. 44 U.S.C. § 3507(a) and (b). OIRA must determine within 60 days whether the proposed collection "is necessary for the proper performance of the functions of the agency, including whether the information shall have practical utility." *Id.* § 3508. If the proposed collection meets that standard, OIRA approves it. The approval is good for up to three years, after which the agency has to seek extension of OIRA approval. *Id.* § 3507(g).

Suppose that OIRA decides that a proposed collection does not meet the "necessary for proper performance" standard. At that point, OIRA's power depends on whether or not a proposed collection is contained in an agency rule. If the proposed collection is *not* contained in an agency rule, OIRA can disapprove the proposed collection outright. This means, for most agencies, that the agency cannot undertake the collection. 44 U.S.C. §§ 3507(c) and 3508. There is an exception for independent agencies, however; they can veto OIRA's disapproval as long as they publicly explain their veto. *Id.* § 3507(f). If a proposed collection is contained in an agency rule, OIRA can file comments on the proposed collection, but its disapproval power is limited. OIRA cannot disapprove the proposed collection in an agency rule merely because it fails the "necessary for proper performance" standard. OIRA can disapprove the proposed collection in an agency rule, however, if the agency's responses to OIRA's comments are "unreasonable." *Id.* § 3507(d)(4)(C). A disapproval in this situation, like the disapproval of a collection that is not in an agency rule, generally means that an agency cannot do the collection. Again, however, an independent agency can veto the disapproval. The bottom line is that OIRA has a large say in whether a government agency can collect information.

Now suppose that 60 days go by without OIRA's (1) disapproving a proposed collection that is not contained in an agency rule, or (2) commenting on a proposed collection that is contained in an agency rule. In those situations, approval is inferred. 44 U.S.C. § 3507(c)(3) and (d)(3). The idea behind this was to ensure that an agency's collection of information is not delayed by OIRA's failure to respond to the proposed collection.

The Act has little to say about judicial review of OIRA decisions on proposed collections of information. All the Act says is that judicial review is not available for a decision by OIRA "to approve or not act upon a collection of information contained in an agency rule." 44 U.S.C. § 3507(d)(6). This may imply that judicial review is available for OIRA's decision to *disapprove* a collection contained in an agency rule. A separate question is whether judicial review is available when OIRA approves, disapproves, or fails to act on collections that are *not* contained in an agency rule. That is unsettled.

In any event, the scarce mention of judicial review in the Act probably reflects Congress's expectation that the Act would be enforced mostly through the political process, rather than the judicial process. That expectation seems to have been accurate so far. OIRA rarely disapproves a collection outright; most problems seem to be worked out through the administrative process established under the Act.

Once OIRA approves of a collection, it must assign the collection a control number. The agency must display this control number whenever it collects the information. For example, if the agency collects information by having people fill out a form, the control number must appear on the form. *See* 44 U.S.C. § 3506(c)(1)(B)(i). In addition, the agency must advise people that if a control number is not displayed, they do not have to provide the information. 44 U.S.C. § 3506(c)(3)(G) and (c)(1)(B)(iii)(V). If the agency fails to display the control number or fails to advise a person that he or she does not have to respond without a control number, the person cannot be penalized for failing to provide information. *Id.* § 3512.

The consequences of an agency's failure to display a control number are dramatically illustrated in *Saco River Cellular, Inc. v. FCC*, 133 F.3d 25 (D.C. Cir.), *cert. denied*, 525 U.S. 813 (1998). *Saco River* involved the FCC's award of a license to provide cellular phone service in Portland, Maine. The FCC initially rejected an application for that license from a company called PortCell because of PortCell's failure to follow an FCC regulation. The regulation required PortCell to submit certain financial information to the FCC when PortCell applied for the license. The FCC later determined that this regulation was a "collection of information" subject to the Paperwork Reduction Act. The regulation therefore should have been submitted to OIRA for review. The regulation had not been submitted for OIRA review, however, and consequently it had never received a control number. After realizing its mistake, the FCC reinstated PortCell's application and awarded the license to PortCell, having previously found PortCell the most qualified applicant. At the same time, the FCC took the license away from the company that had originally gotten it (and was less qualified). The FCC decided that this was necessary to avoid penalizing PortCell for failing to respond to a collection of information that lacked a control number. The D.C. Circuit upheld the FCC's decision. By that time, the company that originally received the license had built a cellular system for Portland, Maine, and had been operating it for almost four years.

In addition to requiring an agency to display a control number, the Paperwork Reduction Act requires an agency to provide some other information when it collects information. (That seems only fair, doesn't it?) For example, the agency must explain why it wants the information; whether providing the information is voluntary, mandatory, or required to get a government benefit; and how long it will take for the person from whom the information is sought to gather the information and report it. 44 U.S.C. § 3506(c)(3)(F) and (G). If you want to see how one agency meets these requirements, look at the instructions that accompany your federal income-tax form. The instructions include a "Disclosure, Privacy Act, and Paperwork Reduction Act Notice." You may be particularly interested in finding out how long the IRS estimates it will take the average person to fill out IRS Form 1040.[5] You should find similar "Paperwork Reduction Act" notices on virtually every other federal form that requires you to provide information.

Legislation enacted in 2000 gave OMB powers to improve the quality of information disseminated by federal agencies. The 2000 legislation is known (interchangeably) as the Information (or Data) Quality Act. It is codified in a note following a provision in the Paperwork Reduction Act. The Data Quality Act requires OMB to issue guidelines to federal agencies "for ensuring and maximizing the quality, objectivity, utility, and integrity of information disseminated by Federal agencies." 44 U.S.C. § 3516 Note. The Act also directs federal agencies to issue their own guidelines. An agency's guidelines must not only ensure information quality but also enable people to "seek and obtain correction of" any information maintained or

5. O.K., we will not keep you in suspense. The government's estimate for the average time needed to complete IRS Form 1040 for the year 2023 was 17 hours.

disseminated by the agency that does not meet OMB's data quality guidelines. Enforcement of these new requirements, like enforcement of the original Paperwork Reduction Act, is likely to occur primarily through the political process; it is unclear to what extent they are judicially enforceable. *See Salt Inst. v. Leavitt*, 440 F.3d 156, 159 (4th Cir. 2006) (holding that Data Quality Act "creates no legal rights in any third parties"); *cf. Miss. v. EPA*, 744 F.3d 1334, 1347 (D.C. Cir. 2013) (reviewing EPA action for compliance with EPA guidelines issued under Data Quality Act).

Example

Miriam Stone, a law student, applied for a federal loan so she could pay for the tuition and expenses of her second year of law school. She filled out a form from the U.S. Department of Education called the "Free Application for Federal Student Aid" (FAFSA). The government loaned her $10,000 less than she wanted. This was apparently because she had a large amount of money in a bank account, reflecting savings from her first career. After studying the Paperwork Reduction Act, she went back and looked at a copy of her FAFSA. She did not see any control number. She has two questions for you (a classmate in her administrative law class):

1. Is the FAFSA subject to the Paperwork Reduction Act?
2. If it is, and her loan information was collected in violation of the Act, is she entitled to get an additional $10,000 loan from the government?

Explanation

1. The FAFSA is precisely the type of form that is subject to the Paperwork Reduction Act. It is a "collection of information" by an "agency," the U.S. Department of Education. For this reason, the actual FAFSA has a control number (1845-0001). The FAFSA also contains the other information required by the Paperwork Reduction Act, such as an explanation of why the government is collecting the information ("to determine if you are eligible to receive financial aid and the amount that you are eligible to receive"); and how long it should take to fill out the current version of the FAFSA (50-55 minutes).
2. If your instincts tell you that Miriam would not get an extra $10,000, you are right. A violation of the Paperwork Reduction Act gives you a *defense* when the government seeks to punish you for not providing information. *See* 44 U.S.C. § 3512. It does not, however, create a private cause of action. *See Util. Air Regulatory Grp. v. EPA*, 744 F.3d 741, 750 n.6 (D.C. Cir. 2014). Under *Saco River*, the most that Miriam can probably ask is that the government re-process her loan application, using a form that complies

with the Paperwork Reduction Act. If she still does not qualify for any more money because of her savings, she is out of luck. Her situation is different from that of PortCell in *Saco River*. Except for PortCell's failure to comply with an information collection that violated the Paperwork Reduction Act, it was the most qualified applicant for the license. That is why it got the license after the FCC reinstated its application.

2. Subpoenas

Agency subpoenas differ from reporting requirements in at least four ways. First, whereas reporting requirements typically apply to whole categories of people, agency subpoenas are directed to specifically named persons. Second, whereas reporting requirements typically require the production of documents, an agency subpoena may require the person named in the subpoena to produce either documents—in which case it is called a "subpoena duces tecum"—or testimony—in which case it is called a "subpoena ad testificandum." Third, an agency does not need express statutory authority to impose reporting requirements; that authority can be inferred, for example, from a broad grant of rulemaking power. In contrast, an agency *does* need specific statutory authority to issue subpoenas. *See Serr v. Sullivan*, 390 F.2d 619 (3d Cir. 1968). Fourth, and perhaps most important, agency subpoenas are enforceable through judicial contempt proceedings. Reporting requirements are usually enforced in other ways. In this last respect, agency subpoenas work somewhat like subpoenas issued under a court's authority.

A typical statute illustrating these features concerns the Federal Trade Commission. The statute gives the FTC "power to require by subpoena the attendance and testimony of witnesses and the production of all such documentary evidence relating to any matter under investigation." 15 U.S.C. § 49. A subpoena issued in aid of an agency's investigation is called an investigative subpoena. In addition to authorizing the issuance of investigative subpoenas, the FTC's statute authorizes it to subpoena documents and testimony for its adjudicative proceedings. The FTC's statute also says that if someone disobeys an investigative or adjudicative subpoena, the FTC "may invoke the aid of any court of the United States." *Id.* This means that the FTC can seek a court order requiring the recipient of the subpoena to comply or else be held in contempt.[6]

6. In this section, we discuss an agency's power to subpoena the information that it wants. An agency also sometimes has a duty to issue a subpoena for information that someone else wants. Specifically, an agency may have to issue a subpoena for evidence needed by the party to an administrative adjudication. For example, when an agency seeks to revoke someone's license, the licensee may have a right to have the agency subpoena evidence that the licensee needs to defend against the revocation. An agency's duty to issue adjudicative subpoenas in this sort of situation is prescribed in the APA. Section 555(d) of the APA says, "Agency subpenas authorized by law shall be issued to a party on request and, when required by

The recipient of an agency subpoena has three options. He or she can comply with it, ignore it, or fight it. When the recipient complies with a subpoena by appearing before an agency to produce documents or testimony, the APA gives the recipient the right "to be accompanied, represented, and advised by counsel or, if permitted by the agency, by other qualified representative." 5 U.S.C. § 555(b).

It is unsettled whether ignoring an agency subpoena can directly result in civil penalties being imposed before an opportunity for judicial review of the subpoena. *See Big Ridge v. Fed. Mine Safety & Health Review Commn.*, 715 F.3d 631, 646 (7th Cir. 2013) (stating that "most administrative subpoenas are not self-executing, meaning that the agency cannot seek penalties for noncompliance until after a judicial officer has ordered compliance"); *see also Los Angeles v. Patel*, 135 S. Ct. 2443, 2453 (2015) (stating that, in general, target of administrative subpoena would be entitled to precompliance review by a "neutral decisionmaker" before being penalized for noncompliance). It is clear, however, that ignoring an agency subpoena cannot result in immediate contempt sanctions. Instead, the agency must go to court to enforce the subpoena before a risk of contempt can arise. Proceedings to enforce subpoenas issued by federal agencies are usually brought in a federal district court. In an enforcement proceeding, the recipient of the subpoena can contest the validity of the subpoena. "On contest," the APA says, "the court shall sustain the subpena[7] or similar process or demand to the extent that it is found to be in accordance with law." 5 U.S.C. § 555(d). The APA also says that, if the court sustains the subpoena, it "shall issue an order requiring the appearance of the witness or the production of the evidence or data within a reasonable time under penalty of punishment for contempt in case of contumacious failure to comply." *Id.* Thus, disobedience of a subpoena ordinarily can result in contempt sanctions only after a court has issued an order

---

rules of procedure, on a statement or showing of general relevance and reasonable scope of the evidence sought." The key word for present purposes is "party." A "party" refers to someone involved in an "agency proceeding." 5 U.S.C. § 551(3). The term "agency proceeding" includes rulemaking, and adjudication, including licensing. *Id.* § 551(12). In practice, however, usually only parties to adjudications have a need for an agency to issue a subpoena on their behalf. The important thing is that people who are merely under investigation by an agency, but not involved in an "agency proceeding" (because, for example, no proceeding has begun), generally have no right to have an agency issue a subpoena on their behalf. Cf. *Jenkins v. McKeithen*, 395 U.S. 411, 431 (1969) (plurality opinion) (suggesting that due process entitled the target of an agency to compulsory process when the agency could "make specific findings of guilt").

7. As you might have guessed, there is no difference between a "subpoena" and a "subpena"; the latter is an alternative spelling that is now obsolete. Notice, however, that the APA refers not only to subpoenas but also to "similar process or demand[s]." This reflects that not all agency demands for information from named people or entities are called "subpoenas." For example, the FTC is authorized to issue "civil investigative demands" that work much like subpoenas. 15 U.S.C. § 57b-1. The Internal Revenue Service is authorized to issue a "summons" that works like a subpoena. *See* 26 U.S.C. § 7602(a)(2).

enforcing the subpoena and the recipient of the subpoena has violated that court order. Agencies do not have the power by themselves to hold someone in contempt for disobeying an agency subpoena.

If the recipient of a subpoena decides to fight it, he or she usually need not, and should not, wait until the matter gets to court. Many agencies, including the FTC, have an administrative process for contesting agency subpoenas. *See* 16 C.F.R. § 2.7(k) (petitions to quash investigative subpoenas); 16 C.F.R. § 3.34(c) (motions to quash subpoenas issued in connection with FTC adjudications). Equally important, most agencies will meet informally with the recipient of a subpoena in an attempt to work out the recipient's objections to the scope of the subpoena or the deadline for complying with it. If the recipient cannot resolve things with the agency, then she can disobey the subpoena and wait for the agency to go to court to enforce it. The recipient usually cannot take the initiative by seeking judicial review of an agency subpoena before the agency seeks judicial enforcement. *See, e.g., Schulz v. IRS*, 395 F.3d 463 (2d Cir. 2005), *on reh'g*, 413 F.3d 297 (2005).

When an agency seeks judicial enforcement of a subpoena, the recipient can challenge the subpoena on the same two grounds that apply to other coercive agency methods of collecting information: the recipient can argue that the subpoena exceeds the agency's authority or that it violates affirmative legal restrictions. Arguments about the agency's authority will ordinarily focus on the specific statute granting subpoena authority and any regulations implementing that authority. Affirmative legal restrictions on agency subpoenas, as well as on agency reporting requirements, include restrictions imposed by the Fourth and Fifth Amendments. We turn to those next.

B. Fourth Amendment Limits on Reporting Requirements and Subpoenas

When an agency inspects a workplace or other private premises, it is obviously conducting a "search" that is subject to the Fourth Amendment. It may be less obvious why the Fourth Amendment applies when, instead of going out and getting information through an inspection, the agency requires the information to come to it, pursuant to a reporting requirement or an agency subpoena. In the latter situation, the agency is not "searching" any place or person in the usual sense. Nor is it "seizing" anything from anybody; rather, someone is handing over information to the agency (albeit under compulsion). The Supreme Court has accordingly characterized administrative subpoenas as entailing only "constructive" searches. *See, e.g., Oklahoma Press Publishing Co. v. Walling*, 327 U.S. 186, 202 (1946). The Court has not required agencies to obtain a warrant, or to demonstrate probable cause, in order to issue subpoenas. Nonetheless, the Court has construed the

Fourth Amendment to put some limits on agency subpoenas, as well as on reporting requirements. The Fourth Amendment limits on agency subpoenas and reporting requirements, however, are much less stringent than the Fourth Amendment limits on administrative inspections.

This laxness has not always existed. Early Supreme Court cases suggested that the Fourth Amendment significantly restricted an agency's power to compel people to produce information. The leading case was *Federal Trade Commn. v. American Tobacco Co.*, 264 U.S. 298 (1924). In that case, the Court held that FTC subpoenas to tobacco companies exceeded the FTC's statutory authority. The Court narrowly construed the statute under which the subpoenas were issued. The Court determined that a narrow construction was necessary to avoid the Fourth Amendment problem that would be caused by interpreting the statute "to direct fishing expeditions into private papers on the possibility that they may disclose evidence of crime." *Id.* at 306.

The Court abandoned its stringent approach to the scope of agency subpoena power in later cases, the most important of which is *United States v. Morton Salt Co.*, 338 U.S. 632 (1950). In *Morton Salt*, the Court upheld FTC orders requiring salt producers to file reports proving compliance with a prior court decree. The Court assumed that the FTC was "engaged in a mere fishing expedition" in the sense that it had no evidence that the salt producers were violating the decree. The Court made clear that such evidence is not necessary. It explained that an agency like the FTC, which has investigative subpoena power, is more like a grand jury than a court. Like a grand jury, such an agency "does not depend on a case or controversy for power to get evidence but can investigate merely on suspicion that the law is being violated, or even just because it wants assurance that it is not." *Id.* at 642-643. The Court confirmed that an agency's exercise of this investigative power to compel production of information is subject to the Fourth Amendment. The Court determined, however, that the Fourth Amendment will be satisfied "if the inquiry is within the authority of the agency, the demand is not too indefinite and the information sought is reasonably relevant." *Id.* at 652. The Court summarized that "the gist" of the Fourth Amendment is "that the disclosure sought shall not be unreasonable." *Id.* at 652-653. *See also Oklahoma Press Publishing Co. v. Walling*, 327 U.S. 186 (1946).

The *Morton Salt* test construes the Fourth Amendment to impose three limits on agency subpoenas. First, the subpoena must fall within the agency's authority. This means that the subpoena must be issued for the purpose for which the agency is authorized to issue subpoenas, and it must be issued using proper procedures. Second, the subpoena cannot be too indefinite and, relatedly, it cannot be overly burdensome. *See Donovan v. Lone Steer, Inc.*, 464 U.S. 408 (1984). Third, the subpoena must seek information that is relevant to a proper subject of investigation for the agency. *See Endicott Johnson Corp. v. Perkins*, 317 U.S. 501 (1943).

Courts rarely invalidate agency subpoenas under the *Morton Salt* test. Invalidation is rare partly because subpoenas are almost always issued before the agency has finished its investigation or other proceeding. Thus, judicial challenges to the subpoenas are interlocutory. If courts regularly decided interlocutory challenges to the agency's authority, the administrative process would severely bog down. Similarly, it can be hard for a court to determine the relevance of the information sought before the outcome of the agency's investigation or proceeding is known. Finally, courts tend to take claims that a subpoena is too indefinite or oppressive with a grain of salt. Courts realize that agency subpoenas must be somewhat indefinite, since the agency would not ask for information if the agency already knew it. Courts also realize that agency investigations, like other legal proceedings, almost invariably impose some burdens. Usually, a court will find a subpoena too burdensome only if compliance with it "would threaten or seriously disrupt . . . normal business operations." *EEOC v. Ranstad*, 685 F.3d 433, 452 (4th Cir. 2012) (internal quotation marks omitted).

Nonetheless, there are cases invalidating agency subpoenas under each of the *Morton Salt* requirements. For example, courts occasionally invalidate a subpoena because it has been issued for an improper purpose. In particular, it is improper for an agency to issue a subpoena for the purpose of harassment. *See United States v. LaSalle National Bank*, 437 U.S. 298 (1978). Once a court decides that an agency has identified a proper purpose for its subpoena, the court will use that purpose to judge the relevance of the information sought. As long as the agency does not articulate the purpose of its investigation too broadly, courts will usually reject relevance challenges as long as information sought might be relevant to that purpose. An agency can sometimes get into trouble when it describes the purpose of its subpoena too broadly. For example, the D.C. Circuit invalidated an administrative subpoena issued for the purpose of uncovering "wrongdoing as yet unknown." *In re Sealed Case (Administrative Subpoena)*, 42 F.3d 1412 (D.C. Cir. 1994). Even when an agency has a legitimate purpose for the subpoena, it can run into trouble if the subpoena's demand is too vague or onerous. For example, the Eleventh Circuit refused to enforce an EEOC subpoena that had, at most, a "tenuous" connection to a legitimate subject of investigation and imposed a "significant" compliance burden. *EEOC v. Royal Caribbean Cruises, Ltd.*, 771 F.3d 757, 763 (11th Cir. 2014). These are rare cases, though, for the reasons that we discussed in the last paragraph.

Although *Morton Salt* involved an investigative order issued by an agency to specified artificial entities, the *Morton Salt* test has been applied outside that setting. First, the Court has applied the *Morton Salt* test to review a Fourth Amendment challenge to a statutory reporting requirement. *California Bankers Assn. v. Shultz*, 416 U.S. 21 (1974) (upholding the Bank Secrecy Act of 1970).[8]

---

8. In a later case under the Bank Secrecy Act, the Court held that a bank customer could not challenge a subpoena to his bank for his bank records. *See United States v. Miller*, 425 U.S. 435 (1976). The Court based that holding on the principle that the Fourth Amendment protects

Second, the lower courts have applied the *Morton Salt* test to agency subpoenas directed to human beings. *See, e.g., United States v. Gurley*, 384 F.3d 316 (6th Cir. 2004) (applying *Morton Salt* test to EPA information demand served on individual). Thus, *Morton Salt* establishes a Fourth Amendment test for a wide variety of agency subpoenas and other regulatory demands for information.

To sum up, the Fourth Amendment has something to say about agency investigative demands. But it does not speak in the familiar language of warrants or probable cause. Instead, the overarching requirement under the *Morton Salt* test is one of "reasonableness." It is rare for a court to find that an agency subpoena is unreasonable under that test. Consider how the test applies in the following examples.

Example

The Equal Employment Opportunity Commission (EEOC) has authority to investigate charges that an employer has discriminated against an employee because of her sex. As part of this authority, the EEOC can subpoena an employer for documents pertinent to a charge of employment discrimination.

The EEOC receives a written complaint from Tanya Shelton, a partner in the law firm of Toodles and Prigg, charging the firm with discriminating against her and the other female partners. The EEOC issues a subpoena to the firm seeking a massive amount of documents related to the treatment of the firm's partners. Toodles and Prigg refuses to comply with the subpoena, and so the EEOC files an action in federal district court to enforce the subpoena. In that action, Toodles and Prigg argues that the federal employment discrimination statute does not apply to it because the partners are not in an employer-employee relationship. Assume that this argument is at least plausible. Should the court consider it in the subpoena-enforcement proceeding?

Explanation

Most courts would not consider Toodles and Prigg's argument because it is not the type of argument that courts will address in a proceeding to enforce a subpoena. The firm argues that the statute that it is suspected of violating does not cover the firm. The Supreme Court, however, has held that courts generally should not consider arguments about statutory coverage in proceedings to enforce an agency subpoena. *See Endicott Johnson Corp. v. Perkins*, 317 U.S. 501, 508-509 (1943). The "coverage" question is an issue on the

---

only information that a person reasonably expects will stay private. The Court in *United States v. Miller* ruled that, once you turn information over to a third party, such as a bank, you cannot reasonably expect the information to remain private. You can appreciate the importance of this ruling if you think about how much personal information you give to third parties such as banks, credit card companies, health care professionals, and so on.

merits. In other words, it is a defense that Toodles and Prigg can raise if, after completing its investigation, the EEOC or Ms. Shelton brings a proceeding to hold the firm liable for sex discrimination. A liability proceeding may never happen. Indeed, after it reviews the subpoenaed documents, the EEOC may agree with Toodles and Prigg that it is not subject to the employment discrimination law. Before the EEOC gets those documents, however, the agency may not have the evidence it needs to litigate the coverage issue. *See, e.g., EEOC v. Sidley Austin Brown & Wood*, 315 F.3d 696 (7th Cir. 2002).

Example

The Occupational Safety and Health Act requires employers to provide "employment and a place of employment which are free from recognized hazards." 29 U.S.C. § 654(a)(1). To enforce this duty, the Occupational Safety and Health Administration (OSHA) can "investigate . . . any" place "where work is performed by an employee of an employer." *Id.* § 657(a). OSHA also can issue subpoenas "[i]n making [its] investigations." *Id.* § 657(b).

OSHA receives complaints from two employees of the Precise Printing Company. The employees complain that they have back and neck problems from their jobs at Precise Printing, which require them to sit in front of a computer screen all day. In response to the complaints, OSHA begins an investigation of Precise Printing. As part of that investigation, OSHA subpoenas from Precise Printing all documents related to any back or neck injuries suffered by any of its white-collar employees in the last five years. In resisting judicial enforcement of the subpoena, Precise Printing makes two arguments. First, it claims that the subpoena is too broad, because it is not limited to investigating the two employee complaints that prompted OSHA's investigation. Second, it claims that compliance with the subpoena is too burdensome. To support that claim, it submits the affidavit of an office manager estimating that it will take 200,000 hours to search for responsive documents. OSHA responds that the first argument is wrong as a matter of law and the second argument is factually flawed because the 200,000-hour estimate is inflated. Should the court enforce the subpoena?

Explanation

The court will probably enforce the subpoena. Unlike the subpoena challenge in the last example, Precise's challenge does not concern the merits; Precise is not arguing about whether it is covered by the statute that the agency seeks to enforce or whether Precise has violated any statute. Instead, Precise is arguing that the subpoena is too broad and burdensome. Because these arguments do not concern the merits, the court will consider them, but it will also almost certainly reject them.

Precise's argument about the breadth of the subpoena goes to relevance. It argues that the only relevant documents are those related to the two employee complaints. The problem with this argument is that OSHA's statutory subpoena power is not limited to investigating complaints. Instead, it can subpoena any documents relevant to an employer's duty to provide a workplace "free from recognized hazards." 29 U.S.C. § 654(a)(1). In this respect, OSHA has broader subpoena power than the EEOC, the agency involved in the last example. The EEOC's statutory subpoena power is limited by its more limited statutory power to investigate only specific charges of discrimination. The upshot is that "relevance," for purposes of the *Morton Salt* Fourth Amendment test for subpoenas, varies with the scope of an agency's statutory powers of investigation. *See EEOC v. United Air Lines, Inc.*, 287 F.3d 643, 652-653 (7th Cir. 2002). Most federal agencies that have subpoena power, such as the FTC, have broader subpoena power than the EEOC has. *See also EEOC v. Shell Oil Co.*, 466 U.S. 54 (1984).

OSHA's subpoena power not only differs from the subpoena power of the EEOC; OSHA's subpoena power also differs from OSHA's inspection power. Courts have generally held that, when OSHA gets a warrant to inspect a workplace that is based on employee complaints, the inspection is limited by the scope of those complaints. *See Trinity Industries, Inc. v. OSHRC*, 16 F.3d 1455 (6th Cir. 1994). OSHA's subpoena power is not so limited. This difference between OSHA's subpoena power and its inspection power is partly the result of difference in the statutes prescribing those powers. *Compare* 29 U.S.C. § 657(b) *with id.* § 657(f). It is also partly the result of the Fourth Amendment's differing treatment of subpoenas and administrative inspections. Subpoenas are only "constructive" searches, whereas inspections are actual searches.

As sympathetic as it might seem, Precise's claim of burdensomeness will also probably fail. For one thing, courts tend to be skeptical of an employer's estimate of the burden of complying with a subpoena. We would need more information about the basis for Precise's estimate and about OSHA's reasons for disputing the estimate to know if skepticism is warranted here. In any event, the sheer number of hours that it will take to comply with the subpoena is not as important as its effect on the business. As we mentioned, courts ordinarily require proof that compliance will unduly impair the operation of the business. *See, e.g., EEOC v. Quad/Graphics*, 63 F.3d 642, 648-649 (7th Cir. 1995) (rejecting claim of burdensomeness based on estimate that compliance would take 200,000 hours).

C. Fifth Amendment Limits on Reporting Requirements and Subpoenas

The Fifth Amendment guarantees that "[n]o person . . . shall be compelled in any criminal case to be a witness against himself."[9] You might wonder why this privilege against compelled self-incrimination even comes up in the study of administrative law. After all, the Fifth Amendment could be read to apply only when compulsion is exerted *in a criminal proceeding;* it refers to being "compelled in any criminal case." The Supreme Court has not interpreted the Amendment so narrowly, however. Instead, the Court has held that it protects people from being compelled in *civil* proceedings to give information that could incriminate them in a *future* criminal proceeding. Thus, the privilege can be invoked in administrative proceedings. For example, the Court has held that police officers suspected of misconduct could claim the privilege in an administrative investigation by the state Attorney General. *See Garrity v. New Jersey*, 385 U.S. 493 (1967). The Court has held that prisoners can do likewise in prison disciplinary proceedings. *See Lefkowitz v. Turley*, 414 U.S. 70, 77 (1973). Similarly, attorneys can claim the privilege in disbarment proceedings. *See Spevack v. Klein*, 385 U.S. 511 (1967).

Furthermore, the Court has construed the Fifth Amendment to reach government compulsion that takes the form of a "threat of substantial economic sanction." *Lefkowitz*, 414 U.S. at 82. For example, a government employee cannot be prosecuted based on incriminating information that he or she gave under threat of being fired. *See, e.g., Uniformed Sanitation Men Assn. v. Commissioner of Sanitation*, 392 U.S. 280 (1968). Similarly, a person who holds a government license, such as a license to practice law, cannot be prosecuted based on information that he or she gave under the threat of losing that license. *See Spevack v. Klein*, 385 U.S. 511 (1967). When a person incriminates herself under the government's threat of losing her job or professional license (not to mention the threat of being prosecuted), she is being "compelled" within the meaning of the Fifth Amendment.

As a result of these holdings, the Fifth Amendment can sometimes protect a person from complying with an agency subpoena or other demand for information. To understand the classic situation in which the protection is available, suppose that the FTC subpoenas the owner of a business to testify before the FTC during an FTC investigation of unfair trade practices. If the FTC asks the business owner a question the answer to which could be used to prosecute her for a crime, she can "take the Fifth" and refuse to answer the question. The agency cannot prosecute the witness for

---

9. The Fifth Amendment, like the Fourth Amendment, applies to state and local governments because it is incorporated by the Fourteenth Amendment. *See, e.g., Andresen v. Maryland*, 427 U.S. 463, 470 (1976).

her refusal to answer the question. Nor, if she answers the question under the compulsion of some threatened non-criminal sanction, can the answer be used to prosecute her. Sometimes, to compel a witness to answer an incriminating question, the government must give the witness immunity by promising her that it will not use her answer or any information derived from it to prosecute her. *See* 18 U.S.C. § 6002.

Outside of this situation, however—which involves compelling a person to give oral testimony that could incriminate her—the Fifth Amendment seldom provides protection from agency demands for information. Its limited scope is the result of several features. For one thing, the Fifth Amendment protects only human beings; it does not protect artificial entities such as corporations and partnerships. Thus, when an agency issues a subpoena to a corporation or partnership, that entity cannot resist the subpoena on the ground that the documents or testimony sought by the subpoena could expose the entity to criminal prosecution. *See Wilson v. United States*, 221 U.S. 361 (1911).

Of course, an artificial entity cannot comply with a subpoena without human aid. That is why, when an agency issues a subpoena to a corporation seeking corporate records, for example, the burden of complying with the subpoena falls on the custodian of corporate records. The corporate documents sought under the subpoena will sometimes incriminate the individuals responsible for producing those documents. If so, can these individuals use the Fifth Amendment to resist producing the documents? The answer is usually no, because of three limits on the Fifth Amendment's protection of individuals.

First, a person cannot use the Fifth Amendment to resist producing a *voluntarily prepared* document on the ground that the contents of the document would be incriminating. For example, suppose that a taxpayer voluntarily makes and keeps records revealing that her income was larger than the amount she reported to the IRS. She cannot resist an IRS demand for those records on the ground that their contents would incriminate her of tax crimes. Her Fifth Amendment claim would be rejected because she did not prepare the records under compulsion. *See, e.g., Smith v. Richert*, 35 F.3d 300 (7th Cir. 1994).

Second, a person usually cannot resist producing even documents that the law has *required* her to keep on the ground that the contents of the documents would incriminate her. This is because of the "required records" doctrine. The case establishing this doctrine is *Shapiro v. United States*, 335 U.S. 1 (1948). In *Shapiro*, the Court held that a business owner could be compelled to produce records that he was required to keep under the federal Emergency Price Control Act. Under *Shapiro*, courts have held that the government can compel people to keep records for a legitimate administrative purpose and compel their production even for use in criminal prosecutions. The required records doctrine operates as an exception to the Fifth Amendment.

The primary limitation on the required records exception is that the government cannot target recordkeeping requirements to a "selective group inherently suspect of criminal activities." *Marchetti v. United States*, 390 U.S. 39, 57 (1968). Based on that principle, the Court in *Marchetti* struck down a federal law that required professional gamblers to register with the government and pay an occupational tax. The Court likewise struck down a federal law that required the owners of sawed-off shotguns to register those illegal weapons and pay a license fee. *Haynes v. United States*, 390 U.S. 85 (1968). This limitation on the required records exception to the Fifth Amendment prevents the government from using administrative reporting requirements as a pretext for enforcing the criminal laws. In that sense, the limitation is analogous to the Fourth Amendment principle that an administrative inspection cannot be a pretext for a traditional law-enforcement search for evidence of a crime.

Third, the Fifth Amendment does not prevent the government from compelling person *A* to provide information that incriminates person B. The Supreme Court made this limitation clear in *Fisher v. United States*, 425 U.S. 391 (1976). In *Fisher*, the government subpoenaed an accountant for records that would incriminate a taxpayer (but not the accountant). The Court rejected the taxpayer's Fifth Amendment challenge to the subpoena. The Court explained that the Fifth Amendment only protects a person from being compelled to be a witness "against himself." In *Fisher*, the taxpayer was not being compelled to do anything; the compulsion (i.e., the subpoena) was directed at the accountant. The information sought would incriminate not the accountant but the taxpayer. When the person who is compelled is different from the person who would be incriminated, the Fifth Amendment does not apply. *See SEC v. Jerry T. O'Brien, Inc.*, 467 U.S. 735, 742 (1984).

When these limits are combined, they leave only one main situation in which the Fifth Amendment protects people from agency demands for incriminating documents. That is when the documents are prepared voluntarily and the mere act of producing them would tend to incriminate the person who is being compelled to produce them. The "act of production" doctrine was first articulated clearly in *Fisher, supra*. We will illustrate the act of production doctrine using a variation on the facts of *Fisher*.

Suppose that the IRS demanded that a taxpayer produce all of the records in her possession that relate to her income-tax report for the year 2019. Also suppose that one of those documents showed that the taxpayer's income for that year was $100,000, and not $50,000, as she had reported to the IRS. Further, assume that the taxpayer was not required by law to create or keep this incriminating document. The taxpayer could not resist producing this document on the ground that its *contents* would incriminate her. (Because she had prepared the incriminating document voluntarily, the

Fifth Amendment does not entitle her to withhold it on the ground that the contents are incriminating.) The taxpayer might be able to resist producing the incriminating document, however, on the ground that the mere act of producing it would incriminate her. Her production of the document would implicitly "testify" that (1) the document existed; (2) the document was authentic—e.g., not a forgery; and (3) that she had possession of the document at the time of production. In some cases, one or more of these three items of information could be incriminating. Recall that in our example the document made it clear that the taxpayer's income in 2019 was $100,000, and not the $50,000 previously reported. From the taxpayer's possession of that record, a jury might infer that she knew its contents—i.e., knew her true income—an inference that could defeat her defense that her under-reporting of income was just a mistake. Since the act of producing the document could imply guilty knowledge, the taxpayer may well be able to resist producing it based on the "act of production" doctrine of the Fifth Amendment. *See, e.g., United States v. Ponds*, 454 F.3d 313 (D.C. Cir. 2006). *See also United States v. Hubbell*, 530 U.S. 27 (2000).

When all is said and done, the Fifth Amendment influences administrative law mostly when an agency compels someone to testify under the threat of a significant economic sanction. The Fifth Amendment only rarely restricts the power of agencies to compel the production of documents. The restrictions on compelled document production that do exist stem mostly from the "act of production" doctrine.

The following example gives you practice identifying whether any Fifth Amendment restrictions arise in administrative settings.

Example

The State of West Carolina requires the sellers of used automotive parts to have a license and to keep a record of every auto part that they receive. Each record must indicate whether any serial number or other identification number on the auto part "has been altered, defaced or removed." If a licensee fails to keep records that include this information, the licensee is subject to civil fines and license revocation. In addition, the State makes it a felony for a person to receive an auto part "with knowledge that the identification number of the part has been removed or falsified."

Helen Bright is a licensee and the sole proprietor of Barely Used Auto Parts. Helen wants to challenge the provision requiring her to indicate whether a part that she receives has had its serial number or other identification number altered, defaced, or removed. She would argue that this provision violates her privilege against compelled self-incrimination. Is that argument valid?

Explanation

The state law would violate a sole proprietor's privilege against compelled self-incrimination. To begin with, the state law clearly implicates the privilege. It exerts compulsion by threatening Bright with civil fines or the loss of her license if she refuses to produce the records. The threat of a significant economic sanction is one type of compulsion that the Fifth Amendment protects against. Furthermore, the state is compelling Bright both to keep the records, which are a form of "testimony," and to produce them. Finally, these compelled acts could incriminate Bright of a felony; they could indicate that she has knowingly received a part that has had its serial number or other identification number removed or falsified.

Even so, the state law would not violate the Fifth Amendment if it falls within the "required records" exception. West Carolina's law probably would not fall within that exception. As the court explained in the case on which this example is based: "The determinative factor . . . is that [the law] is both directly incriminatory and aimed at a select group suspected of criminal activities. Recording that a serial number has been defaced or altered, without more, subjects the automotive parts proprietor to criminal penalties." *Bionic Auto Parts & Sales, Inc. v. Fahner*, 721 F.2d 1072, 1083 (7th Cir. 1983). In other words, the West Carolina law works like the law struck down in *Marchetti*, which required professional gamblers to identify themselves as such, and the law struck down in *Haynes*, which did the same for people in illegal possession of a firearm. *See also In re Grand Jury Subpoena Duces Tecum to John Doe 1*, 368 F. Supp. 2d 846 (W.D. Tenn. 2005) (holding that required records exception did not apply to federal statute requiring producers of sexually explicit material to keep records of age and identity of participants when requirement was aimed at identifying producers of illegal child pornography).

This conclusion does not prevent West Carolina from getting the information that it wants. West Carolina can still require the sellers of parts to keep records indicating whether the parts that they receive have had the serial numbers removed or altered. The Fifth Amendment will simply prevent West Carolina from using those records or any information derived from them to prosecute the sole proprietors who are required to keep the records.

We should emphasize that it is rare for a law to be invalid under the *Marchetti/Haynes* line of cases. To be distinguished from the laws struck down in those cases, as well as the law that would be struck down in this example, is the law that was upheld in *California v. Byers*, 402 U.S. 424 (1971). In *Byers*, the Court rejected a Fifth Amendment challenge to a California "hit and run" law. The California law made it a crime for someone to leave the scene of a car accident without giving his or her name and address to everyone involved in the accident. The law merely helped the police find people who had committed traffic-related crimes such as drunk driving. It was not targeted, however, at "a highly selective group inherently suspect of criminal activities."

CHAPTER 9

Public Access to Government Information

A popular government without popular information or the means of acquiring it is but a prologue to a farce or a tragedy or perhaps both.

—*Letter from James Madison to W.T. Barry, August 4, 1822*

I. INTRODUCTION

Through the methods described in Chapter 8, the federal government collects much information from the public for various governmental purposes. In addition, the federal government generates much information about its own processes. As a result, the government is a vast storehouse of information that makes the Library of Alexandria look like a little free library.[1]

While the government's collection of private information can be burdensome to the people from whom the information is collected, the resulting collection of information can also be quite valuable. The information in the government's possession can have both commercial value and democratic value. For example, the government may have financial information about Company *A* that would help Company *A*'s competitor, Company B.

1. The Library of Alexandria in Egypt was the largest library of the ancient world. It was reported to have had about 500,000 "books" as of the third century B.C. In contrast, little free libraries are a relatively recent, American invention.

Or the government might have information about the environmental impact of Company *A*'s operations that an environmental organization would want to know. To give a third example, the government undoubtedly has information about the government's own process for regulating Company *A*. Public access to that information can reveal government corruption and incompetence or at least shed light on how the government works.

Even so, public access to information in the government's possession must take into account privacy concerns. For example, some of the information that the government has about Company *A* may constitute trade secrets that should stay confidential. Some of the information that the government has about its own internal processes may warrant protection from disclosure to ensure that government officials can be candid with each other. Because of concerns like this, public access to information in the government's possession is regulated. Lawyers may become involved in disputes over access to government information on behalf of either clients seeking access to it or clients who want to prevent access to it.

Public access to information in the government storehouse is governed primarily by statutes. This chapter discusses four of the major federal statutes governing public access to government information. The first is the Freedom of Information Act (FOIA). Among other things, the FOIA requires federal agencies, with certain exceptions, to give any records they have to anyone who wants them. The second statute is the Government in the Sunshine Act (the Sunshine Act), which, most important to public access, requires independent agencies to open their meetings to the public. The third statute is the Federal Advisory Committee Act (FACA). The FACA regulates groups of people who give the government advice; among other things, the FACA requires those groups to make information about their operations available to the public. The fourth statute is the Privacy Act. In contrast to the first three statutes, its main objective is to limit public access to certain private information.

II. FREEDOM OF INFORMATION ACT

A. In General

The Freedom of Information Act may be the only statute that you will study in administrative law that is well known to people outside the field of administrative law. The FOIA's popularity is no accident. The FOIA was designed for use by anyone who wants information from the federal government. Its purpose "is to ensure an informed citizenry," which is "vital to the functioning of a democratic society." *NLRB v. Robbins Tire & Rubber Co.*,

437 U.S. 214 (1978). The FOIA's general purpose of ensuring open government is qualified, however, by the privacy interests of people that the government has information about and the privacy interests of the government itself. The FOIA attempts to strike a balance between these competing interests.

Whether FOIA strikes the balance properly has been debated since the FOIA was enacted in 1966. No one disputes that the FOIA has often furthered democratic values by informing the public about how the government functions (or malfunctions, in some instances). Nonetheless, the most frequent users of the FOIA are businesses seeking information of commercial value. For example, many businesses use the FOIA to request financial or proprietary information about their competitors. This dominant use of the FOIA worries some people, because the statute was not designed with that use in mind. Another concern is that the government spends more time and money responding to FOIA requests than Congress expected. The unexpected commercial use and high cost of the FOIA led then Professor Antonin Scalia to call the FOIA "the Taj Mahal of the Doctrine of Unanticipated Consequences, the Sistine Chapel of Cost Benefit Analysis Ignored."[2] Supporters of open government recognize that the FOIA can be expensive to administer and that concerns such as national security can justify limitations on disclosure under the FOIA. Supporters contend, however, that the costs of the FOIA are in general outweighed by its difficult-to-quantify benefits and that limitations on disclosure therefore should be as narrow as possible.[3] The differing uses of, and perspectives on, the FOIA are helpful to keep in mind as you learn how the FOIA works.

It may also help you to understand where the FOIA is located and why it is there. The FOIA is codified in Section 552 of the APA. That puts the FOIA right after the APA definition section (Section 551) and before the APA provisions on rulemaking and adjudication (Sections 553 through 557). The FOIA is not the only access statute that has been squeezed between Section 551 and Section 553. In addition to the FOIA (in Section 552), the Privacy Act is codified as Section 552a, and the Government in the Sunshine Act is codified as Section 552b. This organization makes it awkward to flip between Section 551, which defines terms such as "rule making" and "adjudication," and Sections 553 through 557, which describe the rulemaking and adjudication processes. For that reason, the statutory supplements used in courses on administrative law often reproduce Sections 552, 552a, and 552b out of order, after the rest of the 500-series of the APA.

The awkward organization of the current APA reflects the history of statutes regulating public access to government information. The bulk of

2. Antonin Scalia, *The Freedom of Information Act Has No Clothes*, Regulation (1982), at 14.

3. *See* Patricia M. Wald, *The Freedom of Information Act: A Short Case Study in the Perils and Paybacks of Legislating Democratic Values*, 33 Emory L.J. 649, 663-679 (1984).

the FOIA, and all of the Privacy Act and the Sunshine Act, were enacted long after the original APA was enacted in 1946. The original APA had no Section 552a or 552b. The original version of Section 552 of the APA—which, like the current version of Section 552, dealt with public access to government information—was quite short. More important, the original version of Section 552 gave the government great leeway to withhold information from the public. One purpose of the 1966 FOIA, which was enacted as an amendment to Section 552, was to restrict the government's discretion to withhold information. To the same end, the FOIA was significantly amended, and the Sunshine Act and Privacy Act were enacted, during the 1970s, in the wake of the Watergate scandal.[4] All three new statutes were crammed between Sections 551 and 553.

Most people think of the FOIA as a statute that entitles people to get information from the federal government upon request. Actually, the request mechanism is only one of three ways in which FOIA obligates agencies to make information available to the public. The three ways are described in Sections 552(a)(1), 552(a)(2), and 552(a)(3). Section 552(a)(1) requires agencies to publish certain information in the Federal Register automatically, without anyone having to ask for it. This information includes "substantive rules of general applicability," which are also called "legislative" rules. Thus, it is the FOIA that requires, as the last step of rulemaking, the publication of the final rule in the Federal Register. Section 552(a)(2) requires agencies automatically to make certain other information "available for public inspection and copying" (as distinguished from publishing it in the Federal Register). The items that must be made available for public inspection and copying include, among other things, "final opinions . . . made in the adjudication of cases." So you can thank the FOIA for requiring agencies to publish their rules (among other things) in the Federal Register and to make publicly available their decisions in adjudications (among other things).

Section 552(a)(3) contains the FOIA duty that is best-known and the one on which we will focus. Section 552(a)(3) says, with certain exceptions, that,

> (A) . . . each agency, upon any request for records which (i) reasonably describes such records and (ii) is made in accordance with published rules stating the time, place, fees (if any), and procedures to be followed, shall make the records promptly available to any person.

4. The Watergate scandal began in 1972, when White House officials connected with President Richard Nixon engineered a burglary of the offices of the Democratic National Committee located in the Watergate Hotel in Washington, D.C. That burglary, and later attempts by the White House to cover it up, led President Nixon to resign the presidency in August 1974.

An agency's duty under Section 552(a)(3) to make records available upon request is limited in several ways. For one thing, the agency does not have to honor individual requests for information that the agency has already made publicly available under 552(a)(1) or (a)(2). Also, the duty to disclose information on request does not require agencies that have national intelligence responsibilities to provide records to foreign governments or their representatives. *See* 5 U.S.C. § 552(a)(3)(E). Finally, and perhaps most importantly, subsection (b) of Section 552 lists nine categories of information that are exempt from disclosure under any of the three methods of disclosure described in 552(a). These are known as the "FOIA exemptions."

The FOIA also provides a judicial remedy when the government withholds information that is described in subsection (a) and not exempt under subsection (b). The FOIA says:

> On complaint, the district court of the United States in the district in which the complainant resides, or has his principal place of business, or in which the agency records are situated, or in the District of Columbia, has jurisdiction to enjoin the agency from withholding agency records and to order the production of any agency records improperly withheld from the complainant.

5 U.S.C. § 552(a)(4)(B). The FOIA further provides that, in a proceeding under this provision, the court reviews *de novo* an agency's decision to withhold documents. Moreover, the agency bears the burden of justifying its decision. *Id.*

The FOIA exemptions are sufficiently numerous and detailed that we address them in a separate section, after this one. For now, we will focus on the government's basic duty under Section 552(a)(3) to make records "promptly available" upon request. First, we discuss the requirements for triggering that duty. Then we will discuss in more detail the nature of that duty. Finally, we will discuss judicial enforcement of that duty.

To begin with, notice that the government's duty under the FOIA to provide records on request generally does not depend on *who* is making the request or *why*. The FOIA allows a request to be made by "any person." 5 U.S.C. § 552(a)(3). The courts have generally construed this to mean that the person who requests information under the FOIA does not have to show any particular need for the information. The purpose for which a person makes a FOIA request may, however, bear on the fees that an agency can charge for processing the request. It also can affect how "promptly" the agency must process the request. Finally, the purpose of a FOIA request can affect whether the requested information falls into a FOIA exemption. Even with these qualifications, the FOIA is basically an egalitarian statute.

Rather than depending on the purpose for which information is requested, the government's obligation under FOIA depends on four other conditions. First, the obligation extends only to an "agency." Second, the person requesting information under the FOIA must "reasonably describe" the records sought. Third, the FOIA requester must comply with "published rules" that prescribe procedures and fees for making FOIA requests. Fourth, the request must seek "records," a term that the courts have construed to mean only "agency records."

The FOIA contains its own definition of the term "agency" in Section 552(f). The definition of "agency" in Section 552(f) expands the definition in Section 551(1), so "agency" has a broader meaning for purposes of the FOIA than it has for the rest of the APA. Under the FOIA, the term "agency" includes not only executive agencies and independent agencies but also government-owned and government-controlled corporations and the Executive Office of the President.[5] The legislative history makes clear that, while the FOIA's definition of "agency" includes the Executive Office of the President, the FOIA does not apply to the President, his personal staff, or entities that exist solely to advise the President. Under this view, which the Supreme Court has adopted, some entities in the Executive Office are not subject to the FOIA. *See Kissinger v. Reporters Committee for Freedom of the Press*, 445 U.S. 136 (1980). Examples are the National Security Council and the Council of Economic Advisors. Furthermore, the FOIA's definition of "agency" does not cover Congress or the federal courts.

In addition to being directed at an "agency," a FOIA request must "reasonably describe" the records sought. This standard is satisfied, according to the legislative history of the FOIA, if "a professional employee of the agency who was familiar with the subject area of the request [would be able] to locate the record with a reasonable amount of effort." *See, e.g., Ruotolo v. Department of Justice*, 53 F.3d 4, 10 (2d Cir. 1995) (quoting legislative history). While a FOIA requester has to describe the records sought specifically enough to meet this standard, he also has to make the description broad enough to ensure that he gets all of the relevant records. Moreover, the breadth of the request can affect the amount of time that the agency takes to process it. Thus, in drafting a FOIA request, one must sometimes walk a fine line between specificity and comprehensiveness.

A person making a FOIA request must also follow the "published rules" for FOIA requests. Almost every agency has these rules. They are typically published in the Code of Federal Regulations. *See, e.g.*, 28 C.F.R. §§ 16.1-16.11 (FOIA regulations for Department of Justice). Most agencies also publish them on their websites. The rules govern details such as the form

---

5. Section 552(f) says: "For purposes of this section, the term 'agency' as defined in section 551(1) of this title includes any executive department, military department, Government corporation, Government controlled corporation, or other establishment in the executive branch of the Government (including the Executive Office of the President), or any independent regulatory agency."

in which the request must be made; to whom in the agency it should be directed; and the process for an administrative appeal, if the agency initially denies the request. In addition, the rules prescribe the fees for processing FOIA requests and the method for seeking a waiver of fees. Those fees, as well as the availability of a waiver, depend on the purpose for which the request is made. (This is one situation where the purpose for a FOIA request matters.)

Finally, the FOIA request must be for "agency records." This requirement is not apparent from the text of the FOIA; rather, it has been elucidated by federal court decisions. The FOIA provision that describes the government's basic obligation requires the government to provide "records." 5 U.S.C. § 552(a)(3); *but cf. id.* § 552(c) (authorizing agencies to exclude certain "records" as "not subject to" the FOIA). Yet the FOIA provision for judicial enforcement of that obligation authorizes a court to order the government to produce "any *agency* records improperly withheld" from the requester. *Id.* § 552(a)(4)(B) (emphasis added). The Supreme Court has seized on the latter provision to hold that the FOIA obligates an agency to produce only "agency records." The Court has also held that material requested under the FOIA must meet two requirements to be an "agency record." First, the agency must "either create or obtain" the requested material. Second, "the agency must be in control of the requested materials at the time the FOIA request is made." *United States Dept. of Justice v. Tax Analysts*, 492 U.S. 136, 144-145 (1989).

The first requirement—that an agency either "create or obtain" the requested material—is broad in one sense and narrow in another. It is broad in the sense that an "agency record" can include not only material that an agency has created but also material that the agency has obtained from others in connection with agency business. For example, the Court in *Tax Analysts*, *supra*, held that the FOIA obligated the Department of Justice to provide copies of court opinions that it received in the course of litigating tax cases. The definition of "agency record" is narrow in the sense that the FOIA does not require an agency to create a record in response to a FOIA request. Thus, if the requested information is not contained in a previously created (or obtained) record, the requester is out of luck.

The second requirement for "agency record" status—that the agency be in control of the requested material at the time of the request—comes up mostly in two situations. One is where an agency had the requested material at some point but did not possess it at the time of the request. In *Kissinger*, for example, someone asked the State Department for records that Dr. Henry Kissinger had, by then, removed from his State Department office. The Supreme Court held that the FOIA request for the records did not obligate the State Department to bring an action against Dr. Kissinger to get the requested records back. Another situation in which it may be unclear whether a record is in official possession of the agency is when the record has been made by an official at least partly for personal use. For example, an agency official may keep an appointment calendar that records both personal and official appointments. To decide whether the calendar is an "agency record," the D.C. Circuit has considered factors such as whether the calendar was created by an agency employee on agency time, whether it was kept within the agency, whether the agency or an individual controlled the calendar, and how it was used. *Consumer Fedn. of Am. v. Department of Agriculture*, 455 F.3d 283 (D.C. Cir. 2006). These same factors, among others, may be relevant in other situations in which an agency disputes that it has control over a record. *See Judicial Watch, Inc. v. U.S. Secret Serv.*, 726 F.3d 208 (D.C. Cir. 2013) (addressing FOIA request to Secret Service for logs of White House visitors).

Let us now assume that "any person" has made a request to an "agency" that "reasonably describes" the "agency records" sought and that complies with "published rules" for that request. The agency then usually has 20 working days after receiving the request to determine whether to comply with it. Once the agency makes that determination, it must "immediately notify" the requester of the determination. If the agency determines that it will comply, it must make the records promptly available to the requester. If, on the other hand, the agency's determination is adverse—for example, if the agency withholds some or all of the records that are described in the FOIA request—it must tell the requester that he or she can appeal that determination to the head of the agency. The head of the agency usually then has to decide the appeal within 20 working days after receiving the appeal. If the decision on appeal is adverse, the agency must tell the requester that judicial review is available. Both the 20-day period for initial determinations and the 20-day period for determining appeals can be extended by 10 working days under "unusual circumstances." The FOIA defines "unusual circumstances" to mean that the agency has to search and collect records from separate field offices, the agency has to search a "voluminous amount" of records, or there is a need for consultation about the request among separate components of the agency or with another agency. *See* 5 U.S.C. § 552(a)(6)(A) and (B).

If the agency does not meet the FOIA deadlines for processing a request, the requester can go to court. As mentioned above, the court can order an agency to produce agency documents that have been improperly withheld. In theory, therefore, a person should be able to get relief for improper withholdings in no more than 60 working days plus the time consumed by the lawsuit.

The reality is often much different. Many federal agencies take much longer to process FOIA requests, especially requests that require them to search a massive amount of records or that raise difficult legal issues (under the FOIA exemptions, for example). Congress has amended the FOIA to speed up the processing of FOIA requests, but backlogs remain.

Congress has also amended FOIA to take advantage of the Internet. Agencies must assign tracking numbers to certain FOIA requests so that the requester can track its progress by phone or Internet. Agencies must also post on the Internet copies of agency records that are likely to be requested often. This has resulted in the creation of what are called "electronic reading rooms."[6]

The FOIA authorizes a court to order an agency to produce an agency record that the agency has "improperly withheld." If the record is an "agency record" and has been sought in a request that "reasonably describes" the record and that complies with "published rules," it is "improper[]" for an agency to withhold the record after the FOIA deadlines expire unless (1) the record falls within one of the nine FOIA exemptions and (2) the agency can show that releasing the record can reasonably be foreseen to harm the interest protected by the exemption that the agency has relied upon to withhold it. We take up those exemptions in the next section, which follows an example that may come in handy the next time that you discuss the FOIA at a party.

Example

After you describe the FOIA to someone whom you have just met at a party, he says that he would like to find out if the federal government has any records about him. He is willing to pay any reasonable fees that the government might charge for responding to his request. He asks you, though, whether the federal government would honor a FOIA request for any records in the federal government's possession that mention his name. What would you say?

Explanation

Your new friend is a bit too ambitious, but with a little effort he might get at least some of his records from the federal government. For one thing, the FOIA does not let you request records from the entire federal government in one fell swoop. You have to direct your request to a specific federal agency, such as the FBI, and that agency generally only has to search its own records. As a result, your friend will have to send a FOIA request to each agency that he thinks might have records about him. Fortunately for your friend, each agency must post on the Internet a handbook and other information for making FOIA requests to that agency, *See* 5 U.S.C. § 552(g).

6. This nickname reflects that, after the FOIA was first enacted in 1966, many agencies created "FOIA reading rooms," which consisted, typically, of an office at the agency's headquarters where people could go to get the information that the FOIA required the agencies to make publicly available.

Unfortunately, even if he aims his request at one agency at a time, he is not likely to get every single record that mentions his name. An agency has to do a reasonable search for the requested records; it does not have to do the impossible. Depending on how an agency's records are organized and the extent to which they are computerized, it may be impossible for an agency to check every possible piece of paper it has that might bear your friend's name. Indeed, some courts have held that a FOIA request to the Internal Revenue Service for all records mentioning the requester's name did not meet the FOIA's requirements that a request "reasonably describe" the records sought. *See Dale v. IRS*, 238 F. Supp. 2d 99, 104 (D.D.C. 2002). Nonetheless, most agencies that receive a request from someone for records about him will at least run the name through their computers for records that are retrievable by the person's name. *Cf. Nation Magazine v. United States Customs Service*, 71 F.3d 885 (D.C. Cir. 1995) (discussing FOIA request from magazine for all Customs Service records about former presidential candidate H. Ross Perot).

Of course, it is possible that some of the records about your friend that the agency finds will fall within some FOIA exemption, but that is a matter for the next section.

There is one other important thing that you should tell your friend. It, too, foreshadows upcoming matters. In addition to basing his request on the FOIA, he should also invoke the Privacy Act of 1974. As we will discuss, the Privacy Act gives you a right to get records about yourself from federal agencies. The interaction between the FOIA and the Privacy Act is a bit tricky. For now, suffice it to say that people who are interested in getting records about themselves from the federal government generally should invoke both the FOIA and the Privacy Act.

B. Exemptions

FOIA exempts nine categories of records or information from its disclosure provisions. These are the nine FOIA exemptions. If a record falls within an exemption, "that does not end the matter." *Reporters Comm. for Freedom of the Press v. FBI*, 3 F.4th 350, 369 (D.C. Cir. 2021). To justify withholding the record, the agency must also show that it "reasonably foresees that disclosure would harm an interest protected by" the exemption. 5 U.S.C. § 552(a)(8)(A)(i)(I). If the agency can make these showings for only *part* of a record, the agency must disclose any "reasonably segregable portion" of the record that is not exempt. Before it does, though, the agency can delete (or "redact") the exempt information from the record. When an agency deletes exempt information, it must indicate where in the record, and under what exemptions, the deletion (i.e., "redaction") has been made. *See id.* § 552(b).

For example, suppose that someone requested an FBI document that names a confidential informant. The name of a confidential informant would fall within FOIA Exemption 7(D), and the FBI could probably show that it reasonably foresees that disclosure of it could harm an interest protected by Exemption 7(D). If the rest of the document were not exempt and were reasonably segregable from the informant's name, the FBI would have to produce the document. Before doing so, the FBI would redact the document by covering up the informant's name and indicating the claimed exemption in the margin of the document.

In a judicial action to compel the disclosure of an agency record that has been withheld in whole or in part as exempt, the agency bears the burden of justifying its decision to withhold the document. In determining whether the agency has met that burden, courts construe the exemptions narrowly. That is because, as the Supreme Court has said, "disclosure, not secrecy, is the dominant objective" of the FOIA. *Department of Air Force v. Rose*, 425 U.S. 352, 361 (1976).

An agency's burden to justify withholding a document poses a logistical problem. Ordinarily, an agency has to present some information about the contents of the record to show that it is exempt and that its disclosure could reasonably be foreseen to harm an interest protected by the exemption. Yet if the agency reveals too much information about the record to the person who has requested it, the agency will, in effect, lose the benefit of the exemption. As a partial solution to this problem, the FOIA authorizes a court to review withheld records *in camera*. This means that a judge will review them without showing them to the party who requested the records or to anyone else outside the judge's chambers. 5 U.S.C. § 552(a)(4)(B). This is not an ideal solution, though, because it often does not give the requesting party a chance to argue that the records *cannot* properly be withheld. For that reason, instead of reviewing material *in camera*, a court will usually require the agency to file an index of the supposedly exempt records. These are called "*Vaughn*" indices, after the case in which the procedure was devised. *See Vaughn v. Rosen*, 484 F.2d 820 (D.C. Cir. 1973), *cert. denied*, 415 U.S. 977 (1974). A *Vaughn* index must describe each exempt record in enough detail to convince the court that the record falls within one or more exemptions. The index must also identify, for each record, which exemptions the agency claims are applicable. The requesting party gets a copy of the *Vaughn* index, so he or she can challenge the exemption claims. In addition to the *Vaughn* index, the agency might need to file declarations to satisfy the statutory "foreseeable harm" standard discussed above. *See, e.g.*, *Reporters Comm.*, 3 F.4th at 370.

The nine exemptions are set out in Section 552(b). Paraphrasing the statute, the exempt matters are:

(1) classified information;
(2) internal agency personnel rules and practices;
(3) matters that some other statute specifically exempts from disclosure;

(4) trade secrets and certain other privileged or confidential business information that the agency has obtained from someone else;
(5) internal agency documents that ordinarily could not be obtained through discovery in a civil action against the agency;
(6) personnel files, medical files, and similar files disclosure of which would constitute a clearly unwarranted invasion of personal privacy;
(7) records or information that has been compiled for law-enforcement purposes the disclosure of which could cause certain harms;
(8) certain matters related to the regulation of banks and other financial institutions; and
(9) geological and geophysical information and data.

As you can probably tell even from this summary, some exemptions protect not only the government's privacy interests but also the privacy interests of people to whom government records relate. A prime example is Exemption 4, which specifically refers to certain privileged or confidential information supplied to the agency by a person outside the government. Exemption 4 reflects that businesses give the government much information—to get benefits or comply with regulatory requirements, for example—that they want to keep confidential. The government may also want to keep this information confidential, so that, for example, people will not be afraid to give the information to the government. Although an exemption may implicate both government interests and private interests, those interests do not always coincide. For example, a business that has given information to the government may believe that the information falls within Exemption 4, but the government may disagree. Alternatively, the government may agree that the information falls within Exemption 4 but still think that the information should be disclosed to the public.

For this reason, soon after FOIA was enacted, the question arose whether the exemptions were mandatory or discretionary. In other words, did an agency have the discretion to disclose information that fell within an exemption, or was the agency instead required to withhold the information? Some of the lower federal courts concluded that the FOIA exemptions were mandatory. These courts accordingly held that a person who would be hurt by an agency's disclosure of exempt information could enjoin the disclosure. Suits in which that relief was sought are called "reverse-FOIA suits." They are the reverse of the lawsuits explicitly contemplated under the FOIA, in which a FOIA requester sues an agency for withholding the requested information.

In *Chrysler Corp. v. Brown*, 441 U.S. 281 (1979), the Court rejected the legal theory on which prior reverse-FOIA suits had rested, while allowing them to survive on a new legal footing. The Court held that the FOIA exemptions are discretionary, not mandatory; the fact that information falls within a FOIA exemption does not prohibit an agency from disclosing it. The Court also held that the FOIA does not create a private cause of action for a person who wants to prevent an agency's disclosure of information. The Court emphasized, however, that such a person will ordinarily have a cause of action under the APA. The Court explained that an agency's disclosure of information was "agency action" within the meaning of the APA. The APA would therefore generally authorize judicial review of that action by someone who had been, or would be, harmed by it.

Nonetheless, APA review of an agency's decision to disclose information will be watered down compared to review under the legal theory that *Chrysler v. Brown* rejected. According to *Chrysler v. Brown*, a person cannot get relief under the APA merely by proving that the information to be disclosed falls within a FOIA exemption (because the exemptions are discretionary, not mandatory). Relief is available under the APA only if an agency's disclosure of the information would be, to quote the APA, "arbitrary, capricious, an abuse of discretion, or otherwise not in accordance with law." 5 U.S.C. § 706(2)(A). There are some laws that do prohibit disclosure of information, the most important of which is the Trade Secrets Act. A plaintiff who cannot prove a violation of the Trade Secrets Act or some other statute, however, is usually left to argue that the agency's disclosure decision is arbitrary and capricious or an abuse of discretion.

After giving you examples to test your understanding of "reverse FOIA," we discuss the exemptions that are most often studied in courses on administrative law.

Example

The United States Department of Agriculture administers a federal statute called the Pork Promotion, Research, and Consumer Information Act of 1985. The Act creates a marketing program to promote pork. The program is funded by mandatory fees paid by the nation's pork producers. An organization called "the Campaign for Family Farms" (CFF) submits a petition to the Secretary of Agriculture, signed by many pork producers, urging the Secretary to end the mandatory-fee system. Another organization, which is called "the National Pork Producers Council" (the Council) and supports the mandatory-fee system, files a FOIA request for a copy of the CFF petition.

Upon learning that the Secretary intends to honor the Council's FOIA request, the CFF sues the Department of Agriculture for preliminary and permanent injunctions against the disclosure. The CFF contends that the petition falls within FOIA Exemption 6. The CFF recognizes that the FOIA exemptions are discretionary, not mandatory. The CFF argues, however, that a Department of Agriculture regulation requires the Department to withhold material that falls within Exemption 6.

Assume that the CFF correctly interprets a Department of Agriculture regulation to require the Department to withhold information that falls within Exemption 6. If the court agrees with the CFF that the petition falls within Exemption 6, should it set aside the Department's decision to disclose the petition?

Explanation

The court should set aside the Department's decision to disclose the petition because of the regulation that requires the Department to withhold Exemption 6 material. This would be a different case if that regulation did not exist. Under *Chrysler v. Brown*, an agency has discretion to disclose information, even if that information falls within one of the FOIA exemptions. Unless there is some other law that restricts the agency's discretion, a court can set aside the agency's disclosure decision only if it is arbitrary and capricious. In this case, there is another law that restricts the agency's discretion, namely the regulation that makes Exemption 6 mandatory as to the Department. If the Department violates that regulation, its decision is "not in accordance with law" under APA § 706(2)(A). So, assuming that the CFF is right about what the regulation means and right about the petition's Exemption 6 status, this case is resolved by the principle that an agency must abide by its own regulations. *See Campaign for Family Farms v. Glickman*, 200 F.3d 1180 (8th Cir. 2000).

Example

The United States Department of Agriculture (USDA) requires dog breeders to report the number of dogs they buy and sell each year and their annual gross revenue from dog sales. The American Humane Society files a FOIA request with USDA for the reports filed by all dog breeders in Missouri. The USDA solicited comments from the Missouri dog breeders on whether release of the report would cause them competitive harm. After reviewing their comments, the USDA decides to release the reports. Contrary to the breeders' claims, the USDA concludes that the reports did not fall within FOIA Exemptions 4 or 6. The breeders then sued the USDA in federal court to enjoin release of the reports, reiterating their claims that the reports were exempt from disclosure under FOIA Exemptions 4 and 6. Under what circumstances, if any, will the court enjoin release of the reports?

Explanation

This example differs from *Chrysler v. Brown*. In *Chrysler v. Brown*, the Court addressed whether an agency has the discretion to release documents even when the documents are conceded to fall within a FOIA exemption. (The Court answered yes.) In contrast, this Example involves no such concession: the breeders specifically challenge the agency's conclusion that the documents were not exempt from disclosure under FOIA. Even so, in this situation, as in *Chrysler v. Brown*, the APA provides a cause of action for judicial review of the agency's disclosure decision.

The court will enjoin the release of the breeders' reports, however, only if it finds that USDA's decision to release the reports was "arbitrary, capricious, an abuse of discretion, or otherwise not in accordance with law." 5 U.S.C. § 706(2)(A). As the court explained in the case on which this Example is based, this APA standard of review is deferential. The court would not make an independent determination of whether the dog breeders' reports fell within FOIA Exemptions 4 or 6. Rather, the court would review USDA's determination that the reports did not fall within those exemptions, and the court would grant relief only if it found USDA's determination unreasonable or inadequately explained. *See Jurewicz v. USDA*, 741 F.3d 1326 (D.C. Cir. 2014).

Exemption 1 Exemption 1 covers matters that are:

> (A) specifically authorized under criteria established by an Executive order to be kept secret in the interest of national defense or foreign policy and (B) are in fact properly classified pursuant to such Executive order.

5 U.S.C. § 552(b)(1).

Exemption 1 deals exclusively with classified information. That focus may not be entirely clear from the text of Exemption 1. It becomes clear when you understand that the procedures and criteria for classifying information are prescribed primarily by executive orders, and that the key criterion prescribed in those orders for classifying material is that its disclosure would reasonably be expected to harm national-defense or foreign-policy interests. Although the President must issue the executive orders that prescribe the criteria and procedures for classification, the President can delegate to other executive officials the power to determine whether particular documents meet the criteria. *See Environmental Protection Agency v. Mink*, 410 U.S. 73, 82 n.8 (1973).

The executive branch's classification of information is not enough to ensure that it will not be disclosed under the FOIA. Exemption 1 requires that the information have been classified "properly." That requirement was added to Exemption 1 to overrule in part the Supreme Court's contrary interpretation of the former version of Exemption 1 in *Environmental Protection Agency v. Mink*. The "properly classified" requirement means, in theory, that a court can determine whether information requested under the FOIA meets the criteria for classification. In practice, however, courts often defer to the executive branch's classification decisions. *See, e.g., Hamdan v. U.S. Dept. of Justice*, 797 F.3d 759, 770 (9th Cir. 2015). It is therefore rare for someone to get a classified document disclosed under the FOIA.

As the next example illustrates, it can be hard in a FOIA case even to get the government to admit the existence of documents responsive to a FOIA request.

Example

The *New York Times* published an article reporting that the U.S. government had a classified program for carrying out "cyberattacks" on computer systems that Iran was using to develop its nuclear program. A government watchdog group filed a FOIA request with the U.S. Department of Defense (DoD) for documents relating to the alleged cyberattack program. DoD denies the request, citing Exemption 1.

The watchdog group sues DoD to get the documents. In that suit, DoD will not confirm or deny that any documents responsive to the request exist. DoD explains in an affidavit that acknowledging the existence or non-existence of responsive documents would reveal whether or not DoD had a cyberattack program against Iran, which would, in turn, "provide insight into DoD's military and intelligence capabilities and interests." Both DoD and the watchdog group move for summary judgment. How should the court rule?

Explanation

The court should rule for DoD, assuming the standard for summary judgment were met. An agency can refuse to say whether information responsive to a FOIA request exists if the very existence of the information is a properly classified matter. The agency's refusal is known as a "Glomar" response. It takes its name from the "Glomar Explorer," a submarine-retrieval ship the existence of which the CIA refused to admit or deny. *See Phillippi v. CIA*, 546 F.2d 1009, 1010-1011 (D.C. Cir. 1976). Courts will generally uphold a Glomar response based on Exemption 1 if the agency has a reasonable argument about why it would hurt national security for the agency to admit or deny the existence of the requested information. In the example, the DoD's explanation seems reasonable. *Freedom Watch, Inc. v. National Sec. Agency*, 783 F.3d 1340 (D.C. Cir. 2015).

Exemption 2 Exemption 2 covers matters that are:

> related solely to the internal personnel rules and practices of an agency.

5 U.S.C. § 552(b)(2).

The key word in Exemption 2 is "personnel." As the Supreme Court has explained, the term "personnel" limits Exemption 2's scope to documents that concern "employee relations or human resources." *Milner v. Dept. of the Navy*, 562 U.S. 562 (2011). For example, Exemption 2 protects from disclosure documents about "such matters as hiring and firing, work rules and discipline, compensation, and benefits." *Id.* Exemption 2 protects these documents not because of their sensitive nature; on the contrary, their triviality justifies sparing agencies the effort and expense of producing them under FOIA.

In *Milner v. Department of the Navy*, the Court rejected a broader interpretation of Exemption 2 that had prevailed in some lower federal courts for 30 years. The D.C. Circuit and other courts had read Exemption 2 to cover internal agency material that, if disclosed, could be used to circumvent the law. The D.C. Circuit, for example, interpreted Exemption 2 to protect a manual on surveillance techniques used to train agents of the Bureau of Alcohol, Tobacco, and Firearms. *Crooker v. BATF*, 670 F.2d 1051 (D.C. Cir. 1981) (*en banc*). Some other federal courts had followed the D.C. Circuit's interpretation. Under that interpretation, Exemption 2 not only covered documents that were too trivial to warrant disclosure but also documents that were too sensitive to disclose because of their capacity to facilitate illegal conduct. As interpreted to protect such sensitive information, Exemption 2 was known as "High Exemption 2" to distinguish that function of the exemption from its protection of trivial internal agency information, in which role it was known as "Low Exemption 2."

The Court in *Milner* rejected the D.C. Circuit's recognition of a High Exemption 2. First, the "High 2" approach ignored the plain meaning of the term "personnel." In addition, the "High 2" approach ignored that Exemption 2 protects only documents related "solely" to "internal" personnel rules and practices. The High 2 approach allowed agencies to withhold documents that did relate at least partly to interactions (or potential interactions) between the agency and the public. The Court in *Milner* rejected the government's alternative argument that Exemption 2 protects documents that guide agency personnel in performing their duties. The Court explained that Exemption 2 does not protect documents that provide rules or practices *for* agency personnel to follow; it protects certain documents *about* agency personnel: namely, documents relating to their hiring, firing, and conditions of employment.

An earlier decision of the Court on Exemption 2 addressed Exemption 2's protection of only "internal" documents relating "solely" to agency personnel. The Court in the earlier case held that Exemption 2 did not authorize the Air Force Academy to withhold summaries of proceedings to discipline cadets for Honor Code violations. The Court reasoned that, although disciplinary matters concerned internal personnel matters, they also concerned matters of "genuine and significant public interest." *Department of Air Force v. Rose*, 425 U.S. 352, 369 (1976). They were therefore not solely of internal concern. Confirming these summaries' public importance was that they were sought by law students researching an article about the military discipline system.

Example

Jan Sudarkhi, a third-year law student, applied for an attorney job at the U.S. Department of Health and Human Services (HHS). HHS turned her down for the job, selecting instead a classmate who was politically well connected. Ms. Sudarkhi filed a FOIA request for all HHS documents describing rules for contacts between HHS employees involved in making hiring decisions, on the one hand, and applicants for HHS jobs, on the other hand. May HHS rely on Exemption 2 to withhold those documents?

Explanation

Yes, Exemption 2 allows HHS to withhold documents containing rules for contacts between job applicants and HHS employees involved in the hiring process. The documents relate to personnel matters: the hiring of employees. The documents are also presumably internal; they are not made available to the public. It does not matter that Ms. Sudarkhi is a member of the public who is interested in them. That does not give them general public importance; rather, they fall into the category of internal documents whose lack of importance to the general public justifies sparing HHS the effort and expense of producing them.

Example

The Department of Health and Human Services (HHS) often contracts with private organizations to do the initial processing of claims from doctors for reimbursement under the Medicare program. To help the contractors process these claims, HHS has created an internal document known as the "Medicare Policy Guidelines Manual." The Manual divides claims into three categories, which are based on the medical services provided. Claims in one category are automatically paid; claims in a second category are automatically denied; and claims in a third category are closely reviewed. The categories reflect HHS's experience with what types of claims tend to be inflated, fraudulent, or involve services that are not medically necessary.

A group of doctors requests a copy of the Manual under the FOIA. HHS denies that request, invoking Exemption 2. Is the Manual within Exemption 2?

Explanation

The Manual does not fall within Exemption 2, as the Court clarified—and narrowed—that exemption in *Milner v. Department of the Navy*, 562 U.S. 562 (2011). The Manual does not concern the hiring and firing of HHS employees or any other human resources matter. The Manual does guide HHS personnel in performing their duties (assuming the private employees who do the processing qualify as HHS "personnel"). The Court in *Milner* said that this was not enough for a document to be a "personnel" document for purposes of Exemption 2.

In the 1986 case on which this Example is based, a lower federal court held that the HHS Manual was protected by "High Exemption 2," because it could be used to circumvent the law by those wishing to defraud the Medicare program. *See Dirksen v. United States Dept. of Health & Human Services*, 803 F.2d 1456 (9th Cir. 1986). That holding is no longer good law after *Milner*, in which the Court rejected the "High 2" interpretation of Exemption 2. The HHS Manual may, however, be protected from disclosure under some other FOIA exemption. For example, Exemption 7(E) protects certain documents that, if disclosed, could be used to circumvent law enforcement efforts.

Exemption 3 Exemption 3 covers matters that are:

> specifically exempted from disclosure by statute (other than section 552b of this title) [which codifies the Government in the Sunshine Act], if that statute (A)(i) requires that the matters be withheld from the public in such a manner as to leave no discretion on the issue, or (ii) establishes particular criteria for withholding or refers to particular types of matters to be withheld; and (B) if enacted after the date of enactment of the OPEN FOIA Act of 2009, specifically cites to this paragraph.

5 U.S.C. § 552(b)(3).

Exemption 3 incorporates certain federal statutes that prevent public disclosure of an agency's records. To be incorporated, however, a nondisclosure statute must either leave the agency no discretion to disclose the information, or it must specify criteria for withholding information, or it must specify types of matters that should be withheld. These requirements for incorporation were added to Exemption 3 in response to the Supreme Court's decision in *Administrator, FAA v. Robertson*, 422 U.S. 255 (1975), which interpreted the former version of Exemption 3 to incorporate a broad array of nondisclosure statutes. In addition, Exemption 3 was amended in 2009 to require later enacted statutes specifically to refer to Exemption 3 in order to be incorporated into Exemption 3. A nondisclosure statute that meets all requirements for incorporation is called an "Exemption 3 statute."

Even with the addition of these requirements, there are many federal statutes that have been found to be Exemption 3 statutes. For example, the Supreme Court has held that Exemption 3 incorporates statutes governing the disclosure of census data, portions of presentence reports, national security information, and information supplied to the Consumer Product Safety Commission. *See Baldridge v. Shapiro*, 455 U.S. 345 (1982); *United States Dept. of Justice v. Julian*, 486 U.S. 1 (1988); *Central Intelligence Agency v. Sims*, 471 U.S. 159 (1985); *Consumer Product Safety Commn. v. GTE Sylvania*, 447 U.S. 102 (1980). Congress creates new Exemption 3 statutes regularly. For example, after terrorists attacked the United States in September 2001, Congress enacted legislation limiting disclosure of government documents containing "critical infrastructure information." 6 U.S.C. § 133(a)(1)(A). As mentioned above, however, statutes enacted since 2009 must specifically identify themselves as Exemptions 3 statutes to qualify as such.

Analysis under Exemption 3 cannot end with a determination that a statute is an Exemption 3 statute. The question remains whether the requested records were properly withheld under that statute. In the words of Exemption 3, the records must be "specifically exempted from disclosure" by the Exemption 3 statute. A statute may be an Exemption 3 statute but not specifically exempt from disclosure all of the records sought in a particular FOIA request. For example, the Supreme Court in *Julian* held that Exemption 3 incorporates Federal Rule of Criminal Procedure 32, which governs the disclosure of presentence reports on defendants who have been convicted of a federal crime. The Court also held, however, that Rule 32 only authorized the withholding of certain portions of the requested presentence reports. The remaining portions had to be disclosed. *See Julian, supra.*

In the next example, consider (1) whether the statute on which the agency relies is an Exemption 3 statute, and (2) if so, whether the withheld information falls within that statute.

Example

Xan Lu was born and raised in the People's Republic of China (PRC) but now lives in Spain. He has made many speeches charging the PRC government with human rights abuses. He applies to the U.S. State Department for a visa to come to the United States to address the graduating class of the East Dakota University Law School. The U.S. State Department denies his request.

Xan Lu suspects that he was denied a visa because PRC officials have convinced U.S. officials that granting the visa would harm diplomatic relations between the United States and the PRC. Xan Lu files a FOIA request with the State Department seeking all records related to his visa application. The State Department gives him some documents, including a partial copy of the visa application that Xan Lu submitted to the State Department. The State Department has blacked out material in the margins of the application, however.

Xan Lu sues the State Department for release of the withheld documents, including an unredacted version of his visa application. In its *Vaughn* index, the State Department explains that it deleted handwritten marginal notes made by a consular office that concern the visa application. The State Department argues that these handwritten marginal notes are properly withheld under Exemption 3. The supposed Exemption 3 statute on which the State Department relies is 8 U.S.C. § 1202(f), which is entitled "Confidential nature of records" and says:

> The records of the Department of State and of diplomatic and consular offices of the United States pertaining to the issuance or refusal of visas or permits to enter the United States shall be considered confidential and shall be used only for the formulation, amendment, administration, or enforcement of the immigration, nationality, and other laws of the United States, except that in the discretion of the Secretary of State certified copies of such records may be made available to a court which certifies that the information contained in such records is needed by the court in the interest of the ends of justice in a case pending before the court.

Xan Lu responds that Section 1202(f) is not an Exemption 3 statute because it gives the Secretary of State discretion to release visa-related records in some situations. Xan Lu also contends that, even if Section 1202(f) is an Exemption 3 statute, it does not justify withholding from him the marginal notes on his visa application. In support of this contention, he argues that Section 1202(f) is only meant to protect the privacy of the applicant; it is not meant to prevent the applicant himself from finding out why his visa was denied. He says that, in light of this purpose, the term "records" in Section 1202(f) should not be interpreted to prevent him from seeing his own visa application.

Is Xan Lu entitled to an unredacted copy of the visa application that he submitted to the State Department?

Explanation

Xan Lu is not entitled to an unredacted copy of his visa application, because it was properly redacted under Exemption 3. Section 1202(f) is an Exemption 3 statute, and it authorized the State Department to delete the handwritten notes made by a consular office in the margins of Xan Lu's visa application.

To be an Exemption 3 statute, Section 1202(f) has to either "(A) require[] that the matters be withheld from the public in such a manner as to leave no discretion on the issue or (B) establish[] particular criteria for withholding or refer[] to particular types of matters to be withheld." Exemption 3's use of the disjunctive "or" means that a statute will be an Exemption 3 statute if it meets either condition (A) or condition (B). Thus, even if the Secretary's discretion under Section 1202(f) to disclose visa records to a court prevented Section 1202(f) from satisfying condition (A), Section 1202(f) would still be an Exemption 3 statute if it satisfied condition (B).

In any event, the D.C. Circuit has held that Section 1202(f) satisfies condition (A) of Exemption 3. The court observed that Section 1202(f) does not give the Secretary of State any discretion on the issue of whether visa records should "be withheld from the *public*" (emphasis added); it just gives the Secretary discretion to disclose visa records to a *court* in some situations. As to public disclosure, the Secretary of State has no discretion. Section 1202(f) says that visa records have to stay "confidential" and can be used "only" for specified purposes that do not include public disclosure. So Section 1202(f) satisfies condition (A) of Exemption 3.

The D.C. Circuit held that Section 1202(f) also satisfies condition (B) of Exemption 3. That is because Section 1202(f) "refers to particular types of matters to be withheld"—namely, "[t]he records of the Department of State and of diplomatic and consular offices of the United States pertaining to the issuance or refusal of visas or permits to enter the United States." This description is specific enough to satisfy Exemption 3. *See Medina-Hincapie v. Department of State*, 700 F.2d 737 (D.C. Cir. 1983).

The question remains whether the marginal notes were properly withheld under Section 1202(f). The answer is yes. Because the notes were made by a consular office, they fall expressly within Section 1202(f) if they are part of a "record[] . . . pertaining to the issuance or refusal of [a] visa[]." We would commonly think of a visa application as fitting this description. Xan Lu's argument for a narrower interpretation of Section 1202(f) rests on an overly restrictive view of its purpose. Section 1202(f) was certainly intended partly to protect the privacy of visa applicants. It was also intended, however, to protect the State Department's interest in the confidentiality of its process for deciding whether to grant a visa. *See Medina-Hincapie*, 700 F.2d at 744. *See also Badalamenti v. United States Dept. of State*, 899 F. Supp. 542, 547-548 (D. Kan. 1995); *Jan-Xin Zang v. FBI*, 756 F. Supp. 705, 711-712 (W.D.N.Y. 1991).

Exemption 4 Exemption 4 covers matters that are:

> trade secrets and commercial or financial information obtained from a person and privileged or confidential.

5 U.S.C. § 552(b)(4).

Exemption 4 protects three types of business information: (1) trade secrets, (2) commercial or financial information that has been obtained from someone else and that is privileged, and (3) commercial or financial information that has been obtained from someone else and that is confidential. We divide Exemption 4 this way because the courts generally have not treated "commercial" information as being particularly discrete from "financial" information, whereas they have treated the terms "privileged" and "confidential" as distinct.

Even before we get into that, there is some dispute about what constitutes a "trade secret" under Exemption 4. Some courts have used the definition of "trade secret" in the Restatement of Torts. The Restatement defines a "trade secret" to mean information that is secret, used in a business, and gives its owner "an opportunity to obtain an advantage over competitors who do not know or use it." Restatement of Torts § 757, comment b (1939). Other courts, including the D.C. Circuit, have adopted a narrower definition of the term "trade secret" in Exemption 4. These courts impose the additional requirement that the information be directly related to the productive process. *See, e.g.*, *Public Citizen Health Research Group v. FDA*, 704 F.2d 1280 (D.C. Cir. 1983); *see also Herrick v. Garvey*, 298 F.3d 1184, 1190 (10th Cir. 2002). This additional requirement focuses Exemption 4's protection of "trade secret" on things like secret formulas. By the same token, it excludes business information that might fall within the Restatement's definition of "trade secret," such as price lists, customer lists, and sales data. Ordinarily, none of that information relates to the process for producing the goods or services that are being sold.

In addition to protecting trade secrets, Exemption 4 also protects commercial or financial information that is obtained from another person if it is either privileged or confidential. Most courts have held that, as used in Exemption 4, the terms "commercial" and "financial" have their ordinary meaning. *See, e.g.*, *Brown v. Perez*, 835 F.3d 1223, 1230 (10th Cir. 2016). "[F]inancial" information means information about money. "Commercial" information means information about commerce, even if it is supplied by a nonprofit organization. *Brown*, 835 F.3d at 1230-1231. The two terms can, of course, overlap, and the courts seldom need to distinguish between them.

Commercial and financial information is exempt, however, only if it is either "privileged" or "confidential." There has not been much litigation about the term "privileged" in Exemption 4. The legislative history of the FOIA suggests that the term includes commonly recognized ones such as the attorney-client privilege.

Most litigation on Exemption 4 concerns whether commercial or financial information is "confidential." The U.S. Supreme Court addressed the meaning of "confidential" in *Food Marketing Institute v. Argus Leader Media*, 588 U.S. 427 (2019). In that case, a newspaper asked the U.S. Department of Agriculture (USDA) to tell it which grocery stores participate in the food stamp program and how much money they make from food stamps. The USDA identified the stores but withheld information about their food stamp sales. USDA argued that the sales data were confidential under Exemption 4, and observed that USDA had promised the stores that it would keep the data confidential. The Court agreed that the data were confidential. It held, "At least where commercial or financial information is both customarily and actually treated as private by its owner and provided to the government under an assurance of privacy, the information is 'confidential' within the meaning of Exemption 4." *Id.* at 2366.

That holding is significant because it rejects a longstanding interpretation of "confidential" that had been devised by the D.C. Circuit and followed in many other circuits. In *National Parks & Conservation Assn. v. Morton*, 498 F.2d 765 (1974), the D.C. Circuit had established a two-part test under which information was "confidential" only if its disclosure was likely either (1) to impair the government's ability to obtain necessary information in the future, or (2) to cause substantial harm to the competitive position of the person from whom the information was obtained. *Id.* at 770. The Court rejected this test in *Food Marketing Institute* on the ground that it lacked support in the text of Exemption 4.

The following example may not reveal any secrets of the administrative law trade, but it may help you understand Exemption 4. (You do not need to keep it confidential.)

Example

A federal grant program called "Title X" awards money to make affordable family planning services widely available. Until 2011, the federal government awarded Title X grants to New Hampshire for disbursement as subgrants to family planning providers in that state. New Hampshire had consistently awarded subgrants to Planned Parenthood of Northern New England. In 2011, however, New Hampshire refused to award a Title X subgrant to Planned Parenthood because of concern that it was using the money to subsidize abortions, in violation of Title X. The federal government decided in light of that refusal to approve Planned Parenthood's application for a direct Title X grant from the federal government.

New Hampshire Right to Life filed a FOIA request asking the federal government—specifically, the Department of Health and Human Services (HHS)—for documents about Planned Parenthood's application for a direct Title X grant. HHS withheld certain documents claiming they fells within Exemption 4. The withheld documents described Planned Parenthood's business model for operating family planning clinics, including how to determine prices for the clinics' services. Planned Parenthood treated these documents as confidential, not allowing them to be disclosed to people outside the organization. When Planned Parenthood provided these documents to HHS in connection with its grant application, however, Planned Parenthood did not demand, nor did HHS promise, confidentiality. Does Exemption 4 cover Planned Parenthood's business-model and pricing documents?

Explanation

It is unclear whether the documents fall within Exemption 4. Exemption 4 requires that the documents contain (1) financial or commercial information (2) provided by a person that (3) are privileged or confidential. The hard question is whether the information in the withheld documents is "confidential." But first consider the other requirements.

In the case on which this Example is based, the parties disputed whether the withheld documents were "commercial" information. New Hampshire Right to Life (the requesting party) argued that Planned Parenthood could not have "commercial" information because it is a non-profit organization. The U.S. Court of Appeals for the First Circuit rejected that argument, reasoning that "[a]ll sorts of non-profits—hospitals, colleges, and even the National Football League—engage in commerce as that term is ordinarily understood." *N.H. Right to Life v. HHS*, 778 F.3d 43, 50 (1st Cir. 2015).

As to the second requirement for Exemption 4 coverage, Planned Parenthood plainly qualifies as a person, even though it is an organization. Section 551(1) of the APA defines "person" to include "private organization[s]." And Planned Parenthood provided the requested documents to HHS.

Now comes the hard part. In the case on which this Example is based, the First Circuit held that the withheld information was "confidential" under the *National Parks* test. As required by that test, the court determined that disclosure of the information "would likely cause substantial competitive harm" to Planned Parenthood by giving other organizations an off-the-shelf successful business model for running competing family planning clinics and pricing their services. *Id.* at 51. As discussed above, however, the Court in *Food Marketing Institute* rejected the *National Parks* test. The First Circuit's reasoning is therefore no longer valid.

In place of the *National Parks* test, the Court held that "[a]t least where commercial or financial information is both customarily and actually treated as private by its owner and provided to the government under an assurance of privacy," it is "confidential" under Exemption 4. *Food Marketing Institute*, 588 U.S. at 440. This holding refers to two conditions that, together, guarantee confidential status. Planned Parenthood met the first condition; you are told in the Example above that Planned Parenthood kept the information private. But you are also told that Planned Parenthood did not request or get any assurance of privacy when it provided the documents to the government. Does its failure to meet the second condition articulated in *Food Marketing Institute*'s holding disqualify the documents from Exemption 4 protection?

The Court expressly left that question open in *Food Marketing Institute*. The Court said, "At least the first condition has to be [met]; it is hard to see how information could be deemed confidential if its owner shares it freely." 588 U.S. at 434. But the Court did not need to decide whether the second condition is required for information to be "confidential," because the federal government in that case admitted that it had promised confidentiality to the grocery stores that provided the government with data on their food stamp sales. *Id.* Until the Court resolves the matter, lower federal courts must struggle with whether information like Planned Parenthood's business-model and pricing information falls within Exemption 4 even when the government does not promise to keep it confidential.

Exemption 5 Exemption 5 covers matters that are:

> inter-agency or intra-agency memorandums or letters which would not be available by law to a party other than an agency in litigation with the agency, provided that the deliberative process privilege shall not apply to records created 25 years or more before the date on which the records were requested.

5 U.S.C. § 552(b)(5).

The Supreme Court has aptly described Exemption 5 as "somewhat Delphic." *United States Dept. of Justice v. Julian*, 486 U.S. 1, 11 (1988). Its purpose, however, is straightforward: it lets an agency withhold agency documents that ordinarily could not be obtained from the agency through discovery in a civil action.

To fall within Exemption 5, a document must meet two conditions. Its source must be a government agency, and it must be a type of document that could be withheld under a discovery privilege. Thus, Exemption 5 generally covers only documents prepared by someone who works for a government agency. *See Department of Interior v. Klamath Water Users Protective Assn.*, 532 U.S. 1 (2001); *see also Pub. Emps. for Envtl. Responsibility v. U.S. Section, Intl. Boundary & Water Commn.*, 740 F.3d 195, 201-202 (D.C. Cir. 2014) (noting that D.C. Circuit has held that documents provided to agency by consultants can sometimes constitute "interagency" documents). Moreover, even documents prepared by someone working for an agency must be privileged from disclosure in discovery to be withheld under Exemption 5.

Some of the discovery privileges incorporated in Exemption 5 are the type that apply to both government and private entities. For example,

Exemption 5 allows agencies to withhold documents that fall within the attorney-client privilege or the attorney work product doctrine. *United States Fish & Wildlife Serv. v. Sierra Club, Inc.*, 592 U.S. 261, 267 (2021). In a FOIA case in which the government relies on the attorney-client privilege or work product doctrine, the court will often look to cases arising under the discovery provisions of the Federal Rules of Civil Procedure. *See, e.g., Federal Trade Commn. v. Grolier, Inc.*, 462 U.S. 19 (1983).

Perhaps the most important—and certainly the most litigated—privilege incorporated in Exemption 5 is one available only to the government. It is known as the "deliberative process" or "executive" privilege.[7] You will notice that the deliberative process privilege is mentioned in the text of Exemption 5, quoted above; the text limits its applicability to documents created 25 years or more before the request for them.

The deliberative process privilege allows agencies to withhold certain material connected with the government decision making process. The rationale is that the confidentiality of this material ensures frank and open discussion among government officials, which, in turn, enhances the quality of government decision making. The problem is that this desire for confidentiality ultimately runs into the FOIA's policy of open government. In particular, the FOIA requires agencies to make their decisions available to the public, when those decisions have legal effect. *See* 5 U.S.C. § 552(a)(2). Furthermore, the public can benefit from understanding the reasoning behind these decisions.

The Supreme Court has adopted a two-part test to accommodate these competing concerns. To be protected by the deliberative process privilege incorporated in Exemption 5, an inter-agency or intra-agency communication must be (1) "pre-decisional" and (2) "deliberative." "Pre-decisional" means that the communication has to have occurred before the government's final decision is made. Thus, the privilege does not protect an agency memo or letter that is created after an agency decision has been made and designed to explain the decision. "Deliberative" means that the communication has to reflect one or more officials' thoughts about an official matter. Thus, the privilege does not protect purely factual information that is generated during the decision-making process, unless it reveals the thinking behind that process.

The Supreme Court discussed the deliberative process privilege most thoroughly in *NLRB v. Sears, Roebuck & Co.*, 421 U.S. 132 (1975). That case involved a FOIA request for memoranda generated within the National Labor Relations Board. The memoranda were all generated during the Board's process for deciding whether to file an unfair labor practice charge.

---

7. This is not the same as the executive privilege created by the Constitution and construed in cases such as *United States v. Nixon*, 418 U.S. 683 (1974). *See NLRB v. Sears, Roebuck & Co.*, 421 U.S. 132, 151 n.17 (1975).

(When an employer, employee, or union believes that someone has violated the federal labor laws, he, she, or it files an administrative complaint with the Board; it is then up to the Board to decide whether to begin an administrative adjudication—an "unfair labor practice" proceeding—that will determine whether an unfair labor practice has indeed occurred.) The Court held that Exemption 5 did not protect memoranda that announced and explained the Board's decision *not* to file an unfair labor practice charge. These memoranda reflected final agency decisions; they meant that no proceeding would occur. They were therefore not pre-decisional. Moreover, they informed the public of the "working law" that guided those decisions. *Id.* at 153. They were therefore not deliberative. On the other hand, the Court held that Exemption 5 *did* protect memoranda that reflected the Board's decision to begin an unfair labor practice proceeding. These memoranda *were* pre-decisional, because they preceded the ultimate decision by the Board about whether an unfair labor practice had occurred in a particular case. Furthermore, they were deliberative because they reflected the Board's theory of the case.

Although the deliberative process privilege is the main uniquely governmental privilege protected by Exemption 5, it is not the only one. For example, the Supreme Court has held that Exemption 5 authorizes the Air Force to withhold witness statements that it gathered while investigating a plane crash. The Court based this holding on case law predating the FOIA in which lower courts had held those statements exempt from discovery in civil litigation. The Court found that Congress apparently approved of this case law when it enacted the FOIA. *See United States v. Weber Aircraft Corp.*, 465 U.S. 792 (1984). Using similar reasoning, the Court held that Exemption 5 authorized the temporary withholding of government information related to regulation of the monetary system. *See FOMC v. Merrill*, 443 U.S. 340 (1979). These cases show that the Court uses case law on civil discovery as a guide to interpreting Exemption 5, especially when the case law is endorsed in FOIA's legislative history. The Court has also warned, however, that Exemption 5 does not necessarily incorporate all of the discovery privileges. *See Merrill*, 443 U.S. at 354.

The next example requires you to deliberate about the deliberative process privilege.

Example

The EPA proposed for public comment a rule restricting the amount of arsenic that drinking water could contain. EPA received more than 10,000 public comments on the proposed rule. The EPA Administrator told a member of her staff to analyze the most significant public comments. The staff member produced a memorandum that had a summary of each significant comment, followed, in a separate section, by his analysis of that comment.

Now that EPA has published the final rule, a chemical company that plans to bring a lawsuit challenging the rule files a FOIA request with EPA. The request seeks any documents related to public comments on the rule. EPA withholds the staff member's memorandum summarizing and analyzing the comments. The chemical company sues EPA for an order compelling it to produce that memorandum. In response, EPA invokes Exemption 5.

Should the court order EPA to disclose the memorandum in whole or in part?

Explanation

EPA clearly can withhold the portions of the staff member's memorandum that analyze the significant public comments on the proposed rule. Although it is less clear, EPA probably can also withhold the portions of the memorandum that summarize those comments.

The portions of the memo that analyze the public comments fall squarely within the deliberative process privilege. Those analyses are predecisional, because they were prepared before EPA adopted the final rule. They are also deliberative, because they reflect the staff member's thinking about the comments. Notice that, despite what the term "deliberative" might suggest, it does not matter that the memorandum reflected only one official's thoughts. Nor does it matter that the official may have been low in the agency pecking order. What matters is that the memorandum was part of the decision-making process of the agency.

It is a closer question whether EPA can withhold the portions of the memorandum that summarize the public comments. It could be argued that these summaries are purely factual, rather than deliberative, in nature. The better argument is probably that the summaries are deliberative in two ways. First, they reflect the staff member's judgments about which public comments are significant. Furthermore, each summary reflects the staff member's judgment about why the comment is significant. In cases involving similar material, courts have upheld Exemption 5 claims by agencies. *See, e.g., Montrose Chemical Corp. v. Train*, 491 F.2d 63 (D.C. Cir. 1974); *see also Natl. Sec. Archive v. CIA*, 752 F.3d 460, 465 (D.C. Cir. 2014).

Exemption 6 Exemption 6 covers matters that are:

> personnel and medical files and similar files the disclosure of which would constitute a clearly unwarranted invasion of personal privacy.

5 U.S.C. § 552(b)(6).

Whereas Exemption 4 protects commercial and financial privacy, and Exemption 5 protects governmental privacy, Exemption 6 protects personal privacy. The types of personal matters protected by Exemption 6 are suggested by its reference to "personnel and medical files." People who work for the government or get medical benefits from it often give details about their personal history or condition that they do not want spread around. (In this connection, remember that "any person" can make a FOIA request, and it usually does not matter why she is making it.) Exemption 6 covers not only personnel and medical files but also other records that contain information applicable to a particular individual, such as a passport application or the summary of an administrative disciplinary proceeding. *See United States Dept. of State v. Washington Post Co.*, 456 U.S. 595 (1982); *Department of Air Force v. Rose*, 425 U.S. 352 (1976).

Exemption 6 contains an important limit on the protection of personal files. They can be withheld only if their disclosure would cause a "clearly unwarranted invasion of personal privacy." The word "clearly" tips the balance in favor of disclosure. The question remains: how do you decide what is an "unwarranted invasion of privacy"? As you might guess, that question is the subject of most of the litigation on Exemption 6.

The Supreme Court has held that Exemption 6 requires a balancing of the public interest in disclosure against the privacy interest in nondisclosure. The Court has also discussed what qualifies as a valid public interest and a valid privacy interest. The Court has specified that the only relevant public interest is "the citizens' right to be informed about what their government is up to." *United States Dept. of Defense v. FLRA*, 510 U.S. 487, 495 (1994) (internal quotation marks omitted). For example, suppose that an agency record contains much personal information about a Hollywood celebrity but little information about the government's regulation of that celebrity or about government operations in general. There might be a strong public interest in disclosure of that document, as the term *public interest* is commonly understood. Nonetheless, the public interest would be negligible for purposes of determining whether its disclosure would cause a "clearly unwarranted" invasion of privacy. On the other side of the balance, the Court has held that a person may have a strong interest in the government's withholding of even personal information that has previously been made public or that is currently available in some public record. This reflects that, "[i]n an organized society, there are few facts [about an individual] that are not at one time or another divulged to another." *Department of Defense v. FLRA*, 510 U.S. at 500. For example, even though someone's felony conviction is a matter of public record (say, in a local courthouse somewhere), that person may still want to limit the federal government's disclosure of the conviction.

The balancing required under Exemption 6 is illustrated in *United States Dept. of Defense v. FLRA*, 510 U.S. 487 (1994). In that case, a union asked a government agency for the home addresses of certain employees that the union represented. Most of these employees had refused the union's direct request for their home addresses. The Supreme Court held that the agency could withhold the addresses under Exemption 6. The Court determined that there was no strong public interest in disclosing those addresses. The disclosure would not enhance public understanding of what the government was up to. The public interest in disclosure was therefore "negligible." *Id.* at 497, 502. On the other side of the balance, the Court found that the employees had a "nontrivial" interest in the agency's withholding their home addresses. *Id.* at 501. This was true even if those addresses could be found in the phone book or some other public source. The Court observed that "[m]any people simply do not want to be disturbed at home by work-related matters." *Id.* Weighing the "negligible" public interest against the "nontrivial" privacy interest, the Court concluded that disclosure would be "clearly unwarranted." *Id.* at 502.

It is especially worth remembering in connection with Exemption 6 that the FOIA exemptions do not operate in an all-or-nothing way. The FOIA says, "Any reasonably segregable portion of a record shall be provided to any person requesting such record after deletion of the portions which are exempt." 5 U.S.C. § 552(b). This means that, if a record is otherwise subject to disclosure under the FOIA and the deletion of personally identifying information would prevent the disclosure from causing a "clearly unwarranted invasion of personal privacy," the agency must disclose the record after it has made those deletions.

This obligation of partial disclosure is illustrated in *United States Department of State v. Ray*, 502 U.S. 164 (1991). That case involved a FOIA request for records of State Department interviews with people from Haiti who had unsuccessfully sought political asylum in the United States. The State Department had conducted those interviews to ensure that Haiti did not mistreat these people after they were denied asylum by the United States. The State Department disclosed the records of these interviews after deleting from them information that identified the interviewees. The Court upheld those deletions under the same balancing approach that it used in *Department of Defense v. FLRA*. The Court determined that the disclosure of the interviewees' identity would not enhance the public's understanding of what the State Department was "up to." On the other hand, the interviewees had a strong interest in keeping their identities confidential, partly because of the risk of retaliation by the government of Haiti. *See also Department of Air Force v. Rose*, 425 U.S. at 370-382.[8]

8. The Court has often said that, in considering whether the disclosure of information under the FOIA would serve the public interest, courts should not take into account the purpose for which the particular requester has made the request. *See, e.g.*, *United States Dept. of Justice v. Reporters Comm. for Freedom of the Press*, 489 U.S. 749, 771 (1989). Nevertheless, the Court in *Ray* and *Department of Defense v. FLRA* did appear to take the requester's purpose into account in gauging the extent to which disclosure would cause an invasion of privacy under Exemption 6. In a later case, the Court held that a requester's proposed use of information is indeed relevant to whether disclosure "could reasonably be expected to constitute an unwarranted invasion of privacy" under Exemption 7(C). *See National Archives & Records Admin. v. Favish*, 541 U.S. 157 (2004). Although the Court's holding concerned Exemption 7(C), its analysis of privacy interests logically would apply, as well, to Exemption 6.

Of course, courts do not literally balance public and private interests under Exemption 6. "Balancing" is a metaphor, and it is one that may suggest more objectivity than characterizes the actual process. The next example illustrates that point.

Example

From 1981 through 2011, the National Air and Space Administration (NASA) periodically launched space shuttles that went into, and returned from, orbit around the Earth. NASA uses the space shuttles for things like deploying and repairing satellites. In 1986, a space shuttle named the "Challenger" disintegrated soon after taking off, killing all seven astronauts aboard. This event, known as the "Challenger disaster," attracted massive public attention. It was particularly tragic to many people because one of the astronauts who died had been selected to be the first average American in space. She was Christa McAuliffe, a schoolteacher from New Hampshire.

Not long after the disaster, NASA retrieved from the ocean floor an audio recording from the Challenger shuttle. The recording included voice communications among the astronauts and between the astronauts and NASA officials on the ground. The *New York Times* newspaper asked NASA for a copy of the recording under the FOIA. NASA released a written transcript of the recording. NASA refused, however, to release the recording itself on the ground that it fell within Exemption 6.

1. Is the recording a "personnel [or] medical file[s] [or a] similar file[]" within the meaning of Exemption 6?
2. If you represented the *New York Times*, what public interest could you argue would be served by disclosure of the recording, keeping in mind that a transcript had already been disclosed?
3. If you represented NASA, precisely *whose* privacy could reasonably be expected to be invaded, and *how* (still keeping in mind the release of the transcript)?

Explanations

1. The D.C. Circuit held that the recording was a "similar file." The court relied on Supreme Court precedent stating that the determination of whether something is a "similar file" turns, not on the nature of the file, but on the nature of the information in it. The Supreme Court had also said that information merely has to "apply to a particular individual" to constitute a "similar file." Under this broad definition, the D.C. Circuit found that the recording from the Challenger was a "similar file" because it contained information about the astronauts. *See New York Times Co. v. NASA*, 920 F.2d 1002 (D.C. Cir. 1990) (*en banc*).

2. The *New York Times* had trouble establishing a public interest in disclosure of the recording, especially given the Court's narrow concept of public interest and NASA's release of the transcript of the recording. The Supreme Court has narrowly defined the public interest to mean only the public interest in learning what the government is "up to." The recording did not shed much, if any, light on this matter, under the circumstances. The recording did reveal the operation of the shuttle, but that information was already revealed in the transcript of the recording. The D.C. Circuit insisted that the *Times* show that the recording added information of public interest, over and above that supplied by the transcript. The *Times* could not make that showing. This was partly because NASA put on evidence that the background sounds that could be heard on the recording did not reveal anything. So the only value of the recording was to satisfy the perhaps understandable, but legally irrelevant, public interest in hearing people in mortal fear. *Cf. Sikes v. U.S. Dept. of Navy*, 896 F.3d 1227, 1238-1239 (11th Cir. 2018) (holding that public interest in disclosure of suicide note that admiral wrote to his wife was "scant").
3. NASA successfully argued that disclosure of the recording could reasonably be expected to invade the privacy of the dead astronauts' families. The court found that hearing the voices of the astronauts would cause their families pain. This finding reflects a broad understanding of what constitutes an "invasion of privacy," but it finds support in other cases. In addition, the court took into account that disclosure of the recording would expose the families to another round of public attention. Altogether, the court held that the families had a "substantial" privacy interest that could reasonably be expected to be invaded by disclosing the tape. On the other side of the balance, the court found minimal public interest in disclosure. Accordingly, the court held that disclosure would cause a "clearly unwarranted" invasion of personal privacy. NASA was thus entitled to withhold the recording under FOIA Exemption 6. *See New York Times v. NASA*, 782 F. Supp. 628 (D.D.C. 1991); *see also Sikes*, 896 F.3d at 1237-1238 (holding that privacy interests in admiral's suicide note to his wife were "unquestionably strong").

Exemption 7 We will take the last exemption that we will discuss a piece at a time. Exemption 7 protects "records or information compiled for law enforcement purposes," but only to the extent that their disclosure could cause one or more of six harms. Those harms are that disclosure:

(A) could reasonably be expected to interfere with enforcement proceedings;
(B) would deprive a person of a right to a fair trial or an impartial adjudication;

(C) could reasonably be expected to constitute an unwarranted invasion of personal privacy;
(D) could reasonably be expected to disclose the identity of a confidential source, including a state, local, or foreign agency or authority or any private institution which furnished information on a confidential basis, and, in the case of a record or information compiled by a criminal law enforcement authority in the course of a criminal investigation or by an agency conducting a lawful national security intelligence investigation, information furnished by a confidential source;
(E) would disclose techniques and procedures for law enforcement investigations or prosecutions, or would disclose guidelines for law enforcement investigations or prosecutions if such disclosure could reasonably be expected to risk circumvention of the law; or
(F) could reasonably be expected to endanger the life or physical safety of any individual.

5 U.S.C. § 552(b)(7).

This list of harms is daunting, but it may help you to know two things about it up front. First, Congress originally added this list to Exemption 7 in 1974. The original version of Exemption 7 in the 1966 FOIA was blessedly short, but also gave agencies too much discretion to withhold information, in Congress's view. Second, as intriguing as each part of Exemption 7 may be, we will focus only on the portions that have been addressed in Supreme Court decisions.

The threshold requirement for withholding a record or information under Exemption 7 is that it has been "compiled for law enforcement purposes." One question, as you might guess, is: what is a "law enforcement purpose[]"? Specifically, are "law enforcement" purposes limited to criminal laws? The Supreme Court has said no. Law enforcement reaches criminal, civil, and administrative enforcement proceedings. For example, "law enforcement" records include the statements of witnesses that could be called in an unfair labor practice proceeding before the National Labor Relations Board. *See NLRB v. Robbins Tire & Rubber Co.*, 437 U.S. 214 (1978).

Questions have also arisen about what it means for a record or information to be "compiled" for law-enforcement purposes. Specifically, what if the government has originally gathered information for a purpose that is *not* related to law enforcement, but later uses those records for law-enforcement purposes? The Supreme Court held that the purpose of the original compilation does not matter, as long as the later compilation for law-enforcement purposes occurs before the FOIA request is made. *See John Doe Agency v. John Doe Corp.*, 493 U.S. 146 (1990). The later compilation will cause the record or information to be treated as having been "compiled for law enforcement purposes."

The conclusion that information has been "compiled for law enforcement purposes" is not enough to trigger Exemption 7. In addition, its production must cause at least one of six harms. Consistent with its burden under other exemptions, the government bears the burden of proving the applicability of one of the harms specified in Exemption 7. As under some of the other exemptions, however, the government's burden may be eased by the Supreme Court's use of a "categorical" analysis in some situations. The analysis is best explained by describing a case in which the Court has used it.

The Court used the categorical approach in *United States Department of Justice v. Reporters Committee for Freedom of the Press*, 489 U.S. 749 (1989) (a case involving Exemption 7(C)). Exemption 7(C) exempts law-enforcement records the production of which "could reasonably be expected to constitute an unwarranted invasion of personal privacy." In *Reporters Committee*, the government relied on Exemption 7(C) to deny a FOIA request for the "rap sheet" of a man named Charles Medico. A "rap sheet" details all of a person's arrests and convictions. (When the Supreme Court took up this case in 1989, the FBI had rap sheets on more than 24 million people.) The Court held that these rap sheets will almost always fall within Exemption 7(C). In so holding, the Court used the same balancing approach that it uses under the similarly worded Exemption 6. The Court determined, as a categorical matter, that there was no strong public interest in the disclosure of rap sheets; their disclosure typically would not shed light on what the government was "up to." On the other hand, the subjects of the rap sheets had a "strong privacy interest" in preventing their disclosure. This interest, the Court found, existed even though many of the pieces of information collected in rap sheets were available in other public records.

The Court again addressed Exemption 7(C) in *National Archives & Records Administration v. Favish*, 541 U.S. 157 (2004). The Court in *Favish* held that Exemption 7(C) allowed the government to withhold photographs that federal officials took at the death scene of Deputy White House Counsel Vincent Foster. As in earlier Exemption 7(C) cases, the *Favish* Court balanced the privacy interests that, according to the government, would be harmed by disclosure against the public interest that, according to the requesting party (Favish), would be advanced by disclosure. In balancing those interests, the Court announced two important principles. Together, the principles reflect a broad interpretation of Exemption 7(C).

The first principle announced in *Favish* concerns the privacy interests protected by Exemption 7(C). The Court held that they included not only Vincent Foster's privacy interests but also those of his family. The Court determined that "FOIA recognizes surviving family members' right to personal privacy with respect to their close relative's death-scene images." The Court's analysis establishes that the privacy interests protected by Exemption

7(C) can sometimes extend to the family of the person whom the requested records concern.[9]

The second principle announced in *Favish* concerns the public interest in disclosure. The Court held that Exemption 7(C) creates an exception to "the usual rule that the citizen need not offer a reason for requesting the information." Contrary to that usual rule, the Court said, "Where the privacy concerns addressed by Exemption 7(C) are present," the person requesting information "must show that the public interest sought to be advanced is a significant one," and that "the information is likely to advance that interest." Unless that two-part showing is made, the Court concluded, "the invasion of privacy is unwarranted" for purposes of Exemption 7(C). In the case before it, Favish asserted that disclosure would serve the public interest in determining whether any impropriety occurred in the federal investigations of Foster's death. The Court said that, when a request asserts a public interest in exposing official impropriety, "the requester must produce evidence that would warrant a belief by a reasonable person that the alleged Government impropriety might have occurred." The Court found that Favish had not produced any evidence of impropriety. The Court accordingly determined that the public interest would not be served by disclosure. Because disclosure would, on the other hand, harm the privacy interests of Foster's family, disclosure "could reasonably be expected to constitute an unwarranted invasion of personal privacy."

In *Reporters Committee* and *Favish*, the Court interpreted Exemption 7(C) to protect the personal privacy of human beings. More recently, the Court has held that Exemption 7(C) does not protect the privacy of corporations or other artificial "persons." *FCC v. AT&T*, 562 U.S. 397 (2011). In so holding, the Court relied partly on the ordinary understanding of the term "personal privacy" (which is the operative phrase in Exemption 7(C)). The Court also relied on its determination that the term "personal privacy" in Exemption 6, which was enacted before Exemption 7(C), plainly refers to the privacy of individuals, not artificial entities.

The next example focuses on two parts of Exemption 7: 7(A) and 7(C). It also requires you to think about the relationship between Exemption 7(C) and Exemption 6.

---

9. Family privacy can also presumably be considered in appropriate cases under Exemption 6, as it was in the Challenger disaster case that we described in connection with Exemption 6. Indeed, the Court in *Favish* cited with apparent approval the lower court decision in the Challenger disaster case.

Example

On September 11, 2001 ("9/11"), foreign terrorists hijacked commercial airplanes and flew them into buildings in New York City and Washington, D.C., killing thousands of people. In the investigation of the 9/11 attacks, U.S. officials detained (arrested) more than 1,000 people. Several public interest organizations made a FOIA request for information about the detainees, including their names, the dates and locations of the arrests, and the reasons for their detention.

The government denied the request for detainee information, citing, among other exemptions, Exemptions 7(A) and 7(C). In support of its Exemption 7(A) claim, the government argued that disclosure would interfere with its investigation of the 9/11 attacks. For example, it could reveal to those who planned the attack which of their accomplices had been detained. In addition, information about the detainees could be used to determine the process and direction of the government's investigation. In support of its Exemption 7(C) claim, the government argued that the detainees had a substantial privacy interest in their identity and the circumstances of their detention because release of the information could cause them to be associated with the 9/11 attacks, thereby injuring their reputation and even possibly endangering their personal safety. To establish the public interest in disclosure, the requesters submitted press reports of suspected mistreatment of the detainees by the government.

1. Is any of the detainee information within Exemption 7(A) or 7(C)?
2. Why did the government rely on Exemption 7(C) instead of Exemption 6?

Explanations

1. This is a close case. To begin with, however, the information about the post 9/11 detainees met the threshold requirement for withholding under Exemption 7. It plainly was "compiled for law enforcement purposes," even though the national security implications of the 9/11 attack made the investigation quite different from an ordinary law enforcement investigation. *See Center for National Security Studies v. U.S. Dept. of Justice* ("CNSS"), 331 F.3d 918, 926 (D.C. Cir. 2003). The question remains, however, whether disclosure of the detainee information "could reasonably be expected to interfere with enforcement proceedings," and therefore be withheld under Exemption 7(A), or "could reasonably be expected to constitute an unwarranted invasion of personal privacy," and therefore be withheld under Exemption 7(C).

   A majority of the court in CNSS held that the detainee information fell within Exemption 7(A). The court initially determined that the information could qualify for Exemption 7(A) even though no "enforcement proceedings" were then pending. The court found it sufficient that the 9/11 investigation was likely to lead to such proceedings. The court then determined that there was a "reasonable likelihood" that release of the detainee information could interfere with the 9/11 investigation and, consequently, with enforcement proceedings that were likely to arise from that investigation. In making that determination, the court gave great deference to the government's assessment of the potential for interference. Granting that deference, the court credited the government's concern that disclosure would enable terrorists "to map the course of the investigation and thus develop the means to impede it." The court also found reasonable the government's judgment that disclosure could deter detainees and other, as-yet-unknown witnesses from cooperating with the government.

The dissent in *CNSS* criticized the majority's Exemption 7(A) analysis for treating disclosure as an "all or nothing" proposition. The dissent closely examined the declarations that the government submitted to explain the potential harms that disclosure could cause. The dissent found that the declarations did not justify withholding every category of information requested for every single detainee. For example, the dissent did not believe any harm could come of releasing the names of detainees who were found not to have any connection to terrorism. More generally, the dissent did not believe that the court owed great deference to the government's assessment of the risks of disclosure. *CNSS*, 331 F.3d at 939-941 (Tatel, J., dissenting).

Having determined that the detainee information fell within Exemption 7(A), the majority in *CNSS* found it unnecessary to decide whether the information also fell within Exemption 7(C). The dissent addressed the government's Exemption 7(C) claim, however, and rejected it. The dissent recognized that in some cases courts had allowed the government under Exemption 7(C) to withhold the identity of people contacted during government investigations. The dissent did not believe that this case law automatically extended to the identity of people who have been "arrested and jailed," because arrests and incarceration are official acts that are traditionally made public. *CNSS*, 331 F.3d at 945-946 (Tatel, J., dissenting). In addition, the dissent found significant public interest in disclosure because of what it considered "ample evidence of agency wrongdoing" in the treatment of the detainees. *Id.* at 946.

2. The government invoked Exemption 7(C) instead of Exemption 6 because it is easier for the government to justify withholding information under Exemption 7(C) than under Exemption 6 (assuming the withheld information was compiled for law-enforcement purposes). To justify a withholding under Exemption 6, the government has to show that disclosure "would constitute" a "clearly unwarranted" invasion of privacy. In contrast, Exemption 7(C) requires the government to prove

only that disclosure "could reasonably be expected to cause" an "unwarranted" invasion of privacy. Thus, Exemption 6's wording tilts more in favor of disclosure than that of Exemption 7(C).

III. GOVERNMENT IN THE SUNSHINE ACT

The Government in the Sunshine Act (the Sunshine Act) was enacted in 1976. This was about the same time as the FOIA was significantly amended and not long after the enactment of another access statute that we will explore, the Federal Advisory Committee Act (FACA). The Sunshine Act arose from the same belief in the need for open government as did the FOIA and the FACA. Reflecting that belief, the Sunshine Act says that "every portion of every meeting of an agency shall be open to public observation." 5 U.S.C. § 552b(b). In addition, it requires agencies to give advance public notice of their meetings. *Id.* § 552b(e). Despite the apparent breadth of these obligations, they are limited in several major ways.

First, the Sunshine Act defines "agency" quite narrowly. To fall within the Act, an agency must be "headed by a collegial body composed of two or more individual members, a majority of whom are appointed to such position by the President and with the advice of the Senate." 5 U.S.C. § 552b(a)(1). This means that the Act applies only to the multi-member bodies that head the independent agencies. Examples of such bodies are the Federal Communications Commission, the Securities and Exchange Commission, the Nuclear Regulatory Commission, and the Federal Trade Commission. The Act does not apply to the Executive Departments such as the Department of State (or their components), because they are each headed by one person. The idea behind the limited definition of "agency" was to open up the deliberations of the collegial bodies that make the ultimate decisions for independent agencies. (In contrast, the solitary head of an agency has no colleagues of equal status in the agency with whom to deliberate.)

The Act also defines a "meeting" quite narrowly. A "meeting" means, with some exceptions, "the deliberations of at least the number of individual agency members required to take action on behalf of the agency where such deliberations determine or result in the joint conduct or disposition of official agency business." 5 U.S.C. § 552b(a)(2). This definition has three requirements for a gathering of agency members to constitute a "meeting." The requirements relate to (1) the number of agency members who gather, (2) the necessity that they deliberate, and (3) the effect of the deliberations. One thing that the definition does not require is that the gathering be physical. For example, a telephone or video conference call could be a "meeting." The requirements that do apply can be a bit tricky, so they are each worth a bit of discussion.

First, enough agency members must gather to constitute a quorum of either the entire agency membership or of a subpart that has power to act "on behalf of" the entire membership. 5 U.S.C. § 552b(a)(2). For example, the Act would not apply if only two members of a five-member agency met to discuss agency business without having power to act for all five members. This means that an agency might be able to avoid the Act through a "divide and decide" strategy. For example, an agency's chairperson could probably meet one-on-one with every other member without triggering the requirements for a "meeting."

Second, the Act applies only if the agency members gather to "deliberat[e]." 5 U.S.C. § 552b(a)(2). For example, the Act would not apply if the members of the agency threw a birthday party for one of the members and did not talk agency business. More subtly, the Act probably would not apply to gatherings in which agency members discuss only logistics, such as when to hold their next substantive meeting. *See Washington Assn. for Television & Children v. FCC*, 665 F.2d 1264 (D.C. Cir. 1981).

Third, the deliberations must "determine or result in the joint conduct or disposition of official agency business." 5 U.S.C. § 552b(a)(2). The Supreme Court has explained that this excludes "informal background discussions" that merely "clarify issues and expose varying views of official agency business." On the other hand, a "meeting" can occur even if it does not result in an official agency decision. What is required is that the discussions be "sufficiently focused . . . as to cause or be likely to cause the individual participating members to form reasonably firm positions regarding matters pending or likely to arise before the agency." *Federal Communications Commn. v. ITT World Communications, Inc.*, 466 U.S. 463, 471 (1984) (internal quotation marks omitted). Thus, the fact that a discussion is "pre-decisional" does not exclude it from the Act.

Even when a covered "agency" holds a covered "meeting," the meeting can be closed to the public if it is likely to involve any of ten exempt matters. Seven of those exemptions track those of the FOIA. Specifically, meetings can be closed if they are likely to:

(1) disclose classified information;
(2) relate solely to internal personnel rules and practices of the agency;
(3) disclose matters that are specifically exempted from disclosure by some other statute;
(4) disclose trade secrets or commercial or financial information that is privileged or confidential;
(5) disclose information of a personal nature if disclosure would constitute a clearly unwarranted invasion of personal privacy;
(6) disclose investigatory records compiled for law-enforcement purposes, if disclosure would cause any of six specified harms; or

(7) disclose certain types of information related to the government's regulation of banks and other financial institutions.

In addition to these FOIA-inspired exemptions, the Sunshine Act allows meetings to be closed if they:

(8) involve accusing someone of a crime or censuring someone;
(9) disclose information that, if disclosed prematurely, would "be likely to significantly frustrate implementation of a proposed agency action," or, in the case of agencies that regulate the currency or other financial matters, would be likely to "lead to significant financial speculation" or "significantly endanger the stability of any financial institution"; or
(10) specifically concern the agency's issuance of a subpoena or its participation in various types of civil or criminal proceedings.

None of these exemptions protects the deliberative process, as does FOIA Exemption 5. *See* 5 U.S.C. § 552b(c). Thus, meetings cannot be closed to protect the participants from revealing their interpersonal deliberations. Moreover, an agency's meeting cannot be closed to protect revealing that agency's recommendation to another agency, even though, once the recommendation is in writing, it might be exempt from disclosure under Exemption 5. *See Common Cause v. Nuclear Regulatory Commn.*, 674 F.2d 921 (D.C. Cir. 1982).

Similar to the FOIA, the Sunshine Act entitles "any person" to bring a federal-court suit for a violation and puts the burden on the agency to justify its action. 5 U.S.C. § 552b(h). The relief available in a suit under the Sunshine Act will depend on the nature of the violation and the timing of the suit. For example, if an agency announces that it is going to close a meeting, a person may be able to get a preliminary injunction requiring the meeting to be open. On the other hand, if the person sues after a closed meeting has occurred, the person may only get a court order requiring the agency to release a transcript of the meeting. *Cf. Common Cause v. Nuclear Regulatory Commn.*, 674 F.2d 921, 927 (D.C. Cir. 1982) (vacating as too vague an injunction against agency's closing meetings "similar to" prior meetings held in violation of Sunshine Act). In any event, a court cannot invalidate an agency action on the grounds that the agency took that action at a meeting held in violation of the Act. *See* 5 U.S.C. § 552b(h)(2).

To wrap up, the Sunshine Act does not turn the federal government into a sun-beaten beach but into a series of glades. In those glades the public can watch the multi-member heads of independent agencies deliberate about agency business. The public can only watch, though; the Sunshine Act itself does not allow the public to participate in or influence those deliberations.

In this respect, the Sunshine Act works like the FOIA and unlike the Federal Advisory Committee Act (FACA), to which we turn after an example that, we hope, sheds more light on the Sunshine Act.[10]

Example

The Nuclear Regulatory Commission is an independent agency that is subject to the Government in the Sunshine Act. The Chairman of the Commission would like to hold as few "meetings" as possible. He asks you, as his special assistant, to advise him whether any of these decision-making techniques would be a "meeting" subject to the Act:

1. The staff of each of the five commissioners meets to discuss commission business. After each meeting, the staff brief their respective commissioners. Each commissioner instructs the staff on his or her views. The staff of all the commissioners then meets again to air these views. Staff meetings continue until it is apparent that a majority of the commissioners has agreed on a decision. The commissioners then hold a "meeting" subject to the Sunshine Act in which the decision is formally made after minimal deliberation.

2. The commissioners all meet informally to discuss matters that will be taken up in future "meetings." At the informal meetings, the commissioners fully debate each matter. They do not take any vote, however, and none commits to any final position.

3. The commissioners make decisions exclusively through circulation of written memoranda, in which they express views and cast written votes on matters.

Explanations

1. The staff probably can meet and decide things by proxy without triggering the Sunshine Act. The Sunshine Act applies only when the commissioners themselves meet. The Act does not apply to meetings of the staff. Some courts might bristle at such an obvious circumvention of the Act, but most courts would not consider this a violation of the Act. Instead, the majority probably would take a view similar to that expressed by the D.C. Circuit in a FOIA case against the NRC: "We know of no provision in FOIA that obliges agencies to exercise their . . . authority in a manner

10. In addition to creating the open-meeting provisions that we have discussed in this section, the Sunshine Act also added provisions to the APA that restrict ex parte communications. *See* 5 U.S.C. §§ 551(14) and 557(d). These provisions are discussed in Chapter 3.

that will maximize the amount of information that will be made available to the public. . . ." *Critical Mass Energy Project v. NRC*, 975 F.2d 871, 880 (D.C. Cir. 1992) (*en banc*), *cert. denied*, 507 U.S. 984 (1993).

2. The second meeting-avoidance technique is questionable. This technique, unlike the first, does involve a gathering of the members of the agency. Moreover, those members plainly deliberate at the informal meetings. The tough question is whether those deliberations "determine or result in the joint conduct or disposition of official agency business." If not, the informal meetings are not "meetings" as defined in the Act.

   The issue could be argued either way. Since the commissioners do not vote at the informal meetings, those meetings arguably do not "result in . . . disposition of official agency business." On the other hand, the informal meetings do arguably "result in the joint conduct" of agency business. The informal meetings also may, as a practical matter, "determine . . . [the] disposition" of agency business. The Supreme Court has construed the Act to be triggered by deliberations that "effectively predetermine official agency actions" or that are "likely to cause" members to form "reasonably firm positions" on official agency matters. *See FCC v. ITT World Communications, Inc.*, 466 U.S. 463, 471 (1984). Given the Chairman's motivation for proposing these informal meetings, at least some courts would conclude that they were "likely to cause" (since they seem intended to enable) the commissioners to form "reasonably firm positions" on official agency matters.

3. The third meeting-avoidance technique, in which decisions are made exclusively through the exchange of written memoranda, has the blessing of courts and the Sunshine Act's legislative history. *See, e.g.*, *Common Cause v. NRC*, 674 F.2d 921, 935 n.42 (D.C. Cir. 1982). That is because, although it may produce a meeting of the minds, it does not involve a physical meeting.

IV. FEDERAL ADVISORY COMMITTEE ACT

The chances are good that, unless you have studied political science or worked in the federal government, you have not run across "federal advisory committees" before. Basically, they are groups of people, at least some of whom are from the private sector, that advise the executive branch about law or policy. They furnish yet another way in which the federal government collects information. The information that comes from advisory committees, though, is usually oriented more toward law or policy than toward pure facts (though this need not be the case).

Although most people have never heard of them, advisory committees have been around since the federal government began. They grew in number and influence after World War II. In the last 30 years, however, the federal government has tried to reduce their number and tame them somewhat. As of 2024, there were still about 1,000 federal advisory committees.[11] They continue to influence the administration of federal law. That is why they are studied in many courses on administrative law.

The main statute governing federal advisory committees is the Federal Advisory Committee Act (FACA). The FACA was enacted in 1972 out of three main concerns. One concern was that advisory committees had until then operated mostly in secret. Another concern was that many advisory committees were unnecessary or at least inefficient. A third concern was that some advisory committees were dominated by "special interests," especially business interests. It is no coincidence that the FACA was enacted to deal with these concerns during about the same period as the FOIA was significantly amended (1974 and 1976) and the Sunshine Act was passed (1976). All of these statutes are often described as "good government" laws; they aim to make the government more open and accountable to the public.

Probably the biggest challenge for newcomers to the FACA is figuring out what an "advisory committee" is. (That can be a big challenge for FACA "experts" and courts, too.) We begin with that subject. Then, in keeping with the topic of this chapter, we turn to the public-access provisions of the FACA. Thereafter, we briefly discuss other provisions in the FACA that control existing advisory committees and limit the creation of new ones.[12]

The keystone of the FACA, and the subject of most of the litigation over it, is its definition of "advisory committee." The FACA defines an advisory committee to mean, with some exceptions:

> any committee, board, commission, council, conference, panel, task force, or other similar group, or any subcommittee or other subgroup thereof . . . , which is:
>
> (A) established by statute or reorganization plan, or
> (B) established or utilized by the President, or
> (C) established or utilized by one or more agencies
>
> in the interest of obtaining advice or recommendations for the President or one or more agencies or officers of the Federal Government.

11. *See* FACA Database, available at https://www.facadatabase.gov/FACA/s/.

12. In keeping with the relative obscurity of advisory committees, the FACA was initially even codified in an obscure place: in the appendix to title 5 of the U.S. Code. In 2022, Congress moved it to 5 U.S.C. §§ 1001-1014, but in keeping with the pre-2022 convention you'll find in most judicial decisions, we cite the FACA as "FACA §."

FACA § 3(2). The Act excepts some groups from this definition. Two exceptions are especially important. One exception is for "any committee that is composed wholly of full-time, or permanent part-time, officers or employees of the Federal Government." *Id.* The other exception is for advisory committees established or utilized by the Central Intelligence Agency or the Federal Reserve System. FACA § 4(b)(1).

Roughly speaking, the FACA's definition of an "advisory committee" has three elements. First, an advisory committee must be a group of people at least one of whom is not a federal employee. Second, the group must be either (1) established by a statute or reorganization plan; or (2) "established or utilized" by the President or other federal official or federal agency. Third, the group must give advice or make recommendations to the President, another federal official, or a federal agency.

The first element of the definition was at issue in a case involving the National Energy Policy Development Group (NEPDG), which President George W. Bush created to develop a national energy policy. The NEPDG satisfied the second and third parts of FACA's definition of an "advisory committee." It was "established . . . by the President," and it gave him advice (by submitting a report to him). The question was whether the NEPDG was "composed wholly of" federal employees, in which case it was exempt from the FACA, or instead had some members who were not federal employees, in which case it was an "advisory committee" subject to the FACA. All of the officially designated members of the NEPDG—which included Vice President Richard Cheney as the chair—were federal employees. Nonetheless, several organizations sued under the FACA claiming that people from the private sector, including members of the energy industry, participated in the NEPDG's deliberations as "de facto" members. On that theory, the NEPDG was not exempt from FACA because it was not "composed wholly of" federal employees but instead included (de facto) members from the private sector.

The case went to the Supreme Court after the lower federal courts denied Vice President Cheney and his co-defendants relief from the plaintiffs' discovery requests. The Supreme Court remanded the case, instructing the lower courts to evaluate the government's "weighty separation of powers objections" to discovery. *See Cheney v. U.S. District Court for the District of Columbia*, 542 U.S. 367 (2004). On remand, the *en banc* D.C. Circuit rejected the plaintiffs' "de facto membership" argument. The court initially determined that the application of the FACA to advisory committees established by the President raises "severe" separation-of-powers concerns. This is because the FACA's regulation of the conduct and composition of presidential advisory committees arguably restricts the President's freedom to get advice from whomever he chooses. To avoid this separation-of-powers concern, the court interpreted the FACA strictly.

Specifically, it held that the only people who could be considered "members" of the NEPDG were those given "a vote in or, if the committee acts by consensus, a veto over the committee's decisions." *In re Cheney*, 406 F.3d 723, 729 (D.C. Cir. 2005). The court found that everyone given a vote or veto in the NEPDG's decisions was a federal official. Thus, the NEPDG was exempt from the FACA because it did not meet the first element of the definition of an "advisory committee": it did not have at least one member who was not a federal employee.

Separation of powers concerns also played a big role in a case involving the second element of the FACA's definition of "advisory committee," under which a group may be an advisory committee if it is "established or utilized by the President." The case was *Public Citizen v. United States Dept. of Justice*, 491 U.S. 440 (1989).

The case concerned the American Bar Association's Standing Committee on the Federal Judiciary. For a long time, presidents have relied on the Standing Committee's evaluation of people that the President is considering nominating to be federal judges. The organization Public Citizen argued that the Standing Committee was "utilized by" the President and thus subject to the FACA. The Court rejected that argument partly because, if accepted, it "would present formidable constitutional difficulties." *Public Citizen*, 491 U.S. at 466. Specifically, the Court was concerned that, if applied to the Standing Committee, the FACA would interfere with the President's constitutional power to nominate federal judges. In light of that concern, the Court thought that the term "utilized" in the FACA was best read to "encompass groups formed indirectly by quasi-public organizations such as the National Academy of Sciences 'for' public agencies as well as 'by' such agencies themselves." *Id.* at 462. This interpretation excluded from the FACA groups such as the Standing Committee, which was created by and operated independently of the government. The Court did not explain whether this narrow interpretation of the term "utilized" applies only to advisory bodies that the President himself uses or also to advisory bodies used by other government officials and agencies.

Given the constitutional doubts that courts have expressed about a broad reading of the FACA, you may be wondering how, exactly, the FACA interferes with interactions between the executive branch and advisory committees. Consistent with the concerns that prompted its enactment, FACA does three main things. First, it opens up the operation of advisory committees to public scrutiny and to limited public participation. Second, it controls their operation in other ways designed to make them more efficient and effective. Finally, it limits the creation of new advisory committees and the renewal of existing ones, to achieve, among other goals, a "fair balance" of views on each advisory committee.

The FACA contains several provisions designed to enhance public scrutiny of and participation in advisory committees. The FACA states, as a general rule, "Each advisory committee meeting shall be open to the public." FACA § 10(a)(1). To make this rule meaningful, the FACA generally requires an advisory committee to give advance public notice of its meetings. *Id.* § 10(a)(2). The FACA also requires an advisory committee to give "interested persons" a chance "to attend, appear before, or file statements with any advisory committee," subject to regulations of the Administrator of General Services. *Id.* § 10(a)(3). The committee must keep and publish minutes of each meeting. *Id.* § 10(c). It must also make publicly available all other documents that were "made available to or prepared for or by" the committee. *See* FACA § 10(b).

These public-access provisions are subject to exceptions. Specifically, an advisory committee meeting can be closed to the public on the same grounds as can an agency meeting under the Government in the Sunshine Act. FACA § 10(d); *see also* 6 U.S.C. § 133(b) (exempting certain "critical infrastructure information" from the FACA). Similarly, an advisory committee can withhold documents that are exempt from disclosure under the FOIA. *Id.* § 10(b). Furthermore, an advisory committee does not have to give advance public notice of a meeting "when the President determines otherwise for reasons of national security." *Id.* § 10(a)(2). So, like the FOIA and the Sunshine Act, the FACA strikes a balance between open government and privacy concerns.

In addition to exposing advisory committees to public scrutiny and input, the FACA aims to weed out unnecessary ones. To that end, the FACA requires congressional committees periodically to review each advisory committee under their jurisdiction. In that review, the congressional committees must determine whether the advisory committee should be abolished or merged with another advisory committee; whether the advisory committee's responsibilities should be revised; and whether the advisory committee performs a necessary function not already being performed. Similarly, ongoing review is supposed to be done by the Administrator of General Services for all federal advisory committees and by the head of each agency for every advisory committee that serves that agency. *See* FACA §§ 6-8.

Advisory committees that survive the review process operate on a short leash. An advisory committee cannot meet or take any action until it has filed a charter with the congressional standing committees that have jurisdiction over it, as well as with the Administrator of General Services (if it is a presidential advisory committee) or the head of the agency to which it reports. The charter must detail the committee's objectives and duties and the scope of its activities, among other things. An advisory committee cannot meet except with the approval of "a designated officer or employee of the Federal Government." FACA § 10(f). In addition, an advisory committee must have that officer or employee approve the agendas for its meetings, unless it is a presidential advisory committee. No advisory committee can meet unless a designated federal officer or employee attends the meeting. That officer or employee can adjourn the meeting "whenever he determines it to be in the public interest." *Id.* § 10(e). Finally, virtually all advisory committees expire two years after their creation, unless they are renewed for another two years by the President, the head of an agency, or Congress. When an advisory committee is renewed, it must file a new charter. *See generally* FACA §§ 9, 10, and 14.

Potential new advisory committees face an uphill battle. The FACA requires congressional committees to consider certain factors when they consider legislation creating a new advisory committee. The congressional committee must consider, among other things, whether the functions of the proposed new advisory committee could be performed by an agency or an advisory committee that already exists. Furthermore, legislation proposing a new advisory committee must contain, among other things, a "clearly defined purpose" for the advisory committee. Such legislation must also require the membership of a new advisory committee "to be fairly balanced in terms of the points of view represented and the functions to be performed." In a similar vein, the legislation must ensure that the advisory committee's advice "will not be inappropriately influenced by the appointing authority or by any special interest"; instead, the advice should be "the result of the advisory committee's independent judgment." FACA § 5(b)(3).[13]

Judicial enforcement of the FACA raises many questions, partly because the FACA does not address judicial review. There is no question that a plaintiff with standing has a private cause of action for violations of at least some of the FACA's provisions. Questions have arisen, however, about whether some of the FACA's provisions are judicially enforceable and what judicial remedies are appropriate for the FACA violations. *See Manshardt v. Federal Judicial Qualifications Committee*, 408 F.3d 1154, 1156 n.3 (9th Cir. 2005). Specifically, some courts have held that claims based on the FACA's "fair balance" provisions are nonjusticiable; that appears to be a minority view, however. *See Ctr. for Policy Analysis on Trade & Health v. Office of U.S. Trade Rep.*, 540 F.3d 940 (9th Cir. 2008). In addition, courts have disagreed about when it is appropriate to enjoin an agency from using advice from a group that has violated the FACA. *See Cargill, Inc. v. United States*, 173 F.3d 323, 341-342 (5th Cir. 1999).

13. Over and above the statutory provisions governing advisory committees, the Executive Branch has put additional restrictions on agencies that want to create or maintain advisory committees. For a complete discussion of both the FACA and the executive material, *see* Steven P. Croley & William F. Funk, *The Federal Advisory Committee Act and Good Government*, 14 Yale J. on Reg. 451 (1997).

See also Alabama-Tombigbee Rivers Coalition v. Department of Interior, 26 F.3d 1103 (11th Cir. 1994).

The next example should help you think about how to identify the rather esoteric animals known as advisory committees and how they can be brought to heel.

Example

The federal government owns about 24 million acres of forest land in the states of Washington and Oregon. For years, there was a dispute about how this federally owned land should be used. The main disputants were environmentalists, on one side, and people involved in the timber industry, on the other. President Bill Clinton formed two bodies to try to resolve the dispute.

One body was the Forest Conference Executive Committee. The Executive Committee was chaired by the Director of the White House Office of Environmental Policy, which is part of the Executive Office of the President. The other members of the Executive Committee were all high-level officials in the Department of Interior and other Cabinet-level agencies. The Executive Committee had the job of supervising the second body.

The second body was the Forest Ecosystem Management Assessment Team (FEMAT). FEMAT's job was to give the President a list of options for managing the federal forest land in Washington and Oregon. About 600 people contributed to FEMAT's work, but there was dispute about which of these people were "members" of FEMAT. It was undisputed, however, that the members of FEMAT included five professors, three from Oregon State University and two from the University of Washington. None of these professors took leaves of absence from their schools while they worked for FEMAT. While they worked for FEMAT, their schools continued to pay their full salaries.

Under the Executive Committee's supervision, FEMAT produced a report for the President. The report identified ten options for managing the government's western forest lands. The President adopted one of the options identified in the report, with some changes. The Executive Committee and FEMAT disbanded.

An industry association sued the government, asserting claims under the FACA. It was undisputed that neither the Executive Committee nor FEMAT followed the FACA.

1. Is either the Executive Committee or FEMAT an "advisory committee"?
2. If the court finds a violation of the FACA, what is the appropriate remedy?

Explanations

1. The Executive Committee is not an advisory committee, but FEMAT is. The Executive Committee is not an advisory committee because it is made up exclusively of full-time federal employees. That is not true of FEMAT because of the presence of the state university professors. Moreover, FEMAT meets the other criteria for an advisory committee. It was established by the President for the purpose of giving him advice. Indeed, it ended up giving the President advice, which he took.

2. It is unclear what relief the court should grant. Now that FEMAT has finished its work and disbanded, there is no reason for an injunction compelling future compliance with the FACA. Certainly, the materials that would have been made public had FEMAT complied with the FACA should now be required to be made public, if they have not already been. The tough question is whether the court should enjoin the government from relying on the FEMAT report to implement the President's plan. Unlike the Government in the Sunshine Act, the FACA itself does not provide for judicial enforcement. Instead, persons seek relief for FACA violations under either the APA or the mandamus statute. Also unlike the Government in the Sunshine Act, the FACA does not expressly preclude injunctions against agency actions arising out of violations of the FACA. Thus, courts are left to decide for themselves whether such an injunction is appropriate. In the case on which this example was based, the court refused to issue such an injunction, primarily because of separation-of-powers concerns. The court said that it was "aware of no authority upon which it could confidently rely in concluding that it may forbid the President and his Cabinet to act upon advice that comes to them from any source, however irregular." *Northwest Forest Council v. Espy*, 846 F. Supp. 1009 (D.D.C. 1994). On the other hand, in a case in which a group prepared recommendations to the U.S. Fish and Wildlife Service in violation of the FACA, the Eleventh Circuit enjoined the Service from using any of the information generated by the group in determining whether to list certain species as endangered. *See Alabama-Tombigbee Rivers v. Department of Interior*, 26 F.3d 1103 (11th Cir. 1994). The D.C. Circuit in one case refused to enjoin the use of the information, but it reserved the right to do so in a case where to deny such an injunction "would effectively render FACA a nullity." *California Forestry Assn. v. United States Forest Service*, 102 F.3d 609, 614 (D.C. Cir. 1996). In short, the appropriate remedy may depend on the court and the circumstances.

V. THE PRIVACY ACT

The Privacy Act of 1974 does both less, and more, than protect privacy. The Act gives people some protection from the government's release of personal information about them; however, there are major exceptions to this protection. In addition to protecting personal privacy (somewhat), the Privacy Act enables individuals to get access to, and to correct, some of the information that the government has about them. Because of the access feature of the Act, a person who wants government records about herself should request them under both the Freedom of Information Act and the Privacy Act, as we mentioned in an earlier example. The interaction between the FOIA and the Privacy Act is discussed in greater detail in this section.

A. General Rule Against Disclosure

The Privacy Act says, as a general rule, "No agency shall disclose any record which is contained in a system of records." 5 U.S.C. § 552a(b). This rule covers the same agencies that are covered by the FOIA. *See id.* § 552a(a)(1). To understand why this rule protects personal privacy at all, you have to understand the Act's definition of "record." To begin to appreciate the scope of the Act's protection of personal privacy, you have to know what a "system of records" is.

The Act defines "record" to mean information that an agency maintains about an individual and that identifies the individual by name or in some other way. The definition explains that this information can include, for example, someone's "education, financial transactions, medical history, and criminal or employment history." Thus, the term "record" in the Privacy Act focuses on personal information; this is narrower than the concept of "record" reflected in the FOIA. *See* 5 U.S.C. § 552a(a)(4).

The Privacy Act's general rule protects a record from disclosure only if it is "contained in a system of records." The Act defines a "system of records" to mean a group of records under the agency's control "from which information is retrieved by the name of the individual" or by some other identifying particular. This definition reflects that Congress was mostly concerned in the Privacy Act with personal information maintained by the government in computer databases that were searchable using a person's name or some other individual identifier. (It is worth mentioning at this point that the Act protects only individuals, not artificial entities such as corporations.) *See* 5 U.S.C. §§ 552(a)(2) (defining "individual") and 552(a)(5) (defining "system of records").

So the basic rule of the Privacy Act is that agencies should not disclose information that they maintain on individuals in a form that is searchable by reference to the individual.

B. Exceptions

The general rule prohibiting agencies from disclosing "records" in their "systems of records" is subject to many exceptions. Some are quite large.

One sensible exception is that an agency can disclose records about a person with that person's prior written consent or on that person's written request. This exception, for example, lets prospective employers and schools check the records of an applicant after he has signed a consent form. *See* 5 U.S.C. § 552a(b).

Another exception allows the agency to disclose records for a "routine use." To take advantage of this exception, an agency must first publish in the Federal Register a description of the "routine uses" that it makes of the records in any system of records that it maintains. *See* 5 U.S.C. § 552(b)(3). For example, some time ago the Social Security Administration (SSA) adopted a "routine use" to authorize disclosure of misconduct by attorneys and others who represent people applying for social security benefits. 80 Fed. Reg. 919 (Jan. 7, 2015). This routine use enabled the SSA, for example, to report an attorney's misconduct to a state bar's disciplinary authorities.

Besides the "routine use" exception, other exceptions allow agencies to disclose records for, among other things, law-enforcement purposes, census-taking purposes, and statistical research. *See* 5 U.S.C. § 552a(b)(4), (5), and (7).

Perhaps the most important exception allows an agency to disclose records in its systems of records if disclosure is "required" under the FOIA. 5 U.S.C. § 552a(b)(2). This means that if someone requests a record about someone else under the FOIA, the agency must disclose that record unless it falls within a FOIA exemption. Moreover, an agency cannot withhold the record on the grounds that Exemption 3 of the FOIA incorporates the Privacy Act; the Privacy Act is not an Exemption 3 statute. *See id.* § 552a(t)(2). Thus, when a record covered by the Privacy Act is requested under the FOIA, an agency must disclose it—despite the Privacy Act's general rule barring disclosure of records—unless the record falls within some FOIA exemption other than Exemption 3 or some nondisclosure statute other than the Privacy Act that is incorporated by Exemption 3. The main FOIA exemptions that might at least partly protect records subject to the Privacy Act from disclosure are Exemptions 6 and 7(C). *See United States Dept. of Defense v. FLRA*, 510 U.S. 487 (1994).

C. Other Functions

The Privacy Act does more than restrict agencies' disclosure of records about a person to other people (or other agencies). It also entitles a person to (1) request copies of the records in a record system that pertain to him, and (2) ask the agency to amend those records if they are inaccurate. These rights of access and amendment can be limited in some situations. Specifically, an agency can promulgate a regulation exempting its system of records from the access and amendment requirements. The agency can do so, however, only to protect certain types of information, such as classified information or certain law-enforcement information. *See* 5 U.S.C. §§ 552a(j) and 552a(k).

One other function of the Privacy Act deserves mention. Section 7(b) of the Act applies whenever a federal, state, or local agency requests that someone disclose his or her social security number. When the agency makes that request, Section 7(b) requires the agency to tell the person whether disclosure is voluntary or mandatory, under what authority the agency is making the request, and what uses the agency will make of the social security number. 5 U.S.C. § 552a Note. Unlike other provisions of the Privacy Act, Section 7(b) is not limited to federal agencies. *But cf. Gonzalez v. Village of West Milwaukee*, 671 F.3d 649, 660-662 (7th Cir. 2012) (discussing case law holding that Section 7(b), despite its text, applies only to federal agencies). The Supreme Court held that in order to recover the statutorily set $1,000 minimum award for violations of Section 7(b) (in that case, a violation by a federal agency), a person must prove actual damages. *See Doe v. Chao*, 540 U.S. 614 (2004).

D. Judicial Relief

An agency can violate the Privacy Act in three main ways, and judicial relief is available for each type of violation. An agency can violate the Act by (1) improperly disclosing a record about someone to someone else; (2) refusing to let someone see her own records; or (3) refusing to amend inaccurate records. The judicial relief available for these violations varies accordingly. For an improper disclosure, the person injured by the disclosure can get a minimum of $1,000 for actual damages if the disclosure was "intentional or willful." For an improper refusal to let someone see her records, the court can order disclosure of the records. Finally, for an improper refusal to amend someone's records, the court can order the agency to make the amendment. For all three types of violations, courts can sometimes award attorneys' fees. *See* 5 U.S.C. § 552a(g).

E. Summary

The Privacy Act has three main features. First, to a modest extent, it bucks the open-government trend created by the other access statutes that we have studied, such as the FOIA and the Sunshine Act. It is only a modest bucking, though, because of the Privacy Act's many exceptions to the rule against disclosure of records. Second, while limiting public access to personal records somewhat, the Privacy Act ensures that a person generally can obtain access to records pertaining to himself or herself. Third, the Privacy Act recognizes and tries to remedy the inaccuracies that creep into some of the government's records on individuals. The following examples illustrate some of these features of the Act.

Example

Jane Austin applies to the Social Security Administration (SSA) for disability benefits and is turned down. She asks the SSA for copies of her medical files under both the Privacy Act and the FOIA. SSA denies the request on the ground that the files fall within FOIA Exemption 6. SSA concedes that the files would otherwise be disclosable to Austin under the Privacy Act. Is Austin entitled to disclosure of her files? In answering that question, assume that Austin's request complies with all applicable rules for FOIA and Privacy Act requests.

Explanation

SSA must disclose the files even if they fall within FOIA Exemption 6. The Privacy Act says, "No agency shall rely on any exemption contained in [the FOIA] to withhold from an individual any record which is otherwise accessible to such individual under the provisions of this [Act]." 5 U.S.C. § 552a(t)(1). SSA was right, by the way, to concede that Austin was entitled to her medical records under the Privacy Act. Those records clearly were "records" within the meaning of the Privacy Act and were maintained by SSA in a "system of records." They were "records" because they contained personal information about Austin and, no doubt, personally identified her in some way (even if only by a claim number). They were maintained in a "system of records" because SSA no doubt retrieved records like hers by using some personally identifying set of words or numbers (such as her name or her claim number). Agencies can exempt some types of records from disclosure under the Privacy Act, but Austin's records are not one of those types. Cf. *Warren v. Colvin*, 744 F.3d 841 (2d Cir. 2014) (holding that Privacy Act did not entitle son to get his dead father's disability records).

This example involves a situation in which a person may not be entitled to her records under the FOIA, but she clearly is entitled to them under the Privacy Act. Some cases involve essentially the opposite situation: a person is entitled to her records under the FOIA but is not entitled to them under the Privacy Act. The Privacy Act has a provision dealing with that situation, too. It says, "No agency shall rely on any exemption in this section to withhold from an individual any record which is otherwise accessible to such individual under the provisions of [the FOIA]." 5 U.S.C. § 552a(t)(2).

The upshot is that a person who requests her records under both the Privacy Act and the FOIA is entitled to those records unless they are exempt under *both* statutes. That is why a person who wants records about herself should request them under both the Privacy Act and the FOIA.

Example

Dwight Slocum, a law student and Army veteran, applied to the Veterans Administration (VA) for a loan to buy a house. During a random audit of his loan application, the VA determined that he had lied on the application by falsifying his income. The VA official who investigated Slocum's case learned that Slocum was planning to take the Nevada bar examination after finishing law school. The official wrote a letter to the Nevada Board of Law Examiners stating that Slocum had falsified a loan application to the VA.

When Slocum later applied to take the Nevada bar exam, the Nevada Board of Law Examiners sent the VA a letter asking the VA for more information about its investigation of Slocum. Attached to the Board's request was a form signed by Slocum allowing government agencies to disclose information about him to the Board. The VA sent the Board a second letter in which it gave details of its investigation. After considering that information, the Board refused to allow Slocum to take the Nevada bar exam, finding him morally unfit.

Slocum sued the VA, claiming that the VA's two letters to the Nevada Board of Law Examiners violated the Privacy Act. He also claimed that the VA's disclosures were "intentional or willful," entitling him to $10 million in actual damages. In defense, the VA argues that Slocum consented to the disclosures and that they fell within a "routine use." The second argument rested on a regulation that permits the VA to respond to a state agency's request for information relevant to the state's decision whether to license someone.

Did either of the VA's two letters to the Board violate the Privacy Act? In answering that question, assume that the information disclosed by the VA constituted "records" maintained in a "system of records."

Explanation

The first (unsolicited) VA letter did violate the Privacy Act, but the second (solicited) VA letter did not. The second VA letter disclosed information with Slocum's "prior written consent," thanks to the consent form that Slocum signed when he applied to take the Nevada bar exam. Furthermore, the second letter was independently permissible as a "routine use." In contrast, the first VA letter did not occur with Slocum's *prior* consent, nor did it occur in response to a state agency's request for the information. It therefore did not fall within the exceptions for consented-to disclosures or routine uses.

Despite the violation caused by the VA's first letter, Slocum may have trouble getting any relief against the VA. The Privacy Act authorizes damages only for "intentional or willful" violations. The courts have construed this to mean "something greater than gross negligence." *See, e.g., Tijerina v. Walters*, 821 F.2d 789, 799 (D.C. Cir. 1987), on which this example is based. Whether Slocum can meet that standard will depend on more facts than we have given you. *See Beaven v. U.S. Dept. of Justice*, 622 F.3d 540 (6th Cir. 2010) (court must examine agency's entire course of conduct to determine whether its violation was intentional or willful).

Example

Sally Roe worked at a Veterans Administration (VA) hospital. Roe's supervisor at the VA hospital was Dr. Dale, a physician whom Roe and other employees often saw for minor medical complaints. During a medical appointment with Dr. Dale, Roe mentioned that she had tested positive for human immunodeficiency virus (HIV) and smoked marijuana to alleviate some HIV symptoms. Dr. Dale recorded these facts in Roe's medical record. Later, Roe met with Dr. Dale to discuss Roe's frequent absences from work. Roe brought her union representative to that meeting. During the meeting, Dr. Dale mentioned Roe's HIV-positive status and her marijuana use. Roe sues the VA, claiming that Dr. Dale violated the Privacy Act by disclosing information in Roe's medical records. The VA concedes that the records are "contained in a system of records" and therefore subject to the Act. The VA argues, however, that Dr. Dale did not disclose information in those records because he had independent knowledge of Roe's HIV-positive status and marijuana use. Is there a Privacy Act violation here?

Explanation

Dr. Dale's disclosure did not violate the Privacy Act, according to the Eighth Circuit. *Doe v. Department of Veterans Affairs*, 519 F.3d 456 (8th Cir. 2008), *cert. denied*, 555 U.S. 1136 (2009). The court relied on precedent in which it held that "the only disclosure actionable under [the Privacy Act] is one resulting from a retrieval of the information initially and directly from the record contained in the system of records." *Id.* at 461. Here, Dr. Dale retrieved the information not from Roe's medical records but from his own memory of his conversation with Roe. Roe argued that, even though Dr. Dale disclosed information from his memory, his disclosure violated the Privacy Act because he prepared the protected record that contained that same information. The Eighth Circuit rejected this argument for what it called a "scrivener's exception" to the Privacy Act limitation on actionable disclosures. *Cf. Bartel v. FAA*, 725 F.2d 1403, 1411 (D.C. Cir. 1984) (holding that an FAA official may have violated the Privacy Act when he disclosed the results of an investigation that he ordered and that was the subject of a protected record).

Table of Cases

Index